THE FIRST AND SECOND PARTS

of

John Hayward's

THE LIFE AND RAIGNE OF KING HENRIE IIII

edited with an introduction by

JOHN J. MANNING, M.A., Ph.D.
The University of Connecticut

CAMDEN FOURTH SERIES
VOLUME 42

D0002863

LONDON
OFFICES OF THE ROYAL HISTORICAL SOCIETY
UNIVERSITY COLLEGE LONDON
GOWER STREET WC1E 6BT
1991

British Library Cataloguing in Publication data
Hayward, John
  The first and second parts of John Hayward's
  The life and raigne of King Henrie IIII. –
  (Camden. Fourth series)
  I. Title   II. Manning, John J.   III. Series
  942.041092
  ISBN 0-86193-129-7

Printed and bound in Great Britain by
Butler & Tanner Ltd, Frome and London

CONTENTS

ACKNOWLEDGEMENTS

I am deeply indebted to several people, both colleagues and strangers (and often to the institutions they serve), for generous help with particular problems that arose during completion of this book, and I have tried to acknowledge their contributions in the notes. Over the project's several years, however, it became evident that the assistance and suggestions of many others had come gradually to inform the work as a whole in more widespread fashion. They rightly share any credit for advancing our understanding of John Hayward and his history.

In the United Kingdom these include Ann Saunders, of the London Topographical Society; David G.C. Allan, of the Royal Society of the Arts; The Trustees and staff of London House for Overseas Graduates; Katherine S.H. Wyndham; Tony North; Sarah Barter-Bailey, of H.M. Armouries, Tower of London; Blair Worden and Michael Jones, of the Royal Historical Society; the staff of the Institute of Historical Research, and the Brotherton, Bodleian, Cambridge University, Lambeth Palace and Pembroke College, Cambridge, libraries.

In the United States they include Julius Elias, Tom Giolas, William Moynihan, Richard Peterson, Milton Stern, and Frank Vasington, all colleagues at the University of Connecticut; Phyllis Deutsch; Edmund Creeth; Helen Apthorp Greenspan; O.B. Hardison, Jr., of the Folger Shakespeare Library, for permission to use its MS materials, and Giles Dawson, for assistance in working with them there; and the Babbidge, Houghton and University of Michigan libraries.

And I am especially grateful to G.B. Harrison, this project's first begetter, and Laura A. Manning, *femme sage* and midwife to its birth, many seasons ago.

J.J.M.
Storrs, Connecticut
October 1991

INTRODUCTION

1 John Hayward and his *Life of Henry IV*

Dr. John Hayward – civil servant, lawyer, historian and author of the texts presented here – complained to the Prince of Wales in 1612 that

> men might safely write of others in manner of a tale; but in manner of a history, safely they could not: because, albeit they should write of men long since dead, and whose posterity is clean worn out; yet some alive, finding themselves foul in those vices which they see observed, reproved, and condemned in others, their guiltiness maketh them apt to conceive, that, whatsoever the words are, the finger pointeth only at them.[1]

Hayward's cynicism was rooted in experience. That writing history could prove a thankless craft, even a dangerous one, he had learned first-hand. Thirteen years before, in 1599, the publication of his first historical work, *The First Part of the Life and Raigne of King Henrie IIII*, had subjected him to frightening scrutiny by powerful officials, who suspected him of collusion with the Earl of Essex, to whom he had dedicated the book in excessively flattering terms. His book (fairly titled, for it covered only 'the first part' of Henry's career: the causes and highlights of his insurgency and the events of his first regnal year) was burned and suppressed. In 1600, after Essex's disgrace, Hayward was imprisoned in the Tower, where he remained during the earl's rebellion and the subsequent trials and executions. He was released only after the death of the queen, who in 1599 had herself accused him at least twice of sedition.

Several publications, especially those promoting unacceptable views on the succession question, upset Elizabeth greatly during the 1590s, and she despised Hayward's history in particular. Sensitive in her declining years to an array of criticisms, she was especially angered by efforts to compare her to Richard II, whose misfortunes occupy such a large part of Hayward's book; she tended to see in the disgraceful behaviour of Essex, once her favourite, something of Henry Bolingbroke. 'I am Richard II, know ye not that?' she remarked

---

[1] Hayward reports this conversation with Prince Henry in his dedication (to Prince Charles) of *The Lives of the III Normans, Kings of England* (London, 1613).

I

bitterly, only a few months after Essex's execution.[2] Of her special
and outspoken aversion to Hayward's book, voiced in 1599 (several
months after its suppression, but more than a year before Essex would
take to the streets of London with an armed band), Francis Bacon
supplies a detailed account:

> Her majesty being mightily incensed with that booke which was
> dedicated to my lord of Essex, being a storie of the first yeare of
> king Henry the fourth, thinking it a seditious prelude to put into
> the peoples heades boldnesse and faction, said, she had an opinion
> that there was treason in it, and asked me if I could not find any
> places in it that might be drawne within case of treason: whereto I
> answered: 'For treason surely I found none, but for fellonie very
> many.' And when her Majesty hastily asked me 'wherein?' I told
> her, the author had committed very apparant theft: for he had
> taken most of the sentences of Cornelius Tacitus, and translated
> them into English, and put them into his text.

Elizabeth would not be put off lightly; Bacon reports her continued
irritation with Hayward and his book:

> Another time when the Queen would not be perswaded it was his
> writing whose name was to it, but that it had some more mischievous
> author; and said, with great indignation, that she would have him
> racked to produce his author: I replyed, 'Nay, madame, he is a
> doctor, never rack his person, but rack his stile; let him have pen,
> inke, and paper, and help of bookes, and be enjoined to continue
> the storie where it breaketh off, and I will undertake by collecting
> the stiles to judge whether he were author or no.[3]

As Bacon suggested, the very title of *The First Part* seemed to promise
more to come. And indeed, many were calling for more of the story
but, as we shall see, for reasons other than Bacon's. 'No book ever
sold better,' recalled John Wolfe, its publisher, in testimony given the
following year. 'The people divers times since called to procure the
continuation of the history by the same author,' claimed Wolfe, who

[2] This remark to Willam Lambarde, her Keeper of the Rolls (4 August 1601), was
first reported by John Nichols in *The Progresses and Public Processions of Queen Elizabeth*
(2nd ed., 1823), iii, 552; cited by E. K. Chambers, *The Elizabethan Stage*, (4 vols.,
Oxford, 1961), ii, 206; See also Historical MSS Commission, *Fourth Report* (1874), col.
330. The exchange with Lambarde, cited by almost all commentators upon perceived
parallels between Richard and Elizabeth, includes the queen's celebrated remark
connecting the Essex rebellion with the theatrical popularity of the Richard story: '...
this tragedy was played 40 times in open streets and houses.'

[3] *Sir Francis Bacon his Apologie, in Certain Imputations Concerning the Late Earle of Essex*
(1604), 34–5. Bacon dates the exchange at about the middle of Michaelmas term, 1599.

'entreated him to go forward with it, and thinks he hath done some part of it.'[4]

Wolfe – who probably knew more than he cared to admit – was correct in that belief. After all, he had published Hayward's effort under a title that anticipated a sequel. And Bacon seems to have at least suspected that Hayward had more to offer about Henry. He had noticed that Hayward's story, as published, does not *terminate* with the quarto text, but abruptly 'breaketh off.'

The modern reader who would rack the doctor's style will have the advantage both of Bacon and of Wolfe's customers, for Hayward did in fact continue the controversial story 'where it breaketh off.' The suppression of *The First Part* effectively doomed publication by Hayward of anything further on Henry IV, so the anticipated continuation never saw print. But that sequel, which I have short-titled *The Second Part*, now appears for the first time below. The present edition, by marrying in print Hayward's two sequential texts as one continuous account, thus completes a union that for almost 400 years has remained *ratum, sed non consummatum*.

The discovery of a sequel to Hayward's provocative published segment on Henry IV affords us a wider lens through which to survey an early modern historian's early work. To present both segments for the first time in a useful modern format is the principal goal of the present edition. The significance of this amplified material for the modern student is manifold, and it is hoped that this edition will stimulate a reassessment of this interesting historiographer.

A good deal of the attention Hayward has received until now has understandably been focussed upon extrinsic matters. As set forth below, some of his contemporaries, with only *The First Part* to guide their judgments about his work, found it more political than scholarly, and it was their continuing emphasis upon its topicality that prompted the bitterness Hayward expressed to Prince Henry. It is difficult to fault them. The queen would naturally have thought a book focussed upon the overthrow and murder of a legitimate prince 'a seditious prelude.' Her attorney-general, Edward Coke, was deeply suspicious of a book limited to 'that story only' (a phrase repeated often in the record of offical inquiries into Hayward's motives); he wondered, in 1600, why Hayward selected 'a storie 200 yere olde, and publisheth it this last yere.'[5]

The controversy that greeted its publication (described below) secured *The First Part* not only a spectacular popularity, but incidentally an unusual bibliographical history as well. Its first edition sold

[4] Wolfe's testimony, July 1600: PRO SP 12/275, no. 28.
[5] PRO SP 12/275, no. 25. (Coke's investigation of the Hayward case is detailed below.)

a thousand copies, before a much-altered second edition, reportedly an even larger press-run, was banned and burned. Even after its immediate notoriety had passed and Elizabeth and Essex were dead, the book continued to acquire fresh political topicality. Several more editions, some counterfeit, were brought out during the next forty years in defiance of the early suppression order, and it was eventually published in 1642 as a companion-piece to Sir Robert Cotton's *Life of Henry III* (a deliberately topical book, itself unlicensed when it appeared in 1627). This uncommon notoriety offers the modern reader – as it imposed upon Hayward – dramatic instruction about public attitudes and preoccupations between the 1590s and the 1640s. By itself, *The First Part* affords a case study of certain Elizabethan licensing practices, of interesting (and illegal) aspects of the book-printing trade, and of official sensitivity to history as a form of propaganda. It specifies something of the Elizabethan court's nervousness about rebellion and the uncertainties associated with identifying her successor. And the continued popularity of this Elizabethan book during the forty years that followed the queen's death offers useful glimpses into the intensifying quarrel between the Stuart kings and Parliament.

The availability of *The Second Part* in the present edition will perhaps shift attention to the intrinsic worth of Hayward's history. Although it is understandable that modern commentators – much like the prosecutors at the Essex trials – have been inclined to see *The First Part* principally as an exhibit in a famous political dispute, the broader documentary evidence offered in the present edition might profitably deflect inquiry into other important dimensions of Hayward's work on Henry IV.

The sequel text reveals an historian as cheerless about Henry as he had been in *The First Part* about Richard and his flatterers. He dismisses Henry's title claims, and his assessments of the new king's subsequent administration are neither anti-Ricardian nor pro-Lancastrian. He is generous with criticism of Richard's successor, of the remnants of the Ricardian faction, and of the rebellious Percies alike. At the very least, *The Second Part* suggests that *The First Part* was intended as part of something more than a 'seditious prelude.'

More significantly, although only a secondary source for its late medieval subject matter, Hayward's study of Henry IV constitues a primary source in early modern intellectual history. Students of the period's then rapidly developing but still embryonic historical profession will recognize in Hayward's treatment of his material useful examples of prominent trends in late Tudor and Stuart historiography. Of particular note is Hayward's role in the revival of interest in Tacitus, a development under Elizabeth a matter of scholarly dispute, but under the Stuarts a matter of serious political division.

(For a professed admirer of Tacitus like Hayward to express dismay that his work's topicality overshadowed its scholarship, is itself an irony worth pondering.) The period of Richard's fall and Bolingbroke's accession, seminal to the fifteenth-century civil wars, had acquired wide appeal during the sixteenth century: students of Elizabethan literature – particularly drama – will recognize familiar subject matter here. Taken together, for example, the two texts presented in this edition span almost precisely the material exploited by Shakespeare in *Richard II* and *1 Henry IV*. (And, like Shakespeare's *1* and *2 Henry IV*, *The Second Part* invites the question whether the author had conceived it from the outset as part of a larger continuum, or undertook it only after *The First Part's* success had prompted a sequel.)

The first portion of the present edition (whose principles are described below) is based upon the piece published by Wolfe in 1599: *The First Part of the Life and Raigne of King Henrie IIII* (qto., 149 pp.; *STC* 12995 ff.). Apart from a photographic facsimile in 1975 of an edition from c. 1610 (see 'Bibliographical History,' below) it has been neither edited nor republished since 1642. The present edition's second element is based upon a MS scribal copy (Folger Shakespeare Library MS G. a. 12; 73 fols.) of Hayward's unpublishable *continuation* of the published initial segment. The authenticity of this piece, a fair copy made from Hayward's own MSS shortly after his death, is supported by its provenance (see below), by the intrinsic evidence of its intertextual connection with *The First Part*, and by a stylistic similarity to the published portion that would have satisfied Bacon about its authorship, if not the queen. This second text, about two-thirds the length of *The First Part*, extends Hayward's account through the fourth year of Henry's reign, to slightly beyond the battle of Shrewsbury, leaving ten years of Henry's life about which no trace of any further work by Hayward remains. In this respect it is much like his *Annals of Elizabeth* (the other Hayward text published in the Camden Series), which is similarly abbreviated.

2 Hayward and his Contemporaries

For an author to have a lifetime's work eclipsed by a single notable title is not rare, and *The First Part* has naturally absorbed most of the modern attention Hayward has received. Moreover, the stir attending its publication has inclined modern readers to associate its author with misadventure and disappointment, an impression not diminished by the tone of aggrieved long-suffering in which he often later indulged. But the facts of his subsequent career, the intellectual circles in which he moved, and critical assessments of his work by contemporary and other early scholars, all invite, as we shall see, a less sharply politicized appraisal of his contribution. *The First Part,* probably Hayward's first book,[6] was followed by nine other titles, some matching it in popularity and reprinted frequently, even after his death. A two-volume collection of his *Works* appeared in his own lifetime. Viewed in this light, the season of his difficulties with *The First Part* takes on the appearance of an unfortunate early parenthesis in a career of more than modest civic and intellectual accomplishment.

Hayward was about thirty-five when *The First Part* appeared, old enough to allow his claim that he had conceived it more than 'a dozen years' before it appeared.[7] He was born in the town of Felixstowe on the Suffolk coast (or possibly Walton, then a neighbouring parish),[8] most probably in 1564, the year of Shakespeare's birth. His own will[9] makes reference to certain Felixstowe property inherited from his father, suggesting a not altogether penniless background, but in that will he also acknowledges that his boyhood parish undertook to subsidize his education.[10]

That education was at Cambridge, where he graduated B.A. in 1581, and M.A. in 1584. College and university records reveal only the dates of his degrees,[11] which reasonably support assignment of his

---

[6] He was back in print even before the Essex rebellion, with a lengthy devotional piece written no later than autumn, 1600. Although the first (1599) edition of *The First Part* is Hayward's first *extant* published title, the 1601 edition of *The Sanctuarie of a Troubled Soul* (STC 13003.5), entered to John Wolfe, 13 Nov. 1600 (and Wolfe with Burby, 19 Jan. 1601) advertised itself as 'newly enlarged and revised,' suggesting a previous edition, conceivably even earlier than *The First Part.* See Arber, Edward, *A Transcript of the Registers of the Company of Stationers of London 1554–1640* (London, 1875–7), iii, 176, 179, hereafter cited as Arber, and below, 'Chronology of Hayward's Publications.'

[7] PRO SP 12/278, no. 17. Specifically, Hayward testified that he began to write it about a year before its publication, 'but had intended it a dozen years before, although he acquainted no man therewith.'

[8] Norman Scarfe, 'Sir John Hayward, his life and disappointments,' *Proceedings of the Suffolk Institute of Archaeology and Natural History,* No. 25 (1950), 79. No baptismal records for either place survive, nor does clear documentary evidence of the Haywards of Felixstowe, but in Walton the property of a Thomas Harward (the historian's grandfather?) was valued at £2 in 1524, and of a John Haywarde (his father?) at £4 in 1568.

[9] Hayward's will (PCC: Skynner 67), dated 30 March 1626, is reprinted in full by J. Bruce in his edition of Hayward's *Annals of the First Four Years of Queen Elizabeth* (Camden Series, 1840), xli–xlvi.

[10] 'I give to the poor of Felixstowe, in the County of Suffolk, out of which parish I received the means of my education, twenty pounds to remain as a stock, and the profits thence arising to be converted to the use of the poor there for the time being.'

[11] John and J. A. Venn, *Alumni Cantabrigiensis,* Part I (Cambridge, 1922), ii, 342; and *The Book of Matriculations and Degrees in the University of Cambridge from 1544 to 1659* (Cambridge, 1913), 335; Hayward later sought incorporation as D.C.L. at Oxford in 1616: whether he achieved it is unknown: see Anthony A. Wood, *Fasti Oxoniensis; Annals of the University of Oxford,* New ed., additions by Philip Bliss (1815), I, 368. See also Joseph Foster, *Alumni Oxoniensis: The Members of the University of Oxford, 1500–1714* (Oxford, 1891–2), ii, 682.

birth to 1564. One independent notice of his time in Pembroke College surfaced later, ironically in Samuel Harsnett's disclaimer of blame for having licensed *The First Part*.[12]

For several years Hayward remained at Cambridge, becoming Doctor of Laws in 1591. This period of academic seasoning marked a professional beginning, as well. The LL.D. (or D.C.L., at Oxford) degree was the statutory qualification for inclusion among the civil lawyers, who during this period enjoyed exclusive rights to practise in the array of jurisdictions and tribunals, many of them ecclesiastical, where the more numerous barristers, trained up in the common law traditions of the Inns of Court, had no standing.[13] Hayward was actively engaged in this civil practice at least as early as 1595, when the Archbishop of Canterbury issued a warrant for his admission as advocate to the Court of Arches, the province's highest ecclesiastical court.[14] When *The First Part* appeared in 1599, Hayward could already claim several years' experience in a public and very contentious profession.

His choice of profession had much to do with how he viewed his world, and it is difficult to overemphasise the heavy influence it exerted upon his formation as an historian. The civil jurisdiction derived its authority from the deductive traditions of the Justinianic Code, from ancient commentaries, and from canon law. Its secular opposite had developed by induction, upon the cases and precedents of common law. Hayward's understanding of history's purposes and uses, his style, and his handling of source materials all reflect the very qualities prized in civil advocacy.[15] The way others saw him was probably influenced by his professional identity, as well. Although the

[12] PRO SP 12/275, no. 31 (see below).
[13] The Act of 1545 allowed Doctors of Civil Law, although laymen and married, to exercise ecclesiastical jurisdiction. About two dozen civilians were in active practice at the turn of the century, and never numbered more than 70 at a time, whilst the barristers numbered at least 400 at the same time. Besides serving in the archbishop's courts (the Courts of the Arches and of Audience, the Prerogative Court, the Court of Peculiars and the Court of the Vicar General), and as ecclesiastical officials of various kinds, civilians were judges in Admiralty and peculiar jurisdictions, and masters in courts of Requests and Chancery, and the courts of high commission. See Brian Levack, *The Civil Lawyers in England, 1603–1641* (Oxford, 1973), 7–49; *also* Levack, 'The English Civilians, 1500–1750,' 109, 112, 119; and Wilfred Prest, 'The English Bar, 1550–1700,' 67; both in W. Prest, ed., *Lawyers in Early Modern Europe and America* (1981). See also W.S. Holdsworth, *A History of English Law*, 7 vols. (1924), i, 593.
[14] Lambeth Palace Library, MS 1351; *Whitgift Register* ii, fol. 132.
[15] In BL MS Lansdowne 418 (402) ('Dr. Hayward touching remaunding of prisoners') we see a remarkable illustration of the civilian's respect for the force of historical authority in legal pleadings. Here Hayward, in an opinion drafted for a case in admiralty (8 July 1618), reaches for instructive principle back to the Samnites, the Lacedaemonians, the Israelites and King Herod.

civil advocates, ranking closest to the legal profession's elite, the
Serjeants-at-Law, claimed a higher social status, they were as a whole
far less representative of 'country' than the barristers, and their
number included proportionately more sons of commoners such as
Hayward.[16] In consequence, they tended more than the barristers to
depend upon their profession for upward mobility. It was still the case
when Hayward took up the practice of law that only civilians were
eligible for appointment to a great number of administrative and
judicial posts in those courts whose tradition reflected not the common,
but the civil (or canon) law.[17] The result was 'a profession of civil
servants,'[18] who looked to the archbishop and the crown for protection,
income and advancement. This relationship became more dependent
under James I and Charles I, whose reigns developed into something
like a continuing lawsuit between crown and parliament, and whose
autonomy was increasingly baulked in the common law courts.[19]
Throughout his professional lifetime Hayward was joined to an elite
but increasingly pressured group. Most of them, like Hayward, were
prompted by either background or professional self-interest to favour
the Stuarts. On the whole, he and his fellow civilians occupied a
lucrative but certainly controversial patch of ground increasingly
isolated and exposed to professional, political and religious crossfire.

But he was also more than a lawyer. In fact, during the months
when official scrutiny of his book on Henry was growing most severe,
another book by Hayward, quite unlike *The First Part*, began to
compete successfully for the reading public's attention. This was *The
Sanctuarie of a Troubled Soule*,[20] entered to John Wolfe 13 November

---

[16] Levack, *Civil Lawyers*, 3–9.

[17] The jurisdictions in which the civilians practised or held official posts – chancery,
admiralty, the ecclesiastical courts – handled an enormous portion of the capital's legal
work. Under More (C 1529–32) Chancery heard about 500 cases. Under the chancellors
(or Lords Keeper) of James I, the same tribunal heard over 32,220 cases, an average
of nearly 1500 per year (Holdsworth, i, 409). The adjudication and administration of
matters pertaining to wills, family law and other proceedings depending for legitimacy
upon the crown prerogative – like the peculiars and the courts of High Commission –
similarly belonged almost exclusively to the civilians. The church courts were themselves far-reaching, handling cases of ecclesiastical property as well as persons. This
great body of legal activity, which until the time of Elizabeth's grandfather and the
last of the churchmen-chancellors had been guided by canon law and chancery
procedures, was by now nominally secularized, but Henry VIII's statute dismantling
the canon law in England had been quickly recognized as unfeasible, and its chief
effect was a charge to the universities to replace the training of 'canon' lawyers with
the training of 'civil' lawyers.

[18] The phrase is Levack's, in *Civil Lawyers*, 7; 'English Civilians', 117.

[19] F. Smith Fussner, *The Historical Revolution: English Historical Writing and Thought,
1580–1640* (1962), 118, and esp. Ch. 5.

[20] STC 13003.5.

1600, and to Wolfe with Burby 19 January 1601.[21] Its publication, if not its authorship,[22] evidently dates from the early months of Hayward's imprisonment. Its durable popularity is attested by a dozen editions by 1636. During his lifetime it brought him more acclaim than his histories, and in his later years he followed it with other similarly successful devotional titles: *David's Teares* (1622), and *Christ's Prayer upon the Cross for His Enemies* (1623). It was later claimed that he was 'accounted a learned and godly man, being better read in theological authors than in those belonging to his own profession.'[23]

None of the unpleasant consequences of *The First Part's* publication, including nearly three years' imprisonment, appear to have outlived the queen. Released from the Tower upon her death, or upon James's accession,[24] he wrote on 6 June 1603, to the new king, urging the importance of contemporary historiography, and dedicating to him his scholarly skills;[25] if his pen had incriminated him under Elizabeth, it would exculpate him under James. Only fourteen days after Elizabeth's death, his *An Answer to the First Part of a Certain Conference Concerning Succession* was entered for printing,[26] and published not much later that same year.[27] In this book he argues the Stuart case against the Spanish preferences of the Jesuits, turning his scholarly weapons against the infamous Father Parsons. It was a learned and lawyerly brief, deriving from ancient authorities and the *Corpus Juris Civilis* the validity of discerning in the English throne the Roman imperial authority of an earlier age.[28] *A Treatise of the Union of the Two*

[21] Arber, iii, 176, 179.

[22] The title-page of the (first extant) 1601 edition proclaims itself an enlarged and emended edition, and another edition in 1602 identifies itself as 'a third time enlarged;' this suggests a lost first edition, from 1600, or earlier.

[23] Wood, *Fasti*, I, 368.

[24] PRO E407/56, pt. 2, fols. 93–98 (details below).

[25] Bodl. MS Smith, 70, fols. 23–5.

[26] 7 Apr. 1603; Arber, iii, 94.

[27] At the new king's accession, Catholic apologists disputed the justification of the new king's authority, whilst Puritans found fresh opportunity to dispute royal supremacy and episcopal jurisdiction in religious matters. Levack (*Civil Lawyers*, 88–9) notes that several civilians, including Hayward, 'provided James with considerable intellectual assistance in his attempt to counter these claims.' See also G. L. Mosse, 'The Influence of Jean Bodin's *République* on English Historical Thought,' *Medievalia et Humanistica*, V (1948), 73–83, esp. 80.

[28] This may have been a disingenuous undertaking: by rebutting 'Doleman,' Hayward put some distance between himself and Essex, to whom the *Conference on Succession* had been dedicated. On the other hand, the Essex connection would not, on the whole, have been entirely objectionable to James. Not incidentally, its dedication (to James) enabled Hayward to make, with benefit of hindsight, an exculpating claim about the politics of *The First Part*: 'I here present unto your majesty this defence, both of the present authority of princes, and of succession according to proximity of blood: wherein is maintainted that the people have no lawful power to remove the one or repel the

Realms of England and Scotland appeared in 1604, followed by *A Report of a Discourse concerning Supreme Power in Affairs of Religion* in 1606, in which he concentrates on the important point that 'the political government in ecclesiastical affairs should be a point of regality.'[29] This flurry of historiography applied to political dispute, certainly pleasing to James, reflected thoughtful and carefully prepared scholarship, pressing ancient authority to the service of legal disputation in the best tradition of the civil lawyers. In his writings of this period, Hayward emerged as a vigorous advocate of protestant royalism and its theoretical underpinnings. These three titles were in effect briefs arguing a basis in civil law for the absolute authority of the king.[30]

If a subtext of such briefs was to reestablish himself with those in power, Hayward succeeded. By the end of the new century's first decade, when he was 46, his protestant orthodoxy and political reliability had earned his appointment as one of two official historiographers of the king's new college in Chelsea. A project urged by Matthew Sutcliffe, Dean of Exeter, the college was intended for the study of 'polemical divinity'; it would be a community close to Whitehall and Westminster where learned divines would seek the 'advancement of reformed religion, and in defence thereof from the attacks of the church of Rome.' To its initial membership the king named Sutcliffe as provost, sixteen churchmen as fellows, and the laymen Camden and Hayward: 'their employment was to consist in recording the principal historical events which might occur during the time that they remained in office.'[31]

During the ensuing decade, Hayward's appointment to several judicial posts credits him with a respectable level of professional

other: in which two points I have also heretofore declared my opinion, by publishing the tragical events which ensued the deposition of King Richard and usurpation of King Henry the Fourth. Both these labours were undertaken with particular respect to your majesty's just title of succession in this realm.' Lily B. Campbell, *Shakespeare's 'Histories,' Mirrors of Elizabethan Policy* (San Marino, 1947), 186, for comment upon Hayward's claim that both *An Answer* and *The First Part* were intended as rejoinders to Parson's assertion that Richard II's deposition offered useful guidance in choosing Elizabeth's successor.

[29] This was republished in 1624 as *Of Supremacie in Affaires of Religion*. Its sub-title summarizes accurately the book's argument: 'Manifesting that this power is a right of regalitie, inseparably annexed to the soveraignty of every state: and that it is a thing both extreamely dangerous, and contrarie to the use of all aunceint empires and commonwealths, to acknowledge the same in a forraigne prince.'

[30] Levack, *Civil Lawyers*, 86–117; F. J. Levy, *Tudor Historical Thought* (San Marino, 1967), 263.

[31] Thomas Faulkner, *An Historical and Topographical Description of Chelsea and its Environs*, (2 vols., Chelsea, 1829), ii, 218–34. Faulkner describes the difficulties the college encountered: one of eight planned wings was actually built, and a programme carried out for several years, but in the absence of adequate funding it could not survive King Charles's indifference.

accomplishment, and confirms his good opinion at James's court. There is evidence of his holding certain prerogative court appointments as early as 1609 when, besides occasional pleadings in Admiralty and in the Court of Common Piracy, he appears as Commissioner of Admiralty for Middlesex.[32] By 1613 he was serving in the Court of Delegates (the post-Reformation court of ecclesiastical appeals which had replaced the appellate tribunal of the papacy), and as Commissioner for Policies and Assurances.[33] By around 1617 he was Commissioner for Shoreham and Croydon Peculiars.[34] Although scattered, such evidence is persuasive that his professional fortunes were steadily rising. He was becoming one of the small coterie of civilians who dominated London civil practice during the period.[35]

Between 1616 and 1619 Hayward's accomplishments were ratified in very public ways. The cap of Master in Chancery, with which he was ritually adorned on 13 November 1616, ultimately confirmed him as a senior legal officer in the Crown's service.[36] There were twelve such Masters, who assisted in the hearing of cases as deputies to the Lord Keeper, and in whose gift lay their appointment. It was regarded as a lucrative post: Hayward probably paid about £250 to secure and maintain it. The twelve Masterships were reckoned to bring the Lord Keeper about £3000 per year, and the post may have been worth £2000 per year to Hayward.[37] At about this time his name surfaces among investors in the Bermuda and Virginia ventures.[38] In

[32] PRO HCA 1/32/1, fols. 38,55; HCA 24/73, fols.10, 110, 262, 266.

[33] PRO DEL 5/5–6; DEL 8/70, part ii.

[34] PRO C. 181/2, fols. 101v, 194, 213, 214, 219v, 220.

[35] Although strictly speaking not Crown appointments, each of his assignments represented advancement within the patronage system governing nomination and confirmation of officials in these courts, and indicates a degree of security within the central government's judicial civil service. Such appointments were commonly obtained – and maintained – upon substantial payment to the Crown official in whose gift they lay: Hayward's very ability to capitalize his advancement argues a degree of success. Moreover, the readiness of candidates to invest in such positions reveals something of their value. Officers like Hayward were paid in fees and gratuities, not salaries or wages, and the very volume of court business whose execution they supervised ensured a rather good living for most civilians who secured such posts.

[36] Holdsworth, i, 417; Edward Foss, *The Judges of England* (1857), 8–9.

[37] G.E. Aylmer, *The King's Servants: The Civil Service of Charles I, 1625–1642* (London, 1961), 238.

[38] His name appears among investors with 'several summes adventured' in certain of the speculative ventures in the New World. Although the evidence is scattered, he seems to have backed both the Bermuda and Virginia Companies (1615, 1618), and he is very likely the 'Maister John Hayward' entered for the latter company as late as 1620. Susan M. Kingsbury, *The Records of the Virginia Company of London*, (4 vols., Washington, 1906–35), iii, 84, 327; iv, 306, 365. Theodore K. Rabb, *Enterprise and Empire: Merchant and Gentry Investment in the Expansion of England, 1575–1630* (Cambridge, Mass., 1967), esp. 233–410.

1616 he was also admitted to Doctors' Commons (5 August) and later to Gray's Inn (1 August 1619, possibly an honorific admission).[39] He was granted arms,[40] and he was knighted by James at Whitehall on 9 November 1619.[41]

During the 1620s, and perhaps earlier, Hayward served on the High Commission,[42] the very investigative and judicial mechanism by which he had been ground in 1599 and 1600. Both Chancery and the High Commission were closely and specifically associated with crown prerogative. During Hayward's lifetime, Chancery itself became a fiercely contested jurisdictional ground between 'Crown and Country', resented, like Admiralty and the ecclesiastical courts, by common lawyers ('jealous of every jurisdiction not their own')[43] and by Puritans and other supporters of anti-clerical and anti-royalist

[39] Lambeth Palace Library, Register of Doctors' Commons, fols. 47v, 108; C. Coote, *Sketches of the Lives and Characters of Eminent Civilians, etc. . . . to the Close of the Year 1803* (1804), 73-4; Joseph Foster, *The Register of Admissions to Gray's Inn, 1521-1889* (1889), 154.

[40] Joan Corder, *A Dictionary of Suffolk Arms* (Suffolk Records Society, vii, 1965), 295.

[41] DNB; Venn, ii, 342; Coote, 73; Foster, *Alum. Ox.*, ii, 682.

[42] Toward the end of his life, Hayward's posts as Master and Commissioner brought him nearer to centre stage as early scenes of the estrangement between parliament and crown were acted out. One victim of parliamentary displeasure thinly disguised as judicial reform was Chancellor Bacon, charged with financially exploiting his office, and particularly its fee and gratuity system. He and civilian officials like Hayward were said to have evaded recent statutory efforts to limit the fee abuse in Chancery and other prerogative courts. As part of this complicated business a charge was brought in the Parliament of 1621 that 'Sir John Bennet, as Judge of the Prerogative, of Delegates, as Chancellor to the Queen, as Master of Chancery and as High Commissioner' had 'deeply offended' by collecting extortionate fees. Hayward was named, on 19 April, as the deputy who took £40 in a probate case for delivery to Bennett. See W. Notestein, F. H. Relf, and H. Simpson (eds.), *Commons Debates, 1621* (New Haven, 1935), 5:337-8, and *Proceedings and Debates of the House of Commons in 1620 and 1621, Collected by a Member of that House* (Oxford, 1766), 279-80, 304. Four days later in the Commons were singled out 'the Masters in Chancery charged with taking fees contrary to the Statute: Sir John Bird, Sir Edward Thelwel, Sir John Hayward and James Hussey.'(Notestein, 6:92) The target was Bacon, not the Masters, and his fall left his Masters in place. Five years later another Commons, more jealous than its predecessor of its prerogatives, reacted fiercely against an action in which the High Commission (of which Hayward was by now a member) excommunicated and imprisoned a sitting member, Sir Robert Howard, despite his claim of parliamentary privilege. On 3 May 1626, Hayward was grilled about his role in the affair: 'Sir Jo. Hayward called in about Sir Ro. Howard his Business, and interrogated, by Mr. Speaker, divers questions: Answereth, he was not present, when Sir Ro. Howard was committed close Prisoner. That he was present at the Excommunication: he saw Sir Ro. Howard tender a Paper to the Lord Keeper, but heard no Word of Privilege of Parliament spoken of . . .' (*Journal of the House of Commons,* i, 854; also 858, 861, 869, 871.) As before, Hayward and his colleagues seem not to have been penalized. See also *Bulstrode Whitelock's Journal of the Parliament of 1626* (in CUL *Compiled Parliamentary Journals*, Dd 12. 20-2.), fols. 175v, 176.

[43] Holdsworth, v, 257-61 and 423-4.

views. Coke's downfall in 1616 devolved from his challenge to prerogative authority; on the other side, Francis Bacon's enemies found
his administration of Chancery the most strategic point at which to
attack him a few years later. Despite such turmoil Hayward, having
gained his Mastership under Egerton (C 1596–1617), outlasted both
Bacon (C 1617–21) and Williams (C 1621–25), and until his death in
1627 served under Coventry (C 1625–40) as well.

Hayward was an acknowledged member of London's intellectual
elite from the early days of James I's reign. An unsigned petition
(probably drafted by Henry Ferrars in 1617) to reconstitute the
Elizabethan Society of Antiquaries, suppressed in 1604, recommends
for a proposed Academy Royal a list of 27 'names I have seen quoted,
and heard often-times cited as authoritative.' In this cross-section of
intellectual Stuart London, among 'incomparable' Camden, Fulke
Greville, Francis Tate, George Buck, Bulstrode Whitelock, John
Selden, Sir Edward Coke, Sir Peter Manwood and Sir Henry Savile
we find 'Mr. John Hayward, Doctor of Laws, a fair and learned
historian.'[44] Meetings at which antiquarian topics were set for debate
reflected the professional and intellectual vitality of the participants,
among whom Hayward was featured in at least one such session: *Of
the precedencye of Doctors and Masters of the Chauncerye before Serieaunts att
Lawe, with the arguments for both sides, collected by Sir John Hayward, one
of the Masters of said Courte, and answered by Mr. Francis Tate of the Middle
Temple. 22 January 1604.*[45] Hayward's own account of a dinner at
Bishop Toby Mathew's house provides a hint of the society in which
he was circulating by early 1606.[46] Degory Wheare, the Camden

[44] *Archaeologia*, i (1770), 'Introduction: containing an historical account of the origin
and establishment of the Society of Antiquaries.' xv-xxi. (The petition, possibly by
Henry Ferrars, is unsigned.) See also Ethel M. Portal, 'The Academy Roial of King
James I,' *Proceedings of the British Academy, 1915–16*, 189–208. She cites Edmund Bolton's
proposed membership list of '84 essential members,' which does not include Hayward,
and in which many of Bolton's Catholic associates have displaced several earlier
nominees. See also BL Harl MS 5177 (1591?), fol. 171, which offers a similar list,
including a 'Dr. of Lawes' who might be Hayward.

[45] BL Additional MS 22587, fols. 33–6. This MS, probably an abstract of such a
session, is dated retrospectively (Hayward was neither knight nor Master until much
later). Tate was well known as a learned barrister and member of Middle Temple.
Until Elizabeth's reign the Masters in Chancery had enjoyed an unquestioned social
ascendancy over the Serjeants-at-law, the officers of the Court of Common Pleas whose
position was most analogous to the Masters' own. Their contest for precedence was an
early emblem of a rivalry that would flare into open resentment under Egerton and
Coke, and it reflected the contending constitutional assumptions of both parties about
Crown prerogative and common law.

[46] In *A Reporte of a Discourse concerning Supreme Power in Religion* (1606; see above). In
this 'symposium' piece, dinner-table conversation initiates Hayward's discourse, which
becomes a carefully-argued, citation-laden brief supporting supremacy in religion as a
point of regality. Mathew, himself a notable civilian, was Bishop of Durham and

Reader in History at Oxford, thought him in 1623 a 'very candid, true and learned writer.'[47] And Roger Ley, whose assessment of bishops, divines and scholars notable principally during his own lifetime conveys a sense of first-hand authenticity, groups '*excertatissimus Johannes Haywardus*' with Thomas Bodley, John Cowell and William Camden. '*Nam claruit his temporibus,*' he says, '*et libros eruditissimos composuit*'*;* he enumerates several of Hayward's contributions to history, Stuart orthodoxy and devotional literature, and confirms that these earned Hayward his lucrative appointment as commissary to the Dean and Chapter of St. Paul's.[48]

Hayward was undoubtedly close to the young Henry, prince of Wales; he may have exercised a tutorial role in the prince's education. He describes in detail how the prince urged him to publish *The Lives of the III Normans, Kings of England.* Apparently, *The Beginning of the Reigne of Queene Elizabeth* (eventually published with *The Life and Raigne of King Edward the Sixt* after Hayward's death) owed something to the prince's encouragement as well.[49] Before his death at eighteen, Prince Henry had assembled a personal court of politically engaged and artistically accomplished men. Some had been closely associated with Essex. Others, by virtue of talent irrespective of politics, found either patronage or employment in the household of a young prince celebrated for his interest in arts and learning. Hayward, like Francis Bacon, Walter Raleigh and Inigo Jones, was suited to these favoured and prominent groupings on both counts: association with Essex, and a scholarly and literate protestantism.[50]

eventually Archbishop of York, while several dinner guests sound like thoroughly royalist Protestants.

[47] Degory Wheare, *The Method and Order of Reading Both Civil and Ecclesiastical Histories ... etc.* (1685), 171. Originally published as *De Ratione et Methodo Legendi Historias* (1623).

[48] BL MS Stowe 76, fols. 257–7b.

[49] Hayward records (in the Dedication of *The Lives of the III Normans, Kings of England,* 1613) that the prince asked if he 'had wrote any part of our English history.' Hayward told him of his work on the *III Normans,* but expressed a preference for writing upon contemporary matters. The prince desired to see both sorts, and Hayward readied for his inspection both the *III Normans* and 'certain yeares of Queene Elizabeth's reigne' (edited for the Camden Society in 1840 by J. Bruce as *Annals of Elizabeth*). 'At his return from the progress to his house at St. James, these pieces were delivered unto him; which he did not only courteously, but joyfuly accept: and, because this [*III Normans*] seemed a perfect work, he expressed a desire that it should be published. Not long after he died; and with him died both my endeavours and my hopes.' One of 'these pieces' may have been the large-copy reprint of *The First Part* (see Prof. Jackson's remarks, below, in 'Bibliographical History').

[50] Sir Roy Strong, *Henry, Prince of Wales, and England's Lost Renaissance* (1986). Associates of Essex in Henry's circle included the Earl of Southampton, Thomas Chaloner, Walter Ralegh, Lionel Sharp, Inigo Jones and Francis Bacon; the prince also encouraged the poets Joseph Hall, Sir Arthur Gorges, Samuel Daniel, Michael Drayton, George

In the years after Henry's death, as the Jacobean court became marked by extravagance and by the Duke of Buckingham's political dominance, the gravitational pull of disaffection helped reshape earlier associations. Hayward's emphatic preference for traditional values over upstarts, and his firmly held view of the importance of honour, with its implicit argument on behalf of government by a talented and hereditary aristocracy (both views thematic to his work on Henry IV), were as appealing to James and Arundel as they had been to the Essex faction.[51] Many who had been on familiar terms with the late Prince of Wales were drawn to the circle of the Earl of Arundel,[52] who shared Henry's interest in antiquity and its cultural importance, and who resisted the mainstream trends of Jacobean politics. Jones, Hayward and Ben Jonson had been part of Prince Henry's circle. John Selden, close to Jonson, was Arundel's lawyer. Robert Cotton, especially close to the earl, undertook research commissions at Arundel's request, as did Camden and Hayward.[53]

The relationship between Camden and Hayward is difficult to piece together from available evidence. Camden mentions *The First Part* and its dedication in his account (itself Tacitean) of the Essex trial, but appears to hold Hayward free from much blame, distinguishing him from the immoderate elements of the Essex faction, and describing him as a learned man who suffered an unfortunate reprisal brought about by choosing the wrong season in which to publish his book.[54] Hayward relied upon certain material in Camden's possession for his *Lives of the Three Normans, Kings of England*, written before 1612, with

Chapman (who made his translation of Homer at Henry's urging) and Sir William Alexander.

[51] Mervyn James, 'At a crossroads of the political culture: the Essex Revolt, 1601,' in *Society, Politics and Culture: Studies in Early Modern England* (Oxford, 1986), 416–65. James argues that the Essex revolt, 'like that of Hayward's Henry of Lancaster, had honour as its constitutive principle' (423). He analyses 'the secular, politic and Tacitean formulation of these attitudes undertaken by the intellectuals in the ambience of Essex House, of whose work Hayward's *First Part* was an outstanding instance' (437). See also his 'English politics and the concept of honour, 1485–1642', ibid. 308–415.

[52] Kevin Sharpe, 'The Earl of Arundel, his circle and the opposition to the Duke of Buckingham,' in K. Sharpe, ed., *Faction and Parliament: Essays in Early Stuart History* (Oxford, 1978).

[53] Most of Cotton's work in the 1620s resulted from his connections with other of Arundel's friends and household. Kevin Sharpe, *Sir Robert Cotton, 1586–1631: History and Politics in Early Modern England* (Oxford, 1979), 208–9.

[54] It is in the context of discussing Meyrick's seditious intent in reviving the Richard play that Camden mentions Hayward's book: '*Liberque paullo ante eodem argumento ab Haywardo erudito viro editus, & Essexio dicatus, eandem judicii aleam subiit, quasi in documentum & incitamentum Reginam solio deturbandam scriptus; infelici auctoris fato, qui diturno luit intempestivam editionem, & haec verbula in Praefatione ad Essexium, Tu magnus spe, major futuri temporis exspectatione.*' In Thomas Hearne, ed., *Annalium Rerum Anglicarum et Hibernicarum Regnante Elizabetha* (3 vols., 1717), 867–8.

which Camden implies a certain professional familiarity in an undated letter to Sir Robert Cotton.[55]

Hayward's association with Cotton is better known. Their collaboration on the Earl Marshal Arundel's commission to prepare a carefully researched account of his ancestors, is documented from 1613 and endured into the 1620s.[56] Although during the last decade of his life Hayward appears to have given over the writing of British history for general publication, he edited Sir Roger Williams's *The Actions of the Lowe Countries*, published in 1618.

The commoner's son from Felixstowe died on 27 June 1627, possessed of substantial wealth. In his will he describes the parish of St. Bartholomew the Great, Smithfield, as a venue 'where I have long remained.'[57] When he moved there is unknown, but it is certain that he resided in Bartholomew Close from 1622, when he took out a forty-year lease, until his death in 1627. His house was itself evidence of respectable prosperity. It was one of the largest and most expensive of the old glebe houses,[58] in a neighbourhood containing many spacious homes clustered about the church.[59]

[55] BL MS Cotton Julius C III, f. 60: 'Good Sir Cotton: Mr. Bill sent to me 2 Copies Rexs Normannicarum, but without Titles, Praefaces, or Lettre. I doubt not but they were sent by Mr. Peiresc, or by Chesne, to you and me, and therefore have sent you one of them. I hope I shall not be seen in the matter of Arundell. *Tuus tuo merito, Guil. Camdenus.*' This is undated, but Hayward's book was first published in 1613. Bill, printer to the king, would become Hayward's publisher during the 1620s, and his mortgagee as well. Camden's somewhat cryptic remark about 'the matter of Arundell' may refer to the ancestral research commissioned by the Earl Marshal from Cotton and Hayward (below).

[56] Arundel (from Padua, 29 August 1613): 'Sir Robert Cotton, I must give you thankes (for the care you please to take nowe) double, because it is for an absent frend, which is not generall in these our times. For Mr. Doctor Haywardes opinnion, to weave in our auncestors lives into the story of the kinges, I should concurre with him, if it were a thinge to be published. But you may lette him knowe that I only intend it as a private memory to befit my house. ... I beseech you the story may goe on, I will sticke no chardge that is fitt' (BL MS Cotton Julius C III, f. 204). And two weeks later, from Venice, another letter to Cotton: 'I beseech you, let the story of my ancestors go on, as I intended, by itself, because (as I wrote unto you) it shall never be published' (ibid. f. 205). Bodl. MS Smith 71, ff. 95, 125.

[57] The will mentions holdings near Wood Green and at Felixstowe, and houses and lands in Kentish Town worth £1300 mortgaged to him by the king's printer, John Bill, and substantial cash bequests.

[58] The elegant scale of Hayward's house is evident not only from area plans, but from its division at his death into three houses, and again into five by 1739. In the late 16th century it brought the highest rental of all the glebe houses. Hayward's rent is not recorded, but before 1622 it brought £4 p.a., and upon expiration of his lease in 1662 it was let again at £16 p.a. E. A. Webb, *The Records of St. Bartholomew's Priory and of the Church and Parish of St. Bartholomew the Great, West Smithfield*. (2 vols., Oxford, 1921), ii, 224, 274.

[59] It had been a fashionable address for many years, during which period Sir Walter Mildmay, Sir Thomas Neale, Sir Henry Carey, Sir Roger Manwood and Sir Thomas

But despite wealth, despite professional and scholarly recognition, despite his knighthood and his holdings, Hayward carried an aggrieved tone to his grave. Pointed instructions in his will to spurn both his wife and his daughter's relatives by marriage in favour of his granddaughter sound vindictive, particularly from an author celebrated for godly writings. It seems ironically consistent with his characteristic pessimism that the granddaughter died as a child, and that despite both his insistent precautions against body-snatchers and his related demands for an elaborate monument at St. Bartholomew's (both carefully specified in his will), no indication of his place of burial there survives.

3 The Publication and Suppression of The First Part

What befell *The First Part of the Life and Raigne of King Henrie IIII* and its author between 1599 and 1603[60] affords a useful glimpse of a world where 'men might safely write of others in manner of a tale; but in manner of a history, safely they could not.' The events of this period were painful, and ten years would elapse before Hayward would be induced, by Prince Henry, to publish another of his historical writings (*The Lives of the III Normans, Kings of England*, 1613), with a dedicatory preface reporting his complaint to the prince about readers who discovered unintended meanings in histories. His histories of Edward VI and Elizabeth never appeared in his lifetime. In what follows, I have attempted to sketch how his work on Henry IV came to achieve such unsought consequences.

The episode began late in 1598, when Hayward requested John Wolfe 'to print the book entitled Henry IV.'[61] On 9 January 1599

Walsingham had maintained their residences there. The nearby Charterhouse had become, after the dissolution, the residence of the Duke of Norfolk; Lord Rich, Chancellor under Edward VI, had lived near Hayward's house. The district, as Bruce points out (p. xxxiv), was 'a situation well suited to the practice of [Hayward's] profession, and containing, at that time, many excellent family mansions.' The site of Hayward's home, later nos. 92 and 93 Bartholomew Close, was damaged by German bombs in both wars. See Webb, ii, 222, 224, 274–5.

[60] For many years the fullest account of these events was Margaret Dowling's 'Sir John Hayward's troubles over his *Life of Henry IV*,' *The Library*, 4th ser., 11 (1930), 212–24.

[61] Wolfe's account of the book's origins, of his role in its publication and of its removal from circulation is found in a summary transcript of his interrogation (13 July 1600), PRO SP 12/275, no. 28. Wolfe was apprenticed in 1562 and first appears as a printer in Florence in the mid-1570s. He caused a stir in London in the early-1580s by challenging press monopolies by illegally printing titles reserved by Queen's Privilege to others. The Stationers appear to have co-opted him: by 1587 he was beadle of the company. After 1593, when he became Printer to the City, he worked exclusively as a publisher, contracting his printing work to other shops. He printed or published over 400 titles, including many in Italian, and was a principal source of books reporting on the Protestant-Catholic struggles in France. His name is linked to several surreptitious

Wolfe secured his copyright and authorization to print, 'under the hands of Master Harsnet and the Wardens' of the Stationers' Company.[62] Unlike Samuel Harsnett, the bishop's *censor deputatus* who licensed it routinely but would later regret that action,[63] Wolfe recognized in Hayward's history the potentially strong popular appeal it soon demonstrated. It was evidently Wolfe who suggested its dedication to the Earl of Essex.[64] The earl was, as Wolfe later pointed out, 'a martiall man,' and by January 1599 everyone expected the queen to appoint him leader of her forces against the Irish rebels. The book's dedication, laced with superlatives, seemed to forecast enlargement of the controversial nobleman's political importance: '. . . *Optimo &* *Nobilissimo (inquit Euripedes) ex qua sententia tu primus ac solus fere occur- rebas (illustrissime comes) cuius nome si Henrici nostri fronte radiaret, ipse & laetior & tutior in vulgus prodiret. Magnus siquidem es, & presenti iudicio, & futuri temporis expectatione. . . .*'

But the anticipated patronage of Essex soon proved troublesome. When the printshop work was finished in early February, Wolfe left a copy of *The First Part* for the earl at Whitehall, Hayward being ill. At about the same time, the book went on sale. By mid-February there had been no word from Essex, but an eager public was snatching up copies. It was awkward to have a book so dedicated in the hands of so many readers, with no sign that the powerful earl approved of such wholesale capitalization on his name. Wolfe's repeated inquiries were deflected by intermediaries.[65] It was claimed later that Essex purposely waited until the book's widespread circulation was assured

editions of Machiavelli, to certain notable civilians (especially Aretini), and to both the Marprelate and Harvey-Nashe-Greene controversies (Harvey was a close associate). Wolfe died in 1601. The fullest account of his career is by Clifford C. Huffman, *Elizabethan Impressions: John Wolfe and His Press* (New York, 1988), although mention of Hayward's book is restricted to a single note (p. 180). For more on Wolfe's work, see Harry R. Hoppe, 'John Wolfe, printer and publisher, 1579–1601,' *The Library*, 4th ser., xiv (1933), 241–88; H. Sellers, 'Italian books printed in England before 1640,' *The Library*, 4th ser., v (1924–5), 107; R. B. McKerrow, ed., *A Dictionary of Printers and Booksellers in England, Scotland and Ireland, and of Foreign Printers of English Books, 1557– 1640* (London, 1919), 296–8. See also H. R. Plomer, 'An examination of some existing copies of Hayward's "Life and Raigne of King Henrie IV,"' *The Library*, 2nd ser., iii (1902), 13–23.

[62] Arber, iii, 134.

[63] A detailed account of Harsnett's involvement appears in W. W. Greg, 'Samuel Harsnett and Hayward's *Henry IV*,' *The Library*, 5th ser., xi (1956), 1–10.

[64] PRO SP 12/275, no. 28, Wolfe: 'it had no epistle dedicatory or to the reader when first brought to him; after some conversation between them, it was dedicated to the Earl of Essex.'

[65] PRO SP 12/275, no. 28. He 'went three or four times, by direction of the doctor, to the Earl, he being then at the Court at Richmond, to learn what he thought of it, but was always put off by some of his men that his Lordship was much busied about his voyage to Ireland, and so never spoke to him.'

before responding to the extravagant dedication.[66] When it did come, his response was troubling: before February was out, he wrote to Archbishop Whitgift, suggesting an inquiry into the matter of the book's dedication. Whitgift soon obliged: within three weeks of publication, Wolfe later testified, 'the wardens of the Stationers' Company received order from my Lord of Canterbury that the epistle dedicated to the Earl should be cut out.'[67]

Despite this mutilation (if it occurred: although Wolfe later insisted that he complied with the episcopal order, no extant copy lacks the dedication page),[68] demand remained steady. Wolfe clearly had a best-seller on his hands. About half the edition had been sold, and the remaining five or six hundred would soon be bought up. Wolfe's commercial sense was vindicated, since a press run of a thousand copies was no small investment. In his words, 'no book ever sold better'.

The book's sudden popularity seemed to centre on two issues, one Hayward's apparent political encouragement of an ambitious but controversial earl, the other its potentially allusive subject matter. Either matter invited questions about the timing of the publication, and early public opinion seems divided: by 1 March, John Chamberlain had bought a copy to send to his friend Dudley Carleton in Ostend:

> ... for lack of better matter I send you three or four toys to pass away the time. ... The treatise of Henry the fourth is reasonably well written. The author is a young man of Cambridge toward the civil law. Here hath been much descanting about it, why such a story should come out at this time, and many exceptions taken, especially to the epistle which was a short thing in Latin dedicated to the Earl of Essex, and objected to him in good earnest, whereupon there was a commandment that it should be cut out of the book, yet I have got you a transcript of it that you may pick out the offence if you can. For my part, I can find no such bugswords, but that everything is as it is taken.[69]

For Chamberlain, the magnet of contemporary interest seems to have been the dedication. Indeed, the promptness of Whitgift's suppression order, and the earl's own complaint (both of which addressed *only* the dedication), support the view that in February the book's association

---

[66] PRO SP 12/278, nos. 54, 63, 94; and below, 26–7, 33.
[67] PRO SP 12/275, no. 28.
[68] The dedication page contained on its verso a list of 'Faultes escaped in the printing' (see text), a practical reason for preserving it. But Coke's notes (PRO SP 12/275, 25) seem to confirm the excision, as does Chamberlain's letter to Carleton, below.
[69] *The Letters of John Chamberlain*, ed. N.E. McClure (Philadelphia, 1939), i, 70.

with Essex invited much more suspicion than its contents. On the one hand, *Magnus . . . futuri temporis expectatione* was not an unreasonable plaudit for the hero, especially by comparison with dedicatory flattery then in vogue. Furthermore, the previous year Richard Grenewey had dedicated to Essex his translation of the *Annals* of Tacitus, issued in a double volume with Sir Henry Savile's *The Ende of Nero and the Beginning of Galba,* and Savile's translation (dedicated to the queen) of the *Histories* of Tacitus, whose prefatory 'A.B. to the Reader,' extolling the virtues of Tacitean history, is generally thought to have been written by Essex.[70] On the other hand, dedications could prove troublesome, particularly if they implied the dedicatee's endorsement of a text's argument. As recently as 1595 Essex had been endangered by *A Conference about the Next Succession to the Crown of England,* a polemic in two volumes by one 'R. Doleman' (understood to be the Jesuit Robert Parsons), who argued that claims to the English succession ought to rest upon more than blood descent. It was a candid discussion of the relative merits of likely claimants, and concluded that civil war would surely follow the death of Elizabeth. Worse, the entire treatise was dedicated to Essex, in words of praise that bordered upon the damning:

> I thought no man more fit than your honour to dedicate these two books unto, which treat of the Succession to the Crown of England, for that no man is in more high and eminent place and dignity at this day in our Realm, than yourself, whether we respect your nobility, or calling, or favour with your Prince, or high liking of the people, and consequently *no man like to have a greater part or sway in deciding of this great affair (when time shall come for that determination) than your Honour,* and those that will assist you and are likeliest to follow your fame and fortune.[71]

---

[70] *The Ende of Nero and Beginning of Galba. Fower Bookes of the Histories of Cornelius Tacitus. The Life of Agricola* (STC 23643) and *The Annales of Cornelius Tacitus. The Description of Germanie* (STC 23644; both 1598). At the time of the Essex rebellion, in Feb. 1601, Savile spent a short time in private custody. Grenewey's dedication calls history 'a true and lively pattern of things to come . . .;' the same volume's 'A. B. to the Reader' tells us 'For Historie . . ., what studie can profit in so much, as that which gives patterns either to follow or to flee. . .?' *The First Part's* introductory 'A. P. to the Reader' praises historians for setting forth 'unto us not onely precepts, but lively patterns, both for private directions and for affayres of state,' a purpose to which Elizabeth's officials later proved explicitly unsympathetic.

[71] (Italics mine.) Elizabeth's refusal to settle the succession question enabled her to keep competing interests, domestic and foreign, at bay. Parson's advertisement of the question's implications was accordingly seditious. She objected as well to the dedication, with its suggestion of a subject sharing in her own prerogative. Although she did raise the matter with Essex, she apparently never doubted his loyalty. The incident so shook the earl, however, that he fell ill and kept to his bed for several days.

Whatever the interpretation of such extrinsic links between Essex and certain books, Hayward's subject matter – especially his treatment of the politics of Richard's downfall – would also have resonated suggestively among both the earl's supporters and his enemies. A recurrent theme in Hayward's book is that of honour, a quality that he (much like Essex) argued to be inherent in the ancient nobility, but absent in the *arrivistes* who counselled Richard (much Essex's view of the Cecils).[72] Elizabeth's wry remark to Lambarde about the Richard parallel had not yet been made, but no one in Hayward's circle could have been ignorant how open to misconstruction the topic of Richard's deposition had already become during her waning years. Like Richard, the childless queen had been plagued by Irish troubles, the unpopularity of the government's response to financial exigencies, much unwanted advice about a foreign marriage, and the fact that close advisers were despised by some as upstarts.[73] (On the other hand, the acquisition of the throne by the queen's grandfather in 1485 bore striking resemblances to Bolingbroke's success, and James VI of Scotland was warned of being treated like Richard II, as well.) The government had already reacted to specific and highly public invocations of the Richard story. The details of his deposition, for example, thoroughly described in the 1577 edition of Holinshed's *Chronicles*, had been censored from the 1587 edition; of three editions of Shakespeare's *Richard II* to appear during Elizabeth's lifetime, none printed the deposition scene in Act 4.[74] A play about Richard (probably not Shakespeare's) became known as a favourite of Essex,[75]

---

[72] See James, 'Crossroads,' 437. An example of Hayward's preoccupation with this subject is his somewhat unfair characterization of de la Pole as a 'merchant's sonne of London,' below, 72.

[73] As early as 1578 her relative, Sir Francis Knollys, found the phrase 'Richard the Secondes men' a readily understood shorthand for the favouritism he found rampant at Elizabeth's court: Thomas Wright, *Queen Elizabeth and Her Times*, 2 vols. (London, 1838), ii, 75. Ten years later Henry Carey (father of the Lord Chamberlain and Essex's great-uncle) protested his own political virtue with the comment 'I was never one of Richard II's men.' Cited by Agnes Strickland, *Lives of the Queens of England*, 12 vols. (New York, 1840–48), iii, 540.

[74] For a thorough commentary on the corruption of the quarto texts of the depositon scene, see A. W. Pollard's introduction to his facsimile edition of Q3 (London, 1913).

[75] A much discussed point. An abstract of testimony at the *first* Essex trial (5 June 1600), alleges that 'Essex's own actions confirm the intent of his treason. His permitting underhand that treasonable book of Henry IV to be printed and published; it being plainly deciphered, not only by the matter, and by the epistle itself, for what end and for whose behalf it was made, but also the Earl himself being so often present at the playing thereof, and with great applause giving countenance to it.' (PRO SP 12/275, no. 35). This comment, by Coke, has been taken by some scholars as indication of a connection between Hayward's book and Shakespeare's play, but the dating of both makes that unlikely. Evelyn May Albright, 'Shakespeare's *Richard II* and the Essex Conspiracy,' *PMLA*, 42, 628–720; R. Heffner, 'Shakespeare, Hayward and Essex,'

and Robert Cecil would later claim[76] that for years the earl had been devising ways of emulating Bolingbroke. By any measure, the Richard-Bolingbroke story was widely identified by 1599 as a sensitive one, a fact itself probably enough to account for 'much descanting ... about why such a story should come out at this time.'

If some connection, however ambiguous, between the earl and Hayward's book was a source of public titillation, the fact remains that the authorities refrained at this point from further action. It is even possible that the connection with Essex forced them to defer judgment. On 27 March, to the encouragement of crowds lining the streets to cheer their hero,[77] Essex set out on his Irish mission. Throughout the spring, matters went well for him in Ireland: he crowned a decisive campaign near Waterford on 27 May with the taking of Castle Cahir. The rebels were retreating, and Essex seemed to be making good his promise to rid the queen of her Irish problem. As Professor Greg observes, 'no doubt Hayward's choosing for literary embellishment an historical episode concerning which Elizabeth's reactions were well known was open to misconstruction, and so was his dedication of it in adulatory terms to the ambitious favourite. But as yet there was no suggestion that Essex would one day aspire to play the part of Bolingbroke.'[78] Despite the official attention it had drawn in late February, the book was allowed to circulate freely throughout March and April, and into May.

The 'descanting' reported by Chamberlain made a good market. The book's first edition, presumably now lacking its dedication, was well along toward a sale of a thousand copies, and Wolfe was preparing a second edition to meet the demand. That he and Hayward discussed substantial textual alterations for the second edition, however, is clear indication of a new sense of caution engendered by the first edition's popularity. Around Easter (8 April) Wolfe 'obtained a new edition of the doctor, wherein many things were altered from the former.' The

---

PMLA, 45, 754–80; Miss Albright's reply, 'Shakespeare's *Richard II*, Hayward's History of Henry IV, and the Essex conspiracy,' *PMLA,* 46, 694–719; more by Heffner and a counter by Miss Albright in *PMLA* 46, 898–901. Heffner's view seems the more likely: that the Essex clique privately staged a pageant recreating essentially the same material covered both in Shakespeare's play and *The First Part*.

[76] PRO SP 12/278, no. 94, in 1601 (see below). As late as 1615 Francis Bacon, prosecuting Oliver St. John for sedition, could charge, 'I see you follow the example of them that brought him [Richard II] upon the stage and into print in Queen Elizabeth's time,' in J. Spedding, R.L. Ellis and D.D. Heath, eds., *Works* (1857–74), xii, 145.

[77] Much as they had thronged the departure of the popular Bolingbroke, as Shakespeare describes it in *Richard II*, II, iv; (see also *Henry V* , V, prol.). Everard Guilpin's account in *Skialetheia*, 'Satire I' (1598), named in the 1 June suppression order (below), appears to characterize the Essex departure in similar terms.

[78] Greg, 2.

author, according to Wolfe, 'understanding that many had spoken against the former edition, made an epistle apologetical to set to the second edition.'[79] In this epistle Hayward makes no reference to the dedication to Essex, but asserts that in the new edition he has tried to 'overlook and overlicke' his historical text from the beginning, 'thereby both in portion and proportion to amend the same.'[80] This may reflect decisions – not necessarily recent ones – already taken to expand the work beyond Henry's first regnal year, and to reapportion *The First Part* accordingly. But on the question of any intended topicality, he is quite firm:

> I have purposely passed over many imputations, and some secret sences which the deep searchers of our time, have framed rather than found: partly on the science of mine own conscience, and partly seeing no reason wherefore they should be more applied to this book than to the original authors out of which it hath been gathered.

Having said this, he devotes the epistle's argument to proving his support of the sovereign's right to levy taxes. *The First Part's* account of Richard's irregular methods of raising money had evidently proved to be a sensitive topic:[81] he expresses irritation that 'certain oppressions' had been taken by people intent on 'quarellous conceits,' to have been 'meant of another time (although nothing like) than that whereof it was reported.' This is characteristic of Hayward the historian, distressed that his readers would trivialize his scholarship by politicizing it. But it also raises interesting questions that derive, like Hayward's predicament itself, from the conundrum embedded in any historiography patterned upon Tacitus. The Elizabethan mind, already conditioned to discern patterns shared among variant orders of experience, would not deny the contemporary applicability of earlier political events themselves. Hayward stresses, in his preface and throughout *The First Part*, that the past holds a message for the present, but he naturally deplores society's inclination to execute the messenger bringing the tale. This is why Hayward argues that the charge of topicality is not to be *more* applied to his book than to

---

[79] PRO SP 12/275, no. 28.

[80] The full text of this 'epistle apologetical' is given in the present edition.

[81] Wright (*Queen Elizabeth*, ii, 25–6) cites a comment as early as 1575 by Nicholas White in a letter to Burghley, complaining of the queen's 'letting of the realme to farme,' like 'benevolence' a complaint lodged with notorious regularity to Richard's mismanagement. Such terminology was already familiar in the anonymous play *Woodstock*, V, i, as it was in Shakespeare's *Richard II*, I, iv, 45–7; II, i, 58–60, 110, 113, 250, 256. Hayward later was taken to task for similar references, and admitted under questioning (PRO SP 12/278, no. 17), to certain anachronistic lapses in his handling of sources on the topic; see below.

the historical events themselves, and adds the disclaimer that historical *conditions* 200 years before were 'nothing like' the world of his contemporaries. Nevertheless, in a world where such reactions were commonplace, few observers could have been startled when, a few days after Whitsun (27 May, the day Essex captured Cahir), *The First Part* was seized by the authorities.

On 1 June 1599 there issued to the Stationers an order mandating a comprehensive sweep of London booksellers, and aimed at the suppression of certain carefully defined classes of book. Hayward's, although not named, was certainly one of its targets. Among its prohibitions was the decree 'that noe English historyes be printed except they be allowed by some of her maiesties privie counsell.'[82] The order was uncommonly proscriptive, and unmistakably authoritative: it appeared over the signatures of both Bishop Bancroft of London and Archbishop Whitgift of Canterbury. A procedural rule promulgated in its final paragraph seems aimed at the very sort of casual licensing practice which had offered no obstacle to *The First Part* in January:

> That thoughe any booke of the nature of theise heretofore expressed shalbe broughte unto yow under the hands of the Lord Archebisshop of CANTERBURYE or the Lord Bishop of LONDON yet the said booke shall not bee printed untill the master or wardens have acquainted the said Lord Archbishop, or the Lord Bishop with the same to knowe whether it be theire hand or no.[83]

Such a hypothetical case came very near the circumstances of Samuel Harsnett's approval of *The First Part*. Harsnett, who later came to regret very much his prompt licensing of Hayward's manuscript, had approved the book in Bancroft's name.[84] The newly-required vetting of signatures seems aimed not at the unlikely event of a printer forging an episcopal hand, but at ensuring bureaucratic caution as a safeguard against routine actions like Harsnett's.

The order concluded with a post-script linked in its effect directly to the second edition of *The First Part*: 'such bookes as can be found or are already taken of the arguments aforesaid or any of the bookes above expressed lett them be taken presentlye broughte to the Bishop

---

[82] Arber, iii, 677–8.

[83] Arber, iii, 677.

[84] Nominally, censorship was controlled by the Star Chamber, of which Bancroft became a member in February 1599/1600, whence emanated censorship regulations and orders for their administration. But their execution devolved upon the High Commission where Bancroft, as Bishop of London, was the acutal as well as nominal head. R. G. Usher, *The Rise and Fall of the High Commission* (2 vols., Oxford, 1913), i, 101–12, and *The Reconstruction of the English Church* (2 vols., 1910), i, 119, 128. Harsnett's defence is described below.

of LONDON to be burnte.'[85] Four days later the Company reported that the 'foresaid Commaundementes' had been published, 'and especiyally' to fourteen irregular printers, among whom was Edward Allde.[86] It was Allde who had printed Hayward's book for Wolfe.[87]

The 1500 copies of the second edition being readied for sale by Wolfe 'were taken by the wardens of the stationers, and delivered to the Bishop of London.'[88] Hayward's new 'epistle apologetical' was turned over in manuscript to the authorities. Wolfe reluctantly 'delivered the original of the first edition, which was interlined and altered according to the second, to Mr. Barker, registrar of the high commission.'[89] The pile of books was burned at the Bishop of London's house in Fulham. The altered edition never reached the public; no known copies survive.

Although certainly a target of the decree, *The First Part* appears to have escaped, in June 1599, the highly specific taint of treason it suffered later. The order names several titles, but makes no direct mention of Hayward's book; its proscriptions seem more generic than specific. It aims at tightening procedures against further lapses, like Harsnett's apparent inattentiveness in licensing *The First Part*. Harsnett would continue as censor, and would be startled to learn more of the matter over a year later. Hayward appears to have gone practically unnoticed; despite Elizabeth's later remarks to Bacon, the doctor would not be arrested until a year had passed, when political developments would bring him under a sort of retrospective suspicion. Although official censure had touched *The First Part* for the second time in four months, the Earl of Essex would have to fall decisively from favour before expressions of official irritation would be transformed into prosecution of an author for sedition.

But events developing in Ireland would reopen official interest in the book, and in Hayward's motives in writing it. For Essex and his campaign, the summer months became a season of frustration and failure, during which the earl's relationship with his queen and her councillors turned very bitter. At court, his behaviour was perceived as increasingly erratic. He defiantly promoted his protege, Southampton; he sent Elizabeth and her council increasingly intemperate

---

[85] Arber, iii, 677.
[86] Arber, iii, 678.
[87] 'Bibliographical History,' below. Wolfe ceased printing his own books in 1594; Hoppe, 267.
[88] Wolfe's testimony (PRO SP 12/275, no. 28).
[89] PRO SP 12/275, no. 28. Edward Barker was 'register and actuarie' of the 'court of commission' which was 'kept the next day forenoon after the delegates court in the consistorie of Paules' (BL MS Cotton Cleo. F III, f. 152). The High Commission, originally constituted *ad hoc* as ecclesiastical investigations were needed, had by 1592 become a permanent court, no longer vistitational, but judicial.

complaints about his lack of logistical support and the political antag-
onism of suspected rivals at home. His early military success was not
repeated. A bitter exchange of letters ended on 19 July, when the
queen tersely enjoined him to make good his military boasts; she
expressly forbade him to leave Ireland without her invitation. In
August a large English force was shamefully defeated near Athlone,
and on 7 September, after a parley with the rebel Tyrone, Essex
concluded a truce. Despite all this, he knighted 59 of his soldiers, an
action very near to the royal prerogative. The queen was furious; the
earl's patience broke. At least briefly, he discussed with his lieutenants
the prospect of an armed rebellion. Finally, in direct violation of
orders, he set out for London. His rash and empty-handed return set
in motion 'the greatest downfall of a great man in living memory.'[90]

Under house arrest after the end of September, on 29 November
Essex suffered the extraordinary humiliation of a public dressing-
down by the Star Chamber for his failures in Ireland. It was recommended then that he be relieved of his command, and the queen's
officers were charged, with ominous and thinly-veiled references to
his conduct, to search out sedition in the land. His health declined
sharply, and his partisans, many of them dissidents both political and
religious, encouraged popular sympathy by painting him as a noble
victim of the queen. Pulpits and street-corners echoed dissatisfaction
with her treatment of the popular hero.[91] Although for several weeks
his apparent nearness to death mooted the need for further proceedings against him, by late winter of 1599–1600 his restored health
made formal resolution of his case a matter of urgency. Crown officials
resumed preparation of their case, and on 5 June 1600, the earl was
summoned before eighteen special commissioners, to hear Attorney-
General Coke accuse him formally of five separate offences: defiance
in making Southampton General of the Horse; refusal to prosecute
the Ulster campaign as directed; the creation of so many knights; his
dishonourable parley with Tyrone; and his disobedient return to
Court. (Significantly, he was not charged with disloyalty.) The proceedings culminated in a presentation by Francis Bacon. After describing some of Essex's immoderate comments made during his
estrangement from the queen two years earlier, Bacon put heavy
emphasis on Hayward's *The First Part*, exploiting popular suspicion
that the earl had encouraged the book in furtherance of his own
designs: 'Who was thought fit to be patron of the book,' Bacon asked
the tribunal, 'but my Lord of Essex, who after the book had been out

[90] G.B. Harrison, *The Life and Death of Robert Devereux, Earl of Essex* (New York, 1937), 254.
[91] Camden, *Annales*, ii, 185.

a week wrote a cold formal letter to my Lord of Canterbury to call it in again, knowing belike that forbidden things are most sought after?' These comments, from a man formerly Essex's adviser and confidante, had telling effect.[92] In fact, they provided the hearing's climax: soon the commissioners recommended that Essex be barred from his offices, and imprisoned at the queen's pleasure. But the queen would require more detailed advice before resolving her uncertainty about what course to take with a man, however exasperating, whom she still admired.

In preparing the Crown's case, considerable effort was made to probe the connection emphasised by Bacon between the earl and Hayward's book. Investigators had examined the two MS copies of Hayward's 'Epistle Apologeticall'[93] intended for the now impossible second edition, and the text revised by Hayward for that edition. Both Coke and the Lord Chief Justice Popham reviewed the whole of Hayward's text with some care, and made notes citing passages they found objectionable.

Popham's notes, less extensive than Coke's, took the form of interrogatories[94] to be addressed to Hayward; they provide the earliest particulars of the government's objections to *The First Part*. Of fourteen questions raised, nine address passages Popham deemed misleading, or susceptible to seditious interpretation, *e.g.*, 'What moved him to maintain ... that it might be lawful for the subject to depose the king?,' and 'What moved him to allow that it is well for the common weal that the king was dead?' But he appears even more troubled by the possibility that off-stage figures had prompted Hayward. The first of Popham's questions, 'Who made the preface to the reader?' initiated a recurring theme: that Hayward, as author, was not his own man. 'What was the true cause of setting forth this single story ...?' Popham demanded to know whom the historian 'had made privy to his purpose of writing this history, and what allowance they made of it, where and when?' More bluntly, 'Who were his animators to set it forth?'

---

[92] Bacon later sought to minimize his part in the proceedings, claiming that he took part only at the queen's own insistence. Although he stressed that the Hayward affair was merely incidental to the much larger matter of Essex's disgrace, we have only his own testimony that he entered the business reluctantly. '... it was allotted to me, that I should set foorth some undutifull cariage of my lord, in giving occasion and countenance to a seditious pamphlet, as it was tearmed, which was dedicated unto him, which was the booke before mentioned of king Henry IV. Whereupon I replyed ... That it was an old matter, and had no maner of coherence with the rest of the charge, being matters of Ireland: and therefore, that I having bene wronged by bruites before, this wold expose me to them more; and it would be said that I gave in evidence mine own tales.' (*Apologie*, 223–4).
[93] PRO SP 12/274, nos. 59, 60.
[94] PRO SP 12/274, no. 58.

This line of questioning would dominate official scrutiny of Hayward's book over the next several months.

The record of Coke's own investigations, during this period of accelerated inquiry into Hayward's book, reveals extensive research into *The First Part*. Coke made lists, much more extensive and detailed than Popham's interrogatories, of passages that he found objectionable or suggestive.[95] Together, they yield a thorough brief of the government's misgivings about Hayward.[96] An early draft by Coke[97] lists general objections: '1. What reason moved him to select this history out of all the cronicle? 2. With whome he conferred in writinge of it; 3. Whome he acquainted before he published it? 4. Who corrected it, and wherein?' Other notes, more carefully prepared and subsequently annotated with marginal commentary, enlarge upon the former and amount to a bill of particulars, endorsed later by Coke as 'the matters wherewith D: Hayward was charged . . . .'[98]

Hayward was invited to assist the authorities with their enquiries at this stage: on 11 July he appeared at court before the Lord Keeper, the Lord Admiral, the Secretary and the Chancellor of the Exchequer, all thoroughly briefed by Popham and Coke. In an abstract apparently prepared for this session, Coke notes: '1. he selecteth a story 200 yere olde, and publisheth it this last yere, intending the application of it to this tyme 2. maketh choice of that story only, a kinge is taxed for misgovernment, his council for corrupt and covetous for their private, the king censured, for conferring benefits of hateful parasites and favourites, the nobles discontented, the commons groning under continuall taxations. Hereuppon the king is deposed by an erle and in the ende murdres.'[99]

[95] PRO SP 12/274, nos. 61, 62; 12/275, no. 25.I.

[96] The date assigned by the *Calendar of State Papers* to PRO SP 12/274, no. 58 (Popham) and to four others relevant to this stage of the Hayward proceedings (nos. 59 and 60, the MS 'Epistle Apologeticall,' and nos. 61 and 62, notes by Coke) is 'Feb.?' 1600. Other similar notes by Coke (PRO SP 12/275, no. 25.I) are dated 11 July 1600. At Hayward's later hearing in January, 1601 the framework of his testimony (PRO SP 12/278, no. 17) appears to have been dictated point by point by Popham's interrogatories, with Coke's, reportedly prepared in July 1600, as a supplement. Although it is likely that crown officials prepared their questions well before this January 1601 inquisition, February 1600 seems altogether too early; Hayward was not arrested until July of that year. It is more likely that Popham and Coke prepared their interrogatories at roughly the same time, during the investigation (spring/summer 1600) surrounding the first Essex trial, after which Hayward was first questioned and imprisoned. The queen's uncertainty about how to proceed with Essex may have made it unneccessary to question the principals exhaustively, until Essex's activites in January/February, 1601 reactivated the business, and caused officials to reapply their earlier inquiries with renewed vigour.

[97] PRO SP 12/275, no. 25.I.

[98] PRO SP 12/274, nos. 61, 62.

[99] PRO SP 12/275, no. 25.I.

Evidently all the issues briefed by Coke and Popham were not pursued at this session, which seems to have been aimed principally at collecting evidence against Essex. Hayward was challenged about arguments he attributed to the Archbishop of Canterbury defending the subject's right to rebel, and about his anachronistic use of the term 'benevolence.' But he was also asked why he had invented the 'consultations' that argued various viewpoints on the Irish question,[100] an issue repeatedly noted in Coke's memoranda, and arguably linked to Essex's conduct of the Irish war. Hayward's 11 July confession, endorsed by Coke, touches only these three matters, although he acknowledged another point of obvious interest to Coke: that 'presently after the book was printed Woolfe the printer thereof carried the same to the erle of E:, and about a moneth after the epistle was taken out.'[101]

Hayward was remanded to the Tower on 13 July,[102] and on the same day Coke examined John Wolfe.[103] The printer was naturally eager to distance himself from the affair, and the notes on his testimony about the book's uncommon first few weeks reveal a subtext of injured innocence. They also reveal his interrogators' drift: Wolfe was called upon first for an account of how the idea for the book arose, then to review the matter of its revisions, and finally to provide information about Essex's relationship to its publication. 'Dr. Hayward requested him to print the book. ... It had no epistle dedicatory or to the reader when first brought to him; after some conversation between them, it was dedicated to the Earl of Essex, he being a martial man, and going into Ireland, and the book treating of Irish causes.' Wolfe told of delivering it to Essex, of the order to cut out the dedication, of his compliance with the order after 500 or 600 copies had been sold, and of the sale of as many thereafter. 'The people calling for it exceedingly, about Easter, obtained a new edition of the doctor, wherein many things were altered from the former, and yet the volume encreased.' He told of the new epistle, and described the seizure of the 1500 copies of the new edition. He 'does not remember the alterations in the latter edition, and has not now any copy. Thinks the apology was only to

<hr/>

[100] Below, 109–10.
[101] PRO SP 12/275, no. 25.
[102] J.R. Dasent, ed., *Acts of the Privy Council of England* (1905), new ser., xx, 499 (13 July 1600, letter to Sir John Peyton, L. Lt. of the Tower): 'Her Majesty's pleasure is you shall receave into your charge and custodye the person of Doctor Heiward, and to see him safely kept under your charge untill you shall receave other dyreccon.' See also Carleton's comment (SP 275, no.37) on 26 July 1600: 'My Lord of Essex remains prisoner, but at his owne custody. The Queen had given him libertie to go into the countrie, but recalled it againe upon the taking of Dr. Haywood who for writing Henry the fourth is committed to the tower.'
[103] A full transcript of Wolfe's testimony, from which the following are drawn, is in PRO SP 12/275, no. 28.

satisfy the people of the author's meaning in writing the book; the doctor, when told that some fault was found, desired to know what they misliked, that he might express his meaning therein.'

Perhaps as an afterthought, perhaps in reply to a question about Hayward's choice of 'this single story,' Wolfe revealed one feature of the historian's work now confirmed by what we know of *The Second Part:* 'The people having divers times since called to procure the continuation of the history by the same author, entreated him to go forward with it, and thinks he has done some part of it.'

Wolfe reported how frustration dogged his efforts to secure some response from Essex about the dedication. He vouched for the authenticity of the MS epistle apologetical intended for the second edition, and described how he turned over the first edition MS, with its alterations intended for the second edition, to the High Commission. His closing testimony was that of the aggrieved entrepreneur: 'Since the last edition was suppressed, a great number have been for it. Had no recompense for printing either edition, save a few copies of the work. Was committed 14 days for the printing of the last edition, and lost all the books.' Wolfe, no stranger to official scrutiny, appears to have brought this off reasonably well. There is no further record of harrassment of the printer by the authorities.

Later in July Coke got around to Samuel Harsnett, who had been licensing books for less than a year when he authorized Hayward's first edition in January 1599.[104] Coke probably had little interest in involving Harsnett directly in the Hayward affair, but he would learn what he could about the book's early history. He wrote to Harsnett to demand an account of why he had failed to stop publication of what had become such a troublesome book.

Harsnett's anxious reply[105] sought to excuse his approval of *The First Part* on the grounds that he had been informed, 'by a gentleman in my Lord of London his [Bancroft's] house' that the book was only 'a cantel of our Englishe chronicles phrased and flourished over onlie to shewe the Author his pretie witt.': Harsnett also claimed that when

---

[104] Prof. Greg's article, cited above, is concerned chiefly with Harsnett's reply to Coke as an example of the actual practices current among Elizabethan censors. He concludes, in part: 'Making allowance for Harsnett's anxiety to minimize his responsibility, and admitting that as an examiner he may, at least at the beginning of is career, have shown a disregard of duty surprising in one in his position, it is nevertheless impossible to avoid the impression that at the end of Elizabeth's reign ecclesiastical licensing for the press was more casual and less effective than the authorities can have intended or perhaps realized. This was probably inevitable in view of the output of the press and the inadequate provision for control, but it is a fact that bibliographical criticism should bear in mind.' (8–9).

[105] PRO SP 12/275, nos. 31, 31.I (30 July 1600), from which the following citations are drawn. Greg's article contains a full discussion of these two documents.

approved, the book 'was hedlesse without epistle, preface or dedication at all which moved me to thinke it was a meer rhetorical exornation of a part of our Englishe history to shewe the foyle of the Author his witt.' He had therefore not read more than 'one page of the hedlesse pamphlett,' before granting it his signature for printing. Hindsight encouraged him to add that 'the Author foysted in an Epistle dedicatorie to the Earle of Essex which I neither allowed nor saw, and which if I had seen I protest I shold never have allowed the rest of the Pamphlett.' He claimed that Hayward had avoided meeting him when license was sought, even though he and the lawyer had been 'both students togither in Pembrook hall in Cambridge, & both of a tyme and standing in the Colledge.' None of this helped Hayward, but neither did it reveal anything new to Coke. Wolfe had already testified that the dedication and epistle had been afterthoughts.

Hayward remained in the Tower. It was the unresolved Essex question that worried the Crown, and as summer turned to autumn pressures became severe upon both the queen and her fallen favourite.[106] When in October she finally decided to draw the line by refusing to renew his patent to collect duties on certain wine imports, his financial ruin was assured. Essex House was now a haven for malcontents, political and religious – Camden's *homines male feriati* – and by January 1601, a crisis seemed imminent. Essex appeared to be holding a rival and hostile court. Analogies to Richard and Bolingbroke, once the private asides of partisan cynics, now sounded ominously at large. It was decided to summon the earl to appear again before the council.[107]

It was in this atmosphere that Hayward was re-examined at great length before Coke and Sir John Peyton at the Tower, on 22 January. He was pressed hard on the twin themes of his book's sponsorship and his real motives in writing it. The interview[108] (evidently as much dispute as interrogation) ran roughly parallel to the lists of questions drafted months earlier by Popham and Coke. Much of it focussed upon positions Hayward – or at least his characters – asserted upon matters of political theory, which in turn invoked the very nature of Tacitean historiography. For such disputes there was little official patience. On particulars that seemed to promise evidence of either collusion with Essex or of seditious intent, Hayward seems to have held his own. Pressed several times about the circumstances of the

---

[106] Bacon reports in the *Apology* many instances of the queen's uncertainty about what course to take; the exchange with Bacon (above) in which she suggested that Hayward be tortured to reveal his book's true origins took place during Essex's confinement, when she was clearly perplexed about what to do with the earl.

[107] PRO SP 12/278, no. 49.

[108] PRO SP 12/278, no. 17.

book's publication, he acknowledged the preface to the reader, but insisted that his admiration for history's utility was general praise, not an urging aimed at present particulars. He had acquainted no one of his undertaking, begun about a year before its publication but conceived a dozen years previously, before bringing it to Wolfe, from whom he received nothing.

Coke's preoccupation with the earl generated other topics at this session. In defending his account of Hereford's claim that the King's Council accounted the ancient nobility vain, and virtue the ready way to destruction – a complaint notoriously bruited by the Essex faction – Hayward was able to cite Hall, Vergil and other sources. He was also questioned, doubtless with Essex in mind, about Bolingbroke's reported currying of public favour. But this had been exhibited upon the stage by Shakespeare, and Hayward was able to cite Hall for at least the substance, if not the detail, of his description of the earl.

He admitted to certain anachronisms, particularly in assigning 'benevolences' (a subject raised twice during the interview) to Richard's reign, but so had Shakespeare. Other difficulties of that reign, like the Irish rebels and excessive crown indebtedness, he was able to justify out of Walsingham. And he was able to cite several sources (Foxe, Hall, Polydore Vergil, Bodin) for the general tone of his account, if not for the details, and asserted several others whose names escaped him.

For Coke, as for Popham, Hayward's narrow selectivity of subject matter had been as damning as his book's congeniality to Essex. 'He selecteth a story 200 yere old,' he 'maketh choice of that story only' (Coke).[109] 'What was the true cause of his setting forth that story only?' (Popham).[110] 'What reason moved him to select this history out of all the cronicle?' (Coke).[111] On this important question why he chose the unfortunate Richard for his subject, he had a ready answer. He had 'selected out this single hystorie' because Hall had begun his account of Henry IV with Richard's downfall – and Roger Ascham commended Hall above all others. Specifically, he asserted that 'he had an intention to have continued the hystorie.' But here the record inserts, tellingly, the examiner's afterthought: 'as he saith.'

Little more than a fortnight later, Coke's apprehensions about the Bolingbroke story came to pass. On Saturday, 6 February, occurred the celebrated incident where the earl's supporters, led by Sir Gilly Meyrick, persuaded Shakespeare's company to present a play called *Richard II*, despite the players' reluctance to stage an out-of-date

109 PRO SP 12/275, no. 25.I.
110 PRO SP 12/274, no. 58.
111 PRO SP 12/275, 25.I.

production. Once again the Richard story had been resurrected, this time to set a theme for events to occur the following day. On Sunday the ill-starred Essex rebellion flared briefly, and then burned out. After false starts, a skirmish at Ludgate, and utter failure to reach the court, the conspirators surrendered to the Lord Admiral before the day was out. There remained only the job of trying the earl and his followers for treason.

In preparing the Crown's case, officials brought Hayward's book and its Essex connection once more to centre stage. By 14 February directions were circulated to the preachers of London, cautioning them about what they might profitably say to their congregations: these directions read, in part:

Two years since a history of Henry IV was printed and published, wherein all the complaints and slanders which have been given out by seditious traitors against the government, both in England and Ireland are set down and falsely attributed to these times, thereby cunningly insinuating that the same abuses being now in the realm that were in the days of Richard II, the like course might be taken for redress. This book was no sooner published but the earl, knowing hundreds of them to be dispersed, would needs seem the first that disliked it, where he has confessed that he had the written copy with him to peruse 14 days, plotting, how he might become another Henry IV. ... If he had not been prevented there had never been a rebellion since Richard II more desperate or dangerous.[112]

Cecil declared, in Star Chamber, that Essex had 'kept the book 14 days to peruse, and when he knew how many copies were dispersed, sent to the metropolitan to have it called in as a dangerous book.'[113] Then, a deeper thrust: 'It is to be remembered there was a book of Henry IV with many things to make those times seem like these, and himself like Henry IV, which he countenanced while pretending to disapprove it. ... He would have removed Her Majesty's servants, perhaps let her continue a time, and then stepped into her chair and put her where Richard II was.'[114] Essex was executed. Hayward remained in prison, not to be released until the season of the queen's death, two years later.[115]

[112] PRO SP 12/278, no. 63; see also Hussey's rough notes describing the 13 February Star Chamber session, calendared at 12/278, no. 94.
[113] PRO SP 12//278, no. 54.
[114] PRO SP 12/278, no. 94.
[115] The 'list of traitors' connected with Essex given in the *Acts of the Privy Council*, ed. J.R. Dasent (London, 1906), 261–2, 159–60, 483–9 are surely complete, but do not include Hayward's name. Hayward, like Southampton, was released from the Tower between Christmas 1602 and June 1603. The 'Demands of Sir John Peyton knight lieutenant of the Tower of London for the dyettes and chardges of prysoners in his

It was Coke who provided an interesting postscript to Hayward's hapless role in this monstrous affair. After his 22 January session with the historian in the Tower, he had jotted down a set of observations,[116] intended for his report to the council, which appear to encapsulate his assessment of Hayward. Three of his points are clear and unambiguous: 'He pretende to wright a history past but entend to point at this very time;' 'he presupposed that there should be ill success in Ireland;' and 'he writing his booke in 99 after the archtraitor was in his strength.' These, he noted, exhibited Hayward's 'outward pretence and his secret drift.'

But on this crucial matter of the principles by which Hayward chose the deposition and murder of Richard as material to publish in 1599, Coke's words in January 1601 were very carefully chosen. He drafted a concluding comment to summarize his overall impressions of Hayward's complicity, but then made certain corrections to it suggesting his own ultimate ambivalence about the precise character of Hayward's culpability. First he wrote, 'to *quo animo* & to what end he *selecteth* this only bloody story of the deposition of a lawful kinge. ...' Then he went back, deleted a couple of words and made two insertions, so that his final draft then read: 'to *quo animo* & to what end he selecteth *this bloody story out of all the rest* of the *unlawfull* deposition of a lawful kinge that had long raignes by an erle I must leave in the ende to your lo.'[117]

4 Hayward and Early Modern Historiography

For Coke, Hayward's 'secret drift' ('in 99 after the archtraitor was in his strength') was threatening in very practical ways. But as that threat dissipated, it became apparent that Hayward, with *The First Part*, had introduced an approach to historiography fundamentally more significant and enduring than its capacity to provoke topical connections, however remarkable the latter. With four centuries' hindsight and access to much more textual evidence than Coke possessed (we have the present edition's greatly expanded text on Henry IV, together with six other political and historical books by Hayward), the modern student will very likely assess the historian's work in

custodye ...' for the Michaelmas quarter, 1602, include: 'Doctor Hayward – Item – ffor the dyett and chardge of John Hayward, for the foresaid time at xv(s) the weeke – xxv(li) Item for his washinge and to the Barber x(s)... xxv li x s....' Southampton's expenses for the same quarter were £33.6.8. (PRO E407/56 pt. 2, fo 96, endorsed 'Jo: Cant, Tho Egerton, W Knollys, Ro Cecill.) There is no mention of Hayward in such records before June 1600; records from June 1600 to Michaelmas 1602 (fols 94–95) are missing; he is not mentioned in the quarter St John/Michaelmas 1603.
[116] Marginal annotations to PRO SP 12/274, no. 61.
[117] PRO SP 12/274, no. 61; italics mine, showing change of emphasis.

less politicized terms than did Elizabeth's attorney-general.[118] Coke's
questions, 'to *quo animo?*' and 'to what end?' have separate answers.
Although Hayward was surely self-promoting and ingratiating with
prospective benefactors like Essex (and later, Prince Henry), and
uncommonly sententious, he was not, as he completed work on *The
First Part* in 1598, attempting to topple a government.

In the Epistle Apolgeticall written for the second edition before its
suppression, Hayward dismisses in a single sentence the subject of
'secret sences' reportedly discovered in his book: he sees 'no reason
wherefore they should be more applied to this book than to the original
authors out of which it hath been gathered.' Later, he repeated this
defence before Coke, arguing that *The First Part* relies upon material
already in the public domain. This was certainly true. For source
materials he depends almost exclusively upon published accounts such
as Hall's *Union*, Polydore Vergil's *Anglicana Historia*, Walsingham's
Historia Anglicana, and William of Malmesbury. (Under Coke's questioning he testified that he began the story where Hall had begun it,
because Ascham commended Hall above all others.)[119] Indeed, most
of the raw material for his book was already commonplace, widely
available in print; much of it had been acted upon the London stage,
as well. Particularly in this first historical undertaking, Hayward is
less a scholarly researcher into primary sources (like his friends
Camden and Cotton) than an analyst and commentator.

But to claim his published sources as exculpating precedents avoided
acknowledgment of the disruptive element his text introduced to
British political discourse. Like Bacon, whose theory of historiography
would in later years be more widely noted, Hayward placed critical
emphasis upon 'the proper treatment of facts rather than on their
collection.'[120] True to his training as a civilian, he found history more
a source of principle, than of precedent. This is precisely what Bacon

[118] Hayward's historical theory and its significance has not had the benefit of much
modern commentatary. S. L. Goldberg, 'Sir John Hayward, 'politic' historian,' *Review
of English Studies*, NS 6 (1955), 233–44, and F.J. Levy, *Tudor Historical Thought* (San
Marino, Calif., 1967), esp. 259–69, are the most comprehensive treatments. L.F. Dean,
in 'Sir Francis Bacon's theory of civil history writing,' *ELH*, 8 (1941), 161–83, treats
Hayward's theory of history mainly in relationship to Bacon's. E.B. Benjamin offers a
brief but very useful survey of Hayward's stylistic dependence upon Savile's translations
of Tacitus in 'Sir John Hayward and Tacitus,' *RES*, NS 8 (1957), 275–6. Mervyn
James (noted above) mentions Hayward's reliance upon honour as a central theme.
D. R. Woolf, Change and Continuity in English Historical Thought, c.1590–1640
(unpublished D. Phil. thesis, Oxford, 1983), gives a general summary of Hayward's
historiography. Lily B. Campbell analyses *The First Part* and the topicality of its themes
in *Shakespeare's 'Histories'*, 168–212, in a chapter that elaborates her earlier article 'The
use of historical patterns in the reign of Elizabeth,' *Huntington Library Quarterly*, 1 (1938),
135–69.
[119] PRO, SP 12/278, no. 17.
[120] Dean, 170–1.

had noticed about Hayward's historiography, and intimated to the queen: the historian had 'taken most of the sentences of Cornelius Tacitus . . . and put them into his text'.[121] He was much more interested in history's capacity to furnish glosses upon the human political condition, than in the discovery of events themselves.

This inclination carried his book far beyond topicality, and in large part accounts for why neither the death of Essex nor the book's suppression terminated *The First Part's* publication history. It was republished six times over the next forty years. Such continued popularity reflected both a steady growth of interest in the Tacitean history of utility ('politic' history, of which *The First Part* is the first book in English) and a deepening related fondness for parallels to be drawn between autocratic English monarchs who, influenced by self-seeking flatterers, failed to govern well.[122] In 1599, the fashion for drama drawn from Tacitus (beginning in 1603 with Jonson's *Sejanus His Fall*) had not yet developed. The efforts of James I to neutralize the political effects of a Tacitean history that personalized and penetrated the mystique of statecraft, (and of his son to suppress them altogether) were also in the future.[123] Hayward was the first after Savile's 1591 translation of Tacitus to develop in English the implications of Tacitean historiography on a British topic. This innovative historiographical approach, evident in both *The First Part* and *The Second Part*, is modelled upon the practical, evaluative method of Guicciardini, Machiavelli and Bodin.[124] Hayward was quite willing

[121] According to Benjamin, a complete list of Hayward's borrowings in *The First Part* from Sir Henry Savile's translations of the *Histories* and *The Life of Agricola*, and from Savile's *The Ende of Nero to the Beginning of Galba* (both cited above) would run to a dozen pages, particularly in the identification of 'political aphorisms and maxims used to interpret and clarify the events of Richard's reign.' Benjamin gives the following examples (his page references are to the quarto editions of Savile (1598) and Hayward (1599): *Aphorisms and maxims:* S (p) 165, H (pp) 1–2; S 137, H 135; S 199–200, H 12, 54; S 201, H 50, 52; S 6, H 59; S 2,1,2,17, H 64, 65, 66, 67–8. *Broader historical parallels:* S 190, 191, 192–3, 194, 196, 189, H 56, 57, 58, 60. *Battle scenes:* S 135–6, H 31; S 110–11, H 142; S 131, H 148. *Characters:* S 1, H 4; S 139, H 130. (Savile was himself imprisoned briefly at the time of the earl's trial.)
[122] One example: a diary-entry of Sir Symonds D'Ewes (23 May 1623): 'I studied a little, and lighting by chance upon Heiwards Henrye the fowerth, read somewhat in it and was the rathre drawen to reed further, because his raigne came somewhat neare our hard times.' Elisabeth Bourcier, ed., *The Diary of Sir Simonds D'Ewes, 1622–1624* (Paris, Sorbonne, 1975), 138, also 34. Note also its 1642 publication in a double volume with Sir Robert Cotton's intentionally topical *Life of Henry III* (Wing, C6494; see below, 'Bibiliographic Comment,' item *F.*).
[123] Alan T. Bradford, 'Stuart absolutism and the 'utility' of Tacitus,' *Huntington Library Quarterly*, 46 (1983), 127–55.
[124] Benjamin (275) points out that Hayward's assessment of Richard's banishment of Bolingbroke is based on Machiavelli's *Discourses*, ii, 13, and that the Bishop of Carlisle's long speech amounts to a 'direct translation of the part of Bodin's *République* (ii, 5) that distinguishes between elective and hereditary monarchy.'

to admit to Coke that he was influenced in his handling of source material by Foxe's *Actes and Monuments*, by Bodin's *République*, and of course by Tacitus.[125] Hayward is an analyst of political behaviour, and his historiography is accordingly much more the product of how he employed his sources, than of how he chose them.

In a letter written to Sir Robert Cotton in 1621, in connection with their collaboration on the Arundel family history, Hayward reveals something of the perspective he brought to the writing of history, and particularly to the handling of sources:

> I desire to understand ... whether in good earnest you intende to make anye collections touching the houses of Northfolke and Arundell. ... *Doe you your part in bringing materiall, I will doe mine in making the structure.*[126]

The division of labour proposed here constitutes an altogether apt summary of Hayward's historical method. 'Making the structure' was for Hayward a task essential to the historian's purpose: the framing of what he termed elsewhere 'a true caryed history.'[127] By this he meant that historical narrative ought to follow a dramatic trajectory: he strove not only for narrative coherence, but to discern in his material (or impose upon it) a sense of movement from agent cause to final outcome. To this purpose, matter was subordinate to form, and his recognition of this principle was acknowledgment of an essential element of the new 'rational' English historiography.

One consequence of this dramatic sensibility at work is the symmetry of framework he seeks to impose upon his material. The narrative of *The First Part*, for instance, falls naturally into three chapters, in length proportional both to each other, and to each of the annualized segments of *The Second Part*.[128] If the resulting narrative is more

---

[125] PRO, SP 12/278, no. 17.

[126] BL MS Cotton Julius C III, f.191 (14 Oct. 1621). Italics mine.

[127] Hayward asserts in *The Life and Raigne of King Edward the Sixt* (1630), that the reporting of Acts of Parliament unrelated to main political events, is 'fruitlesse & improper to a true caryed history' (p. 47). He asserts elsewhere that 'in all Histories three things are especially required, Order, Poyse, and Truth.' See the introduction to his edition of Sir Roger Williams' *The Actions in the Low Countries* (London, 1618). See also Goldberg, 236–43; Dean, 177. But John Strype, *Ecclesiastical Memorials* (1822) II, ii, 186–7, adds this to the other faults he found in Hayward's writing.

[128] Although the quartos do not mark these divisions, I have marked them in the present edition of *The First Part* as a convenience to the modern student. Hayward's inclination to cast material into a dramatic structure is not limited to his retelling of the Henry IV story. It is even more evident in *The Life and Raigne of Edward the Sixt* (1630), where he explicitly refers to such segmentation ('And now to begin the third act of this tragedie...'); on this point see Levy, 265–8. See also below, 166: '... and in his person ... the tragedie did end.'

engaging, it is also correspondingly less accurate. Hayward is inclined to subordinate historiographical precision – and completeness – to the aim of dramatic effect. The modern reader will be struck by a selectivity in Hayward's narrative that in a playwright we might assign to dramatic license. French expeditions surface in Henry's second regnal year that probably occurred later; several campaigns in Wales are compressed into a couple of seasons; the span of Glendower's career is similarly truncated; Henry appears to wed rather earlier than in fact he did. Further, the child Isabel declaims tragically to her royal persecutor before the entire court at the age of ten; the other royal child, the Earl of March, takes prudent political decisions philosophically, but suffers the defeat and capture actually incurred by his uncle. Hereford himself leads an expedition to Africa that he never undertook in fact.[129]

Another narrative device – particularly objectionable to Coke and other critics – reflects an even more characteristic inclination to fashion source material into dramatically effective commentary upon the human condition (and thus upon man's political nature). This is his readiness to invent or embroider speeches giving dramatic force to known views held by the figures he describes.[130] He was challenged repeatedly on this technique at his Tower hearing, and was quite adamant about its justification:

> Being demanded what was the reason why he sett forth the orations of the B of Caunterbury & the erle of Dearby, seing that they tende to greate ill & to thinges most unlawfull, sayeth that *there can be nothing done be it never so ill or unlawfull but must have a shadowe, and every counsell must be according to the action.*[131]

---

[129] Hayward's confusion about Bolingbroke's military expeditions in 1390 (to Prussia) and 1392 (to Jerusalem), offer an example. He incorporates details (from Walsingham) of the siege of Vilna, a feature of the 1390 campaign (in which Derby participated) into his account of the Anglo-French raid on Tunis and the Barbary pirates (in which he did not). For interesting comment upon Hayward's mishandling of this account, see Lucy Toulmin Smith, ed., *Expeditions to Prussia and the Holy Land made by the Earl of Derby*, Camden Society Publications new ser., no. 52 (1894), p. xxxviii.

[130] This inclination was not uniformly admired by 18th- and 19th-century observers. Bishop Nicolson noted that Hayward 'had the Repute (in those Days) of a good clean pen, and smooth style; tho' some have since blam'd him for being a little too Dramatical,' in *The English, Scotch and Irish Historical Libraries, Giving a Short View and Character of Most of our Historians, ... etc.* (London, 1736), 821. Strype reports that 'his style and language is good, and so is his fancy too; only he makes too much use of it for an historian: which puts him sometimes to make speeches for others which they never spake, nor perhaps thought on ...' (*Ecclesiastical Memorials*, II, ii, 179.). The *Fasti Oxoniensis* (I, 368) observes that 'some have wished that in his *History* of Hen. 4 ... he had not changed his historical stile into a dramatical....' Oldys, in the *Harleian Miscellany* (London, 1809), repeats Strype's view, noting that 'Kennet terms him, a professed speech-maker' (438).

[131] SP 12/278, 17 (italics mine).

Hayward was defending, for his English text, the very approach that Bacon would admire in certain classical and continental writers.

The issues of *The First Part*, for example, clearly turn upon the moral quality of both Richard's government and Bolingbroke's insurrection, the classic dilemma of other Renaissance analyses of the Wars of the Roses. Hayward gives this problem a dramatic architecture by making so much of his narrative's development depend upon the matching speeches of Archbishop Arundel, Bolingbroke's theoretical apologist, and the Bishop of Carlisle, well known to readers of Shakespeare's dramatization. Although Coke had objected strongly to the Arundel passage, Hayward argued that the longer Carlisle passage effectively contradicted Arundel's arguments favouring rebellion, and the reader caught up in the full trajectory of the narrative will most likely agree.[132] And in *The Second Part*, the scaffold address of Sir Roger Clarindon becomes a commentary upon the repressions of the new king's government (and perhaps a pointed rejoinder to Hayward's contemporaries who thought *The First Part* seditious, as well). The battlefield speeches of Henry and Hotspur before Shrewsbury become benchmark passages in Hayward's transformation of military history into tragedy: here the personalities of both hero and antagonist, differentiated with a playwright's skill, contribute significantly to the battle's outcome.

In his preface to *The First Part* ('A. P. to the Reader'), he seems to anticipate Coke's later demand for justification of this technique. He is inclined, he claims (after approving Alexander the Great's anger at a too-flattering historian), to take up at length the principles of good historiography, including '... what liberty a writer may use in framing speches, and declaring the causes, counsailes and eventes of thinges done.' Since 'this were a field too large to enter in,' he conveys the prudent impluse only in *praeteritio*. Later, in January 1601, he asserted before Coke that 'it is a liberty used by all good writers of history to invent reasons and speeches;' and that 'it is lawful for an historian' to put words in a speaker's mouth, as he had in the speeches of Arundel and Carlisle, in order the better to convey the speakers' arguments: he did so 'after the example of the best historians.' Hayward's repeated defence – that this was a technique practised by all the best authors – will be familiar to students of Bacon's ideas about writing history, even if such dramatic license was not admired by government officials examining a text for seditious intent. Such an approach invites a sharp distinction between the 'facts' of history and their instructive employment, and was not entirely congenial to an

---

[132] Campbell (*Shakespeare's 'Histories,'* 185) argues Hayward's side.

earlier tradition that saw the workings of Providence inexorably operative in events themselves.

Hayward's historical method accordingly dictated a highly selective employment of source materials; he tended to cull them for episodes that yielded useful pronouncements (Tactitean *sententia*) upon the human political condition. The political even-handedness Hayward achieves in *The First and Second Parts* is the cumulative result of combining narrative elements compiled judiciously from mutually uncongenial sources, with commentary and speeches of his own invention. Walsingham's antipathy is apparent – often as verbatim borrowings – in material exposing the young king's personal and administrative deficiencies; Hayward then specifies the character of the king's minions concretely in an invented passage where they offer him poor advice (74). By omitting the readily available details of Richard's coronation, he avoids early emphasis on the legitimacy of his rule, thus beginning his account, like Hall (whose narrative framework is especially discernable in *The First Part*) with a *de facto* king. He gives dramatic weight to Richard's over-reaction to the appellants by rehearsing in detail both the judicial deliberations and the resulting bill of particulars indicting them for treason. In contrast to Richard's administrative weakness, he goes beyond his sources to particularize Hereford's virtues, notably his clemency (85) and his military skill (83, 89). He relies heavily upon Hall from the Mowbray–Hereford conflict onward for both narrative and attitude, but any sense of Lancastrian bias fades with the introduction of Hereford's titular claims. Here Hayward's own sense of priorities overpowers his sources: he turns contrastively to the resulting injustice to the young Mortimer, and devotes considerable energy to the closely argued (and annotated) speech of Carlisle demolishing Hereford's claims. In brief, Hayward's sources are at every turn made to conform to his own sense of the human tragedy being played out in his dramatic narrative.

The reader willing to consider the whole instead of its parts will accordingly discover that the narrative content of *The First Part*, separated from the political distractions that developed after its publication, is not only resistant to sinister interpretation,[133] but actually

---

[133] Annabel Patterson, *Censorship and Interpretation: the Conditions of Writing and Reading in Early Modern England* (Madison, 1984), 46–8. A capacity of early modern texts to resist unambiguous interpretation of arguably anti-government statements is typical of the uneasy balance between author and censor during this period. Prof. Patterson focusses upon *The First Part* and discerns in Chamberlain's letter about the book (cited above) the principles governing a broad mutual understanding between authors and readers of the period concerning controversial topics: 'topical (and hence exciting) reading may be present, but cannot be proven to be so.' She argues that 'this indeterminacy is central to the hermeneutics of censorship,' or, as Chamberlain puts it, 'every thing is as it is taken.'

quite even-handed. Carlisle's oration (142–9) is much more carefully crafted than the Arundel speech it refutes. In the quartos it bears elaborate marginalia documenting the bishop's (Hayward's) ancient sources; its civilian author clearly intended it as a legal brief arguing against the Lancastrian succession. The invented protestations of the Aquitanes (152–4), Hayward's dismissal of Henry's title claims (138, 140–1) and his assessment of how Richard's murder was eventually avenged upon Henry VI (165–6), all indicate something less than Lancastrian partisanship. And in *The Second Part*, his editorial excursion upon the evils of rebellion (199–200) is as critical of Henry's takeover as his apostrophe on the tragedy of Shrewsbury: 'O pore England, how unhappie wert thou to incurre the errour by dismounting thy naturall prince, & stouping under the soveraigntie of one who had noe right, whereby thy limmes were oftentimes in this sorte bathed in the bloud of thy children, & such as might have sufficed to encounter the proudest enemie in the world!' (249). However severe he had been on Richard's failings, Hayward's generally censorious presentation of Henry's political predicament as an illicit succesor conveys unmistakable disapproval of the Bolingbroke insurgency. In S. L. Goldberg's words, 'Even though the book has been mistaken for a history of Richard II, it is what it purports to be: the first part of a biography of Henry, in which is traced how "the follies of one, were either causes or furtherances of the fortunes of the other." '[134]

Like his continental models, and like other Englishmen such as Bacon, Ralegh and Daniel who brought to historical undertakings the relative objectivity of the new learning, Hayward is inclined to separate the factual from the moralistic, the 'is' from the 'ought to be.' This is not to say that he scants the latter: like Tacitus (as Bacon suggested to Elizabeth), he is often overly sententious. But he tends to reserve his critical asides for particular actions and judgments, and normally avoids sweeping characterizations. Like any Tacitean historian, he knew very well that his book's themes and examples could be applied to his contemporary environment. But telling unpleasant truths does not demand a sinister spirit: lessons are found in history because they are there. Like Shakespeare in the history plays, in his analysis of particular characters or events he resists pointed political advocacy: his reference point is the human condition. Hayward 'is always concerned to probe beneath the surface of events, to show how the past illustrates the permanent realities of human nature and politics, and to draw conclusions about them.'[135] If Hayward's history struck some politicians as finger-pointing, it was because it reflected

[134] Goldberg, 238, citing *The First Part*, 69.
[135] Goldberg, 235.

these permanent realities, not because it mirrored events which, when he wrote it, were yet to occur. His fascination with the human causality behind events makes him disapprove of those historians who, 'if they speake of any publicke affaires, they discerne nothing but the outside: not unlike to beggars, who traverse over many countries, from dore to dore, and touch as many faire buildings, but observe nothing either of the persons, or furniture, or order within.'[136] This concern to focus upon the moral causality of political outcomes explains his effort to capture the conditions of character and attitude that gave rise to individual historical events. His characters – like Shakespeare's – are independent agents exercising their will upon the national stage, not fatal victims: they neither piece out blindly the designs of an intervening providence, nor mimic anachronistically the themes of subsequent political interpretation. Earlier writers' providential sense of history gives way in Hayward's work to a sensibility much like Shakespeare's: it is character that is fate.

Hayward was approaching history in a novel way, and this yielded the sort of history where meaning was easily overtaken by events, even submerged by them. What Hayward could not anticipate was that the society to whom he offered the counsels of history would change its frame of reference significantly during the two years between his book's publication and the Essex revolt. The reader will note that Hayward was not imprisoned until seventeen months *after* his book's publication, and seven months *before* the Essex rebellion.

5 Bibliographical History and the Texts of the Present Edition

Between 1599 and 1642, six editions of *The First Part* were published, of which the first (*A*, below, on which the first part of the present edition is based), the third (*C*) and the fifth (*E*) were reissued. The second edition, suppressed in June 1599, is lost. New editions and issues (all counterfeits purporting to have been printed in 1599) followed in 1604–10?, 1610?, 1623, 1625, 1628–9, and 1639; a wholly new edition came out in 1642. The extant copies printed before 1640 are recorded in the revised *Short-Title Catalogue* with the numbers 12995 to 12997a.5.[137] The 1642 edition is a part of Wing C6494.[138]

---

[136] Hayward's most extensive commentary upon historiography and historians appears in the introduction he wrote for his edition of *The Actions of the Lowe Countries*, by Sir Roger Williams (London, 1618), quoted here.

[137] A. W. Pollard and G. R. Redgrave, *A Short-Title Catalogue of Books Printed in England, Scotland and Ireland and of English Books Printed Abroad, 1475–1640* (2nd ed., 2 vols., 1986, 1976, eds. W. A. Jackson, F. S. Ferguson, K. F. Pantzer).

[138] D. Wing, *Short-Title Catalogue of Books Printed in England, Scotland, Ireland, Wales and British America . . . 1641–1700* (3 vols., New York, 1972).

The First Part has gone unedited since 1642 (although an unedited and unannotated photographic reproduction of the third edition (*C*) was issued in 1975).[139]

Apart from the 1642 edition (octavo) and a few large-paper copies of the third edition (noted below), all extant copies of the book are quartos and, regardless of their true provenance or year of publication, bear the imprint of John Wolfe and the date '1599.' W. C. Hazlitt, in 1876, left modern textual critics the first hint, faint and generally unsatisfying, that the imprint and date might for most copies be unreliable. 'Of this exceedingly common book,' he wrote, 'the copies, though all purporting to be printed by John Wolfe in 1599, vary in date from 1599 to 1630, having been reissued from time to time with the old imprint retained.'[140]

H. R. Plomer argued in 1902 that Hazlitt was mistaken, and that all the available copies were indeed printed in 1599, and under Wolfe's auspices.[141] The records of the Stationers' Company, however, show that the book remained a marketable property as late as 1639, and that after Wolfe's death (1601) at least four printers successively paid for the right to publish it.[142] Professor Jackson observed (1934) the improbability that 'publishers of the day would continue to pay out sixpences to register the ownership of the copyright of a book which was completely dead.'[143] Moreover, in variant copies of *The First Part*, Jackson had noticed clear evidence of counterfeit in the reproduction of devices and other printers' ornaments. Ornaments appearing in many copies bearing the 1599 imprint were of a much later date, and were used commonly by printers subsequent to Wolfe and Edward Allde, whose print-shop assisted in producing the first edition. Besides establishing the fact that Hayward's book was reprinted often, Jackson's article offered interesting comments on the dishonest practices

---

[139] *The English Experience, its record in early printed books published in facsimile, No. 742* (Amsterdam, Walter J. Johnson Inc., 1975). Its modern title-page bears the (erroneous) imprint '1559.'

[140] W. C. Hazlitt, *Collections and Notes, 1867–1876* (1876), 205.

[141] 'An examination of some existing copies of Hayward's "Life and Raigne of King Henrie IV",' *The Library*, New (2nd) Series, iii (1902), 13–23. Plomer's investigation was limited to copies held by libraries in the U.K.: six in the British Museum, three in the Bodleian, two each in the Lambeth and Dyce and Forster Libraries, and single copies in the Sion College, Trinity College (Camb.) and Lincoln's Inn Libraries. Although it suggested that the first edition required the use of more than one press, his survey did not include copies such as the one held by the Huntington Library (see below). Examining copies of *D, E* and *E2*, would have forced him to expand his article's categories of classification.

[142] Arber, iii, 232, 621 and iv, 153, 459.

[143] W.A. Jackson, 'Counterfeit Printing in Jacobean Times,' *The Library*, 4th ser., xv (1934), 376.

of early Jacobean print-shops. I have incorporated his conclusions in many of the descriptive notes that follow.

Because they constitute a monument to the counterfeiting skills of certain Jacobean print-shops, the bibliographical description of these variant copies is at once interesting and important. All extant quartos after the first and its re-issue were counterfeited paginary reprints: as late as 1639, copies were printed with the intent of passing them off as first editions. Even where their ornamentation is variant, it is not obviously so, and it was certainly consistent enough with its earlier model to have permitted booksellers to offer later copies as originals. I have sketched here briefly the bibliographical characteristics of the extant editions and issues, partly with a view toward documenting the title's rather consistent popularity, as outlined earlier. I have also incorporated in the following material the identification and, where appropriate, some description of unusually prominent variants, such as ornamentation and certain characteristics of the preliminary pages (a few of which are cited by the *Short Title-Catalogue*) that enable the modern reader to differentiate conveniently among quarto copies. (For speedy reference, note that four words on sig. A2 (the dedication page), characteristically variant among the editions, invite comparison with the descriptions that follow: 'Louein,' γενναιοτάτῳ, 'fronte,' and 'Teucer.')

The First Part of the Life and Raigne of King Henrie IIII

A. First edition, February, 1599; STC 12995. 'THE / FIRST PART / OF / THE LIFE AND / raigne of King *Henrie* / *the IIII*. / Extending to the end of the first / yeare of his raigne. / *Written by* I. H. / [Wolfe's device – McKerrow no. 294[144] – of a fleur-de-lis in an ornate border, with the initials 'I. W.'] / Imprinted at London by Iohn Woolfe, and / are to be solde at his shop in Popes head Alley, / neere to the Exchange. 1599.'

Collation: Twenty gatherings (fours), A1 (title-page) to V4v; A1v, V4 and V4v are blank. The text proper comprises B1 to V3, paginated 1–149, with catchwords and italic running-title: '*The Life and raigne of* / *K. Henrie the fourth.*' The text is for the most part set in small roman type, 35 lines to the page. *Colophon* (V3v): '[Row of blocks] / *LONDON.* / Printed by John VVolfe, and are / to be sold at his shop in Popes / head alley, neere the / Exchange. / 1599. / Row of blocks.' *Other notable characteristics:* A2: Dedication (roman and italic); 'Louein,' γενναιοτάτῳ, 'fronte,' 'Teucer' [first 'e' properly formed]; distribution

[144] Ronald B. McKerrow, *Printers' and Publishers' Devices in England and Scotland, 1485–1640* (1913).

of lines 10–13 irregular in some later editions. A2v: List of '*Faultes escaped in the Printing.*' A3: Head-piece and ornamental initial 'A'; here begins 'A. P. to the Reader,' which continues through A4v.[145] B: Head-piece and ornamental initial 'T'; title 'THE / FIRST PARTE / OF THE LIFE AND / RAIGNE OF KING / Henry the fourth, / *Extending to the end of the first / yeere of his raigne.*' V3: Tail-piece.

Notes: Although the list of 'faultes' recorded on A2v appears in all extant copies, only in this first edition does it serve its announced purpose of correcting textual errors. In all subsequent quartos this list, though retained to suggest authenticity, has been made redundant by the textual corrections incorporated in the text by later printers.[146] Its unique relevance to *A* helps to establish *A's* textual priority.

The figured head-piece on A3 has been identified by McKerrow as belonging to Edward Allde.[147] The heavily-decorated initial 'A' that begins the Preface was also Allde's. Showing two seated figures reading, flanking the letter 'A' within a beaded border, this device has been identified by Professor Jackson as one employed in Allde's edition of Norman's *The New Attractive* (1596).[148] Use of these devices shows that Wolfe drew on the resources of Allde's print-shop in the production of the first edition. The factotum on A2 was also used by Allde in the work by Norman. The head-piece on B is of lacy, finely-cut printers' blocks. The initial 'T' with which the text proper begins is open and floriated, with a height of about eight lines of type. V3 bears the tail-piece identified by McKerrow as Allde's.[149] On the basis of this evidence Professor Jackson concludes that the first edition was set up by Allde, under Wolfe's auspices; the latter owned the rights to the book in 1599. Some copies of this edition lack the date in the colophon.

A2. Another issue of the first edition, with new preliminary pages, c. 1604–1610; STC 12995.5. 'THE / FIRST PART / OF THE LIFE AND / Raigne of King Henrie the / *fourth: extending to the end* / of the

---

[145] It was doubtless here, between gatherings A and B, that Wolfe intended to insert Hayward's 'Epistle Apologeticall,' prepared for the second (suppressed) edition. For its text, see below.

[146] To leave the page blank would have given obvious evidence that the edition thus marked was not original; to cancel the leaf would also have meant loss of the dedication page, the reverse of which bears the list of 'faultes.' Most probably the list was retained by subsequent printers to suggest authenticity, but Plomer ('Examination,' 23) advances an opposite theory to account for his understanding that no extant copies lacked the dedication page, despite the early order from the censor: to cancel the dedication would have meant cancelling the list of errors.

[147] 'Edward Allde as a Typical Trade Printer,' *The Library*, 4th ser., x (Sept. 1929), 150–1.

[148] 'Counterfeit Printing,' 373.

[149] McKerrow, 'Edward Allde,' 161.

first yeare of his / raigne. / *Written by* I. H. / [ornamental volutes] / Imprinted at London by *Iohn Wolfe,* and are / to be sold at his shop in Popes-head / Alley neere to the Exchange. / 1599.'

Notable characteristics: Title-page, dedication (A2) and colophon. This is a unique copy of the first edition, and is in the library of University College, London. Its text is clearly identical to that of *A,* and is throughout clearly the original Wolfe/Allde edition.[150] It is distinguished from other copies of that edition, however, by unique preliminary pages. The title-page, completely reset, shows in place of the Wolfe device a pair of volutes, used by the printer George Eld in the first decade of the seventeenth century.[151] The dedicatation page has been totally reset as well, although there has been no tampering with the text. The colophon (V3v), although identical in other respects to that of the Wolfe/Allde printing, omits the date, and the lower line of printer's blocks has been adjusted to compensate for that omission.

The title-page of this copy bears the inscription 'Geo: Buc: liber eius quoted by him,'[152] together with a partly illegible notation referring to p. 50 of the quarto text (where Hayward characterizes Bolingbroke's departure into exile). 'H.' has been expanded (in MS) to 'Haywarde.' On p. 149 (V3), below the tail-piece, appears Buck's MS notation: 'D. Jon Hayward the Author of this history was comitted to the tower for writing it Because it was apatern of sedition the effects wherof appeared shortly after in his movings to whom it was dedicated. G. B.'

B. Second edition, printed but suppressed May 1599; no surviving copies known. Despite the lack of any extant copy, both its printing and the fact that it contained substantial editorial revisions is amply documented by contemporary testimony (see above). In these bibliographic comments I have therefore designated the missing second edition of *The First Part* as *B*, the third (second extant) edition as *C*, and so on, as the most expedient way of minimizing the confusion prompted by lack of agreement on this point by earlier commentators.

C. Third (second extant) edition, c. 1610; STC 12996. 'THE / FIRST PART / OF / THE LIFE AND / raigne of King *Henrie* / the IIII. / Extending to the end of the first / yeare of his raigne. / *Written by* I. H. / Wolfe's device / Imprinted at London by Iohn Wolfe, and

---

[150] I am grateful to Mr. J. Scott, Librarian of University College, for comments about this unique copy and its characteristics. Although not known to Prof. Jackson when his article appeared in 1934, it has been incorporated in the *STC* revision, with the number 12995.5.

[151] I found this observation in Prof. Jackson's notes at the Houghton Library; I am grateful to Miss Mutchow of the library's staff for calling this material to my attention.

[152] Buck, a contemporary of Hayward, was a prominent lawyer and antiquarian, and Master of the Revels.

/ are to be solde at his shop in Popes head Alley, / neere to the Exchange. 1599.'

Collation: As in *A* above, wholly reset. *Colophon:* As in *A* above, wholly reset. *Notable characteristics:* 'Louen,' γενν(α)ιστάτῳ, 'fronte;' first 'e' in 'Teucer' inverted. This edition is a very careful reprint of the first edition. Although the collation is in every respect identical to *A* (even to the list of 'faultes' which textual corrections have rendered unnecessary), the text has clearly been completely reset. Despite Wolfe's device, imprint and the '1599' date on the title-page, this is a new edition.[153]

Prof. Jackson takes the ornaments and initials of this edition to have been copied from those used by Allde in the first edition (*A*). After Wolfe's death (1601) his 'I.W.' fleur-de-lis device passed to John Windet;[154] *C* was most probably printed by Windet, or his successor William Stansby, about 1610. The factotum on A2 was used by Windet, and the 'Apostle' intitial 'A' (on A3) and the floriated 'T' (on B) were used by Stansby.[155] The headpiece on A3 and the tail-piece on V3 were, according to Jackson, copied from McKerrow-Allde nos. 4 and 2, in simulation of the ornamentation of *A*.[156]

These observations make it clear that *C* was a product of the Windet-Stansby establishment around the end of the first, or early in the second decade of the seventeenth century. The copyright to *The First Part* had passed from the Wolfe family on 14 April 1603, when Wolfe's widow transferred the rights to C. Burby. By the time the title next appeared in the Stationers' records (2 March, 1618) it had become the property of W. Welby, for it was he who sold it on that

---

[153] Jackson points out ('Counterfeit Printing,' 374) that 'there are large paper copies of this edition in the British Museum (Grenville), Lambeth (Archbishop Abbot), and Harmsworth (Augustine-Sheldon-Scott-Heber-Britwell) Libraries, of which the Grenville, which measures 9 1/4 by 7 inches, is the tallest. As it is the only edition of which LP copies are known it was presumably issued with the connivance of the author who, in the dedication of his *Lives of the III Norman Kings*, reports that Prince Henry 'questioned, whether I had wrote any part of our English Historie, other then that which had been published, which at that time he had in his hands; ...' It is possible that, after the accession of James, the author still mindful of his examination at the hands of Justice Coke ... but desirous of having copies for presentation to those who might assist him in his ambition to become tutor to the Prince of Wales and a member of James's projected Chelsea College, induced Windet to counterfeit the original edition so that he might present copies as 'one of a few remaining.' Such an explanation is, of course, highly conjectural, but it is difficult otherwise to account for such a phenomenon as a LP. counterfeit.' See also Levy, 263.

[154] Jackson cites several instances of Windet's use of the device, 373.

[155] Windet used the factotum in his edition of Daniel's *Tethys Festival* (1610); Stansby the initial 'A' in his edition of Johnson's *Seven Champions*, Part II (1626) and the 'T' in Cortes' *The Art of Navigation*, which he printed in 1615. Jackson, p. 373.

[156] Jackson, 373–4.

date to T. Snodham.[157] Although Burby or Welby apparently owned it when the Windet/Stansby edition appeared, there is no evidence linking either owner to that publication.

C2. This third edition also appears as a re-issue in a singular example of Stuart printing published by John Bill, the king's printer. This is a two-volume issue of Hayward's *Collected Works,* which appeared in 1623, about four years before the author's death. Each of the two volumes is a unique copy.

'The First Volume / OF THE / WORKES / OF / Sir IOHN HAYWARD Knight / hitherto unpublished' (STC 12987.3) is in the National Library of Wales. Its title-page originally called for five parts; the fifth has been cut, and the volume contains only four texts: *The Lives of the III Normans, Kings of England* (1613); the third edition, reissued *(C2),* of *The First Part; An Answer to the First Part of a Certaine Conference, Concerning Succession* (1603); and *A Treatise of Union of the Two Realmes of England and Scotland* (1604). The missing fifth title may have been *A Reporte of a Discourse Concerning Supreme Power in Affaires of Religion* (1606). The title-page imprint is 'Collected by IOHN BILL. / M. DC. XXIII.'

'The Second Volume / OF THE / WORKES / OF / Sir IOHN HAYWARD Knight / hitherto unpublished' (STC 12987.5) is in the library of Pembroke College, Cambridge. Its title-page calls for *A Sanctuary of of a Troubled Soule* (1623 – another edition of Hayward's most popular book); *David's Tears* (1623); and *The Prayer of Christ upon the Crosse for his Enemies* (1623). Imprinted similarly to Volume I, it includes the texts of only the first two of the three titles.

John Bill printed several of Hayward's titles, and Hayward's will (above) reveals that Hayward held Bill's mortgage for certain properties in Middlesex which became part of the historian's estate.

D. Fourth (third extant) edition, c. 1625; STC 12997. 'THE / FIRST PART / OF / THE LIFE AND / raigne of King *Henrie* / *the IIII.* Extending to the end of the first / yeare of his raigne. / *Written by* I. H. / square of printer's blocks / Imprinted at London by Iohn Wolfe, and / are to be solde at his shop in Popes head Alley, / neere to the Exchange. 1599.'

Collation: As in *A* and *C,* but completely reset. *Colophon:* As in *A* and *C,* completely reset; printer's blocks variant.

Notable Characteristics: A2: 'Louen,' γενναισάτῳ, 'fronti,' inverted first 'e' in 'Teucer' (as in *C,* despite the resetting; an unusually dramatic example of the pains taken to invest a counterfeit with authenticity). B: Head-piece badly worn; initial 'T' bordered, but variant.

---

[157] Arber, iii, 621.

V3: Tail-piece unique to this edition. V3v: Blocks framing colophon variant. Copy in the Huntington Library.

Clearly another edition, this betrays much less concern for faithful replication of the earlier editions' ornamental details, although it is, like the other quartos, a paginary reprint of *A*. It was set from *C*. The apparent Allde headpiece and initial 'A' on A3 are counterfeit. Although the headpiece of printers' blocks on B appears identical with that of *A* and *C*, here the blocks are broken and worn from long use. The open, floriated 'T' of *A* and *C* becomes here a clearly bordered and poorly cut block. Possibly intended clumsily as an imitation of the earlier edition's model, it is somewhat smaller (about seven lines high), poorly set in the forme, and fitted awkwardly into the oversized space allotted it by the carefully imitated lineation of *A* and *C*.[158]

The tail-piece on V3, unique in extant editions of *The First Part*, is a winged angel head in a stylized framework. Professor Jackson identifies this as a counterfeit copy, made by Creede, after a block owned by Thomas Eld, and used extensively by Creede in 1615.[159] Alsop was Creede's successor, and the likely printer of this edition. The evidence of textual transmission makes it clear, at any rate, that *D* was consequent upon *C*. A date in the mid-twenties is most likely.

E. Fifth (fourth extant) edition, c. 1638–39; STC 12997a. 'THE / FIRST PART / OF / THE LIFE AND / raigne of King *Henrie* / the *IIII*. / Extending to the end of the first / yeare of his raigne. / *Written by* I. H. / square of printers' blocks / Imprinted at London by Iohn Wolfe, and / and [sic] are to be solde at his shop in Popes head Alley, / neere to the Exchange. 1599.'

Collation: As in *A, C, D* but, again, completely reset. *Colophon:* '[Row of blocks] / *LONDON,* / Printed by *John VVolfe,* and are to / be sold at his Shop in Popes / head alley, neere the / Exchange. / 1599. / Row of blocks.' *Notable characteristics:* A1: Title-page, set in close imitation of *D*; the blocks, though similar, are badly worn. A2: Dedication page. 'Louen,' γενναισάτῳ, 'fronti,' 'Teucer.' A3: Head-piece of badly-worn printers' blocks; initial 'A' variant. B: Head-piece of blocks, as in *D*; initial 'T' variant, open. V3: Tail-piece variant.

Professor Jackson believes this edition to have been printed 'by one of the succession of printers who occupied a shop in Cow Lane near Holborne Conduit, viz. William White, John White, Augustine Mathews, or Marmaduke Parsons, according to the date at which it was printed. The ornaments are to be found in their work; the tail-

---

[158] Jackson (375) notes these characteristics, and observes that this block was used frequently by both Bernard Alsop and Thomas Creede from 1593 onward. Its deterioration here suggests that it was used for *D* some time after its use in Alsop's edition of Phaer's *Aeneid* (1620).

[159] p. 375.

piece at the end, for instance, was used by William White almost with
the regularity of a device.'[160] The rights to the book were sold to R.
Bishop on 4 March 1639, by W. Stansby,[161] who had acquired them
from T. Snodham's widow on 23 February 1626.[162] It was Bishop who
would print edition *F* in 1642. *E* may have been printed as late as
1638 or 1639. One extant copy was dated, in a contemporary hand,
'April 1639,' and two other copies have a cancel title-page with the
imprint: 'London. / Printed for William Sheares and are / to be sold
at his shop in Coven-Garden neare / the new Exchange. /
MDCXXXIX.'[163]

The lineation of *E* on fols. A3 and B differs from that of *A, C* and
D. The floriated initial 'T' on B bears little resemblance to those of
earlier editions, and the title on that page shows the spelling 'yeere.'
Although a fairly faithful paginary reprint of its predecessors, it reveals
the printer to have been frequently innovative in his spelling and
type-setting; his orthography shows a marked preference for forms
which eventually fell out of use.

E2. Another issue of *E,* c. 1639; STC 12997a.5. 'THE / FIRST
PART / OF / THE LIFE AND / raigne of King *Henrie* / *the IIII.* /
Extending to the end of the first / yeare of his raigne. / Written by I.
H. / [Wolfe's device] / Imprinted at London by Iohn Wolfe, and /
are to be sold at his shop in Popes head Alley, / neere to the Exchange.
1599.'

Collation (except title-page) *and Colophon:* identical with *E.* The title-
page is a cancel from *C* (above).

F. Sixth (Fifth extant) edition, 1642; Wing, C6494. 'THE / HIS-
TORIES / OF THE / LIVES AND RAIGNES / OF / HENRY /
THE THIRD, AND / HENRY / THE FOURTH. / Kings of *England.*
/ [rule] / *Written* by / SR. ROBERT COTTON, / and / SR. IOHN
HAYVVARD, / Knights. / [Rule] / *London,* printed for *William
Sheares,* and are to be / sold at his Shop in *Bedford-Street,* in *Coven-* /
garden neere the new Exchange, at the / signe of the Bible, *An.* 1642.'

Collation: Octavo, with one preliminary leaf, 45 pp., constituting
the Cotton text; then seven preliminary leaves; then 318 pp. numbered
separately, constituting the Hayward text.

Notable characteristics (Hayward Text): A faithful reprint of the
earlier quartos, it includes the dedication to Essex. A thoughtless
editorial change in the final sentence of the text brings Hayward's
account of Henry's life to a surprisingly abrupt conclusion: instead of
'And with these troubles the first yeere of King *Henrie:* the fourth

---

[160] p. 375.
[161] Arber, iv, 459.
[162] Arber, iv, 153.
[163] Jackson, 375.

ended,' *F* reads 'And with these troubles the Life and Raigne of King *Henry* the fourth ended.' (Henry ruled for over thirteen years.)

The importance of this edition is political and historical: the fact of its existence, and in what company, makes it remarkable. But it lends nothing to a useful text of Hayward's work, and I have made no effort to incorporate its characteristics in the present edition.

The (MS) Second Part of the Life and Raigne of King Henrie IIII

Hayward's continuation of *The First Part*, which covers the second and third years of Henry's reign (and much of the fourth), is a MS held by the Folger Shakespeare Library in Washington, D.C. (Folger MS G. a. 12.). The MS is clearly a scribal copy of Hayward's own material: although its style and tone are unmistakably Hayward's, the MS errors and corrections are those of a copyist, not of an author. It comprises 157 quarto-sized pages, 33 lines to each page, in a clearly legible secretary hand. Its final page (f. 73) bears the notation, 'I found this peece among Sir John / Haiwoods papers which I / bought written in his owne / hand. 1628 Out of which this was coppied.' It is bound as the third piece in a volume also containing the unlicensed 1627 edition of Cotton's *Life of Henry III*[164] and the 1625 edition (*D*) of *The First Part*.

Until its sale in 1924, this unique volume, evidently bound with some care and more than usual expense, was held in the library of the Drake family, at Shardeloes, near Amersham, Buckinghamshire.[165] The professional connections of this family make it probable that Hayward's papers found their way into the Drake library directly upon his death. William Tothill (1557–1626), son of the printer and, like his brother-in-law, William Pennyman, one of the Six Clerks in Chancery, purchased Shardeloes in 1595; his daughter married Francis Drake of Exeter (d. 1633), a member of the Inner Temple

---

[164] The Cotton title-page reads: 'A SHORT / VIEVV OF THE / Long Life and Raigne of / *HENRY* the Third, King / of *ENGLAND*. / *Presented to King IAMES*. in / the yeare 1614 by / Sir Robert Cotton. / *Printed*. (I) I) cxxvII.' It comprises 49 pages of poorly set, large Roman type, 24 lines to each page, in fours, with the last two leaves blank. It obviously had at one time been bound separately before its private inclusion with the two Hayward pieces that follow it.

[165] This volume was offered for sale in Sotheby's *Catalogue* for 15 April 1924, one of almost 200 'Interesting Books Selected from an Old Country House' (Shardeloes), as lot 319. Other titles offered in the collection illustrate a previous owner's interest in Stuart historiography: a quarto containing Daniel's *The First Part of the Historie of England* and Hayward's *The Lives of the III Normans, Kings of England* (1612); a book containing *The Lamentation of Doctors' Commons for their Downfall* (1641); Bacon's *History of Henry VII* (1629); Mathieu's *The Heroyck Life and Deplorable Death of Henry the Fourth*, trans. E. Grimeston (1612), and a copy of Greneway's translation of Tacitus's *Annales* (1622).

and Gentleman Pensioner of the Royal Household.[166] The volume
containing *The Second Part* MS was certainly at Shardeloes in 1730,
for it appears in a careful inventory of the library prepared that
year.[167]

Beside the known dates of the volume's two printed components,
handwritten notations made throughout all three texts (including the
dated note concerning the MS's provenance) suggest a date within a
year or so of Hayward's death in 1627 for the private juxtaposition
and rebinding of this tripartite material (i.e., about fifteen years *before*
the appearance of *F*, which first coupled the Cotton and Hayward
histories publicly). All three texts are underscored frequently throughout, calling attention to passages readily applied to contemporary
political argument. Two interesting notations appear on the first leaf
(the Cotton title-page). They appear to be in the same hand, although
made at separate times.[168] The first is a Latin inscription thoroughly
applicable to both the Cotton and Hayward materials: '*Si ulla quidem
res prudentiam publicam, privatamque facit, facit historia, eademque ad civilem
hanc partem utilissima.* Lipsius 1628.' Below this is the note, '*Lenta
festinatione quieta cum industria.*' The title-page of *The First Part* has been
emended in the same hand to acknowledge the inclusion of the MS
Second Part as its sequel: the word 'first' has been struck and replaced
by 'fourth,' to read '... Extending to the end of the fourth yeare
of his raigne.' The author's surname initial has been amplified to
'H[ayward].'

To bind the MS *Second Part* with the printed *First Part* was a
convenient and natural step for the owner who 'found this peece,' and
probably accounts for his having had it 'coppied' in quarto. The two
texts join seamlessly: the MS *Second Part* takes up without preliminaries
the details with which *The First Part* concludes. The heading on f. 1
('The Seconde Yeare of King Henrie the Fourth. written by the
foresayd author.')[169] indicates that the MS was intended as a fair copy

[166] Tothill had married Catherine, daughter of Chief Baron Sir John Denham and
sister of the poet. For notes on such family connections and the early history of
Shardeloes, see G. Eland, *Shardeloes Papers of the Seventeenth and Eighteenth Century* (Oxford,
1947).

[167] The Brotherton Collection MS *No. (35) Catalogue of Mr. M. G. Drake's Books, etc.,
... 4th. Augt. 1730*, which lists 'Cottons Life of Hen: ye 3d. - and Hawards Life of Hen.
ye 4th. Lon: 1627.' I am greatly indebted to H. A. Hanley and Sarah Charlton of the
Buckinghamshire Records Office for their assistance in tracing this MS, and to C.D.W.
Sheppard, of the Brotherton Library at the University of Leeds, for locating it and
making it available to me.

[168] Mr. Giles Dawson, Curator of MSS at the Folger Library, concurred in this
judgment.

[169] 'The thirde yeare of K. Henry the fourth' begins on fo 26, and 'The Fourth yeare
of King Henrie the fourthe' on fo 47v. These titles are not later interpolations: they
were centered by the copyist at the head of each announced annual segment.

to be paired with the printed copy of *The First Part,* whose text it extends, and upon whose closing pages the intelligibility of the opening MS passage depends. Immediately below this heading, the MS text begins *in medias res,* with the words 'Now the king had dischardged himselfe of his troupes but not of his troubles, his mind being perpetuallie perplexed with an endlesse and restlesse chardge, either of cares, or griefes, or suspicions, or feares.' This is clearly retrospective, a linking sentence. Henry had 'discharged' his army only three (quarto) pages earlier (*The First Part,* 147); the statement, 'And with these troubles the first yeere of King Henrie the fourth ended' is the quarto's final sentence (149). The immediate textual dependence of its opening sentence upon the closing passages of *The First Part* identifies the MS material as an uninterrupted sequel to the quarto text.

Coke clearly mistrusted Hayward's testimony that when *The First Part* went to press, its continuation was truly intended. Having denounced Hayward for selecting, for *The First Part,* 'this only bloody story' (i.e., Richard's deposition and murder), he later emended that to read '. . . he selecteth this bloody story out of all the rest. . . .' It is tempting to discover in this phrasing a finding by Coke that Hayward and Wolfe had indeed published only the initial segment of a lengthy MS, but there is no evidence that Coke ever examined the text of *The Second Part,* or that Hayward in January 1601 had even begun to write it. Indeed, Hayward's testimony seems to imply that he had not.[170] But in July 1600, Wolfe had already testified that a continuation was under way, although he conveyed the impression to Coke the idea that the decision to continue *The First Part* was commercially motivated.[171] This may have been disingenuous; by characterizing a continuation that might exist as something of an afterthought, he made the matter of printing the Richard story seem more the author's choice, not the publisher's. On the other hand, Hayward testified to a dozen years' anticipation of the project,[172] and could have had the MS *Second Part* entirely in hand when he first discussed publication with Wolfe.[173]

Miss Dowling, in 1929, assumed that Hayward 'was interested in Henry IV solely on account of his successful overthrow of Richard, and that the more extensive title of the book was intended to throw

---

[170] 'He [Hayward] had an intention – as he saith [inserted] – to have continued his hystorie. . . .' (PRO SP 12/278, 17.)

[171] PRO SP 12/275, 29.

[172] PRO SP 278/17.

[173] Although E.B. Benjamin's survey of Hayward's reliance upon Savile's *Tacitus* (1598, cited above) would imply that he wrote *The First Part* no earlier than 1598, Savile's first edition, lacking the Grenewey additions, appeared in 1591.

dust in the eyes of the authorities.'[174] But the MS continuation allocates 50 pages to the second year of Henry's reign, 43 to the third, and 64 to the fourth, roughly proportionate to the 44 quarto pages devoted in *The First Part* to Henry's first regnal year. Measured against this editorial apportionment, the 96 quarto pages devoted in *The First Part* to Richard's downfall do not seem a disproportionate introduction to a survey of Henry's reign whose projected scale and scope we may infer from the MS material. And Hayward's intention to continue his narrative well beyond *The First Part* is amply signalled throughout the text itself: 'Henrie Earle of Derby (of whome I purpose chiefly to treate) ... (p. 68)'; 'this Joan was afterwards married to King Henrie, as hereafter shall appeare (p. 167)'; '... his posterities claimed the crowne ... as hereafter more at large shall be declared (p. 167).'[175]

On the other hand, the evidence does not absolutely preclude Hayward's having written *The Second Part* after *The First Part* had appeared. Juxtaposition of *The Second Part* with *The First Part*, as in both the Shardeloes/Folger volume and the present edition, reveals a structural anomaly that invites speculation about how Hayward, to cope with a partial publication, may have decided to handle the transition between them. In the context of this juxtaposition, *The First Part*'s final twelve pages exhibit an unexpected shift of narrative tone. Hayward appears to have reached a natural stopping-place on p. 136 of the quarto (*A*),[176] where he records that 'This yeere Humfrey ... dyed of the plague,' and gives other notable obituaries of that year: Mowbray, John Duke of Brittaine, and Edmund Duke of York, the affairs of whose progeny are summarized in language forecasting more detailed accounts to follow in a later segment: '... as heereafter more at large shall be declared.' These notices, however, do not terminate the first year's account (although similar notices mark the conclusion of the second and third years of Henry's reign in the MS). Instead, Hayward introduces here several new topics that round out the first year's narrative. Compared to other elements of *The First Part*, for the most part extended and dramatic (making for a 'true caryed historie'?), they read like addenda. One of these concluding items, the return of Richard's young widow to her father (quarto pp. 137–9), is summarized and brought to closure here, even though Hayward would reopen and examine it, as if not considered before, in great

---

[174] Dowling, 223.

[175] *The Second Part* similarly offers indications of an intent to extend the narrative beyond the point where it breaks off. One example, of Northumberland after Shrewsbury: 'the variety of fortune which afterwarde he ranne, shallbee declared in the proper place. (251).

[176] Text, below, 167.

narrative detail in *The Second Part* (fols. 4–7).[177] He also reports upon French preparations for invasion; peace negotiations at Boulogne; causes and events of the Welsh uprising, with a detailed character sketch of Glendower and the capture of Mortimer; and the origins and early stages of the Scots invasion, with details of the English siege at Edinburgh and the battle of Nesbitt. These sketches serve to blunt the otherwise strong impression that *The First Part's* dramatic and narrative trajectory was aimed to express the tragedy of Richard's martyrdom, instead of the beginnings of Henry's career. Then, abruptly, in a single sentence it is declared that with these troubles the first year ended.

These pages make it likely that Hayward, with several years of Henry's 'life and raigne' either planned or already in MS, 'selected out' (as Coke put it) a suitable segment for publication. It is also likely that he sought to make this segment's conclusion conform to the politically neutral *terminus ad quem* of Henry's regnal anniversary, by interpolating preliminary notice of certain events intended for (or already accorded) full treatment in *The Second Part*.

The Present Edition

In preparing the text of the present edition, I have compared entirely the four quarto editions described above (*A, C, D* and *E*), as well as selected portions of the first edition's second issue (*A2*), the fourth extant edition's reissue (*E2*) and the sixth (octavo) edition of 1642 (*F*). The evidence of the 'faultes escaped in the printing,' corrected in other editions, offered a reasonable working hypothesis of *A's* priority. After that, although variations among the editions' characteristic ornaments and preliminary pages afforded the most conspicuous means of dating and differentiating, the most consistently reliable evidence was obtained from careful word-by-word comparison of the several texts. Such textual collation confirmed beyond a doubt the priority of *A*,[178] the basis for the text of *The First Part* printed here. I have incorporated the corrections of the 'faultes' listed (sig.A2v) in *A*; I have also printed a few other corrections from subsequent quartos where the *A* reading is obviously faulty. There has been no effort to approximate in this edition the lineation or pagination of the originals. Signature (*First Part*, preliminaries), page (*First Part* text) and folio

---

[177] Text, 168–9 and 180–4, below.

[178] This collation yielded an apparatus of several thousand entries, restricted almost entirely to orthography and pointing variants, but of little other editorial value. The editions were, after all, carefully crafted to pass as specimens of the 1599 edition. I have therefore not included such a bulky apparatus in this edition.

(*Second Part* text) turnings are interposed, in square brackets, in the text.

The editorial task of preserving a sense of authentic stylistic consistency in a work segmented bibliographically but not authorially into two parts, each differing from the other in its extant format, posed minor but interesting difficulties. Each of the separate but sequential segments of Hayward's history already bore its own marks of editorial intervention: *The First Part* had absorbed the normalizing orthographic and pointing conventions of the print-shops commissioned by Wolfe, *The Second Part* those of the scribal MS copyist. To spare the modern reader unnecessary and irritating inconsistencies between the two parts, I have generally chosen to apply to the *Second Part* the print-shop norms of *The First Part*, especially in the expansion of contractions (frequent in *The Second Part* MS, rare in the printed *First Part*). Such contractions are silently expanded ('wch' = 'which,' 'subtes' = 'subjectes'; 'ye' and 'yt,' frequent in the MS, become 'the' and 'that'), as are abbreviations ('K. Rich.' becomes 'King Richard'). Tittles are suppressed and related consonants supplied ('comon' = 'common'). Contracted final syllables (e.g., '-con') are in most cases expanded to normalized equivalents ('suspicon' = 'suspicion;' 'subjeccon' = 'subjection'). Pointing is modernised in both texts to overcome obscurity and ambiguity, and to relieve the effect both of 'comma splicing' which makes many of Hayward's sentences so tedious, and of his idiosyncratic tendency to shift without signal from indirect to direct discourse.

Faults, misprints or other errors in both *A* and the MS are noted where emended below. The items appearing in the list of 'faultes escaped in the printing' (*A*, sig. A2v) are emended in the text, with the original readings given in the notes. (Besides the characteristic variants of the preliminary pages, decribed above, these particulars constitute a useful checklist for authenticating first edition copies, since they were corrected in later quartos.) The reader is reminded that Hayward, aiming for a 'true caryed history' (above), often handles source materials somewhat selectively and, particularly with respect to chronology and sequence, uncritically. Although full critical evaluation of such license and lapses lies beyond the scope of the present edition, the notes do provide (in addition to the original quarto and MS marginalia, of course) sufficient factual references to resolve, it is hoped, the chief items of potential confusion. To the same end, the index gives a measure of biographical information about the principal characters.

I have modernised use of 'i' and 'j,' 'u' and 'v,' and the internal 's' forms, but have retained the ampersand (except where modern repointing places it at the beginning of a sentence). Capitals are modernised. Unless noted, the text otherwise presents the original material without orthographic emendation.

THE FIRST AND SECOND
PARTS

of

John Hayward's

THE LIFE AND RAIGNE OF
KING HENRIE IIII

[A2] Illustrissimo & honoratissimo Roberto Comiti Essexiae & Ewe, Comiti Marescallo Angliae, Vicecomiti Herefordiae & Bourchier: Baroni Ferrariis de Chartley, Domino Bourchier & Lovein: Regiae Maiestati Hyppocomo: Machinarum bellicarum praefecto: Academiae Cantabrigiensis Cancellario: ordinis Georgiani Equiti aurato: Serenissimae Domino Reginae a sanctoribus consiliis; Domino meo plurimum observando.

ΑΡίστω καὶ γενναιοτάτῳ: optimo & nobilissimo (inquit Euripides) ex qua sententia tu primus ac solus fere occurrebas (illustrissime comes) cuius nomen si Henrici nostri fronte radiaret, ipse & laetior & tutior in vulgus prodiret. Magnus siquidem es, & presenti iudicio, & futuri temporis expectatione: in quo, veluti recuperasse nunc oculos, caeca prius fortuna videri potest; dum cumulare honoribus eum gestit, qui omnibus virtutibus est insignitus. Hunc igitur si laeta fronte excipere digneris, sub nominis tui umbra (tanquam sub Aiacis clipeo Teucer ille Homericus) tutissime latebit. Deus opt. max. celsitudinem tuam nobis, reique publicae diu servet incolumem: quo nos vz. tam fide quam armis potenti tua dextra defensi, ultique, diutina cum securitate tum gloria perfruamur.

Honori tuo deditissimus. I. HAYWARDE[1]

[A2v] Faultes escaped in the printing[2]

Page.	Line.	Fault.	Read.
11	23	played	plyed
15	13	pleaseth	please
16	20	present	presents

[1] 'To the most illustrious and most honoured Robert, Earl of Essex and Eu, Earl Marshal of England, Viscount of Hereford and Bourchier; Baron Ferrers of Chartley; Lord Bourchier and Louvain; Master of the Horse to the Queen's Majesty; Master of Ordnance; Chancellor of Cambridge University; Knight of the Order of Saint George; Member of our most gracious Queen's Privy Council; my most highly regarded Lord:

To the best and most noble, says Euripedes, at which thought you first and almost only came to mind, most illustrious Earl, whose name, should it shine on our Henry's forehead, he would more happily and more safely go forth among the people. For you are great indeed, both in present judgment and in expectation of future time, in whom once blind fortune can seem now to have regained her sight, since she moves to heap with honours a man distinguished in all virtues. If, therefore, you would deign to take this up with a happy countenance, it shall rest safely under the shelter of your name, like Homer's Teucer under the shield of Ajax. Long may Almighty God keep Your Highness safe for us and for the state, so that we, avenged and protected in faith as well as in arms by your powerful right hand, may enjoy lasting security and glory. Your Honour's most devoted, J. Hayward.

[2] In the list reproduced here, page and line references are to A. As explained above, these preferred readings have been incorporated in the text of the present edition. The original 'faultes' listed here, useful in identifying copies of the first edition (A), are given in the notes where they occur below.

19	22	sport	sort
19	24	tempored	tempered
37	10	weedlesse	needelesse
41	18	cause	same
43	13	too	two
44	13	in reporting	to reporting
53	08	moved	enforced
55	04	this	his
55	05	chalenged	chalenging
57	27	else	or else
65	20	carried	carry
70	13	lenety	levity
71	35	*Bush*	*Bushie*
75	05	officers if so long	offers of so large
75	12	Castell Trim	Castell of Trim
75	32	of the one,	by the one,
77	32	at men	to men
79	25	increased	incensed
86	13	*Thirminges*	*Thirninges*
86	15	Lophane	Lopham
88	32	confessed	confused
100	10	taking	raking
102	30	or violence	or conceale violence
107	35	is no more	it is no more
127	06	resistance	assistance
127	27	Redding	Reading
130	24	he had	that he had
131	05	hardly	shortly
131	24	was not	he was not
131	27	bloud	bould
148	21	reteyned	he reteyned

[A3–A4v] A. P. to the Reader

AMong all sortes of humane writers, there is none that have done
more profit, or deserved greater prayse, then they who have committed to faithfull records of histories, eyther the government of mighty
states, or the lives and actes of famous men. For by describing the
order and passages of these two, and what events have followed what
counsailes, they have set foorth unto us not onely precepts, but lively
patterns, both for private directions and for affayres of state, whereby
in shorte time young men may be instructed, and ould men more
fullie furnished with experience then the longest age of man can
affoorde. And therefore Cicero reporteth that L. Lucullus, when he

went from Rome to make warre against Mithridates, was altogether
unskilfull in militarie services, yet in the time of his navigation he so
exercised himselfe what with conference, and what with reading of
histories, that when hee came into Asia, by the judgement and confession of that great king hee was preferred before all the commaunders
that were before him. Heereupon when Alexander Severus did deliberate of anye weightie matter, hee would especiallye take advise of
men skilfull in histories, and not without good cause. For if (as Afranius
saith) experience hath begot wisedome, and memory as a mother hath
brought it foorth, who are to be better accompted then they whose
memory is as it were a rich storehouse of the experiences not of one
age or country, but of all times and all nations? And therefore it is no
great marvaile that Zenobia, who after the death of her husband
Odonatus tooke upon her the state, not onely insulted upon the
Romaines, but held the Arabians, the Saricenes, the Armenians and
other fierce and intractible people in such obedience that, although
shee were both a woman and a barbarian, yet they never stirred
against her. For she had perfectly red the Romaine history in Greeke,
and also had herselfe abridged the Alexandrian and all the Orientall
histories, whereby she attained the highest pitch both of wisedome
and authority. For examples are of greater force to stir unto vertue
then bare preceptes, insomuch as Cicero said that nothing could be
taught well without example. Therefore the Lacaedemonians (as
Plutarch writeth) did use upon feastivall dayes to present unto their
sons certayne drunken slaves whom they called ἕιλωτας, that by view
of the vice they might learne to avoide it, and Hismenias the Thebane
would shew to his schollars musitians of all sortes, good and bad,
instructing them to followe the one and not the other. And this is that
which the Apologie telleth of a certaine country woman who, being
hard favoured, and fearing least shee should bring foorth children like
her selfe, got many faire and beautifull pyctures, which shee did dayly
and steedfastly beholde: the meaning whereof is that by setting before
us the actes and lives of excellent men, it is the readiest way to fashion
our qualities according to the same.

Heereupon Cicero doeth rightly call history the witnesse of times,
the light of truth, the life of memory, and the messenger of antiquity.
Heereby wee are armed against all the rage and rashnesse of fortune,
and heereby we may seeme (in regarde of the knowledge of thinges)
to have travelled in all countryes, to have lived in all ages, and to
have been conversant in all affayres. Neyther is that the least benefit
of history, that it preserveth eternally both the glory of good men,
and shame of evill. Some philosophers doe deny that glory is to be
desired, for vertue (say they) is a reward unto it selfe, and must not
be respected for the vaine and titulare blastes of glory. Yet in wryting

these things, they affect that especially, which they especially deprave. And indeed there is no man hath so horny hartstringes (as Persius speaketh) who is not tickled with some pleasure of praise; again, there is no man of so flinty a forehead, who is not touched with some feare of infamy and shame. Doe we thinke that the valiant souldier thinketh no toyle too tough, but boldly adventureth the hazard of all happes, because he is weary of his life? Death commeth by nature to all men alike, onely with difference of memory with posterity.

And I woulde thinke that citties at the first were builded, lawes made, and many thinges invented for the use of men, chiefly for desire of glory; which humour, except the old governours of common wealths had thought necessary, they would never have fostered it as they did, with garlandes, statues, trophies, and triumphes, in which notwithstanding it is but temporary and short, but in histories of worth it is onely perpetual. This Cicero perceiving, he dealt with Luceius to commit his actions to the monuments of his writings; and Pliny the yonger did wish that he might bee mentioned in the histories of Cornelius Tacitus, because he did foresee that they should never decay.

But these are such as are not led away with a lust, eyther to flatter or to deface, whereby the creadite of historie is quite overthrowne. Yet the endevour to curry favour is more easily disliked, as bearing with it an open note of servility. And therefore Alexander, when he heard Aristoblulus read many things that he had written of him farre above truth, as he was sayling the floud Hidaspis he threw the booke into the river, and sayd that hee was almost mooved to send Aristobulus after, for his servile dealing. But envious carping carieth a counterfeite shew of liberty, and thereby findeth the better acceptance.

And since I am entred into this point, it may seeme not impertinent to write of the stile of a history, what beginning, what continuance, and what meane is to be used in all matter; what thinges are to bee suppressed, what lightly touched, and what to be treated at large; how creadit may be won, and suspition avoyded; what is to be observed in the order of times, and descriptions of places, and other such circumstances of weight; what liberty a writer may use in framing speeches, and declaring the causes, counsailes, and eventes of thinges done; how farre he must bend himselfe to profit; and when and how he may play upon pleasure. But this were too large a field to enter into. Therefore, least I should run into the fault of the Mindians, who made their gates wider then their towne, I will here close up, onely wishing that all our English histories were drawne out of the drosse of rude and barbarous English, that by pleasure in reading them, the profit in knowing them myght more easily bee attayned.

[Epistle Apologeticall
(Intended by Hayward for the suppressed second edition) [3]

[Gentle reader, thy friendly acceptance of these loose labors, the accompt of my idle howres from exercises of greater profit and use, hath moved me, before I proceede any further, to overlooke and overlick them once againe, as the beare is said to doe her unformed whelpes, and thereby both in portion and proportion to amend the same. I have purposely passed over many imputations, as some secrete sences, which the deepe searchers of our time have rather framed then found, partly upon the science of myne owne conscience, and partly seeing no reason wherefore they should be more applied to this book, then to the originall authors out of which it hath bene gathered.

[Onely one offence I thought meete to meete with, and that is concerning the rehearsall of certaine oppressions, both unusuall and intollerable, and to no profitable purpose and end; which I heare to be hardly thought of and taken, not in regard of any moderate judgement, which may easily perceive how full it lyeth in the plaine path of history, but for feare of some quarrellous conceits, which may interpret it to be meant of an other tyme (although nothing like) then that whereof it was reported; which in one degree of melancholy further, would imagine the very belles to sound, whatsoever hammereth within their heads.

[For my part, I am of opinion that no imposition[s] at any time have bene either hurtfull to a prince, or hatefull to the people, except two qualities do concurre: first that it be excessive, secondly that it be wildly and wastefully expended. For if the one fayle, it never seemeth greevous; if the other, not odious. But if it be both moderate, and also necessary, or great, joyned with greatnesse and importancy of neede, it standeth neither with reason nor with religion for any subject to repine against it. For the prince is a person of authority & trust, to imploy the goods of the people for their common good, either in maintayning order among themselves, or in repelling the enterprises of their enemies; neither can they possibly be preserved by the prince, if they withdraw their owne endevour and supply. And this the auncient wise men have endeavoured by a fable to make familare:

---

[3] There are two copies of this epistle in PRO, SP 12/275, nos. 59 and 60. It was first transcribed for publication by Miss Dowling, for her article cited above.

[That all the parts of the body were once offended against the stomake, for that they saw themselves vexed with perpetuall travayle & toyle, and the stomake onely not onely to be idle, but to consume all that they could provide. Hereupon they conspired together, that the hand should no more work, nor the feete walk, nor the eye look about, nor the mouth receyve, prepare and send downe foode, so that the stomake, not receyving nourishement, could not impart the same again to every part of the body. Whereby, first they languished and (being neere at the point to perish) at the last perceyved that both their labour to get, and their liberality to geve, in appearance was for the stomack, but in deed for themselves. This tale hath bene verifyed by many truthes, whereof I will rehearse one, and so not exceede the measure of an epistle:

[When the Turk came against the city of Constantinople, the emperor was not able to wage so many souldiers as might stand single upon the walles. Whereupon, he often assembled the wealthy citizens, and sometymes went in person to their houses, leaving nothing undone or unsayd which might be of force to stirre in them either piety or pitty, both for the preservation of their country and frends, and for their owne particuler safeties. But the miserable mony mongers, being as loath to take benefit of their gold as if it had not been their owne, buried it under the ground, and denyed that they were able to make contribution. So, either for want or weakenes of resistance, the Turkes soone became masters of the city. Who in their first fury set all the streetes on streame with bloud, and afterwards, covetousnes succeeding cruelty, they left no closet nor corner unransacked and unrifted, wherein, missing their expected prey, they ripped the bellies and searched the bowels of their wretched captives. Lastly they turned up the foundations of many thousand buildings, and there found such infinite masses of mony as did strike them rather into a maze, then into a merveylle, how so rich a city could possibly be taken.

[I would not wish the like mischance, to our like dull and heavy conceyted repyners, which neyther see nor seeke any other thing but only the stuffing of their owne bags, because it cannot happen unto them without a greater and further mischiefe. But I could wish that they might be fitted as once were the Siracusans, upon whom, when Dyonisius had imposed a contribution, they murmured and complayned, and denyed that they were able to beare that burthen, whereupon, he encreased the imposition and they likewise their complaints. But Dyonisius ceased not to levy it upon them, untill he perceyved them eyther content by being reduced to their duetie, or quiete by being drawne drye.]

The First Parte of the Life and Raigne of King Henry the Fourth,

Extending to the End of the First Year of his Reign.

[I]

The noble and victorious prince, king Edward the third,[4] had his fortunate gift of a long & prosperous raigne over this realme of England much strengthned and adorned by natures supply of seven goodlye sonnes: Edward his eldest sonne, prince of Wales, commonly called the Blacke Prince; William of Hatfield; Lyonel, Duke of Clarence; John of Gaunt, Duke of Lancaster; Edmund of Langley, Duke of Yorke; Thomas of Woodstocke, Duke of Gloucester; and William of Windsore.

These sonnes, during the life of their renowmed father, were such ornaments and stayes to his estate as it seemed no greater could be annexed thereunto. For neither armies nor strong holdes are so great defences to a prince as the multitude of children. [p. 2] Fortes may decay, and forces decrease, and both decline and fall away, eyther by varietie of fortune or inconstancie of mens desires; but a mans owne bloud cleaveth close unto him, not so much in the blisses of prosperitie, which are equally imparted to others, as in the crosses of calamity, which touch none so neere as those that are neerest by nature.

But in succeeding times they became in their ofspring the seminarie of division and discord, to the utter ruine of their families, and great wast and weakening of the whole realme. For they that have equall dignitie of birth and bloud can hardly stoope to termes of soveraigntie, but upon every offer of occasion wil aspire to indure rather no equall then any superiour, and for the most part the hatred of those that are neerest in kinde is most despitefull & deadly, if it once breake forth. The feare of this humor caused Romulus to embrewe the foundations of the cittie and empire of Rome with the bloud of his brother Remus. According to which example the tyrants of Turkie, those butchers of Sathan, doe commonly at this day beginne their raigne with the death and slaughter of all their brethren.

Prince Edward, the thunderbolt of warre in his time, dyed during the life of his father. And although he was cut off in the middle course

---

[4]Pertinent selected biographical information about the more notable persons in Hayward's narrative is given in the index, at the appropriate entry for each.

and principall strength of his age, yet in respect of honour and fame he lived with the longest, having in all parts fulfilled the measure of true nobilitie. He left behinde him a young sonne called Richard, who after the death of King Edward was crowned king in his steade, and afterward died childe-lesse.

William of Hatfield, King Edwards second sonne, dyed also without issue, leaving no other memorie of his name but the mention onely.

Lionell Duke of Clarence, the third sonne of King Edward, was a man of comely personage, of speach and pace stately, in other qualities of a middle temperature, neither to bee admired nor contemned, as rather voide of ill partes [p. 3] then furnished with good.

He had issue Philip his only daughter, who was joined in marriage to Edmunde Mortimer, Earle of March, who in the parliament holden in the eight yeare of the reigne of King Richard, was in the right of his wife declared heire apparant to the crowne, in case the king should die without children.[5] But not many yeares after hee dyed, leaving issue by the said Philip, Roger Mortimer Earle of March. This Roger was slaine in the rude and tumultuous warres of Ireland, and had issue Edmund, Anne and Elienor. Edmund and Elienor dyed without issue. Anne was married to Richard Earle of Cambridge, sonne to Edmund of Langley Duke of Yorke, the fift sonne of King Edward. Of these two came Richard Plantagenet Duke of Yorke, who by the right devolved to him from his mother made open claime to the crowne of England (which was then possessed by the family of Lancaster) first by law, in the parliament holden the thirtieth yeare of the raigne of King Henrie the sixt, where either by right or by favour, his cause had such furtherance that after King Henrie should die, the crowne was entayled to him and to the heires of his bloud for ever. But the duke, impatient to linger in hope, chose rather to endure any daunger then such delay. Whereupon he entred into armes soone after, against King Henrie in the fielde. But being carried further by courage then by force hee coulde beare through, hee was slaine at the battaile of Wakefield, and left his title to Edward his eldest sonne, who with invincible persistance did prosecute the enterprise, and after great varietie of fortune at the last atchieved it.

John of Gaunt Duke of Lancaster, the fourth sonne of King Edward the third, was a man of high and hardie spirite, but his fortune was many times not answerable either to his force or to his forecast. He had two sonnes, Henrie Earle of Derby (of whome I purpose chiefly to treate) and John Earle of Somerset. This John was father to

[5] Hayward probably means the parliament of Oct. 1385, although the report of Mortimer's confirmation as heir presumptive at this session is probably apocryphal. Throughout the text Hayward's references to the Mortimers are somewhat unreliable (see below).

John Duke of Somerset, [p. 4] who had issue Margaret Countesse of Richmond, mother to the noble prince, Henrie the seventh.

Henrie Plantagenet Earle of Derby was likwise, by his mother Blanch, extracted from the bloud of kings, being discended from Edmund, the second sonne of King Henrie the third, by which line the Duchie of Lancaster did accreue unto his house. Hee was a man of meane stature, well proportioned and formally compact, of good strength and agilitie of body, skilfull in armes, and of a ready dispatch, joyntly shewing himselfe both earnest and advised in all his actions. Hee was quicke and present in conceite, forward in attempt, couragious in execution, and most times fortunate in event. There was no great place of imployment and charge which hee would not rather affect for glorie, then refuse either for peril or for paines. And in service hee often prooved himselfe not onely a skilfull commaunder by giving directions, but also a good souldier in using his weapon, adventuring further in person, sometimes, then policie would permit. His expences were liberall and honourable, yet not exceeding the measure of his receiptes. He was verie courteous and familiar respectively towards all men, whereby hee procured great reputation and regarde, especially with those of the meaner sort: for high humilities take such deepe roote in the mindes of the multitude, that they are more strongly drawne by unprofitable curtesies then by churlish benefits. In all the changes of his estate, he was almost one and the same man, in adversitie never daunted, in prosperitie never secure, reteining still his majestie in the one, and his mildnes in the other. Neither did the continuance of his raigne bring him to a proude port and stately esteeming of himselfe, but in his latter yeares he remained so gentle & faire in cariage that therby chiefely hee did weare out the hatred that was borne in him for the death of King Richard. He could not lightly be drawne into any cause, & was stiffe & constant in a good; yet more easie [p. 5] to be corrupted or abused by flattering speeches then to be terrifed by threats. To some men he seemed too greedie of glorie, making small difference of the meanes whereby he attained it; and in deede this humour in noble minds is most hardly over-ruled, and oftentimes it draweth even the wisest awrie. But before I proceede any further in describing either the qualities or actes of this earle, I must write something of the raigne of King Richard the second, his cosin germaine: so farre forth as the follies of the one were either causes or furtherances of the fortunes of the other.[6]

Richard, sonne to Edward Prince of Wales, a little before deceased,

[6] By this device, Hayward reduces his detailed treatment of Richard's downfall, which occupies the next 90-odd quarto pages, to the status of prelimary material, in keeping with his announced purpose of explaining the full career of Henry Bolingbroke.

was after the death of King Edward the thirde crowned king over this realme of England, in the eleventh yeare of his age,[7] at which yeares the minde of man is like to the potters earth, apt to bee wrought into any fashion, and which way so ever it hardneth by custome, it will sooner breake then bend from the same. Now the governaunce of the king at the first was committed to certaine bishops, earles, barons and justices. But either uppon nicenes to discontent the king, or negligence to discharge their dutie, everie one was more ready with pleasant conceites to delight him then with profitable counsaile to doe him good. For smooth and pleasing speaches neede small endeavour, and alwaies findeth favour; whereas to advise that which is meete is a point of some paines, and many times a thanklesse office. Hereupon two daungerous evils did ensue: flatterie brake in, and private respects did passe under publike pretences.

In the thirde yeare of his raigne[8] it was thought meete that this charge should be committed to one man, to avoid thereby the unnecessarie wast of the treasure of the realme by allowing yearely stipend unto many. So by the whole consent of the nobilitie and commons assembled together in parliament, this office was deputed to Lord Thomas Beauchampe, Earle of Warwicke, and a competent pension was assigned him out of the kings eschequer for his paines. [p. 6] But the king, being now plunged in pleasure, did immoderately bend himselfe to the favoring and advansing of certaine persons which were both reproveable in life, and generally abhorred in all the realme. And this was the cause of two great inconveniences: for many yong noble-men and brave courtiers, having a nimble eye to the secrete favours and dislikes of the king, gave over themselves to a dissolute and dishonest life, which findeth some followers when it findeth no furtherancers, much more when it doth flourish and thrive. The king also, by favouring these, was himselfe little favoured and loved of many. For it is oftentimes as daungerous to a prince to have evil and odious adherents as to bee evill and odious himselfe.

The names of these men were Alexander Nevill, Archbishop of Yorke, Robert Veere, Earle of Oxford, Michael Delapoole, afterwards Earle of Suffolke, Robert Trisiliane, Lord Chiefe Justice, Nicholas Brambre, Alderman of London, and certaine others, of no eminencie either by birth or desert,[9] but obsequious and pliable to the kings youthfull humour. These were highly in credit with the king; these were alwaies next unto him both in companie and in counsell; by

[7] 22 June 1377.
[8] 1379–80.
[9] This is the first of many instances exhibiting Hayward's sustained bias in favour of governance by hereditary aristocracy, a theme especially congenial (as noted above, introduction) to the views of the Essex party from before 1599.

these he ordered his private actions; by these he managed his affaires of state. He spared neither the dignitie nor death of any man whose aucthortie and life withstoode their preferment. In so much as in the fifth yeare of his raigne[10] he remooved Sir Richard Scroope from being Lord Chauncellor of England (to which office he was by aucthoritie of Parliament appointed) because hee refused to set the great seale to the graunt of certaine lands which had wantonly passed from the king, alleaging for his denial the great debts of the king, and small demerites of the parties upon whome the king might cast away and consume, but spend in good order he could not, advertising him also to have respect that ryote did not deceive him under the tearme and shewe of liberalitie, and that gifts well ordered procure not so much love, as placed without discretion they [p. 7] stirre envy. This chancellor was a man of notable integrity and diligence in his office, not scornfully turning away from the ragged coat of a poore suppliant, or pale face of a sickely & feeble limmed suter, holding up their simple soiled billes of complaint, nor yet smothering his conscience with partiall maintaining of such as were mighty; but being alike to all, he was soone disliked of those that were bad.

In the eight yeere of this kings reigne,[11] the destruction of the Duke of Lancaster was entended likewise, upon the like dislike. The plot was layde by Justice Trisilian, offences were devised, appellors appointed, and peeres named; he should have bene put under arrest suddenly and foorthwith arreigned, condemned and executed. But the duke, upon privy intelligence of these contrivances, fled to his castle at Pomfret, and there made preparation for his defence against the king.

So this matter began to grow to a head of division, which the common people at that time very busily desired and sought. But the kings mother, travelling incessantly betweene the king and the duke (notwithstanding shee was both corpulent & in yeres), laboured them both to a reconcilement: the king, with regard of the dangerous and discontented times, the duke with resepect of his duty and faith.[12] And so partly by her entreaty and advise, partly by their inclination bending to the safest course, all apparancy of displeasure on the one part, and distrust on the other, was for that time layed aside.

The same year, Michael Delapoole was made Chancellour of England,[13] and created Earle of Suffolke, and Robert Veere Earle of

---

[10] Before the parliament of October 1382.

[11] 1384.

[12] Richard was about seventeen when this crisis with Gaunt erupted. Joan, princess of Wales, 'The Fair Maid of Kent,' exercised a strong influence upon the king until her death in August 1385.

[13] De la Pole actually became chancellor in March 1383.

Oxford was created Marquesse of Dubline, being the first man within this realme that was enobled with that title. But as they grew in honour, so did they in hate; for many noble men did infinitely stomake their undeserved advancements, and with these the favour of the people generally went. But the kings intemperate affection was per[p. 8]emptory and violent, not regarding envy untill he could not resist it.

The yeere next following Robert Veere, the new marques, was created Duke of Ireland.[14] This yere the knights and burgesses of parliament put up many complaints against the Earle of Suffolke, upon which they desired his answeres and triall, namely: how he had abused the king in taking of him to farme all the profits & revenues of the crowne; how wantonly he wasted the treasure of the land in riotous liberalitie and unnecessary charges; how deepe he had dived into the kings debt; how carelesse and corrupt hee was in his office; how greatly he had both deceived and discredited the king in certaine dealings and accounts particularly expressed; with divers other imputations touching dishonour and dishonesty, both in private actions and in office.

This earle was a merchants sonne in London and, growing mighty on the sudden, he could not governe himselfe in the change.[15] But prosperity layed open the secret faults of his minde, which were suppressed and cloaked before; and serving a weake ruler in great place, with an ill minde, he made open sale of his princes honour. Yet the king was willing either secretly to dissemble, or openly to remit these offences, and so passed them over with a short audience (as his maner was in matters of greatest weight) and without examination, shewing himselfe neither grieved at the faults nor well pleased with the complaint.

Afterwards, a subsidie was required, but answere was made that this needed not, since the kings wants might be furnished with the debts which were owing him from his chancellour. Neither was it to any purpose, so long as the money should be ordered by such persons as before it had beene, and at that time was like.

Then were the matters against the Lord Chancellour againe set on foote, and the king perswaded that it was neither honourable nor safe to beare him out: that to private men it was sufficient if them[p.

[14] 13 October 1386.
[15] This seems to be another instance of Hayward overextending his evidence in favour of his notion of aristocratic honour. Although Earl of Suffolk by marriage, and not derived from the ancient nobility, Pole was certainly no mere *arriviste*. The son of a wealthy Hull merchant, he was a knight as early as 1355 and veteran of several foreign military campaigns; Dr. Steel terms him a 'seasoned soldier, diplomat and administrator:' see Anthony Steel, *Richard II* (Cambridge, 1962), 96.

9]selves abstaine from wrong, but a prince must provide that none do wrong under him. For by mainteining or wincking at the vices of his officers, he maketh them his owne, and shal surely be charged therewith when first occasion doth serve against him.

At the last, upon instant importunity of both houses, the king did consent that a commission should goe forth to certaine noble men, giving them authority to heare and determine all matters which were objected against the Lord Chancellour. And then was a subsidie graunted, with exception that the money should be expended by the Lords, to the benefit and behalfe of the realme.

The king did further demaund that the heires of Charles Bloys, who made claime to the Duchy of Britaine, should be sold to the French men for thirty thousand marks, and the money granted to the Duke of Ireland, for recovery of those possessions which the king had given him in Ireland. This was likewise assented unto, upon condition that before Easter the next ensuing the duke should depart into Ireland, and there remaine, at so high a price did they value the riddance of him out of the realme.

The charge of the subsidie money was committed to Richard Earle of Arundell; commissioners for the Earle of Suffolke were appointed: Thomas Duke of Glocester, the kings uncle, and the sayd Earle of Arundell. But during the time of their proceeding, the king kept all off in places farre distant, either to manifest thereby the dissent of his minde, or to avoid the griefe which his neerenesse would increase. And now was the chancellour left unto himselfe to answere those demeanures, wherein he made the kings blinde favour his priviledge and protection, supposing never to see the same either altered or overruled. In the end, being convict of many crimes and abuses, he was deposed from his office, his goods were confiscated to the kings exchequer, & himself was adjudged woorthy of death. Yet was execution submitted to the kings pleasure, and under sureties he was [p. 10] permitted to goe at large.

At the same time John Foorde[16] Bishop of Duresme, another of the kings dainties, was removed also from being Lord Treasorer of England. He was a man of little depth either in learning or wisedom, but one that had the arte of seeming, in making the best shewe of whatsoever he spake or did. And rising from meane estate to so high a pitch of honour, hee exercised the more excessively his ryote, avarice and ambition, not able to moderate the lustes and desires which former want had kindled.

When this businesse was blowne over, the king returned againe to London, and did presently receive the Earle of Suffolke, with the

---

[16] John Fordham, bishop of Durham, was later bishop of Ely.

Duke of Ireland and the Archbishop of Yorke,[17] to greater grace and familiaritie then at any time before. These triumvirs did not cease to stirre up the kings stomake against those noble men whose speciall excellencie had made matter of fame and regarde. Partly for the disgraces which they had received, partly upon malicious emulation to see other so favoured and themselves so odious, and that their private choller and ambition might beare some shewe of publike respect, they suggested unto the king that he was but halfe, yea not halfe a king in his own realme, but rather the shadow and picture of a king. 'For if we respect,' sayd they, 'matters of state, you beare the sword, but they sway it; you have the shewe, but they the authority of a prince, using your name as colour and countenance to their proceedings, and your person as a cypher, to make them great and be your selfe nothing. Looke to the dutie of your subiects, and it is at their devotion, so that you can neither commaunde nor demaunde anything, but with such exceptions and limitations as they please to impose. Come now to your private actions: your liberalitie (the greatest vertue in a prince) is restrained, your expences measured, and your affections confined to frowne and favour as they doe prescribe. What ward is so much under government of his gardian? Wherein will they next, or can they [p. 11] more, abridge you, except they should take from you the place, as they have done the power, of a prince? And in this we thinke they may justly be feared, having so great might joined with so great aspiring mindes. For power is never safe when it doth exceede, & ambition is like the crocodile, which groweth so long as he liveth, or like the ivie which, fastning on the foote of the tallest tower, by small yet continuall rising at length will climbe above the toppe. It is already growne from a sparke to a flame, from a twigge to a tree, and high time it is that the encrease were stayed. Oftentimes such over-ruling of princes have proceeded to their overthrowing, and such cutting them short hath turned to cutting them off. Their minds are suspicious, their power daungerous, and therefore the opportunitie must bee prevented.'

The kings own weaknesse made him apprehensive, and framed his mind to a vaine and needlesse feare. But chiefely, he was moved at the remooving of his chancellour and treasorer out of their offices, and the Duke of Ireland out of the realme, supposing it a restraint to his princely power that he might not absolutely and in things give or forgive as his pleasure served. When these privie incensers perceived the kings humour once sharpned, they so plyed[18] him with plausible perswasions that (although he was naturally of no cruell disposition, as wanting courage) yet they drew him to many violent and indirect

[17] Alexander Neville.
[18] A: 'played,' a listed 'faulte.'

courses, partly upon negligence to search out the truth, partly upon delight to bee flattered and smothly used. Neither did they long deferre their devises.

And first it was appointed that the Duke of Gloucester and certaine others of that part should be invited to a supper within London, & there suddainly surprised and made away. Sir Nicholas Brambre, who the yere before had beene Mayor of London, and in whome abundance of wealth supplyed the want of honest qualities, was a busie agent in this butcherly businesse. But Richard Extone, the mayor of the [p. 12] cittie that yeare, discovered the practise, by whome the duke was warned both to avoide the present perill, and afterwards to be warie of the like.

The yeare next following,[19] Richard Earle of Arundel and Thomas Mowbraye Earle of Notingham had the conduct of a navie committed to their charge. In this viage they tooke above a hundred sayle of the enemies ships, fraughted with wines, and well appointed for fight. They also relieved and fortified Brest, and tooke two fortes which the Frenchmen had raised against it. The earles so behaved themselves in this service that they grew to a verie great estimation, both for curtesie among their souldiers, and for courage against their enemies, & their actions were the more famous, by reason of the infortunate insufficiencie of other commanders, by whose either rashenesse or cowardise many good souldiers were dayly defeated, and every yeare made notorious by one losse or other. Yet, notwithstanding all their good labour and lucke, they were at their returne entertained by the king with great straungnes, both of countenance and speech. Who was so unable to dissemble his dispight that he could hardly deferre it, untill the heate of the honour and love which they had wonne were somewhat abated. So much are men more inclinable to revenge displeasure then rewarde desert; for it is troublesome to bee gratefull, and many times chargeable, but revenge is pleasant, and preferred before gaine.

About the same time, Robert Duke of Ireland forsooke the companie of his lawfull wife, whose mother, Lady Isabel, was daughter to King Edward the third, and in steede of her he tooke unto him a base Bohemian, a taverners daughter.[20] The king little regarded this indignitie done unto his cosin, and in so great confusion of the state let it passe unreprooved, as overshadowed with greater vices. But the Duke of Gloucester, her uncle, tooke it in high disdaine, as injurious to the royall bloud, and did attend upon occasion to worke [p. 13] revenge. This was not secrete from the Duke of Irelande, who likewise

[19] Early 1387.
[20] Robert De Vere, ninth earl of Oxford, was first married to Philippa de Coucy, granddaughter to Edward III; his affair with Agnes Launcecrone began around 1385.

bent al his devises to bring the Duke of Gloucester to his overthrow. The Duke of Gloucester did prosecute this enmitie openly and manlike; the Duke of Ireland closely, and therefore the more daungerously. The Duke of Gloucester was greater in bloud, the Duke of Ireland in favour; he being uncle to the king, this bearing himselfe as the kings fellow. The Duke of Gloucester pretended for the state, the Duke of Ireland for the king. And much private mallice did passe under these publike shewes. But in opposition of such equall powers, there is many times smal difference in harme.

And now was Easter past, the terme assigned to Duke Robert Veere for his departure into Ireland. And, least his stay might breede some stirre within the realme, hee still busied himselfe in preparation for his journie, and at last (although it were long) made a solemne shew of setting forth. The king went in grat state to accompanie him to his shipping, and the Earle of Suffolke, with Justice Trisiliane and the residue of that faction either for favour followed, or for feare durst not stay behinde. So they passed together into Wales, and (whether upon levitie the kings mind changed, or whether it was so contrived at the first, to drawe themselves more seperate from the lords) there the dukes jornie was at an ende. Then they entred into counsell which way the lords might best be suppressed. Many devises were deepely debated; all pleased without respect either of danger or disgrace. But few stoode with likelyhoode of event to their desires, and therefore none was finally concluded. After long time thus frivolously spent, they left Wales and came to the castle of Notingham, where the king caused the high shirifes of all the shires in the realme to be called before him,[21] and demaunded of them what strength they could make on his part against the lordes, if neede shoulde require. Their answere was, that the common people did so [p. 14] favour the lords, and were so well resolved of their love & loyaltie towards the king, that it was not in their power to rayse any great power against them. Then they were commaunded that no knights nor burgesses should afterwards bee chosen to any parliament, but those whome it pleased the king to appoint. Whereto they said that it was a harde matter in those times of jealousie and suspicion to bereave the people of their auncient libertie in choosing knightes and burgesses for the parliament. Some few other matters being either unreasonably required or obtained to small end, the sherifs were licensed to depart.

Then were asembled Robert Trisilian, Chief Justice of the Kings Bench, Robert Belknape, Chief Justice of the Common Pleas, John Holte, Roger Stilthorpe, William Burgh, Knights and Justices also of the Common Pleas, men learned in one rule: chiefely, without differ-

[21] August 1387.

ence of truth or falshoode, to please those in the highest place, enti-
tuling that wisedome, which indeed was but basenesse and feeblenes
of minde. These were charged by the king upon their faith and
legeance, to make true & full answere to those questions following:

1 First, whether the statute, ordinance and commission, made and
set forth the last parliament (whereby was ment the commission aganst
Michael Delapoole, Duke of Suffolke) did derogate from the royall
prerogative of the king.

2 Item, they who procured the said statute, & c. to be made and
set forth, how are they to be punished?

3 Item, how are they to be punished, who provoked the king to
consent to the premises?

4 Item, what punishment have they deserved who compelled the
king to consent to the said statute & c.?

5 Item, how are they to be punished, who resisted or letted the king
in exerciseing his royall power, by remitting any penalties or debts
whatsoever?

6 Item, when a parliament is assembled, and the affaires of [p. 15]
the realme and the cause of assembling the parliament by the kings
commaundement declared, and common articles limited by the king,
upon which the lordes and commons in the said parliament should
proceed; if the lords & commons will proceed upon other articles, and
not upon articles limitted by the king, untill the king hath first given
answere to the articles propounded by them, notwithstanding that
the contrarie were enjoined by the king: whether in this case the king
ought to have the rule of the parliament, and so to order the fact,
that the lordes and commons should first proceede upon the articles
limitted by the king, or that they should first have answere of the king
upon the articles propounded by them, before they proceede any
further?

7 Item, whether may the king when he please[22] dissolve the parliament and commaunde the lordes and commons to depart, or no?

8 Item, since the king may at his pleasure remove any of his officers
and justices, and punish them for their offences, whether may the
lordes and commons without the kings will accuse his officers and
justices in parliament for their offences, yea or no?

9 Item, what punishment have they deserved, who moved in parliament that the statute whereby King Edward Carnarvane was
deposed should be brought forth, by view whereof the new statute,
ordinance and commission aforesaid were framed?

10 Item, whether the judgement given in the last parliament holden

[22] *A*: 'pleaseth,' a listed 'faulte.'

at Westminster, against Michael Delapoole, Duke of Suffolke, was erronious and revocable, yea or no?

These questions or rather quarrelles were drawne by John Blake, a counceller at the law, by direction of Justice Trisilian, whilest the king made his stay in Wales. To the which the justices aforenamed, some in discharge of their owne malice, and some to satisfie the mindes of other, made answere as followeth:

To the first, that they did derogate from the prerogative of the king, because they were against his will.

[p. 16] To the second and third, that they are to be punished by death, except it pleaseth the king to pardon them.

To the fourth and fifth, that they are worthy to be punished as traitours.

To the sixth, that whosoever resisteth the kings rule in that point deserveth to be punished as a traitour.

To the seventh, that the king may at his pleasure dissolve the parliament, and whosoever shall afterwards proceed, against the kings minde, as in a parliament, he is worthy to be punished as a traitour.

To the eighth, that they can not, and whosoever doeth the contrary, he deserveth to be punished as a traitour.

To the ninth, that aswell the motioner as also the bringer of the sayd statute to parliament are worthy to be punished as traitours.

To the tenth they answered, that the said judgement seemed to them erronious and revocable in every part. In witnesse whereof the justices aforesayd, with John Locktone, the kings sergeant at law, have subscribed and set their seales to these presents,[23] & c.

When these bloody sentences of death and treason were under generall & large termes thus fastened upon the lords, the king supposed his attempts against them, whther by violence or by couler of law, sufficiently warranted.[24] But his power both wayes, as it was terrible against weake resistance, so against such mighty defendants it was of

---

[23] A: 'present,' a listed 'faulte.'

[24] By endorsing the charge of treason in these essentially political matters, Richard had reawakened an issue that in his grandfather's reign had caused much bitterness. Since a proved charge of treason could cause certain forfeitures of property, Edward III had found it a powerful weapon against his barons. On the other hand, since the charge could be appealed by combat, its invocation was inherently dangerous to the realm's stability. Edward had eventually agreed to a narrow, and hence infrequently applicable, interpretation of what constituted treason. The verdicts at Nottingham broadened the meaning of the crime once more, thus re-opening the quarrel between crown and nobility at a new level of disruption. An early consequence was the appeal of Vere, Neville, de la Pole, Tresilian and Brembre of treason brought by the duke and earls, with its attendant offer of combat. The confrontatation between Hereford and Mowbray at Coventry was another.

small force to effect that which he so much affected; yet he did not omit his best indevour. And first, accounting the lordes as condemned persons, he made division of their lands and goods among those that he favoured.[25] Then he waged souldiers to be in a readinesse for his assistance, and sent the Earle of Northumberland to arrest the Earle of Arundell at his castle at Reygate, where he then lay. But the Earle of Arundell, either upon advertisement or suspition of the kings minde, banded himselfe so strong that when the Earle of [p. 17] Northumberland came unto him, he dissembled his intent, and left his purpose unperformed.

Thus were these proceedings of the king, as now in counsell, so afterwards in event, not much unlike that which the fable telleth of a certaine hunter, who first solde the skinne of the beare and then went about to take her; but when he came within the forrest, either by unskilfulnesse or misadventure he not onely missed his pray, but fell himselfe into danger of the beast.

The Duke of Gloucester, having secret intelligence of the kings displeasure and his drift, sent the Bishop of London[26] to perswade the king to entertaine a more favorable opinion of him, making faith to the bishop with a solemne oath that he never entended any thing to the prejudice of the king, either in person or state. The bishop, not unskilfull to joine profitable perswasion with honest, declared to the king that his displeasure against the lords was not grounded upon just desert, but either upon false suggestions of their enemies, or erronious mistaking of some of their actions; how desirous they were of his grace and favour; how faithfull and forward they promised to persist in all dutifull service; how honourable this agreement would be to the king, how profitable to the realme; and how daungerous to both, these troubles might encrease.

The king seemed to give good eare & credit to the bishops speech. But Michael Delapoole, a turbulent man, and against quiet counsell obstinately contentious, standing then by the king soone stiffened his minde against all impression of friendship. Heereupon contention did arise betweene the Bishop and the Earle, and brake forth violently into heat of words. The earle applied to the lordes those obiections wherewith great men are usually charged, sparing no spight of speech and using all arte to aggravate matters against them. The Bishop replied that the earle was thus fiercely bent, not upon his owne necessity, nor love to the king, but onely to satisfie his bloody and ambitious humour, wherein he was so immoderate, that ra[p. 18]ther then the lords should not be destroyed, he would overwhelme them

---

[25] *A*: 'favououred.'
[26] Robert Braybrooke.

with the ruines of the state. For tumults might in deed be raised by men of little courage, but must be maintained with the hazzard, and ended with the losse, of the most valiant. That neither his counsell in this matter was to be followed, being the principall firebrand of the disturbance, nor his complaints against any man to be anything regarded, being himselfe a condemned person, and one that held both his life and honour at the pleasure of the king.

At these words the king was exceedinly wroth, and charged the bishop with menacing & threats to avoid his presence. When the Duke of Glocester had knowledge heereof, he signified the daunger to the Earles of Arundell, Warwicke and Derbie, advising them to take armes and unite themselves for their common defence, for in so doubtfull and suspected peace, open warre was the onely hope of safety. These three earles were the chiefest strength to the side, but the Duke bare the most stroke, because he was most bolde, and his greatnesse almost obscured the names of the rest. On the other side the king, thinking separate dealing the onely way to weaken a confederacy, edevoured to prevent the lordes in joyning of their forces. And to that end he sent a strength of men, with charge either to set upon the Earle of Arundell where he did lie, or to intercept him in his passage towardes the Duke. But the earle had traveiled all the night before their comming, and so happily escaped to Haringey Parke, where he found the duke and the other earles with a sufficient company as well to make attempt as to stand upon resistance.

When the king heard hereof, he was disturbed and distracted in minde, being now in choise either to relent or to resist, whereof he much disdained the one, and distrusted the other. His followers also were divided in counsell, some fretting at the disgrace, and some fainting at the daunger. The Archbishop of York[27] perswaded the king that occasion [p. 19] was now offered to shew himself a king indeed, if he would muster a royall armie and by maine might beat downe the boldnesse of this presumption. *Nihil dictu facilius,* sayd another: 'This is more readily devised then done: the army against us is mighty, and the commanders are great men both for courage and skill, and greatly favoured of the common people, whereby that which is accompted so ready pay, may chaunce to proove a desperate debt. Therefore it were better with some yeelding to enter into conditons of quiet, then by standing upon high points of honour to hazard the issue of a battaile, wherein the king cannot winne without his weakning, nor loose without daunger of his undoing.'

There was then in presence a certaine olde knight called Sir Hugh

[27] Alexander Neville.

Linne, a good souldier, but a very madcap,[28] & one that lived chiefly upon the liberalitie of noble men, by vaine jestes affecting the grace of a pleasant conceite. Of him the king demaunded, in mirth, what he thought best to be done? Sir Hugh swore, 'swownes and snayles, let us set upon them, and kill every man and mothers childe, and so we shall make riddaunce of the best friendes you have in the realme.' This giddie answere more weighed with the king then if it had beene spoken in grave and sober sort.[29] And thus it often happeneth, that wisedome is the more sweetly swallowed when it is tempered with folly, and earnest is the lesse offensive, if it bee delivered in jest.

In the end, the devise of raysing armes was laide aside, not as displeasing (being so agreable to former proceedings) but as despayring to prevaile thereby. And the Archbishop of Canterburie,[30] with the Bishop of Ely[31] being Lord Chaunceller, were sent unto the lordes, to understand the cause of their assemblie. Answere was made that it was for the safetie of themselves, the honour of the king, and the overthrow of them which sought the overthrow of both.

At the last it was concluded by mediation of the Bishops that the lordes should come before the king at Westminster, upon promise of his protection, and [p. 20] there have audience concerning their griefes, the Bishop of Ely also making privat faith that he would discover any danger that he could descrie. A little before the time they should come, the Bishoppe of Ely sent word of an awaite that was purposed to be layed for them, at a place called the Mewes, neere London, advising them either to make stay, or to come prepared; but rather to make stay, least further provocation might make reconcilement more hard. Hereupon they came not at the time appointed, and the king, marvailing at their failance,[32] enquired the cause of the Bishop of Ely, who aunswered that the lords found want of true meaning, & that they neither did, nor durst repose assuraunce in the kings word, which they saw to bee used as a meanes to entrape them.

The king made the matter verie strange unto him, affirming with an oath that hee was free from deceite, both in consent and knowledge. And in a great rage, he commaunded the sherifes of London to goe to the place, and slay all those whome they found there in a waite. Whether this was but a countenance of his, or whether he was not privie to the practise, it is not assuredly knowne. And in deede, the matter was not false, but the place mistaken, for Sir Thomas Trivet

---

[28] This characterization of Lynn earned Hayward later criticism: see *Fasti*, I, 368.
[29] *A*: 'sport,' a listed 'faulte.'
[30] William Courtenay.
[31] Thomas Arundel.
[32] Failure, neglect (OED).

and Sir Nicholas Brambre had assembled many armed men at Westminster, with direction to assault the lordes at their best advantage. But, perceiving their deceite to be discovered, they dissolved the companie, and sent them secretely away to London.

Then the lordes, upon new faith for their securitie, came to the king at Westminster,[33] and yet in faith they brought securitie with them, such troupes of men as in a place where they were so entirely favoured, was able to defend them in any suddaine tumult or daunger. The king upon their comming entred into Westminster Hall, apparelled in his royall robes, and when he was placed in his seate, and had composed himselfe to majestie and state, the Bishop of Ely, Lord Chaunceller, made a long oration to the lordes in the [p. 21] kings name, wherein he declared the heinousnesse of their offence, the greatnesse of their perill, how easie a matter it had beene for the king to have levied a power sufficient to distroy them; and yet for the generall spare of his subjects bloud, and in particular favour to the duke and other lords, he made choyse to encounter and overcome them rather by friendship then by force, and therefore was willing, not only to pardon their ryote, but also to heare their griefes, and in a peaceful and quiet manner to redresse them.

The lordes alleaged for causes of their taking armes, first the necessitie of their owne defence, secondly the love both of the king and of the realme, whose fame and fortune did dayly decline by meanes of certaine traytors, who lived onely by the dishonours of the one, and decayes of the other.

Those whom they challenged for traytors were Robert Veere, Duke of Ireland; Alexander Nevill, Archbishop of Yorke; Michaell Delapoole, Earle of Suffolke; Robert Trisiliane, Lord Chiefe Justice; Sir Nicholas Brambre; and certaine others, somewhat secreter, but nothing better. And to justifie this appeale they threw downe their gloves, and offered themselves to the triall by combate. The king replied that often times the causes of actions being good, yet if the meanes want moderation and judgement, the events prove pernicious. And therefore, though these complaints were true, yet were these courses not tollerable which did beare an open face of rebellion, and by licentiousnesse of the multitude might soone have sorted to such an end. For it is more easie to raise the people, then to rule them, whose furie once stirred will commonly be discharged some wayes.

But (sayd he) since we have broken this broile, we will not by combatting give occasion of a new. But at the next Parliament (which he appointed should begin the third day of February next ensuing)[34]

---

[33] 17 Nov. 1387.
[34] Marginal note here: 'Crastino purificationis.'

as well you, as they, shall be present, and justice done indifferently to all.

In the meane time, he tooke all parties into his protection, that none should endanger or endammage another, [p. 22] desiring the lordes to beare in minde that as princes must not rule without limitation, so subiects must use a meane in their libertie. Then he caused the duke and the earles, which all this time kneeled before him, to arise, and went with them into his private chamber, where they talked a while and drunke familiarly together, & afterwards with a most friendly farwell he licenced them to depart. They of the contrarie faction were not present at this meeting, and if they had, it was thought that the presence of the king should little have protected them.

This act of the king was divers waies taken. Some judged him fearefull, others moderate rather, in sparing the bloud of his subjectes. The lordes were verie joyfull of his goodwill and favour, which as by base or bad meanes they would not seeke, so being well gotten they did highly esteeme. Yet they thought it the safest course not to seperate themselves, suspecting the mutabiltie of the king, and the malice of their enemies, of whome they knewe neither where they were or what they did entend. And, being men of great wealth, and great power, and greatly bent to hurtfull practises, they were feared not without a cause. For the Duke of Ireland, either by setting on or sufferance of the king, was all this time mustering of souldiers out of Cheshire and Wales, where hee gathered an armie both for number and goodnesse of men sufficient, if another had beene generall, to have maintained the side.

When the lordes were advertised hereof, they devided themselves & beset all the waies by which the duke should passe to London, determining to encounter him before he did increase his power and countenance his actions with the puissance or name of the king. At the last he was met by the Earl of Derby, at a place called Babbelake, neere to Burforde. And there the earle put his men in array, resolving with great boldnesse to hazard the battaile. His souldiers also were ful of courage and hart, disliking nothing more then [p. 23] delay, as a loosing of time and a hinderance to the victorie. But the duke, being a man not fit for action, yet mutinous, and more apt to stirre strife then able to stint it, upon newes of an enemie would presently have fled.

There was then in the armie as a principall commaunder one Sir Thomas Molineux, Constable of Cheshire, a man of great wealth and of good proofe in service, upon whose leading all that countrie did depend. He perswaded the duke that this was but a part of the forces that were against them, and led onely by the Earl of Derby, a man of no speciall name (at that time) among the lordes, and if they could not beare through that resistance, it was but in vaine to attempt any great atchivement by armes. Hereupon the duke stayed his steps, but his faint spirits were mooved by this speech rather to desire victory, then to hope it. His souldiers also were dul, silent, & sad, and such as were readier to interpret then execute the captaines commandement.

So they joyned battell, but scarse ten ounces of bloud was lost on both sides, before the Duke of Ireland set spurres to his horse, and forsooke the field. His souldiers, seeing this, threw away their unfortunate weapons, more for indignation then for feare, ruffling their rancks and yeelding to the earle the honour of the field.

Sir Thomas Molineux, in flying away, was forced to take a river which was neere, and as he was comming foorth againe a certaine knight, whose name was Sir Thomas Mortimer, pulled off his helmet and stabbed him into the braines with his dagger. The rest submitted themselves to the discretion of the victorours, making them lords over their life and death. But their yeelding was no sooner offered, then it was accepted, the earle presently commaunding that none should be harmed, but those that did make resistance or beare armour, the souldiours also being willing to shew favour towardes their countreymen, as ledde into this action partly upon simplicitie, partly to accompany these which came upon feare.

Then the gentlemen were [p. 24] still reteined in the earles company, the common souldiers were dispoiled of their armour onely, and so returned againe to their peaceable businesse at home. And this was the first acte whereby reputation did rise to the side, and the greatnes began, whereunto the earle afterwards attained.

The Duke of Ireland, at the beginning of his flight, was desirous to have passed the river which ranne by, and comming to a bridge, he found the same broken. From thence he posted to another bridge, which he found guarded with archers. At the last, his fearefulnesse being feared away (as nothing maketh men more desperate upon a doubtfull danger, then feare of that which is certaine), he adventured to take the streame, in the midst wherof he forsooke his horse, and swam to the other side, and so by benefit of the night escaped, and fled into Scotland, and shortly after passed the seas into Flanders, and from thence traveiled into France, where the continuall gall of his griefe soone brought his loathed life to an end. His horse was taken, with his brest-plate, his helmet and his gauntlets, whereupon it was generally supposed that he was drowned. And (as in great uncerteineties it often happeneth) some affirmed that they sawe his death, which men either glad to heare, or not curious to search, did easily beleeve. Whether this were thus contrived of purpose, or fell out so by chance, it was a great meanes of his escape, by staying the pursute after him which otherwise had bene made. His coach also was taken, and certaine of the kings letters found, wherein he desired the duke to come to London with all the power and speede hee could make, and he would be ready to die in his defence. So unskilfull was he in matters of governement, that to pleasure a few, he regarded not the discontentment of all the rest.

The Earle of Suffolke, upon this accident, shaved his beard and in base and disguised attire fled to Calice, and either for feare or for shame never after returned into England. He was a cruell spoiler, and a carelesse spender, in war [p. 25] contemptible, in peace insupportable, an enemie to all counsaile of others, and in his owne conceite obstinatly contentious, of a good wit and ready speach, both which hee abused to the cunning commending of himselfe, and crafty depraving of others. He was lesse loved but better heard of the king then the Duke of Ireland, the more hurtful man & the more hateful, the duke being charged with no great fault, but onely the kings excessive favour. In their course of good and bad fortune, both of them were famous alike.

Also the Archbishop of Yorke, Justice Trisiliane, and others of that faction ran every man, like connies to their coverte. Yea, the king betooke himselfe to the Tower of London, and there made provision for his winter aboade, having all his courses now crossed, first rashnesse in taking armes, and afterwards by cowardise in maintaining them.

The Earle of Darby signified this successe to his associates by letters, yet without any vaunting or enlarging tearms. His speaches also were moderate, rather exstenuating his fact then extolling it. But by stopping his fame, it much increased when men esteemed his high thoughtes by his lowely wordes, and his conceite in great exploites by his contempt of this. Then the lords met, and marched together towards London, whither they came upon S. Stephens day, having almost forty thousand men in their armie, & first they shewed themselves in battaile array, in the fieldes neare unto the Tower, within the viewe of the king. Afterwardes, they tooke up their lodging in the suburbes. The maior and aldermen of the citty came forth and gave liberall allowance of victuall to the souldiers, offering unto the lordes entertainment within the citty, but they did not accept it.

Now this discord seemed to draw to a dangerous distraction of the common-wealth, the vanquished parte being ful of malice, and the conquerors of presumption, the one wanting power, the other right to command and rule. The Archbishop of Canterbury and certaine others of the neutrality, [p. 26] fearing the sequele, perswaded the king to come to a treaty with the lordes. But he made shewe of very light regarde of all these dealings. 'Let them stay,' saide hee, 'untill they have wearied themselves with maintaining this multitude, and then I will talke further with them.' When the lordes understood the drift of his devise, they beset the Thames & all other passages, and protested that they woulde not departe untill they had talked with him to his face. The king, having neyther strength to resist nor scope to scape, consented to a treaty, and to that end desired the lordes to come to him into the Tower. But they refused that place of meeting, upon feare of false measure, untill the king permitted them to search as diligently, and come as strongly, as they thought it meete.

So they came unto the king well guarded, and after a fewe colde kindnesses and strange salutations, they laide before him his proceedings against them at Nottingham; his letters which he sent to the Duke of Ireland, contrary to his worde, for the raysing of armes against them; his agreement with the French king for the yeelding up of Callice and other strong holdes which he possessed in those parts; with divers other pointes of dishonourable dealing and negligent government. What should the king then have said or done? All these matters were so evident and so evill, that there was no place left either for deniall or defence. Therefore ingenuously, first with silence and patience, afterwardes with teares, he confessed his errors. And certainely the stiffe stomack of the lordes relented more to these luke warme drops than they would have done to his cannon shot.

Then it was agreed, that the next day the king should meet with them at Westminster, and there treat further, both of these and other necessarie affaires of the realme. So the duke and the rest of the lords departed, except the Earle of Darby, who stayed supper with the king, and all that time stayed him in his promised purpose. But when hee was also gone, some of the secrete counsailers, or corrupters, rather, [p. 27] and abusers of the king whistled him in the eare, that his going to Westminster was neither seemely nor safe, and would cause not onely to his person present danger and contempt, but also both abasement and abridgement to his authority afterwards.

The kings minde was soon changed. But the lords being now stirred, and feeling the kings hand weake to govern the bridle, became the more vehement, and sent him worde that if hee did jeofaile[35] with them and not come according to appointment, they would chuse another king, who shoulde have his nobility in better regard. This peremptorie message so terrified the king that he not onely went to Westminster, but suffered the lords to doe there even what they woulde. So they caused him, much against his liking, to remoove out of the court Alexander Nevill, Archbishop of Yorke, John Foorde, Bishop of Durisme, Frier Thomas Rushoke, Bishop of Chichester, the kings confessor. Likewise they removed the Lord Souch, the Lord

---

[35] 'Jeofaile' = 'to fail to meet an obligation' (OED).

Haringworth, Lord Burnell, Lord Beaumonte, Sir Albred Veere, Sir Baldewine Bereford, Sir Richard Alderburie, Sir John Worth, Sir Thomas Clifford, and Sir John Lovell, taking suerties for their appearance at the next parliament.

Also, certaine ladies were expelled the court, and put under suerties, to wit: the Lady Mowen, the Lady Moling, and the Lady Ponings, which was the wife of Sir John Woorth. Furthermore, they arrested Simon Burlye, William Elinghame, John Salisburie, Thomas Trivet, James Berneis, Nicholas Dagworth, and Nicholas Brambre, Knights; Richard Clifforde, John Lincolne, and Richard Motford, clearkes; John Beauchampe, the kings steward; Nicholas Lake, Deane of the Kings Chapell; and John Blake, Counceller at the law. All these were committed to divers prisons, where they were forth-comming, but not comming forth, untill the parliament next following.

After the feast of the Purification,[36] the parliament began at London (and yet the king used many meanes either to dash or deferre the same), to which the lordes came, atten[p. 28]ded with the number and strength of a full armie, upon colour to represse any ryote that might happen to arise, but in truth that by this terrour they might draw the whole manage of affaires unto themselves. This assembly continued untill Whitsontide next following, with verie great feare of some men, and hope of others, and expectation of all.

Herein was Justice Trisiliane, by counsaile of the lordes, against the kings minde condemned to bee drawne and hanged, which judgement was presently executed upon him. The like sentence and execution passcd upon Sir Nicholas Brambre, Sir John Salisburie, Sir James Barneis, John Beauchampe, the kings steward, and John Blake, Esquire, who had framed the articles which were exhibited against the lordes at Nottingham. Also the justices who gave their judgement concerning those articles, Robert Belknape, John Holte, Roger Fulthorpe and William Burghe, were condemned to perpetuall exile; and yet they did not interpose themselves, but intermeddle by constraint.

Sir Simon Burlye was also beheaded, who was Keeper of Dover Castle, and had conspired to deliver the same unto the Frenchmen. Hee was infinitely haughtie and proude, equall to the meanest in virtue and and wisedome, but in braverie and traine inferiour to no duke. Divers others were either put to death or banished, and some (as it happeneth when the reyne of furie is at large) without any great cause. The Earl of Derby furthered no mans death, but laboured verie instantly for the life and liberty of many, in so much as hoat speeches did arise betweene the Duke of Gloucester and him, whereby he

---

[36] Marginal note: '1388.' (This was the 'Merciless' parliament, 3 February–4 June 1388.)

purchased a favourable opinion among those of the contrarie part, having caused the death of no man, but onely in the fielde.

Then was an oath exacted of the king, to stand to the government of the lordes, and also an oath was taken of all the subjects within the realme, to be true and faithfull unto the king. The king, in taking this oath of the lordes, bewrayed his inward conceite by his open countenance, loo[p. 29]king pleasantly upon those he favoured, and angerly upon those whome hee hated. By which untimely discovery, hee made them more heedeful, and himselfe more hatefull: which were occasions afterwarde both to prevente the revenge which he much desired, and to procure the mischiefs which hee little feared.

Lastly, a subsidie was graunted; and so the king, comming as it were to a capitulation with the lordes, hee to have the name of a king, and they to have the authority and majesty, the contention for that time ceased.

All this was done in the xj. yeere of the kings reigne,[37] he being yet under age, and in governement of others. But the yeere following[38] he beganne to take upon him more liberty and rule; and upon extreame disdaine that both his pleasure and his power were by the lords thus restrained, he did ever after beare a hard minde against them. And first he assembled them in the councell chamber, and there demanded, of what yeeres they tooke him to be? They answered that he was somewhat above one and twenty.[39] 'Then,' sayd he, 'I am of lawfull age to have the regiment in mine owne hand, and therefore you doe me wrong to holde me still under gouvernement, as though the condition of a king were harder then of a subject.' This the lords were neither willing to grant, nor able to denie, and therefore they either kept silence, or spake little to the purpose. 'Well,' sayd the king, 'since I am no longer an infant, I heere renounce your rule, and take upon me such free administration of the realme as the kings thereof, my predecessours, have lawfully used.' Then presently he began his Phaetons flourish, and commaunded the Bishop of Elie, being Lord Chancellour, to resigne his seale, which the king received, and put up, and therewith departed out of the chamber. But soone after he returned againe, and delivered the same to William Wickham, Bishop of Winchester, constituting him Lord Chancellour thereby. Many other officers he likewise deposed, and placed new in their roome, partly to manifest his autho[p. 30]rity, and partly to satisfie his displeasure. Also he remooved the Duke of Gloucester, the Earle of Warwicke and

[37] Richard's eleventh regnal year, toward the end of which this parliament sat, was 22 June 1387–21 June 1388.
[38] Marginal note: '1389.'
[39] Richard had turned twenty-one on 6 Jan. 1388.

many others from his Privy Councell, and tooke those in their places
which more regarded the humour of the king, but lesse his honour.

Soone after, it was suggested to the king that the Duke of Gloucester
was gathering of forces against him. But upon examination there was
found not onely no trueth, but no shew or colour, of any such matter.
The duke would not quietly have digested the raysing of these reportes,
but the king, whether upon a generall delight to be tickled in the eares
with such tales, or upon particular desire to have some quarell against
the duke, charged him to silence.

In the 13. yeare of the raigne of King Richard,[40] the citizens of
Genua desired his ayde against the barbarians of Afrike, who with
dayly incursions infested and spoyled all the sea coasts & ilands of
Italy and Fraunce which fronted uppon them. The king sent a choyse
companie of souldiers, under the conduct of Henrie, Earle of Derby,[41]
who behaved himselfe in this charge with great integritie & courage,
inciting his men, the good by prayse, the bad by example rather then
reproofe, as more ready to commend the vertues of the one then to
upbraide the vices of the other. And first hee passed into Fraunce,
and there joyned himselfe to certaine French forces, appointed likewise
for this service. Then, with might and minds united, they sayled
together into Afrike.

At their arrivall, the barbarians were ready in armes, to keepe
them from landing. But the earle commaunded his archers to breake
through and make passage, dispising the enemie, whome he knew to
be weake and unskilfull in service, and not to have that advantage in
place which hee had in men. The Frenchmen also sharply set in &
seconded the English, and so whilest both companies contended, the
one to be accompted a helpe, & the other to seeme to neede no help,
the enemies were forced to flie and leave the shoare unto the [p. 31]
Christians.

In this conflict three dukes of the barbarians and above three
hundred souldiers were slaine, and in the flight fower dukes were
taken, and a great, yet uncertaine, number of common people. Then
the Christians marched directly towards Tunis, the head cittie of that
countrie. This they besieged, & in short time tooke, chiefely by the
prowes of the English souldiers, who first scaled the wals and reared
thereon the earls banner. When they were entred the towne, the
Englishmen bent their endevour to the housing of their enemies, and
beating downe of such that made resistance. But the Frenchmen
straight waies turned to their lascivious pleasures, so that there was
presented a spectacle both pitiful and shamelesse: in one place but-

[40] Marginal note: '1390.'
[41] See above, introduction.

chering of men, in another ryoting with women; here streames of bloud & heapes of slaughtered bodies, hard by dissolute and licentious wantonnesses: in some,[42] all the miseries of a cruell warre, and the loosenesse of a secure peace.

Here were slaine and taken above fower thousand barbarians. The kings brother was also slaine, but the king himselfe fled into the castle, which was strongly scited and well fortified and furnished with men. The Christians laide siege to this castle the space of five weekes, during which time they lost many of their men, yet not by sword, but by sickenesse. The barbarians also were distressed with want of victuall, having but little provision, and many unprofitable mouthes to consume it. Hereupon they sent unto the Christians to desire peace, offering them a great summe of money to depart out of their countrie. This the Christians accepted, upon condition that they might freely carrry with them all their pray and prisoners, and that the barbarians should from thenceforth surcease from making spoyle upon any of the coastes of Italy or Fraunce.

Thus had this voyage a prosperous and speedie end, the onely service (as I suppose) which the English and Frenchmen performed together without jotte of jarre. And yet the earle abused not the fortune of this successe to vaine [p. 32] vaunting, or braving in words, but moderately imparted to the rest the honour of the exployt. So by valyantly performing his charge, and sparingly speaking thereof, his glorie encreased, without bit of envie.

In the fifteenth and sixteenth yeres of the reigne of King Richard,[43] certaine causes of discontentment did grow betweene the king and the Londoners, which set the favour of the one and the faith of the other at great separation and distance. One was, for that the king would have borrowed of them a thousand poundes, which they, feeling much and fearing more the kings daily exactions, did not onely deny, but evill intreated[44] a certaine Lumbard who offered to lay out the money.

Another griefe was thus occasioned: one of the Bishop of Salisburies[45] servants, named Romane, meeting in Fleet-street with a bakers man bearing horse-bread, tooke a loafe out of his basket. And by rude demaund of the one, and rough denial of the other, chollar so kindled betwixt them that Romane brake the bakers head. Heereupon the neighbors came forth, and would have arrested this bishops lusty yeoman, but he escaped and fled to the bishops house. The constable followed peaceably, and demaunded a quiet delivery of the offendour.

[42] I.e., 'in sum.'
[43] Marginal notes, '1392, 1393.'
[44] 'evill intreated' = 'evilly treated' (OED).
[45] John Waltham.

But the bishops men shut the gates against him, that no man could come neere.

Then much people flocked together, threatening to breake open the gates and fire the house, unlesse Romane were brought forth unto them. 'What,' sayd they, 'are the bishops men priviledged? Or is his house a sanctuary? Or will he protect those whom he ought to punish? If we may be shuffled off in this sort, not onely our streets, but our shoppes and our houses shall never be free from violence and wrong. This we will not endure; we can not, it standeth not us in hand.'

Heerewith they approched the gates, and began to use violence. But the maior and shiriffes of the citty, upon advertisement of this tumult, came amongst them, crying out that it was [p. 33] not courage but out-rage which they shewed, wherby they would procure both daunger to themselves and displeasure against the whole city; that although wrong had beene received, yet they were not the men nor this the meanes to redresse the same.

So, partly by their perswasions, partly by their presence and authoritie, they repressed the riote and sent every man away, with streight charge to keep the peace.

Here was yet no great harme done, and the quarrell might have bene quieted without more adoe, had not the bishop stirred therein, and kindled the coales of unkindnesse afresh. For the Londoners at that time were not onely suspected secretly, but openly noted to bee favourers and followers of Wickliffes opinions. For which cause, they were much maliced of the bishoppes, and many of their actions interpreted to proceed from another minde, and tend to a worse ende, then was outwardly borne in countenance and shew. And some matters of chaunce were taken as done of purpose.

Therefore the Bishop of Salisburie, called John Waltham, who was also Treasurour of England, made a grievous complaint of this attempt, to Thomas Arundle, Archbishop of Yorke and Lord Chauncellour, affirming that if upon every light pretence the citizens might be suffered in this sorte to insult upon the bishoppes without punishment, without reproofe and blame, they woulde bring into hazzard not onely the dignity and state, but the libertie also of the whole Church. Did they not lately take uppon them the punishment of adulteries, and other crimes appertaining to eclesiasticall jurisdiction, maliciously alleaging that the bishops and their officers, either beeing infamous for those vices themselves, did wincke at the same in others, or else by covetous commutation, did rather set them to sale then carefully represse them? Did they not rudely and unreverently breake open the doores upon the Archbishop of Canterburie and interrupte his proceedings against John Astone, an open follower of Wickliffe?[46]

[46] This had occurred 20 June 1382, during Aston's hearing at Blackfriars, London.

And doe we think that this is the [p. 34] last indignity that they will offer? No, surely, nor yet the least. And if this boldnesse be not beaten downe, our authority will fall into open contempt and scorne, and be made a common foote-ball for every base citizen to spurne at.

Hereupon they went together to the king, and so incensed his displeasure against the Londoners (beeing prepared thereto by former provocations) that hee was in the minde to make spoyle of the citty, and utterly to destroy it. But beeing perswaded to some more moderation in revenge, first hee caused the maior and shiriffes and many of the chiefe citizens to be apprehended and committed to divers severall prisons. Then hee ceazed all the liberties of the citty into his handes, and ordained that no mayor shoulde any more bee elected, but that the king shoulde at his pleasure appointe a warden and governour over the citty. This office was first committed to Sir Edward Darlington, who for his gentlenesse towardes the citizens was shortly after remooved, and Sir Baldwine Radington placed in his roome. Also the king was induced, or rather seduced, by the Archbishop of Yorke, Lord Chancellour, to remoove the tearmes and courtes, to witte: the chauncery, the exchequer, the kings bench, the hamper, and the common pleas from London, to bee kept at Yorke, where the same continued from mid-sommer, in the year 1393, untill Christmasse next following, to the great hinderance and decay of the citty of London.

At the last the king, upon earnest intreaty of the Duke of Lancaster and the Duke of Gloucester, called the Londoners before him at Windsore, where (having first terrified them with the presence and shewe of a greate number of armed men) hee caused all the priviledges of the citty, both olde and newe, to be brought forth, whereof he restored some, and restrained the rest. Yet the Londoners were not fully received to favour; neither recovered they at that time either the person or dignity of their mayor. Shortly after, the king went to London, at whose comming the ci[p. 35]tizens changed all their griefe into gladnesse (as the common sorte is without measure in both), entertayning him with such joyfull triumphes and rich presentes, as if it had beene the day of his coronation. They supposed with these great curtesies and costs to have satisfied his displeasure, but they found themselves farre deceived, for they were not fully restoared to their liberties againe untill they had made fine, to pay unto the king ten thousand poundes.

Thus did the Londoners manifest in themselues a strange diversity of disposition, both licenciously to committe offence, and paciently to endure punnishment; having rashnesse and rage so tempered with obedience, that they were easily punnished who coulde not possibly bee ruled. Yet for this cause, so soone as first occasion did serve against the king, they shewed themselves either his earnest enimies, or faint friends.

King Richard, in the nineteene yeare of his reigne, passed the seas to Calice.[47] The French king also came down to Arde, betweene which two townes a place was appointed, and tentes erected for both kings to meete. After large expenses on both sides, and great honour done by the one king to the other, a surcease of armes was concluded betweene them for thirtie yeares, and King Richard tooke to wife Lady Isabell, the French kings daughter, being not above seven or eight yeeres olde.

The Duke of Gloucester was so offended both with this friendship and affinitie, that he lost all manner of patience, exclaiming that it was more meete to be in armes then in amitie with the French-men who, beeing inferiour to the English in courage, did alwayes over-reach them in craft, and being too weake for warre, did many times prevaile by peace. That now they had got into their handes many townes and holdes appertaining to the crowne of England, they were willing to conclude a peace, to exclude the king thereby from his possessions; but whensoever occasion shoulde [p. 36] change for their advantage, they would be then as ready to start from the freindshippe as at that present they were to strike it. That the French kings daughter, being but a child, was very unmeet for the marriage of King Richard, as well for disparitie of age, as for that the king had no issue by his first wife, and was not like to have any by this, except (perhappes) in his olde and withered yeeres.[48] When the duke saw that with these motives he did nothing prevaile, he suborned the Londoners to make petition to the king that, seeing there was peace with France, he would release them of the subsidie which they had granted to him in regard of those warres. This suite was instantly followed, and much perplexed the king, untill the Duke of Lancaster declared to the people that the king had beene at the charge and dispense of three hundred thousand poundes in his voyage into France, for the procuring of this peace. Whereupon they were pacified, and desisted from their demaund.

The yeere following,[49] Guido, Earle of S. Pauls,[50] was sent into England by Charles, King of France to visit and salute in his name King Richard and Queene Isabell his wife, the French kings daughter.

---

[47] November 1396.
[48] Although Isabell was not yet eight, Richard was himself only twenty-nine at the time of his marriage.
[49] Marginal note: '1397.'
[50] This was Waleran of Luxembourg, who married Richard's half-sister, Maud (Matilda) Courtenay, daughter of Richard's mother Joan and her first husband, Sir Thomas Holland, first earl of Kent.

To this earle the King did relate with what fervencie the Duke of Gloucester contended to make disturbance of the peace betweene England and France: how, because his minde was not therein followed, hee mooved the people to seditious atempts, bending himselfe wholly to maintaine discord and disquiet, rather in his owne countrey then not at all. He further reported what stiffe strifes in former times the duke had stirred, which, howsoever they were done, yet as they were declared they sounded very odious and hard.

When the earle heard this, he presently answered that the duke was too daungerous a subject to be permitted to live; that greatnesse was never safe if it grow excessive and bolde; that the king must not affect the vaine commendation of [p. 37] clemency, with his owne perill; and that it touched him, both in honour to revenge the disgraces which he had received, and in policy to prevent the daungers which he had cause to feare. These words so sharpened the kings displeasure that from thenceafoorth he busied his braines in no one thing more, then how to bring the duke to his end.

Now he began to pry more narrowly into his demeanour, to watch his words, to observe actions, and alwayes to interpret them to the woorst, framing himselfe to many vaine and needlesse[51] feares. Often times he would complaine of him to the Duke of Lancaster and the Duke of Yorke, how fierce and vilolent he was in his speeches, and crosse to him in all matters. The dukes would make answere that the Duke of Gloucester, their brother, was in deed more hoat and vehement than they did commend, yet his fiercenesse was joined with faithfulnesse, and his crosnesse proceded from a care least the commonwealth should decrease either in honour or in possessions; and therefore the king had neither need to feare, nor cause to dislike.

About that time, the Dukes of Lancaster and of Yorke withdrewe themselves from the court, to their private houses. The Duke of Gloucester also went to ly at Plashey, neere Chelmesforde in Essex: upon advantage of which seperation, the king stoode distracted in minde betweene feare to differ, and shame to avow the destruction of the duke, least he mightt happily bee disapointed by the one, or dishonoured by the other. Hereupon he entred into counsaile with John Holland, Earle of Huntington, his halfe brother, and Thomas Mowbray, Earle of Notingham, howe the duke of Gloucester might be suppressed, or oppressed rather. The cruelty which was but wavering in the king, yea wanting by nature, was soone confirmed by evill advise: and being once inclined to bloud, he did not faile either of example of lewd action to followe, or direction of cruell counsaile what to doe.

---

[51] *A*: 'weedlesse,' a listed 'faulte.'

So the plotte was contrived, and according thereto the [p. 38] king and the Earle of Nottingham rode together into Essex, as though it were to disporte themselves in hunting. When they were in the middest of the forrest, the earle made stay, and the king passed forth with a smal and unsuspicious company to the duke, lying at Plashey. There he stayed dinner, and then, pretending occasion of present returne, he desired the duke to accompany him to London. The faire entreatie of a prince is a most forceable commaunde; therefore the duke, supposing that onely to bee intended in deede what was pretended in shewe, went to horse-backe with the king, taking such small attendance as upon the sudden could be in a readinesse, and appointing the rest to come after him to London.

So they rode together, using much familiar talke by the way, untill they came neere the place of await. Then the king put his horse forwarde, and the duke, comming behinde, was suddenly intercepted and stayed, crying aloud and calling to the king for his helpe. The king continued his journey as though he had not heard, and the duke was violently carried to the Thames, and there shipped in a vessell layed for the purpose, and from thence conveyed over to Calice.

When the king came to London, he caused the Earle of Warwicke also to be arrested and sent to prison, the same day that hee had invited him to dinner, and shewed good countenance and promised to be gracious lord unto him. Upon the like dissembled shewe, the Earle of Arundell and his sonne, and certaine others, were arrested also and committed to prison in the Ile of Wight.

The common people, upon the apprehending of these three noble men, whome they chiefely and almost onely favoured, were in a great confusion and tumult, and there wanted but a head to drawe them to sedition. Every man sorrowed, murmured and threatned, and, daring no further, stood waiting for one to leade them the way, all being readie to followe that which any one was loath to beginne.

[p. 39] The Duke of Lancaster and of Yorke gathered a strong armie, and came therewith to London, where they were readily received by the citizens, although the king had commaunded the contrarie. But this seemed to be done rather for garde to themselves, then regarde to any others.

The king all this time kept at a village called Helhame, within foure miles of London, having about him a great power of armed men which he had gathered out of Cheshire and Wales. And to pacifie the common people, hee caused to be proclaimed that the lordes were not apprehended upon olde displeasures, but for offences lately committed, for which they should be appealed by order of law, and receive open triall in the parliament next following. The like message was sent to the Duke of Lancaster and the Duke of Yorke, lying at London, to whome the king made faith for the safetie of their persons, and indemnitie of their goods, and that nothing should be attempted without their privitie and advise. All this was as rashly believed as it was craftily given out. Whereupon the dukes dissembled their feares and dissolved their forces, and remained in expectancie what would ensue.

A little before the feast of St. Michael, the parliament began at London,[52] wherein Sir John Bushie, Sir William Bagot, and Sir Henrie Greene were principall agents for the kings purpose. These were then in all the credite and authoritie with the king, and his chiefest schoolemasters both of crueltie and deceite. They were proude, arrogant and ambitious, and uppon confidence of the kings favour, professed enemies to men of auncient nobilitie: to the ende that, being lately start up, they might become more famous by maintaining contention with great persons.

And first, by their importunate travaile, all the charters of pardon graunted by the king were in this perliament annulled and revoked. Then the prelates did constitute Sir Henrie Percie their procurator, and departed the house, because [p. 40] they might not be present in judgement of bloud. Lastly, the Earle of Arundell and the Earle of Warwicke were arraigned, and for the same offences for which they had bene pardoned (namely for encroaching to themselves royall power in judging to death Simon Burlye, John Berneis and others, without the kings consent) were condemned to be hanged, drawne and quartered. But the king so moderated the severitie of this sentence that the Earle of Arundell was onely beheaded, and the Earle of Warwicke committed to perpetuall imprisonment in the Ile of Man.

The Duke of Gloucester was so greatly favoured that it was thought a point both of policie and peace not to bring him to his open answere, but to put him to death secreately. So he was strangled under a fether-bedde at Calice by the Earle of Nottingham, being then Earle Marshall: which death, howsoever he deserved, yet dying as he did, not called, not heard, he died as guiltlesse.

In this same parliament, Thomas Arundell, Archbishop of Caunterburie, was also accused for executing the comission against Michaell Delapoole, Earle of Suffolke: for which cause his temporalities were seazed, his lands and goods forfeited, as well in use as in possession, and he himselfe was adjudged to exile, & charged to depart the realme within sixe weeks then next ensuing. So hee went into Fraunce, where afterwardes he became a principall mean of the revolt which followed.

[52] 17 September 1397.

Also, the Lord Cobham was exiled into the Ile of Gernsey, and Sir Reinolde Cobham was condemned to death, not for entring into any attempt against the king, but because he was appointed by the lords to be one of his governours, and of his counsaile, in the 11. yeare of his raigne.

Now the king, falsely supposing that he was free from all daungers, and that the humour against him was cleane purged and spent, conceived more secreate contentment then he would openly bewraye: as more able to dissemble [p. 41] his joy, then conceale his feare, being so blinded and bewitched with continuall custome of flatteries, that hee perceived not that the state of a prince is never stablished by cruelty and crafte. On the other side, the comon people were much dismayed, having nowe lost those whome they accompted their onely helpes, and their onely hopes, both for their private affaires and for supporting the state. And because these mishapes hapned unto them, for maintaining a cause of common dislike, the peoples stomacke was stirred thereby to much hate and hearte-burning against the king. And to make their deathes the more odious, the Earle of Arundell was reputed a martyr, and pilgrimages were dayly made to the place of his buriall. The rumour also was current, but without either authour or grounde, that his head was miraculously fastened againe to his body. This, whilest all men affirmed, and no man knewe, the king caused the corpes to bee taken up and viewed, ten daies after it was interred. And finding the same[53] to be fabulous, hee caused the ground to be paved where the earle was layde, and all mention of his buriall to be taken away, forbidding publickly any such speaches of him afterwardes to bee used. But this restrainte raysed the more, and they, who if it had beene lawefull, woulde have saide nothing, beeing once forbidden coulde not forbeare to talke. It was also constantly reported that the king was much disquieted in his dreames with the earle, who did often seeme to appeare unto him, in so terrible and truculent manner that breaking his fearefull sleepe he would curse the time that ever he knew him.

In the one and twenty yeare of the raigne of King Richard,[54] Henry Earle of Darby was created Duke of Herforde, at which time the king created foure other dukes, to wit: Duke of Aumerle, who was before Earle of Rutland; Duke of Southrey, who was before Earle of Kent; Duke of Excester, who was before Earle of Huntington; and Duke of Norfolke, who was before Earle of Notingham. This [p. 42] degree of honour, long time after the conquest of the Normans (whose chiefest rulers had no higher title), was accompted too great for a subject to

[53] *A*: 'cause,' a listed 'faulte.'
[54] Marginal note: '1398.'

beare: the fourme of the common-wealth beeing framed, by the victors, farre from equallity of all and yet, the king excepted, without eminencie of any. At the length, King Edward the third created his eldest sonne Edward, Duke of Cornewale, and made this honour hereditary, conferring it unto many. Since which time, diverse princes of this lande have bene either put, or kept, or hazarded from their estate, by men of that quallity and degree.

The king likewise created the Countesse of Norfolke, Duchesse of Norfolke; the Earle of Sommerset, Marquesse of Sommerset; the Lorde Spencer, Earle of Gloucester; the Lorde Nevill, Earle of Westmerland; the Lorde Scroupe, Earle of Wiltshire; and the Lord Thomas Percy,[55] his steward, Earle of Worcester. Among these hee made division of a great parte of the landes of the Duke of Gloucester, and of the Earles of Arundell and Warwicke, supposing by this double liberality of honour and possessions, to have purchased to himselfe most firme friendships. But bought friendes, for the most parte, are seldome either satisfied or sure, and like certaine ravens in Arabia, so long as they are ful doe yeeld a pleasant voyce, but being empty, doe make a horrible crie.

Now the Duke of Hereford raysed his desires, together with his dignities, and either upon disdaine at the underserved favour and advancement of some persons about the king, or upon open diliske that the king was so dishonourably both abused and abased by them; or else (perhaps) uppon desire to manifest his owne sufficiencie in matters of controwlement and direction, being in familiar discourse with Thomas Mowbraye, Duke of Norfolke, he brake into complaint: How the king regarded not the noble princes of his bloud, and peeres of the realme, and by extreamities used to some, discouraged the rest from entermedling in any [p. 43] publique affaires; how in steade of these hee was wholy governed by certaine new-found and new-fangled favorites, vulgare in birth, corrupt in qualities, having no sufficiencie either of councell for peace, or of courage for warre; who being of all men the most unhonest, and the most unable, with hatefulnesse of the one, and contempt of the other, were generally dispised in all the realme. That hereby, first the honour of the kings person was much blemished, for ungrate and ungracious adherentes are alway the way to hatred and contempt. Secondly, the safetie of his state might bee endaungered, for extraordinarie favour to men apparently of weake or bad desert, doeth breede insolencie in them, and discontentment in others, two[56] daungerous humours in a common-wealth. Thirdly, the dignitie of the realme was much empaired, whose fortune and

---

[55] A: 'Lord Thomas Darcy,' a print-shop error repeated in subsequent quartos.
[56] A: 'too,' a listed 'faulte.'

valour, being guided by the ill chaunce of such unluckie leaders, stood never in the like termes of doubt and distresse, so that matters of peace were tumultuous and uncertaine, and atchievements of warre were never brought to honourable conclusion. That Alexander Severus would have smoaked such sellers of smoake; that Xerxes would have pulled their skin over their eares; and high time it was, that the king should looke unto them. For the nobilitie grew out of hart, the commons out of hope, and all the people fell to a discontented murmuring. And this he said (as he said), not for any grudge, but for griefe and goodwill, and therefore desired the duke, who was one of the Privie Councell, and well heard with the king, to discover unto him these deformities and daungers, that by repayring the one hee might happily repell the other.

These wordes procured to the Duke of Hereforde both great offence, and great glorye. At the delivery whereof, the Duke of Northfolke made shewe of good liking, and promise of sincere dealing. And in deede, if they had bin as faithfully reported by him, and by the king as friendlie [p. 44] taken, as they were faithfully and friendlie meant, many mischiefs might have bene avoyded. But both of these did faile: For the Duke of Norffolke, although in former times he had taken parte with the lordes, yet afterwardes, being desirous to be accompted rather among the great men than the good, he made sale of his honour to maintaine his pleasure, and continue himselfe in grace with the king. To which he was altogether enthralled, insomuch that the murthering of the Duke of Gloucester, and the execution of the Earle of Arundell, was to his charge especially committed.

And supposing upon this occasion to make a free-hold of his princes favour, he grievously aggravated these speeches in reporting[57] them, and yet cunningly, too, with many lyes intermixing some trueths, or making the trueth much more then it was. Againe, the king, not enduring the search of his soares, did bend his minde rather to punish the boldnes, then examine the trueth, of these reproofes. His eares being so distempered with continuance of flatterie, that he accompted all sharpe that was sounde, and liked onely that which was presently pleasant, and afterwards hurtfull. Thus we may dayly observe, that no strange accident doth at any time happen, but it is by some meanes foreshewed, or foretould. But because these warnings are often-times eyther not marked, or misconstrued, or els contemned, the events are accompted inevitable, and the admonitions vaine.

The king being in this sort touched by the one duke, and tickled by the other, was not resolved upon the suddaine what to doe. There-

[57] *A* prints 'in in reporting,' although the list of 'faultes escaped in the printing' has the erratum as 'to reporting.'

fore, he asembled his councell, and called the two dukes before him, and demaunded of the Duke of Norfolke if hee would openly avouch that which he had suggested in secreate. The duke, seeing it was now no time for him either to shrinke or shuffle in his tale, with a bolde and confident courage repeated all that before hee had reported. But the Duke of Hereforde could not bee borne downe by countenance, where his cause was good. [p. 45] And therefore, after a short silence, whereby he seemed rather amazed at the strangenesse of this matter, then abashed at the guilt, he made low obeisance to the king, and greatly both thanked and commended him that hee had not given hastie creadite to matters of such tender touch, as his griefe might have borne out the blame of rashnesse in revenge, desiring him to continue yet a while the respite of his displeasure, and to reserve his judgment free for indifferent audience.

Then he declared, in order, what speech had passed from him, upon what occasion, and to what end. All the rest he stoutely denied, affirming that it was falsely surmised by his adversary, eyther upon malice to picke a quarrell, or upon sycophancie to picke a thanke, and that thereupon he was untrue, unjuste, a forger of slaunderous and seditious lies, whereby he treacherously indeavored to seduce the king, to destroy the nobility, and to raise disturbance within the realme. And this he offered to prove upon him (if the king would permit) by the stroake of a speare, and by dint of sword.

The Duke of Norfolks stomacke, not used to beare scorne, could not disgest these tearmes of disgrace. Whereupon hee stifly stood to his first imputation. And for maintenance thereof, he accepted, and also desired, the combat. The king would some other wayes have quieted this contention, but the dukes would agree to no other kinde of agreement, and thereupon threw downe their gloves, one against the other, for gages. The king, seeing their obstinacy, graunted them the battell, and assigned the place at the city of Coventry, in the moneth of August next insuing; where, in the meane time, he caused a sumptuous theater and lists royall to be prepared.

At the day of combat,[58] the two dukes came, well banded with noblemen and gentlemen of their linage. The Duke of Aumerle, for that day Hie Constable, and the Duke of Surrey for the same time and action High Marshall of England, entred into the lists, with a great troope of men apparelled in [p. 46] silk sendale, embroidred with silver, every man having a tipped staffe to keepe the field in order. About the time of prime, the Duke of Hereford came to the barriers of the lists, mounted upon a white courser, barbed with blew & greene velvet embroidred gorgiously with swans and antilops of

[58] 16 September 1398.

gold-smiths worke, armed at all points, & his sword drawen in his hand. The constable and marshall came to the barriers, and demaunded of him who hee was.

He answered, 'I am Henry, Duke of Hereford, and am come to do my devoire against Thomas Mowbray, Duke of Norfolke, as a traitour to God, the king, the realme and me.' Then he sware upon the Evangelists that his quarrell was right, & upon that point desired to enter the lists. Then he put up his sword, pulled downe his beavier, made a crosse on his forehead, and with speare in hand entred into the lists, and there lighted from his horse & sate downe in a chaire of green velvet, which was set in a traverse of greene & blew velvet at the one end of the listes, and so expected the comming of his enemie.

Soone after, King Richard entred the field with great pomp, both in bravery and traine. He had in his company the Earle of S. Paule, who came purposely out of Fraunce to see this combat tried. He was attended with all the noble peers of the realme, and guarded with tenne thousand men in armes, for feare of any sudden or intended tumult.

When hee was placed on his stage, which was verie curiously and richly set forth, a King at Armes made proclamation in the name of the king, and of the high constable, and of the marshall, that no man except such as were appointed to order and marshall the fielde, shoulde touch any parte of the listes, upon paine of death. This proclamation beeing ended, another herrald cryed: 'Behold here, Henry of Lancaster, Duke of Hereford, appellant, who is entred into the listes royall to doe this devoire against Thomas Mowbray, Duke of Norfolke, defendant, upon paine to be accompted false and recreant.– The Duke of Norfolke was hovering on [p. 47] horsebacke at the entry of the listes, his horse being barbed with crimson velvet, embroadered ritchly with lions of silver and mulberie trees, and when he had made his oath before the constable and marshall that his quarrell was just and true, he entred the fielde boldly, crying aloud 'God aide him that hath the right.' Then hee lighted from his horse, and satte downe in a chaire of crimson velvet, curtained aboute with red and white damaske, and placed at the other ende of the listes.

The lord marshall viewed both their speares, to see that they were of equall length; the one speare he carried himselfe to the Duke of Hereford, and sent the other to the Duke of Norfolke by a knight. This done, a herrald proclaimed that the traverses and chaires of the combatants should be removed, commaunding them in the kings name to mount on horsebacke, and addresse themselves to the encounter. The dukes were quickly horsed, and closed their beaviers, and cast their speares into the restes. Then the trumpetes sounded, and the Duke of Hereforde set forth towards his enimy, about sixe or seaven paces.

But before the Duke of Norfolke began to put forewarde, the king cast downe his warder, and the herralds cried 'Ho.' Then the king caused the dukes speares to be taken from them, and commaunded them to forsake their horses, and returne againe unto their chaires, where they remained aboute two long houres, whilst the king deliberated with his counsaile what was fittest to be done.

At last, the herralds cryed silence, and Sir John Borcy, a secretary of state, with a loude voice read the sentence and determination of the king and his counsaile out of a long roule, wherein was contained: That Henry of Lancaster, Duke of Hereford, appellant, and Thomas Mowbray, Duke of Norfolke, defendant, had honourably appeared that day within the lists royall, and declared themselves valiant and hardy champions, being not onely ready but forward, and desirous to darre in the battel. But because this was a matter of great consequence & import, the king, with [p. 48] the advise of his councell, thought it meet to take the same into his owne hands. And thereupon had decreed that Henrie, Duke of Hereford, because he had displeased the king, and for divers other considerations, should within 15. dayes next following depart out of the realme, and not to returne during the terme of ten yeeres without the kings especiall licence, upon paine of death.

When this judgement was heard, a confused noyse was raysed among the people, some lamenting eyther the deserte or the injurie of the Duke of Hereforde, whome they excedingly favoured, others laughing at the conceite of the king, first in causing and afterwardes in frustrating so great an expectation; wherein he seemd to doe not much unlike Caligula, who, lying in Fraunce with a great armie nere the sea shoare, gave the signe of battell, set his men in aray, marched foorth as if it had bene to some great piece of service, & suddenly commanded them all to gather cockles.

Then the herralds cried again 'Oyes,' and the secretarie did reade on, how the king had likewise ordayned, that Thomas Moubraie, Duke of Northfolke, because he had sowne sedition, by words whereof he could make no proofe, should avoide the realme of England and never returne againe, upon paine of death. And that the king would take the profites and revenues of his landes, untill he had received such summes of money as the duke had taken up for wages of the garison of Calice, which was still unpaide. And that the king prohibited, upon paine of his grievous displeasure, that any man should make suite or entreatie to him on the behalfe of eyther of these two dukes.

These sentences being in this sort pronounced, the king called the two exiles before him, and tooke of them an oth that they should not converse together in foraine regions, nor one willingly come in place where the other was, fearing (as it was like) least their common discontentment should draw them, first to reconcilement, and afterward to [p. 49] revenge.

But this policie was over weake for this purpose. For oathes are commonly spurned aside, when they lye in the way either to honour or revenge, and if their united forces was much to be regarded, their seperate powers was not altogether to bee contemned. Therefore the later princes of this realme have with more safetie wholy abolished the use of abjuration and exile, and doe either by death extinguish the power, or by pardon alter the will of great offenders from entring into desperate and daungerous attempts, which men in miserie and disgrace have more vehemencie to begin, and more obstinacie to continue. When the Samnites had once so enclosed the Romaine legions within certaine streights that thcy lcft thcm neither space to fight, nor way to flie, but without force enforced them to yeelde, they sent to Herennius Pontius, an aged ruler of their state, for his advise, what were best for them to doe. His answere was that the Romaines should be permitted to depart, without any hurt, losse or scorne. This pleased not such as were eyther covetous for spoyle, or cruell for bloud. And therefore they sent unto him the second time, who then returned answere, that the Romanes should bee put to the sworde, and not one man suffered to escape. The contrarietie of these two counsailes brought the olde man into suspition of dotage. But he, comming in person to the campe, maintained both to be good: the first whereof (which hee thought best) would, by[59] unexspected favour, provoke the Romanes to a perpetuall friendship; the second would deferre the warres for many yeares, wherein the enemies should hardly recover strength; third counsaile, there was none that safely might be followed. 'Yes,' said the Samnites, 'to graunt them their lives, yet with such conditions of spoyle and shame as the lawes of victorie doe lay upon them.' 'This is the way,' answered Herennius, 'which neither winneth friends, nor weakeneth enemies, but will much encrease the fury against us, & nothing diminish the force.' And even [p. 50] so, in matters of more particularity, that course of punishment is out of course, which doth neither reclaime the mind of men, nor restraine the might from mischievous endevors. But, againe to our purpose.

The Duke of Norfolke, having now got a fall, where he thought to take his rest, repented his enterprise, and utterly condemned his light conceite of the kings lightnesse. And so, with extreame griefe and anguish of minde, he departed out of the realme into Almaine, and

[59] Quartos: 'be.'

from thence travelled to Venice, where through violence of thought and discontentment, in short time he ended his days. The sentence of banishment was given against him the same day of the yeere wherein the Duke of Gloucester, by his wicked meanes, was strangled to death at Calice.

The Duke of Hereford took his leave of the king at Eltham, who there stroke away foure yeres of his banishment, & even offered himselfe to be fawned upon & thanked for so odious a benefit. And this infortunate adventure he neither bare out vaingloriously, nor yet tooke impatiently: but in the midst of his misery retained still his reputation and honour, shewing no signe of sorow or submisnes in his countenance, nor letting fall any intemperate and unseemly word.

The people, as he departed, by heaps flocked about him, some to see and some to salute him, lamenting his departure in such sort, as though their onely light and delight did then forsake them, not sparing to exclaime that it was aginst the law of armes, against the custome of the realme, and against all right whatsoever, that he should be exiled who had done his honourable endevour for the maintenance of his appeale. This affection was the more excessive, for that the duke was driven into exile by occasion of his liberall speeches against the most hateful persons in all the realme, & being the onely noble man then alive of the popular faction, the love was wholly accumulated upon him which before was devided among the rest.

And thus the duke, leaving England, tooke [p. 51] shipping and passed the seas to Calice, & from thence went into Fraunce, where hee was honourably entertained by Charles, the French king, and found such favour that hee should have taken to wife the onely daughter of John, Duke Berrie, unckle to the King of Fraunce. But King Richarde, fearing the sequel if the favor which was borne to the Duke of Hereford within the realme should be strengthned with so great affinitie in Fraunce, cast such stops in the way that the marriage did not proceede.

This yeare the lawrell trees withered, almost throughout the realme, and afterwardes, against all expectation, recovered life & flourished againe. The same yeare, in Christmasse holy-daies, a deepe ryver which runneth betweene Snedlistorie and Hareswood, neere to Bedford, suddainely stayed the streame, so that for three miles in length, the channell was left drie, and no course of water did hinder passage on foot. This was afterwards interpreted too presage the revolt of the people, & the devision which happened the yeare following. To these wee may adde certaine other prodegies, either forged in that fabulous age or, happening commonly and of course, are then onely noted when any notable accident doth ensue. When King Richard brought his first wife out of Beame, she had no sooner set foote within this land but such a tempest did forthwith arise as had not bene seene many yeares before, whereby divers ships within the haven were quashed to peeces, but especially, and first of all, the ship wherin the queene was carried. This was the rather observed, because such stiffe stormes were likewise stirring when the king brought his second wife out of France, wherein many ships perished, and a great part of the kings fardage was lost.

At Newcastle upon Tine, as two shipwrites were squaring a piece of timber, wheresoever they hewed, bloud issued forth in great aboundance. At one of the kings pallaces, flies swarmed so thicke that they obscured the ayre. These fought together most fiercely, so that sackfuls lay dead [p. 52] upon the ground, and this continued so long that scarce the third part of them (as it was thought) remained alive.

Many like accidents are recorded of that time, but I wil maintaine neither the truth of them, nor what they did portend, being a matter wherein most men are rather superstitious, then not credulous, and doe oftentimes repute common occurrences to be ominous when any strange event doth ensue. Yet, as I am loath to avouch any vaine and trifling matter, so dare I not detract all truth from things anciently reported, although done in an age wherein was some delight in lying. Many do suppose that those things which are fatally allotted, though they never be avoided, yet sometimes are foreshewen, not so much that we may prevent them, as that wee shuold prepare ourselves against them.

[II]

In the two and twenty yeare of the raigne of King Richard, John of Gaunt, Duke of Lancaster, died[60] and was buried on the north-side of the high alter of the cathedrall church of S. Paule, in London. Hee was a man advised and warie in his passages of life, liking better safe courses with reason, then happy by chaunce. Of his owne glory he was neither negligent, nor ambitiously careful. Towards the king he caried himselfe in tearmes honourable inough for a moderat prince, and yet not so plausible as a vaine man would desire; whereby there never happened to him any extraordinary matter, either in prejudice or preferment.

After his death, the Duchy of Lancaster did in right devolve to the Duke of Hereforde, his eldest son. But the king (as the nature of man is inclinable to hate those whome hee hath harmed) seazed all the landes and goodes which appertained to the Duke of Lancaster into his owne handes, and determined to perpetuate the banishment of

[60] 3 February 1399.

Duke Henry, his son, revoking the letters pattents, which were graunted to him at his departure, whereby his generall atturneis were enabled to prosecute his causes and sue liverie of any inheritance which during his exile might fall unto him, his homage being respited for [p. 53] a reasonable fine. The king supposed his estate more safe by the weaknesse and want of the duke, whome he had nowe in some jealousie and doubte. But these violent dealinges were meanes rather to provoake his mischiefes, then to prevent them, for by injurious suppressing of the dukes greatnesse, he greatly augmented the same.

Edmund, Duke of Yorke, the kings onely uncle which remained alive, had hetherto enforced[61] his patience to endure many things against his liking. But nowe, either in disdaine of this indignity, or in distrust both of his owne safety and of the common tranquillity of the realme, hee retired himselfe, with the Duke of Aumerle, his son, to his house at Langley, supposing privatnes to bee the best defense both from danger and blame, where neither the king had judgement to discerne, nor any about him had either hearte or honesty to admonish what was done amisse; where an honourable fame was held suspected, and a good life more in hazard then a bad; protesting that none of these practises were either devised by his counsaile, or done by his consent.

At this time, the whole frame of the state was much shaken, and matters of great weight and moment did hang by a very slender thred. The king was plunged in pleasure and sloath, after whose example others also (as men doe commonly conforme their mindes according to the princes disposition) gave over themselves to delicacie and ease, whereby cowardise crepte in, and shipwracke was made both of manhood and glorie.

The chiefest affaires of state had bene ordered for a long time according to private respects, wherby the common-wealth lost both the fatte and the favour, and seemed, not at seasons and by degrees, but with a maine course and at once, to ruinate and fall. The north parts were many times canvased, and by small yet often losses, almost consumed by the Scots, who had there taken many townes and castles, and defaced all the countrey with slaughter and spoile. Likewise the south partes were often-times wasted [p. 54] by the Frenchmen, and in Fraunce many strong holds were lost. It was also constantly affirmed that the king made agreement to deliver unto the king of Fraunce the possession of Callice, and of other townes which hee helde in those parts, but the performance thereof was resisted by the lords. Whether this was true or surmised probably, as agreeable to the kings loose government, I cannot certainely affirm.

---

[61] 'moved,' a listed 'faulte.'

As for Ireland, which in the time of King Edward the third was kept in order and awe, by acquainting the people with religion and civility, and drawing them to delight in the plenty and pleasures of well reclaymed countries, whereby it yeelded to the kings coffers thirty thousand pounds every yeare, it was then suffered to runne into waste, and the people by rudenesse became intractible, so that the houlding thereof charged the king with the yearely dispence of thirty thousand markes.[62] Many succours had bene sent into these severall countries, but scatteringly and dropping, and never so many at once as to furnish the warres fully.

The king made some expeditions in his owne person, with greate preparation and charge. But, beeing once out of credite, whatsoever fell out well was attributed to others; misfortunes were imputed onely to him. If any thing were happily atchieved by some of the nobility, it was by the kings basehearted parasites, to whom military vertue was altogether unpleasant, so extinuated, or depraved, or envied, that it was seldome rewarded so much as with countenance as with thankes. Yea, sometimes it procured suspicion and danger, the king being informed by a cunning kinde of enemies, commenders, that to be a discreet and valiant commander in the fielde, was a vertue peculiar to a prince, and that it was a perillous point to have the name of a man of private estate famous for the same in every mans mouth. Hereupon, fewe sought to rise by vertue and valure; the readier way was to please the pleasant humour of the prince. Likewise, matters of peace were managed by men of weakest sufficiency, by whose counsell, [p. 55] either ignorant or corrupt, the destruction of the of the best harted nobility was many times attempted, & at the last wrought. The profits and revenues of the crowne were said to bee let to farme, the king making himselfe landlord of his[63] realme, and challenging[64] no great priviledge by his reigne, but onely a dissolute and uncontrouled life. Great summes of mony were yearly rather exacted from the subjects, then by them voluntarily graunted. Whereof no good did ensue, but the maintenance of the kings private delightes, & the advancement of his hatefull favorites.

To these he was somewhat above his power liberall, for which cause he was faine to borrow, begge and extort in other places; but he

---

[62] This comment is the first of several detailed instances of Richard's maladministration that Hayward records in this and in the following four paragraphs; it is also one of the points in this part of the history (like the comment about the Irish forces 'scatteringly and dropping,' in the next sentence) upon which Coke challenged not only Hayward's accuracy, but his motive for including it. Hayward's reply here, that he found in Walsingham the figures upon which he based the comparison of Edward's military expenditures with Richard's, was correct.

[63] A: 'this,' a listed 'faulte.'

[64] A: 'challenged,' a listed 'faulte.'

purchased not so much love by the one, as hate by the other. Besides
the ordinary tearmes of tenthes and fiftenthes, which were many times
paid double in one yeare, divers newe impositions were by him devised
& put in use: sometimes exacting xii. d. of every person throughout
the realme, sometimes of every religious man and woman vi. s. viii.
d., and of everie secular priest asmuch, and of everie lay person,
maried or sole, xii d. Under the favourable tearme of benevolence,[65]
hee wiped away from the people such heapes of money as were litle
answerable to that free and friendly name. He borrowed in all places
of the realme great summes of money upon his privy seales, so that
no man of worth could escape his loane. But he seldome, and to few,
returned payment againe.

This present year hee sent certain bishops, and other personages of
honour, to all the shires & corporations within the realme, to declare
unto the people the kings heavie displeasure against them, for that
they had bin abetters and complices of the Duke of Gloucester, and
of the Earles of Arundell and Warwicke; and that the king was minded
to make a roade uppon them, as common enemies, excepte they would
acknowledge their offence and submit themselves to his mercie and
grace. Hereupon all the men of worth in every shire and towne
corporate made their ac[p. 56]knowledgment & submission in writing
under their seales, & afterwardes were faine to graunt unto the king
such importable summes of money, to purchase againe his favour, as
the land being already greatly impoverished, they were hardly able
to endure.

Then were exacted of them strange & unaccustomed oathes,[66]
which were put likewise in writing, under their seales. They were also
compelled to set their hands and seales to blancke chartes, wherein
the king might afterwardes cause to be written what he would, so that
all the wealth of the realme was in a manner at his devotion and
pleasure. These and such like violences were far wide from the moderate governement of King Henrie the second, whoe, maintaining
great warres, and obteyning a larger dominion then perteyned at any
other time to this realme of England, never demaunded subsidie of
his subjectes. And yet his treasure, after his death, was founde to be
nine hundred thousand poundes, besides his jewels and his plate.

In this sort, the king bearing a heavie hand upon his subjects, and
they againe a heavie hart against him, and being withall a prince
weake in action, and not of valure sufficient to beare out his vices by
might, the people at length resolved to revolt, and rather to runne

---

[65]Another point challenged by Coke, like the comment upon borrowing under the
privy seal, in the sentence next following.
[66]Another item on which Hayward was questioned.

into the hazard of a ruinous rebellion, then to endure safetie joyned with slaverie. So they attended occasion, which shortly after was thus offered.

The king received letters of advertisement out of Ireland (which, being priveledged from other venimous beasts, hath alwaies beene pestered with traytors) how the barbarous Irish had cut in pieces his garrison, and slaine Roger Mortimer, Earl of Marsh (who had beene declared heire apparent to the crowne), exercising all the crueltie in wasting of the country which wrath and rage of victorie could incite a barbarous people to practise. This losse, being great in it selfe, the hard affection of the people did much augment by report. Whereupon the king deliberated whether it were requisite that hee should undertake the warre in person, or [p. 57] commit it to commanders of lower degree? Some perswaded him that wholly to subdue Ireland stoode neither with pollicie, not yet almost with possibilitie. For if it were fully and quietly possessed, some governour might hap to growe to that greatnesse as to make himselfe absolute lord thereof, and therefore it was better to hold it certaine by weake enemies, then suspected by mightie friendes. And yet by what meanes should those bogges & those woods bee overcome, which are more impregnable then the walled townes of other countries? Then, if the purpose were onely to represse the savage people, the war was of no such weight as should draw the king to stand in the fielde. And therefore he might stay in the west partes of England, and from thence make shew of the princely puissance and state, neither venturing his person without cause, and ready at hand if neede should require.

Others were of opinion that to subdue and replenish Ireland was a matter neither of difficultie nor daunger, but both profitable and honourable to the king, and to God very acceptable. For if credite might bee given to auncient histories, this realme of England was once as insuperable, with bogs and woods, as Ireland was then. But the Romane conquerors kept not their presidiarie souldiers in idle garrison, whereby many times the minde grew mutinous and the body diseased, and both unable for the labour and hardnesse of the field; but they held as well them as the subdued Britaines continually exercised, either in building of townes in places of best advantage, or in making of high waies, or else[67] in drayning and paving of bogs. By which meanes the countrie was made fruitfull and habitable, and the people learned the good maners not rudely to repulse the flattering assaults of pleasure, preferring subjection with plentie, before beggerly and miserable libertie. That the same Romaines also kept many larger countries in quiet obedience (so long as they were quiet among

---

[67] *A* omits 'or,' and reads 'of high waies: else in drayning,' a listed 'faulte.'

themselves), without either feare or danger of any governours: first, by deviding them into smal [p. 58] provinces; secondly, by constituting in every province divers officers as lieutenants and procurators, whereof one was able to restraine the other, the first having power over the bodies of the subjects, the second over their goods; thirdly, by changing these officers every yeare, which was too short a time to establish a soveraigntie; lastly, by retaining at Rome their wives and children, and whole private estate, as pledges for their true demeanure. That the daunger was rather to bee feared, least a weake enemie, whilest hee was contemned, should gather strength and be able to stand uppon termes of withstanding. Example hereof happened when the Romaines overcame this iland: for many Britaines who upon no conditions would abide bondage withdrew themselves into the northparts of the land, & by maintaining their auncient custome of painting their bodies, were called of the Romanes Picti. These were neglected a long time, and held in scorne as neither of force nor of number to bee thought worthy the name of enimies. But afterwardes they confederated themselves with other people, and so sharply assaulted the subdued Britaines that, being unable to resist, & the Romanes shrincking from them, they were constrained to desire helpe of the Saxons. And so, betweene their enimies & their aides (being set, as it were, betwixt the beetle and the block),[68] they lost the possession of the best part of their land. That it was a pittifull policy for assurance of peace to lay all waste as a wildernes, and to have dominion over trees and beasts, and not over men. That hereby the king did loose the revenue of a fruitfull countrie, & the benefit of wealthy subjects, which are the surest treasure that a prince can have. That hereby also the majesty of his estate was much impaired, for (as Salomon saith) the honor of a king consisteth in the multitude of subjectes. That the country, being unfurnished of people, was open to al opportunity of forraine enimies. That if none of these respectes would move, yet the king was bounde in duty to reduce those savages to the true worshippe of God, [p. 59] who did then either prophanely contemne him, or superstitiously serve him.

These reasons so weighed with the king, that he gathered a mighty armie, determining to goe in person into Ireland, & to pacifie the country before his returne. But al his provision was at the charge of the subjects: and wheras in time of sedition, a wise prince will least grieve his people, as seeming to stand in some sort at their curtesie, and having to imploy their bodies beside, the king in peace, no stoarer

[68] A 'beetle' was a heavy maul or mallet for driving wedges, setting paving stones, etc., or for crushing or beating material. The phrase suggests being trapped between a crushing force and an immovable surface; it was current by the mid-16th century, and was used again by Hayward in *The Lives of the III Normans*, 274. (*OED*)

for war, was forced to offend, when hee should have bene most carefull
to win favour.

So, about Whitsontide,[69] he set forth on his voyage with many men,
and fewe souldiers, being a dissolute and untrained company, and out
of all compasse of obedience. Hee caried with him his whole treasure,
and all the goods and auncient jewels appertaining to the crowne. In
his company went the Duke of Aumerle, and the Duke of Exceter,
and divers other noble men, and many bishops, and the Abbot of
Westminster. He also tooke with him the sonnes of the Duke of
Gloucester, and of the Duke of Hereford, whose favourers he chiefly
feared.

When hee came to Bristowe, hee was put into suspicion (whether
upon some likelyhood, or meere mallice) that Henry Percy, Earle of
Northumberland, and certaine others entended some disloyall enterprise against him, and for that cause did not folow him into Ireland,
but had fastned friendship with the king of Scots, upon purpose
to retire themselves into his country, if their attempts should faile.
Hereupon the king sent message that the earle should forthwith come
unto him with all the power that he could conveniently make. The
earle returned answere that it was unnecessary in respect of that
service to draw men from such distant places, for the Irish rebels were
neither so many nor so mighty, but the king had strength at hand
sufficient to suppresse them; that it was also daungerous to disfurnish
the north-parts of their forces, and to offer opportunity to the Scottish
borde[p. 60]rers, who were alwayes uncertaine friends in their
extremities.

The king, seeing his commaundement in these termes both contemned and controulled, would not stand to reason the matter with
the earle; neither had he the reason to defer revenge untill hee had
full power to worke it, but presently, in the violence of his fury, caused
the earle and his confederates to be proclaimed traitors, and all their
lands and goods to be seized to his use. The earle tooke grievously this
disgrace, and determined to cure & close up his harme with the
disturbance of the common state. And thus the king, having feathered
these arrowes against his owne brest, passed foorth in his journey into
Ireland.

This expedition at the first proceeded and succeeded exceedingly
well, and the king obtained many victories, even without battell, as
leading his men to a slaughter then to a fight. For the savage Irish
were not under one governement, but were devided into many par-
tialities and factions, and seldome did two or three parts joyne their

[69] Observed 18 May 1399.

common strength and study together. So, whilest one by one did fight, all of them were either subdued or slaine.

But these newes little rejoyced the common people; they lusted not to listen thereto. Their common talke was to recount their common grievances, to lay them together, & aggravate them by construction, every man more abounding in complaints then he did in miseries. Also the noblemen (the principall obiect of cruelty) began to discourse both their private dangers, & the deformities of the state. And upon opportunity of the kings absence, some of them did conspire to cut off that authority which would not be confined, & to cast it upon some other, who was most like to repaire that which King Richard had ruined. 'Or if,' sayde they, 'our power shall come short of so good a purpose, yet will we sell him both our lives & lands with glory in the field, which with certainty in peace we can not enjoy.'

The onely man upon whom all men resolved was [p. 61] Henry, Duke of Hereford (whom since the death of his father they called Duke of Lancaster), not at his own motion or desire, but because he was generally esteemed meet: as being of the royall bloud, and next by discent from males to the succession of the crowne, one that had made honorable proofe of his vertues and valure, the onely man of note that remained alive, of those that before had stood in armes against the king for the behoofe of the common-wealth, for which cause he was deeply touched at that time both in honor and in state.

This attempt pleased, as possible to prove, and of necessity to be followed. Whereupon they secretly dispatched their letters to the duke, solliciting his speedy returne into England, & declaring that aswel for the benefit of the realm, as for their own particular safety, they were forced to use force against King Richard. That if it would please him to make the head, they would furnish him the body of an able army, to expell the king from his unfortunate government, and to settle the possession of the crowne in him, who was more apt and able to sustaine the same; that they would not provide him a base multitude only, & they themselves helpe in bare wishes & advise, but would also adjoyne their hands and their[70] lives, so that the peril should be common to all, the glory only his, if fortune favored the enterprise.

These letters were conveyed by men crafty and bolde, yet of sure credit, and inward in trust with the duke. Who, passing into France, first associated unto them Thomas Arundell, late Archbishop of Canterburie, & at that time (whether deservedly or without cause) an exile in France. Then they travailed by severall waies, and in counterfeit attire, to Parris, where all met at the house of one Clugney, where the Duke then sojourned. After some courtesies of course, with

[70] A: 'theit.'

welcome on the one side, & thankes on the other, and joy of both, the
Archbishop of Canterburie, having obtained of the duke privacie and
silence, made unto him a solemne oration in these words, or to this
sence following:

[p. 62] 'We are sent unto you (right high and noble prince) from
the chiefe lords and states of our land, not to seeke revenge against
our king upon private injury and displeasure, nor upon a desperate
discontentment to set the state on fire, nor to procure the ambitious
advancement of any perticular person, but to open unto you the
deformities and decaies of our broken estate, and to desire your aide,
in staying the ruinous downfall of the same.

'The remembrance of the honourable reputation that our countrie
hath borne, and the noble actes which it hath atchieved, doth nothing
els but make the basenes more bitter unto us, whereinto it is new
fallen. Our victorious armes have heretofore bene famous and memorable, not onely within the bownds of our ocean sea, and in the ilands
adjoyning unto us, but also in France, in Spaine, and in other parts
of Europe, yea in Asia and in Affricke, against the infidels and
barbarians, so that all christian princes have bene either glad to
imbrace our friendship, or loath to provoke us to hostility.

'But nowe the rude Scots, whose spirits we have so many times
broken, and brought on their knees, doe scornfully insult uppon us.
The naked and fugitive Irish have shaken off our shackles, and glutted
themselves uppon us, with massachres and spoiles. With these we
dayly fight, not for glory, but to live, insomuch as we are become a
pitty to our friends, and a verie jeast to our most base and contemptible
enemies.

'Indeed, the king hath both sent and led great armies into these
countries, but in such sort that they have much wasted the realme
with their maintenance, but neither revenged nor relieved it with
their armes. And no mervaile, for all our diligent and discreete leaders
(the verie sinewes of the field) are either put to death, or banished, or
els lie buried in obscurity and disgrace. And the marshalling of all
affaires is committed (without any respect of sufficiency or desert) to
the counsaile & conduct of those who can best apply themselves
to the kings youthfull delightes. Among these, auncient nobility is
accompted a vaine jeast; wealth [p. 63] and vertue are the ready
meanes to bring to destruction.

'It grieves me to speake, but it helpeth not to hide that which every
man seeth. Our auncestors lived in the highest pitch and perfection
of libertie, but we, of servilitie, being in the nature not of subjectes,
but of abjectes and flat slaves: not to one intractible prince onely, but
to many proude & disdainefull favorites, not alwaies the same, but
ever new, & no sooner have we satisfied some, but fresh hungrie

masters are straight waies set upon us, who have more endamaged us by extortion and bribes, then the enemy hath done by the sword.

'What unusuall kindes of exaction are dayly put in practise, without either measure or end, and oftentimes without neede? Or if any be, it proceedeth rather upon ryotus expenses, then any necessary or honourable charge, and great summes of money are pulled and pilled from good subjects, to be throwne away amongst unprofitable unthriftes. And if any man openeth his mouth against these extorted taxations, then either by feined imputation of capital crimes, or by smal matters aggravated, or else by open crueltie and force, his life and libertie is forthwith hazarded. It were too tedious, too odious, too frivolous to put you in mind of particular examples, as though your owne estate, & the lamentable losse of your uncle & other noble friends could be forgotten. Yea, I suppose that there is no man of qualitie within the realme who, either in his owne person, or in his neere friends, doeth not plainly perceive that no man enjoyeth the safeguard of his goods, and suerty of his body; but rich men in the one, & great men in the other, are continually endaungered.

'This, then, is our case, but what is our remedy? We have endured, & we have entreated, but our pacience hath drawne on more heavie burthens, and our complaints procured more bitter blowes: by the one our livings, and our lives by the other, are dayly devoured.

'And therefore we are now compelled to shake off our shoulders this importable yoke, and submit our selves to the soveraigntie of some more moderate and worthy per[p. 64]son: not so much for the griefe of our miseries which are past, nor for the paine of our present distresses, as for feare of such daungers as are most like to ensue. For the king hath cut away the chiefe of the nobilitie, and the commons hee hath pared to the quicke, and still hee harrieth us as a conquered countrie. Whereby we are layd bare to the havoke of al our enemies, & utterly disabled, not onely to recover that which is lost, but also to retaine even that which is left.

'But to whom should we complaine? What succour, whose ayde, should we desire? You are the onely man who in right should, and in wisedome can, and in goodnesse will (we hope) relieve us.

'For you are neerest to the king in bloud, and therefore ought to have the rule of that which his weakenesse cannot wielde. Your yeares are wel stayed from the light conceits of youth, and so spent that all your actions have made proofe of abilitie in government of greatest charge. Nothing past needeth excuse, and feare is vaine for anything to come. The paines and perils which heretofore you have undertaken, for the benefite of your countrie, putteth us also in good hope that in these extremities, you will not forsake us. Wee are all as in a ship that is ready to sinke, as in a house that is ready to fall, & doe most humbly crave and call for your helpe. Now, or else never, shew your selfe in favour of your countrymen, to free us, to free your selfe, to free the whole state from these daungers and decayes, by taking into your hands the scepter and diademe of the realme, and reducing againe the governement thereof to a princely freedome, in combining the soveraigntie of one with the libertie of all.

'Omit not this occasion to set forth to the view of the world, as in a large field, & at free scope, your vertue and courage, by relieving miserable wretches from their oppressors. Which action hath beene so highly honoured, that many heathen men, for the same, have beene accompted as gods.

'This we are constrained to offer and entreate. This is both honorable for you to accept, and easie to be performed. And so much the more, in that no [p. 65] prince by any people have bene desired with greater affection, nor shall be with more dutie obeyed.'

The duke entertained this speach with great moderation of mind, showing himselfe neither disturbed thereat, nor excessive in joy. His aunswere, concerning the king, was respective and wel tempered, rather lamenting his weaknes then blaming his malice. Concerning himselfe, hee spake so modestly that he seemed rather worthy of a kingdome, then desirous.

'The life,' quoth he, 'which hitherto I have led, hath alwaies bene free from ambitious attempts, and the stayednesse of my yeares hath now setled my mind from aspiring thoughts. And experience of former dangers hath bred in me a warie regard in such weightie proceedings.

'For to cast a king out of state is an enterprise not hastely to bee resolved upon, nor easily effected. But suppose that matter not impossible, and perhaps not hard, yet the rarenesse of the like precedents will make the action seeme injurious to most men. And he that shal attaine a kingdome upon opinion of desert, doth charge himselfe with great expectation, and how honourably soever hee carry[71] himselfe, shall never want his deadly enviers. Besides this, in civill dissentions the faith of the whole people is fleeting, and daunger is to bee doubted from every particular person, so that it is possible that al may fall away, and impossible to beware of everyone.

'Therefore, I could rather wish to spend the course of my yeares which yet remaine in this obscure, yet safe and certaine, state, then to thrust my selfe upon the pikes of those perils which, being once entred into, are daungerous to follow, & deadly to forsake. For in private attempts, a man may step and stope when he please; but he that aymeth at a kingdome hath no middle course betwene the life of a prince, & the death of a traytor.'

[71] A: 'carried,' a listed 'faulte.'

The archbishop, hearing this, did as vainly persist in importuning the duke, as he vainly seemed unwilling & strange. 'The state,' said he, 'wherein now you stand is not so safe and certaine as you doe conceive. In deed, by rejecting our re[p. 66]quest you shal avoid certaine dignity, and therewith uncertaine & contingent dangers, but you shal procure most certaine destruction to your selfe and us.

'For this secret can not be kept long secret from the king, and even good princes are nice in points of soveraignty, & beare a nimble eare to the touch of that string, and it more hurteth a subject to be esteemed worthy of the kingdome then it will profit him to have refused the offer. What then will he do, who putteth the chiefest surety of his reigne in the basenesse & barenesse of his subjects, whose head, being possessed with eternall jelousy, maketh every presumption a proofe, and every light surmise a strong suspition against them? Surely, since the generall favour & love which the people beareth you hath bereaved you of your liberty, this their generall desire will not leave your life untouched. As for us, if we either faint in our intent, or faile in the enterprise, *actum est*. We shalbe as lambs among lions, and no conquest can be so cruell as the kings reigne will be over us.

'Certainely, we have gone too far, for to go backe, and the time is past when you for ambition & we for envy might seeme to attempt against the king: the attainment of the kingdome must now be a sanctuary & refuge for us both. The like examples are not rare (as you affirme), nor long since put in practise, nor far hence to be fetched. The kings of Denmarke and of Sweveland are oftentimes banished by their subjects, oftentimes imprisoned & put to their fine. The princes of Germany, about an hundred yeres past, deposed Adulphus the emperour, and are now in hand to depose their emperor Wenceslaus. The Earle of Flanders was a while since driven out of his dominion by his owne people, for usurping greater power then appertained to his estate. The auncient Britaines chased away their owne King Carecious, for the lewdnesse of his life and cruelty of his rule. In the time of the Saxon Heptarchie, Bernredus, King of Mercia, for his pride and stoutnes towardes his people was by them deposed. Likewise Aldredus & Ethelber[p. 67]tus, kings of Northumberland, were for their disorders expelled by their subjects.

'Since the victorie of the Normaines, the lords endeavored to expell King Henry the third, but they were not able. Yet, were they able to depose King Edward the second, and to constitute his young sonne Edward king in his steade. These are not all, and yet enough to cleare this action of rarenesse in other countries, & noveltie in our.

'The difficulty indeede is somewhat, because the excellencie is great. But they that are affraide of every bush shall never take the bird. And your selfe had once some triall hereof, when without battaile, without bloud or blowes, you had the king at such a lift as he held his crowne at your courtesie, even at that time when his grievances were, neither for greatnes nor continuance, so intollerable as now they are growne; and by reason of his tender yeres, not out of al compasse, both of excuse for the fault and of hope for an amendement.'

'Nay,' said the duke, 'where necessity doth enforce, it is superfluous to use speach, either of easinesse or of lawfulnesse. Necessitie will beate thorow brasen walles, and can be limited by no lawes. I have felt verie deeply my part in these calamities, and I would you knew with what griefe I have beheld your.

'For what other reward have I received of all my travailes and services, but the death of my uncle and dearest friends, my owne banishment, the imprisonment[72] of my children, and losse of my inheritance? And what have beene returned to you for your bloud so often shed in his unfortunate warres, but continuall tributes, scourges, gallowes and slaverie? I have made sufficient proofe both of pacience in my owne miseries, and of pittie in your: remedy them hither to I could not. If now I can, I will not refuse to sustain that part which your[73] importunitie doth impose upon me. If we prevaile, we shall recover againe our libertie; if wee loose, our state shall be no worse then now it is. And since we must need perish, either deservingly or without cause, it is more hono[p. 68]rable to put our selves upon the adventure eyther to winne our lives, or to dye for deserte. And although our lives were safe, which in deede are not, yet to abandon the state and[74] sleepe still in this slaverie were a poynt of negligence and sloath.

'It remaineth, then, that we use both secrecie and celeritie, laying hold upon the opportunitie which the kings absence hath now presented unto us. For in al enterprises which never are commended before they bee atchieved, delayes are daungerous, and more safe it is to be founde in action, then in counsaile. For they that deliberate onely to rebell, have rebelled already.'

So the messengers departed into England, to declare the dukes acceptance, and to make preparation against his arrivall, both of armour and of subjection, and desire to obey. Presently after their departure, the duke signified to Charles, King of Fraunce, that he had a desire to goe into Brittaine, to visite John, Duke of Brittaine, his friend and kinsman. The king, suspecting no further fetch, sent letters of commendation in his favour to the Duke of Brittaine. But if he had surmised any dangerous drift against King Richard, who not

---

[72] A misprints by inverting the final 'n:' 'imprisonmeut'.
[73] In A, the 'u' is inverted: 'yonr'.
[74] A misprints: 'state ane sleepe.'

long before had taken his daughter to wife, instead of letters of safe-conducte, he would have found lettes to have kept him safe from disturbing his sonne in lawes estate.

As soone as the duke was come into Brittaine, he waged certaine souldiours, and presently departed to Calice, and so committed to sea for England, giving forth that the onely cause of his voyage was to recover the duchie of Lanchaster, and the rest of his lawfull inheritance, which the king wrongfully deteyned from him. In his companie was Thomas Arundell, the Archbishop of Canterburie, and Thomas the sonne & heire of Richard, late Earle of Arundell, who was very yong, and had a little before escaped out of prison and fled into France to the Duke. The residue of his attendants were very few, not exceeding the number of fifteen lances, so that it is hard to esteeme whether it was greater marvaile, [p. 69] either that he durst attempt, or that he did prevaile, with so smal a company; but his chiefest confidence was in the favour & assistance of the people within the realm. So he did beare with England, yet not in a streight course, but floated along the shoare, making head sometimes to one coast, and sometimes to another, to discover what forces were in a readines either to resist or to receive him.

As he was in this sort hovering on the seas, Lord Edmund, Duke of Yorke, the kings uncle, to whom the king had committed the custody of the realme during the time of his absence, called unto him Edmund Stafford, Bishop of Chichester, Lord Chancellour, and W. Scroupe, Earle of Wiltshire, Lord Treasurour of the realme, also Sir John Bushie, Sir Henry Greene, Sir William Bagot, Sir John Russell, and certain others of the kings Privy Councell, and entred into deliberation what was best to be done. At the last it was concluded, deceitfully by some, unskilfully by others, and by all perniciously for the king, to leave the sea coasts and to leave London, the very walles & castle of the realme, and to goe to St. Albons, there to gather strength sufficient to encounter with the duke. It is most certaine that the dukes side was not any wayes more furthered then by this dissembling and deceivable dealing. For open hostility and armes may openly and by armes be resisted; but privy practises, as they are hardly espied, so are they seldome avoided. And thus, by this meanes, the duke landed, about the feast of Saint[75] Martin,[76] without let or resistance at Ravenspur, in Houldernesse, as most writers affirme.

Presently after his arival, there resorted to him Lord Henrie Pearcie, Earle of Northumberland, and Lord Henry, his son, Earle of Westmerland, Lorde Radulph Nevill, Lord Rose, Lord Willoughbÿ, &

[75] A: 'Saind.'
[76] 4 July 1399.

many other personages of honor, whose company encreased reputation
to the cause, and was a great countenance[77] and strength to the dukes
further purposes. And first they tooke of him an oath, that hee should
neither procure nor permit any bodily harme to be done unto King [p.
70] Richard; whereupon they bound themselves upon their honours to
prosecute all extremities against his mischievous counsailers. And this
was one step further then that which the duke pretended at the first,
when hee tooke shipping at Callice, which was only the recovery of
his inheritance. But that was as yet not determined, nor treated, and
of some perhaps not thought upon, which afterwardes it did ensue.
And so was that place easily insinuated into by degrees, which with
maine and direct violence would hardlier have bin obtained.

Then the common people, desperate upon newe desires and,
without head, head-long to matters of innovation, flocked very fast to
these noble men, the better sort for love to the common-wealth, some
upon a wanton levetie[78] and vaine desire of change, others in regard
of their owne distressed and decayed estate who, setting their chiefe
hopes and devises uppon a generall disturbance, were then most safe
when the common state was most unsure. So, betweene the one and
the other, the multitude did in short time increase to the number of
threescore thousand able soldiours.

The Duke, finding this favour not onely to exceed his expectation,
but even above his wish, he thought it best to followe the current
whilst the streame was most strong, knowing right well that if fortune
be followed, as the first doe fall out, the rest will commonly succeede.
Therefore, cutting of unnecessary delaies, with al possible celerity hee
hastened towardes London, to the end that possessing himselfe thereof
as the chiefe place within the realme, both for strength and store, he
might there make the seat of the warre. In this journey no signe nor
shew of hostility appeared, but all the way, as he passed, the men of
chiefest quallity and power adjoyned themselves unto him, some upon
heat of affection, some for feare, others upon hope of rewarde after
victorie; everie one upon causes dislike, with like ardent desire contending, least any should seeme more foreward then they.

In everie place also where he made stay, rich gifts and pleasant
devi[p. 71]ses were presented unto him, with large supply both of
force and provision, far above his need. And the common people,
which for their greatnesse take no care of publique affaires, and
are in least daunger by reason of their basenes, with shoutes and
acclamations gave their applause: extolling the duke as the onely man
of courage, and saluting him king, but spending many contumelious

[77] *A* inverts the first 'n': 'couutenance.'
[78] *A* inverts a 'u' here: 'lenetie,' a listed 'faulte.'

tearmes upon King Richard, and depraving him as a simple and sluggish man, a dastard, a meycocke,[79] and one altogether unworthy to beare rule; shewing themselves as much without reason in rayling upon the one, as they were in flattering the other.

Again, the duke for his part was not negligent to uncover the head, to bowe the body, to stretch forth the hand to every meane person, and to use all other complements of popular behaviour wherewith the mindes of the common multitude are much delighted and drawne, taking that to bee courtesie which the severer sort accompt abasement. When he came to the citty, he was there likewise very richly and royally entertained with processions and pageantes, and divers other triumphant devises & shewes. The standings in all the streets where he passed were taken up to behold him, and the unable multitude, who otherwise could not, yet by their good wordes, wishes, and wils did testify unto him their loving affections. Neither did there appeare in any man at that time any memory of faith and alleagiance towards King Richard, but (as in seditions it alwaies hapneth) as the most swayed, all did go.

On the contrarie side, the Duke of Yorke with the rest of his counsaile fell to mustering of men at St. Albones for the king. But as the people out of divers quarters were called thither, many of them protested that they would doe nothing to the harme and prejudice of the Duke of Lancaster, who they said was unjustly expelled, first from his country, and afterwardes from his inheritance.

Then W. Scroupe, Earle of Wiltshire, Lord Treasorer, Sir J. Bushie,[80] Sir W. Bagot, and Sir Hen[p. 72]rie Greene, perceiving the stiffe resolution of the people, forsooke the Duke of Yorke and the Lord Chanceller, and fled towards Bristow, intending to passe the seas into Ireland to the king. These foure were they upon whom the common fame went, that they had taken of the king his realm to farme, who were so odious unto the people that their presence turned away the harts of many subjects; yea, it was thought that more for displeasure against them, then against the king, the revolt was made. For being the onely men of credit and authority with the king, under false colour of obedience they wholly governed both the realme & him, to many mischiefs corrupting his mind, & in many abusing his name, either against his wil or without his knowledge, insomuch as he was innocent of much harme which passed under his commandement. But the patience of the people could not endure that two or three should rule al, not by reason they were sufficient, but because they were in favour; and the king, in that he permitted them whom

---

[79] An effeminate person; a coward, a weakling (OED).
[80] A: 'Bush,' a listed 'faulte.'

he might have bridled, or was ignorant of that which he should have knowne, by tolerating and wincking at their faults, made them his owne, & opened therby the way to his destruction. So often times it falleth out to be as dangerous to a prince to have hurtfull and hatefull officers in place and services of weight, as to be hurtfull and hatefull himselfe.

The Duke of Yorke, either amazed at this sodain change, or fearing his adventure if he should proceede in resistance, gave over the cause, and preferred present security before duty with daunger, giving most men occasion to misdeeme by his dealing that he secretly favored the dukes enterprise. Likewise, all other counsailers of that side either openly declared for the duke, or secretly wished him wel &, abandoning all private direction & advice, adjoyned themselves to the common course, presuming thereby of greater safety.

Duke Henry, in the meane time being at London, entred into deliberation with his friends, what way were best to be followed. At the last, having considered the forwardnesse of [p. 73] the people, the greatnes of the perill whereinto they had already plunged, & the kings irreconcilable nature, whereof he made proofe against the Duke of Gloucester & the Earles of Arundel & of Warwicke, they finally resolved to expel him from his dignity, & to constitute Duke Henry king in his sted. And to that end, open war was denounced against the king, and against all his partakers, as enemies to the quiet and prosperity of the realme, and pardon also promised to all those that would submit themselves to follow the present course; otherwise to look for no favour, but all extremities. None of the nobility durst openly oppose himselfe to these designes: some, unwilling to play all their state at a cast, kept themselves at liberty to be directed by successe of further event; others consented coldly, and in tearmes of doubtfull construction, with intent to interpret them afterwards, as occasion should change; but the most parte did directly and resolutely enter into the cause, and made their fortunes common with the duke, in daunger of the attempt, but not in honour. Among whome the duke, standing up, used speach to this purpose:

'I am returned here, as you see, at your procurement, and by your agreement have entred into armes for the common liberty. Wee have hitherto prosperously proceeded, but in what tearmes we now stand, I am altogether uncertaine. A private man I am loath to be accompted, being designed to be king by you; and a prince I cannot be esteemed, whilst another is in possession of the kingdome. Also your name is in suspence, whether to be tearmed rebels or subjects, until you have made manifest that your allegeance was bound rather to the state of the realme then the person of the prince.

'Now you are the men who have both caused this doubtfulnes and must cleare the same. Your parts still remaineth to be performed; your vertue & valure must adde strength to the goodnesse of this action. We have already attempted so farre that all hope of pardon is extinct, so that if wee shoulde shrincke back & breake of the enterprise, no mercy is to be expected [p. 74] but butchery and gibbets, and all extremities. If wee drive of & delay the accomplishment thereof, we shall loose the opportunity which now is offred, and open to our enimies occasion of advantage. For the peoples bloud is up now on our side, and nothing is wanting but our owne diligence & care. Let us not therefore trifle out the time of doing, in talking & deliberating: it is best striking whilst the yron is hoate. Let us set forth roundly, and possesse our selves with speed of al the parts of the realme. And so we shall bee able either to keepe out our concurrent, or els to entertaine him litle to his liking.'

So troups of men were sent in to every quarter of the realm, to secure them for making strength on the part of King Richard. But the people in all places, as men broken with many burthens, did easily entertaine the first commer, and were not curious to side with the stronger. The duke pursued those of the kings privy counsaile which fled away from the Duke of Yorke, bearing himselfe with great cheere and courage, as confident in the cause and secure of the event. When he came at Bristow, he found the castle fortified against him. But in short time he forced it, and tooke therein Sir John Bushy, Sir Henrie Greene, & W. Scroupe, Lord Treasurer, a joyfull pray to the common people, who (fearing that if execution should bee deferred, petitions for pardon might happen to prevaile, and so their cruelties and injuries should bee answered with the vaine title and commendation of clemency) did violently require them unto death: no respite could be obteined, no defence admitted, no[81] answere heard. Yea, their humble and submisse intreaty was interpreted to argue a weak & broken courage upon a guilty conscience, which more incensed the rage of the people, crying out that they were traitours, bloud-suckers, theeves and what other heinous tearmes insulting fury did put into their mouthes. At which clamorous and importunant instance, the day following they were beheaded. Sir William Bagot came not with them to Bristowe, but turned to Chester and, the pursuit being made after the [p. 75] most, he alone escaped into Ireland. This execution, partly because it pleased the people, and partly because it excluded all hope of the kings pardon, caused them to cleave more closely to the duke, which greatly encreased both his glory & his hope, having offers of so large aide,[82] & need of so litle.

[81] A misprints an inverted 'n': 'uo.'
[82] A: 'officers of so long aide,' a listed 'faulte.'

In the meane time, this newes of the dukes arrivall and of other occurrences, part true, part false, and part enlarged by circumstance (as fame groweth in the going), was blowen over to the king, being then entangled with other broyles in Ireland. At the receipt whereof, hee caused the sonnes of the Duke of Gloucester and of the Duke of Lancaster to be imprisoned in the strong castle of Trim,[83] which is in Ireland, & for dispatch to returne into England, left many matters unfinished and most of his provison behind, hasting and shufling up as present necessitie did enforce. So, being both unskilfull and unfortunate himselfe, & devoide of good direction, with more haste then good hap he tooke shipping, with the Duke of Aumerle, Exceter & Surrie, the Bishops of London, Lincolne and Caerliele, and many other men of qualitie, and crossing the seas, landed at Milford Haven in Wales, in which countrimen[84] he alwaies reposed his chiefest suretie & trust. But then he saw, contrarie to his expectation, that as wel there as in all other places, the people by plumps flocked to the duke, & fled from him. Yea, they that came with him began for to waver, no man encouraging them to be constant, but many to revolt.

This suddaine chaunge, not looked for, not thought upon, disturbed all the kings devises, & made him irresolute what hee should doe. On the one side hee saw his cause and quarell to bee right, and his conscience (he saide) cleare from any bad demerite; on the other side hee saw the great stength of his enemies, and the whole power of the realme bent against him, & being more abashed by the one,[85] then emboldned by the other, he stoode perplexed in uncertaine termes, either where to stay, or whether to stirre, having neither skill nor resolution himselfe in cases of difficultie, and ob[p. 76]noxious to hurtfull and unfaithfull counsaile. Some advised him to march forward and pierce deeper into the land, before his owne forces fell from him, affirming that valure is seconded by fortune; that this courage of his would confirme the constancie of his souldiours, and his presence put the people in remembrance of their faith; that in all places he should finde some who for favour, or for hire, or else for duetie, would adheare unto him, whereby hee should soone gather strength sufficient to joyne issue with his enemie in the fielde.

Others perswaded him to retire againe into Ireland, & then, if succour failed him in England, to wage souldiours out of other countries. But the king, being no man of action in militarie affaires, rejected both the counsailes, as neyther venturous enough with the one, nor warie enough with the other. And taking a middle course (which in

---

[83] *A*: 'castle Trim,' a listed 'faulte.'
[84] *A* inverts the 'u': 'conntrimen.'
[85] *A*: 'of the one,' a listed 'faulte.'

cases of extremitie, of all is the worst), he determined to make staye in Wales, and there to attende to what head this humour would rise.

The duke, upon advertisement that the king was landed in Wales, removed with a strong armie from Bristowe towardes Chester, using the first opportunitie against him, and which in deede was the fittest. When Lord Thomas Percie, Earle of Worcester and steward of the kings household, heard of the dukes approach, he brake forth into shewe of that displeasure which before hee had conceived against the king, for proclayming his brother, the Earle of Northumberlande, traytour. And thereupon, openly in the hall, in the presence of the kings servants, he brake his white rodde, the ensigne of his office, and forthwith departed to the duke, willing every man to shift for himselfe in time. By which acte he lost reputation both with the haters & fauourers of King Richard, being accompted of the one a corrupter, of the other a forsaker and betrayer, of the king. After this example, almost all the rest, more fearefull then faithful, scattered themselves every one his way. And they who in the kings flourishing [p. 77] time would have contented to bee foremost, now in his declining estate equally draw backe, and like swallowes, forsooke that house in the winter of fortunes boysterous blasts, where they did nothing but feede & foyle[86] in the summer of her sweete sunne-shine.

And thus, betweene faint souldiers and false friends, the king was abandoned and forsaken, and left almost unto himselfe. Looke on he might, but let it hee could not, as not of force to punish that which he never forced to prevent. His only remedy was pacience (a cold comfort), his only revenge was complaint (a weake weapon), betweene which two, his bitternesse did in this manner breake from him:

'And doe these also,' said he, 'forsake me? Doth their faith & my fortune end together? Wel, if I had forsaken them in time I had not beene forsaken of others who once loved me better, and now are able to harme me more. But now I see the blindnesse of my judgement. I plainely see that there is no friendship in flatterie, nor treacherie in plaine truth. And I would I had as much time to reforme this errour, as I am like to have to repent it, but they would not suffer me to be wise when I might, and now they have made me wretched, they runne from me. They could bee the causes, but they will not be companions of my miseries. Such attendants are crowes to a carcasse, which flocke together not to defend, but to devour it, and no sooner have they layd the bones bare, but straight-wayes they are gone.'

Thus the king, having lost both the feare and love of his subjects, disturbed and distracted in thoughts, without comfort, councell or courage, remained still in Wales, as a stranger at home, as an exile in

---

[86] 'To foyle' = 'to foul,' i.e., to drop excrement (OED).

his owne kingdome, not daring to goe to London, nor any man desirous to come to him; shifting still from place to place and (as it fals out to men[87] distressed & amazed) fearing all things, but most disliking the present.

The duke continually pursued him with a mightie armie. But the kings companie was too small to doe anything [p. 78] by force, & yet too great to remaine in secrete; neither were they in any sort assured unto him, but such as shame and reverence retained a while, bands of small countenance, with men fearfull of danger, & carelesse of credite. At length he came to the castle of Conweye, and there, being utterly destitute of helpe and hope, he stoode devided in mind what way to bend his course; all his followers weare more ready to impugne the opinions of other then to give direction themselves, as seeing better what to shunne then what to follow. And, as it alwaies chanceth in desperate causes, that way was commonly preferred whereof the opportunitie was already past.

Some advised him that it was then time to think rather of saving his life, then recovering his estate. 'You see,' said they, 'how greatly & how wholly your subjects are set against you. It is but in vaine to looke for a suddaine change, or without a chaunge to hope that your purposes may prevaile. Give place for a time to the currant of this furie, let it have the full sway, and when it is at the highest pitch, it will turne againe, and then you shall have the tide as strong on your side as it is now against you. This motion, or rather commotion, of the people is violent and against nature, & therefore (as a stone forced upward) is most stronge at the beginning, and the further it passeth, the more it weakneth, until at last it returne to the naturall course againe.

'Therefore, give a little space for the bad to draw backe, for the good to put forward; treasons prevaile on the suddaine, but good counsailes gather forces by leasure. You have example in your noble progenitor King Henry the third, against whome the lords set up Lewes, the French kings sonne. Conditions were concluded and faith was made that he should be their king. But this purpose lasted not the pulling on, for before they had possessed him of the kingdom, they joyned togither in armes against him, & were as fierce to drive him out of the realme, as they had beene found to draw him in. The like alteration may you likewise not onely hope, but assuredly expect. For [p. 79] the mindes of men are constant in nothing but inconstancie, and persever onely in chaunge; in dislike of things present they desire new, wherwith they rest not long contented, but are many times glutted even with the first sight.

---

[87] *A*: 'at men,' a listed 'faulte.'

'And indeed, how can they long endure the raigne of him who, attaining the kingdome onely by their favour and might, shall holde the same in a manner at their courtesie and will? For everie unpleasant commaund shall be deemed ingratitude, everie suit rejected shal charge him with unkindnesse. Yea, if honor be not offered, they will be discontented; and uppon any occasion of displeasure, thinke themselves as able to displace him as they were to set him up. Therefore, you may for a time returne againe into Ireland, or else passe the seas to your father in lawe, the King of Fraunce. You may assure your selfe of his assistance, to set upon your side, and recover your losses. Times have their turnes, and fortune her course too and fro like the sea, & magnanimitie is shewen by enduring, & not relinquishing when she doth crosse. Onely loose no point of courage, and keepe your person at large, reserving your selfe to that good hope which never dieth whilst life endure.'

Others, who were enemies to all counsaile whereof themselves were not authors, perswaded the king that 'the nobilitie and commons of the realme had attempted so farre, that they would rather dye then desist; not so much for hatred to you, as for feare to themselves, having so deadly incensed[88] your displeasure against them. For it is a hard matter to forgive, and impossible to forget those injuries and indignities which they have offered. And to omit what some princes have done, what all will promise to doe, they will soone find fresh and bleeding examples what you are like to doe. The Duke of Gloucester and the Earles of Arundell and of Warwicke did rise in armes against you, not to remove you from your crowne, but to remove certaine persons from your companie, an action more displeasing then prejudiciall unto you. At the last, a friendship was made and charters of free par[p. 80]don graunted unto them. But what followed? Was ever this breach perfectly made up? Did displeasure dye? Or was it only dissembled? Ah, it grieveth us to thinke how the present want of their lives hath fully revenged their deathes. For if they had lived, their countenance and authority woulde easily have staied these stirs; and the manner of their deaths doth strike an obstinate persistance into all your enemies.

'As for refuge to forren princes, you shall surely receive of them entertainment and allowance, and yet may growe burdensome, and at last perhaps faile. But it is very hard to draw any prince into so dangerous a quarrell, and more harde by that meanes to prevaile. Or, if you should, it is to bee feared that the victorers will hold to themselves the benefit of their conquest, and not yeeld it over unto you. Few countries but have bin under pretence of ayde by forrenners subdued. And this was the only cause which first drew the Saxons

---

[88] *A*: 'increased,' a listed 'faulte.'

into this land, who so assisted the Britaines against their enemies, that themslves could not be resisted from possessing theyr kingdome.

'Yet we doe not altogither condemne the helpe of straungers, in cases of extremity; but doe account it a remedy least to be trusted, and last of all to bee tried. What then if first you should procure a treaty, to see in what terms the people stand against you? It may be that upon some conditions they will submit themselves unto you, as heretofore they have done. Or if they wil needs deforce you from your kingdome, yet if an honourable maintenance may bee assured, what shall you lose thereby? What shall you lack? You have no childe to be disinherited, the chiefest motive which maketh men so greedy to get, and so carefull to keepe. As for your selfe, you shall be removed from a steepe & slippery hill, to a smooth and pleasant plaine, from tempestuous seas to a calme haven, from daungerous travaile to secure rest; & if there be no solace without safety, no felicity without firmnesse, you shall finde the private life not only more sweete, but more high and happy then your princely state. [p. 81] The tallest trees are weakest in the toppes, in widest fieldes are greatest tempests, and envy alwaies aimeth at loftiest marks: so to be placed on high is a false felicity, and a true misery; in shew a rule, but indeed a subjection to all the subjects; having least stay to stand, and most danger in the fall. And therefore, if you come downe safely, you are therein privileged above many other.

'But you shal lose (you will say) the credit & the countenance of a king. So you shal the cares, and so you shall the casualties. The crown & sceptar are things most weighty to weld. If a prince be good, he is laden with labour; if evill, with infamy and reproch; if either, with perils: on every side he is beset with dangerous rocks, with deadly gulfes, & continually tossed with strong and sturdy tempests, so that to be freed from these feares is to be esteemed an escape, and not a losse. This did the stoick philosopher perceive who, seeing Dionysius sit merily & freely conceited in the theater, being a little before expelled his kingdom, greatly condemned the error of his people who had banished him to such liberty, & so preferred him by his punishment.

'These are the dreames of philosophers (you will say), who usually contemne and deprave honor, & yet never lie from honourable mens tables. Let passe then, philosophers: go to vaine and sottish men. Seleuchus, being a king, was wont to say that if a man knew with what cares the diadem was clogged, he would not take it up although it lay in the street. You will say, peradventure, that like the boatman he looked one way, and pulled another, or like the lapwing, he cried most when he was furthest from his nest, vainly dispraising that which hee was loathest to loose.

'What say you then to Antiochus whome, when the Romanes had dispoiled of al Asia, he sent unto them great thanks, that they had rid him of infinit & importable cares, and set him at a moderate quiet? You will say that he made a vertue of his necessity. Well, then, we are somewhat neere your cace, & they that cannot frame their wils to this wisdome, let them thanke their enimies for enforcing them to it. But what say you to Dioclesian, who did voluntarily relinquish[89] not a small and corner kingdome, but the greatest empire that the world did ever beare, [p. 82] and found so sweet contentment in that exchange that when he was importuned by the senate to resume his estate, hes utterly rejected their suite?

'But what need we travell in externe histories for those examples, whereof we have so large supply in our owne? The ancient Saxon kings, Kingilsus, Ina, Ceolulphus, Eadbertus, Ethelredus, Kenredus, Offa, Sebbi, & Sigerbertus did of their owne accord laye downe their diadems and scepters, and betake themselves to solitary & religious lives. Now many princes have helde their estate with better fortune, but none did ever with greater honor leave it, then you should at this present. For others have abandoned their rule, either for desire of ease, or for avoidance of dangers, or upon some sluggish and superstitious devotion. But you, for love to your country, shall forebeare to seek your uttermost remedy in setting up a most cruel war, wherein much English bloud should be spilt, & the realme deprived of many worthy armies. Let others be reported to forsake their kingdoms when they had no longer pleasure to hold them, but your praise shall be for giving over, when it is greatest benefit unto the people. And the more hope you have to prevaile, if you list to contend, the greater commendations will it be to yeeld, as being rather voluntary then by constraint.'

The king commended the courage of the first, but this last counsell best agreed with his faint & feeble spirit, more yeelding to feare then forward in hope; apt by the one to despaire, unable by the other to holde out in any hard adventure, preferring alwayes abject and base safety before hazard with honour. Yet were many ready to reply that al speech of conditions & yeelding was both dishonorable & also dangerous. 'For even in hardest haps,' said they, 'a noble nature wil not presently relinquish, but first endevor either by courage to repell the danger, or by wisdome to decline it. And why should you so litle esteem your glory and fame, as without battel, or blow striken, to bind your hands & yeeld up your weapons, & put your selfe upon miserable mercy? Or if the honor of your noble house doth nothing move you, yet let danger & despaire at least arme you to boldnesse.

[89] *A*: 'relinquisht.'

For neither the duke nor his friends will be so confident [p. 83] as to thinke themselves safe, so long as you shall remaine (although in private state) alive.

'Indeed, you may assure your self that faire words will be given, & large offers made. But the performance shal consist in the courtesy of the conqueror, and nothing will be thought unlawfull to him that hath power. King Edward the second was too heavy to be indured, even of his own sonne; and many have used violence to themselves, rather then they would fall into the power of their concurrents. And do not you expect more favor or greater fortune then other have found: let never that senselesnes possesse your mind to imagine that a prince may live safely in private estate. For in this case there is no meane betweene Caesar & nothing, betweene the highest honor & the deadliest downfall.

'Therefore, omit neither all nor any one meanes unassayed, to maintaine your side by armes. No greater harme can happen at the hardest, then that which wllingly you run into; you can but die if you be vanquished, & die you shall if you do yeeld. But by the one you shall end your life with glory; by the other, with shame & perpetuall reproch. And although you do now esteeme equally of both, yet when you shall see your selfe pent in prison, in dayly feare and expectancy of a bloudy messenger, you shall then perceive a difference in death, and find the weaknesse and fault of the counsell which you are about to follow.'

Many like speeches were with great vehemency often repeated, but the kings eares were stopped against all impression of manhood. And, as he was unable to governe himselfe in his prosperous estate, so was he much lesse sufficient to wind out of these intricate troubles. Therefore, perceiving himselfe so straitly beset that he could hardly either escape away, or shift any longer, he desired speech with Thomas Arundel, Archbishop of Canterbury, & Lord Henry Percy, Earle of Northumberland, of whom the one he had banished, the other he had proclaimed traitor not long before.

These two came unto him, & the king, upon short conference, understanding what stiffe stomacks they bare against him, was content not to demand that which he saw he could not obtaine; & thereupon agreed that he would relinquish his estate, upon condition that an honorable living might [p. 84] be assigned him, & life promised to 8. such persons as he would name, the greatest number whom adversity did not alter.

This was then both readily & faithfully promised by the archbishop and the earle, & afterward solemnly ratified by the duke. The king ceased not to intreat submisly, & promise largely, and (as the nature is of men perplexed with feare) above his ability, & without measure.

The earle incouraged him, and declared that the duke, before he had obtained any aide, secured by his oath the safety of the kings person.

Then the king desired to talke with the duke, which was likewise promised, & so the archbishop & the earle departed, & the king removed to the castle of Flint, about 8. miles distant from Chester, to which place the duke came to him. Here the countenances & words of both were noted by them that were present: the king seemed abject and base, the duke neither insulting nor relenting, but comforting and promising friendly. The king repeated many benefits & kindnesses that he had shewed, how in former time he had spared the dukes own life, & lately his sonnes. In regard whereof he desired him, with such submisnes as was agreeable rather with his necessity than his honour, that he would shew some pitie, where he had received such pleasure, and permit him to injoy his life with such private maintenance as was convenient for his estate. The duke put him in good comfort, promising him assuredly that he would provide for his safety, for which he suffered himselfe to be solemnly thanked, & thought it not much to have it accounted a great benefit. Indeed, from that time the king was kept safe and sure enough from hindring any of the dukes purposes; neither could it so easily have bene discerned what had bene[90] best for him to do, as that this which he did was the very worst: for the same night he was brought by the duke and his army to Chester, and from thence secretly conveyed to the Tower of London, there to be kept safe untill the parliament, which was appointed shortly after to be holden.

Thus the king yealded himselfe the 20. day of August, being the 47. day after the dukes arrivall, so that his journyes considered, from Houldernesse in the north to London, from [p. 85] thence to Bristowe, & so into Wales & backe againe to Chester: a man shal not easily travaile over the land in shorter time then he conquered it. So frienly was fortune unto him that hee eyther found or made a readie passage through al hinderances and lets, & it seemed that he needed onely to open his armes to meete and receive her, as she offered herselfe unto him. All the kings treasure & jewels, with his horses and all his fardage came to the dukes hands, and many that were in his companie were afterwards also despoyled by the souldiours of Northumberland and Wales.

Some writers affirme that the king did not yeald himselfe, but was forelaied & taken as he was secretly passing from Flint to Chester. But the authoritie of others who lived in that time, eyther in the plaine viewe or certaine intelligence of these affaires, who for their place could not but knowe, and for their profession would not but deliver

---

[90] *A* inverts the 'n': 'beue.'

the very truth, hath drawne me to follow their report, which I find
also received by some late wrighters, of as great deapth in judgement
and choice as any (without exception) that this age hath brought
forth.

As the king was carried towards London, certaine citizens conspired
to lay themselves in a wait by the way, and sodainly to slay him,
partly for private grievances, & partly for the cruelty that he had used
towards the whole citty. But the maior, upon intelligence, prevented
the practise, and rode forth in person with a convenient company to
conduct him safely unto the Tower.

Shortly after, the duke came to London in solemn estate, and sent
forth summons in the kings name for a parlament to be holden at
Westminster, the last day of September in the same yeare. In the mean
time, he deliberated with his kindred and kind friends concerning the
order of his proceedings. The Duke of Yorke (who a litle before had
bene governour of the realm for the king & then was the chiefest
directer of the duke) thoght it best that King Richard should both
voluntarily resigne & also solemnly be deposed, by consent of all the
states of the realme. For resignation only would be imputed to feare,
and deprivation to force; whereof the one is alwaies pitied, and the
other en[p. 86]vied. But if both concurre, and his desire be combined
with his desart, being willing to forsake that which he is adjudged
worthy to forego, then shall it appeare that he neither is expelled his
kingdom by meere constraint, nor leaveth it without just cause.

This advice pleased the rest, and for executing therof upon the day
of S. Michaell[91] (which was the day before the parlament should
begin) there assembled at the Tower Thomas Arundell, Archbishop
of Canturbury; Richard Scroupe, Archbishop of Yorke; John, Bishop
of Hereford; Henry, Duke of Lancaster; Henry, Earle of Northumberland; Radulph, Earle of Westmerland; Lord Hugh Burnell,
Lord Thomas Berkley, Lord Rose, Lord Willoughby, Lord Abergeiny;
the Abbat of Westminster; the Prior of Canterbury; William Thirn-
inges[92] and John Makeham, Chiefe Justices; Thomas Stoke and John
Burbacke, Doctours of Law; T. Herpingham and T. Gray, Knights;
W. Ferby and Dionise Lopham,[93] publike notaries; and divers others
either not noted or not remembred. When all were set in their places,
King Richard was brought foorth apparelled in his royall robe, the
diademe on his head and the scepter in his hand, and was placed
amongst them in a chaire of estate. Never was prince so gorgeous,
with lesse glory and greater griefe; to whom it was not disgrace

---

[91] 29 September.
[92] A: 'Thirminges,' a listed 'faulte.'
[93] A: 'Lophane,' a listed 'faulte.'

sufficient, to lose both the honour and ornaments of a king, but he must openly, to his greater scorne, renounce the one and deliver the other. After a little pause and expectation, the king arose from his seat, and spake to the assembly these words, or the very like in effect:

'I assure my selfe that some at this present, and many hereafter, will accompt my case lamentable: either that I have deserved this dejection, if it be just or, if it be wrongfull, that I could not avoide it. Indeede, I doe confesse that many times I have shewed my selfe both lesse provident and lesse painfull for the benefite of the common-wealth then I should, or might, or intended to doe hereafter; and have in many actions more respected the satisfying of my owne particular humour then either justice to some private persons, or the common good of al. Yet I did not at any time either omit dutie, or commit grievance, [p. 87] upon natural dullnesse or set malice, but partly by abuse of corrupt councellers, partly by errour of my youthfull judgement. And now the remembrance of these over-sights is so unpleasant to no man as to my selfe; and the rather because I have no meanes left either to recompence the injuries which I have done, or to testifie to the world my reformed affections, which experience and stayednesse of yeares had already corrected, & would dayly have framed to more perfection. But whether all the imputations wherewith I am charged be true, either in substance or in such qualitie as they are layd, or whether being true, they be so heinous as to inforce these extremities; or whether any other prince, especially in the heate of youth, and in the space of two and twentie yeares (the time of my unfortunate raigne) doth not sometimes either for advantage, or uppon displeasure, in as deepe maner grieve some particular subject, I will not now examine. It helpeth not to use defence, neither booteth it to make complaint. There is left no place for the one, nor pity for the other. And therefore, I referre it to the judgement of God, and your lesse distempered considerations.

'I accuse no man, I blame no fortune, I complaine of nothing. I have no pleasure in such vaine and needlesse comforts; and if I listed to have stood upon tearmes, I know I have great favourers abroad, and some friends (I hope) at home, who would have beene ready, yea forward, on my behalfe to set up a bloudy and doubtfull warre. But I esteeme not my dignitie at so high a price, as the hazard of so great valure, the spilling of so much English bloud, and the spoile and waste of so flourishing a realme, as thereby might have bene occasioned. Therefore, that the common-wealth may rather rise by my fall, then I stand by the ruine thereof, I willingly yeeld to your desires, and am heere come to dispossesse my selfe of all publike authority and title, and to make it free and lawfull for you to create for your king Henry, Duke of Lancaster, my cousin germaine, whom I know to be as worthie to [p. 88] take that place, as I see you willing to give it to him.'

Then he read openly and distinctly the forme of his cession, wherein he did declare that he had discharged his subjectes from their oathes of fealtie and homage, and all other oathes whatsoever; and of his owne will & free motion did abdicate the title, dignitie, and aucthoritie of a king; and rendred up the possession of the realme, with the use and title thereof, and all the rights thereunto appertaining. To this the king subscribed and was sworne; and then hee delivered with his owne hands the crown, the septer, and the robe to the Duke of Lancaster, wishing unto him more happinesse therewith then had ever happened unto himselfe. Then he did constitute the Archbishop of Yorke and the Bishop of Hereford his procurators, to intimate and declare this his resignation to all the states of the realme, which should be assembled together in parliament. Lastly, he gave all his riches and goods, to the summe of three hundred thousand pounds in coyne, besides his jewels & plate, for satisfaction of the injuryes that hee had done, desiring the duke & al the rest that were present, severally by their names, not altogether to forget that he had beene their king, nor yet too much to thinke upon the same; but to retaine of him a moderate remembrance, and in recompence of the ease that hee had done them by his voluntarie yeelding, to permit him to live safely, in a private and obscure life, with the sweetenesse wherof he was so possessed that from thenceforth he would preferre it, before any preferment in the world.

All this was delivered and done by the king, with voyce and countenance so agreeable to his present heavinesse that there was no man to unmindefull of humane instabilitie, which was not in some measure moved thereat; insomuch as a fewe secrete teares melted from the eyes of many that were present, in whose mindes a confused[94] and obscure alteration alreadie ganne to beginne. So prone and inclinable are men to pitie miserie, although they have procured it, and to envie prosperitie, even that which they have raysed.

[p. 89] Upon Munday next following, the parlament began at Westminster, and the Archbishop of Yorke and the Bishop of Hereford (the kings atturneys for this purpose) declared openly to the states there assembled the kings voluntarie resignation, and demaunded whether they would assent and agree thereunto. The barons of the realme by severall and particular consent, the commons with one generall voyce, did expreslye accept and admit the same. Then it was thought meet that certaine defects and misdemeanures concerning matters of government should be objected against the king, for which

[94] *A*: 'confessed,' a listed 'faulte.'

he should be adjudged as unworthy as he seemed unwilling, to reteine the kingdome. To this purpose certaine articles were engrossed, and openly read, in which was conteyned, how unprofitable the king had bin to the realme, how unjust and grievous to the subjectes, contrarie both to his honour, and to his oath; the chiefest of which articles are these that follow:

1 First, that King Richard did wastefully spend the treasure of the realme, and had given the possessions of the crowne to men unworthy, by reason whereof new charges were dayly laide on the neckes of the poore comminaltie.

2 Item, where divers lords, as well spirituall as temporall, were apointed by the high court of parlament to commune and treate of matters concerning the state of the realme, and the commonwealth of the same, they being busied about the same commission, he with others of his affinitie went about to impeache them of treason.

3 Item, that by force and menace, he compelled the justices of the realme, at Shrewsburie, to condiscend to his opinion for the destruction of the said lords: insomuch as he began to raise warre against John, Duke of Lancaster, Thomas, Earle of Arundell, Richard, Earle of Warwicke, & other lords, contrarie to his honor and promise.

4 Item, that he caused his unckle, the Duke of Glouce[p. 90]ster, to be arrested without lawe, and sent him to Calice, and there without judgement, murthered him; and although the Earle of Arundell, upon his arraignement, pleaded his charter of pardon, he could not be heard, but was in most vile and shamefull manner sodainely put to death.

5 Item, he assembled certaine Lancashire and Cheshire men, to the intent to make warre on the foresaid lords, and suffered them to robbe and spoile, without correction or reproofe.

6 Item, that although the king, flatteringly and with great dissimulation, made proclamation throughout the realme that the lords aforenamed were not attached for any crime of treason, but onely for extortions and oppressions doone within the realme, yet he laide to them in the parlament rebellion and manifest treason.

7 Item, he hath compelled divers of the said lords servants, by menace, to make great fines & extreame paiments, to their utter undooing; and notwithstanding his pardon to them graunted, he made them fine a new.

8 Item, where divers were appointed to common of the estate of the realme, and the commonwealth of the same, the king caused all the roules & records to be kept from them, contrary to his promise made in parlament, to his open dishonor.

9 Item, he uncharitably commaunded that no man, upon paine of

losse of life and goods, should once entreate him for the returne of Henrie, now Duke of Lancaster.

10 Item, where the realme is houlden of God, and not of the Pope, or any other prince, the said King Richard, after he had obteyned divers acts of parlament for his owne peculiar profit and pleasure, then he procured bulles and extreame censures from Rome, to compell all men streitly to keepe the same, contrary to the honour and auncient priviledges of this realme.

11 Item, although the Duke of Lancaster had done his devoyre against Thomas, Duke of Northfolke, in proofe of [p. 91] his quarrell, yet the said king without reason or ground banished him the realme for ten yeares, contrarie to all equitie.

12 Item, before the dukes departure he, under his broad seale, licenced him to make atturneys to prosecute and defend his causes; the said king, after his departure, would suffer none atturney to appeare for him, but did with his at his pleasure.

13 Item, the said king put out divers shiriffes lawfully elected, and put in their roomes divers others of his owne minions, subverting the lawe, contrarie to his oath and honour.

14 Item, he borowed great summes of money, and bound himselfe under his letters patents for the repayment of the same, and yet not one peny paide.

15 Item, he taxed men at the will of him and his unhappy counsaile, and the same treasure spent in folly, not paying poore men for their vittaile and viand.

16 Item, he said that the lawes of the realme were in his head, and sometimes in his brest: by reason of which phantasticall opinion he destroyed noble men, and impoverished the poore commons.

17 Item, the parlament setting and enacting divers notable statutes for the profit and advancement of the commonwealth, he by his privie friends and solicitours caused to be enacted, that no acte then enacted should be more prejudiciall to him then it was to his predecessours; thorow which proviso he did often as he list, and not as the lawe ment.

18 Item, for to serve his purpose, he would suffer the shiriffes of the shires to remaine above one yeare or two in their office.

19 Item, at the summons of parlament, when the knights and burgesses should be elect, and the election had fully proceeded, he put out divers persons elected, and put in others in their places, to serve his will and appetite.

20 Item, he had privie espials in every shire, to heare [p. 92] who had of him any communication, and if he communed of his lascivious living and outrageous dooing, he straightwayes was apprehended and made a grievous fine.

21 Item, the spiritualitie alledged against him that he, at his going

into Ireland, exacted many notable summes of money, beside plate and jewels, without lawe or custome, contrary to his oath taken at his coronation.

22 Item, when divers lords and justices were sworne to say the trueth of divers things to them committed in charge, both for the honor of the realme and profit of the king, the said king so menaced them with sore threatnings that no man would or durst say the right.

23 Item, that without the assent of the nobilitie, he caryed the jewels and plate and treasure over the sea into Ireland, to the great impoverishing of the realme; and all the good recordes of the common wealth against his extortions, he caused privily to be embeasled[95] and caryed away.

24 Item, in all leagues and letters to be concluded and sent to the sea of Rome and other regions, his writing was so subtill and darke that no other prince durst once beleeve him, nor yet his owne subjects.

25 Item, he most tyranouslie and unprincely said that the lives and goods of all his subjects were in the princes hands, and at his disposition.

26 Item, that he, contrarie to the Great Charter of England, caused divers lustie men to appeale divers olde men, upon matters determinable at the common law, in the Court Marciall, because that in that court is no triall but onely by battaile; whereby the sayd aged persons, fearing the sequell of the matter, submitted themselves to his mercie, whom he fined and ransomed unreasonably at his pleasure.

27 Item, he craftily devised certaine privie oathes, contrarie to lawe, and caused divers of his subiects first to be sworne to observe the same, and after bound them in bands for surer keeping the same, to the great undooing of many [p. 93] honest men.

28 Item, where the chancellour, according to lawe, would in no wise graunt a prohibition to a certaine person, the king graunted it unto the same person under his privie seale, with great threatnings if it should be disobeyed.

29 Item, he banished the Bishop of Canterburie, without cause or judgment, and kept him in the parlament chamber with men of armes.

30 Item, the bishops goods he graunted to his successor, upon condition that he should maintaine all his statutes made at Shrewsburie, Anno. 21., and the statutes made Anno 22. at Coventree.

31 Item, uppon the accusation of the archbishop, the king craftily perswaded the said bishop to make no answer, for he would be his warrant, and advised him not to come to the parlament; and so, without answere, he was condemned and exiled, and his goods seazed.

---

[95] Embezzled.

Foure other articles were laide, which particularlie did concerne the said archbishop, by whose dooing chiefly the king was utterlie undone.

Then was demaunded of the nobilitie and commons of the realme, what they judged both of the trueth and desert of these articles; who all agreed that the crimes were notorious, and that King Richard was worthie for the same to be deposed from his princely dignitie. The noble men gave their voyces, part corrupted by favour, part awed by feare; and the commons are commonly like a flocke of cranes: as one dooth flye, all will follow. Hereupon commissioners were appointed by both the houses, who pronounced sentence of deposition against King Richard, in manner and forme as followeth:

'In the name of God, Amen. We, John, Bishop of S. Asses; J[ohn], Abbote of Glastenburie; Thomas, Earle of Gloucester; Thomas, Lord Berkley; Thomas Erpinghame, Thomas Graye, Knights; William Thirninge, Justice; commisioners for the matters here[p. 94]after specified by the lords spirituall and temporall of the realme of England and the commons of the said realme, representing all the states of the saide kingdome, specially deputed, sitting in seate of judgement and considering the manifold perjuries, and cruelties, and many other crimes and offences by Richard, late king of the saide realme, committed and doone contrarie to good governement, in the realmes and dominions aforesaide, during the time of his reigne; also considering the articles which were openly exhibited and red before the said states, which were so publicke, notorious, manifest and famous, that they could nor can by no avoydance and shift be concealed; also considering the confession of the saide king, acknowledging and reputing and truly upon his certaine knowledge judging himselfe to have been and to be altogether insufficient and unskilfull for the rule and government of the realmes and dominions aforesaid and of any parts of them, and not unworthy to be deposed for the notorious demerites by the said Richard first acknowledged, and afterward by his will and mandate before the said states published, and to them opened and declared in the English tongue.

'Upon these and other matters which were done concerning the same business, before the said states and us, by the diligent place, name, and authority to us in this part committed, in aboundance and for a cautele[96] we pronounce, decree and declare the saide Richard to have beene and to be unprofitable, and unable, and altogether insufficient and unworthie for the rule and governement of the said realmes, and of the dominions, rights and parts of them; and in regarde

---

[96] A reservation or provision made for precaution's sake. This legal language reflects the 'constitutional' concerns of some of Henry's party.

and respect of the premises, worthily to be deposed from all kinglie dignitie and honour (if any such dignitie and honour remaineth in him); and for the like cautele wee do depose him by our sentence definitive in this writing; inhibiting from hencefoorth expressely all and singular lords, archbishops, bishops, prelates, dukes, marquesses and earles, barons, knights, vassalles, and all other persons whatsoever, of the saide realmes and dominions, and other places to the said realmes and dominions appertaining, the subjects and liege people of the same, and every of them, that from henceforth none obey, or in[p. 95]tend to obey, the foresaid Richard, as king or lord of the realmes and dominions aforesaid.'

Then the same commissioners were by the consent and suffrages of both houses constituted procurators, joyntlye and severally for all the states of the realme, to resigne and surrender unto King Richard, for them and for all other homagers of the realme, all the homages and fealties which were both due and doone unto him as king and soveraigne, and also to declare unto him al the premises concerning his deposition.

Now Henrie, Duke of Lancaster, that he might be reputed, or reported at the least, not to attaine the kingdom by intrusion and wrong, was counsailed by his friends to pretend some lawfull challenge and claime thereunto; and being in power, it was no sooner advised what was to bee doone, but it was presently devised how to doe it. So a title was drawne from Edmund, sonne to King Henrie the third, whom they surnamed Crowch-backe, affirming that he was the eldest sonne of King Henrie, and that for his deformitie he was put from his right of succession in the kingdome, which was for that cause given to his yonger brother, King Edward the third. To this Edmund the duke was next of bloud by his mother Blanche, sole daughter and heyre to Henrie, the first Duke of Lancaster, and sonne to the saide Edmund. This cunning conceit was perceived of all men, but seeming not to perceive it was a point of friendship in some, and of obedience in the rest. Therefore, the kingdome of England being then thought vacant, both by the resignation and also by the deposition of King Richard, Duke Henrie arose from his seate and, standing in view of the lords, crossed himselfe on the forehead, and on the brest, and spake as followeth:

'In the name of God, Amen. I, Henrie of Lancaster, claime the realme of England, & the crowne, with all the appurtenances, as I that am descended by right line of the bloud royall, comming from that good lord, King Henrie the third, and through the right [p. 96] that God of His grace hath sent mee, with the helpe of my kindred and of my friendes, to recover the same; which kingdome was in point to be undoone, for default of good government and due justice.'

After these wordes, it was demaunded in both houses, of the nobility & of the commons which were assembled, whether they did consent that the duke should raigne. Who all with one voyce acknowledged and accepted him for their king. Then the Archbishop of Canterbury tooke him by the hand, and placed him on the throane of estate, The Archbishoppe of Yorke assisting him, and all the assemblie testifying their owne joy, and wishing his.

Then the archbishop made an oration, and tooke for his theame this place of Scripture: 'See, this is the man whom I spake to thee of, this same shall raigne over my people. I. Reg. 9. 17.' After all this he was proclaimed King of England, and of Fraunce, and Lord of Ireland. And the common people, which is voide of cares, not searching into sequels, but without difference of right or wrong inclinable to follow those that are mighty, with shoutes and clamours gave their applause, not all upon judgement or faithfull meaning, but most onely upon a received custome to flatter the prince whatsoever he be.

Yet, least the heate of this humour should allay by delay, it was foorthwith proclaimed in the Great Hall that upon the 13. day of September[97] next ensuing, the coronation of the king should be celebrated at Westminster. These matters being thus dispatched, the king proclaimed arose from his seate, and went to White Hall, where he spent the rest of the day in royall feasting, and all other complementes of joy; notwithstanding there appeared in him no token of statelynesse or pride, nor any change, in so great a change.

Upon Wednesday next following, the procurators before mentioned went to the presence of King Richard, being within the Tower, and declared unto him the admission of his resignation, and also the order and forme of his depo[p. 97]sition, and in the name of all the states of the realme, did surrender the homage and fealty which had been due unto him: so that no man from thence foorth would beare to him faith and obedience, as to their king. The king answered that he nothing reguarded these titulare circumstances, but contented himselfe with hope that his cousen would be gracious lord and good friend unto him.

So, upon the 13. day of October, which was the day of the Translation of Edward the Confessour, the duke was, with all accustomed solemnities by the Archbishoppe of Canterbury sacred, annointed and crowned king at Westminster, by the name of King Henry the fourth, upon the very same day wherein the yeere before he had been banished the realme. Hee was annoynted with an oyle which a certaine religious man gave unto Henry, the first Duke of Lancaster (grandfather to

---

[97] The coronation was actually set for 13 Oct. This lapse, common to all the quartos, is put right in the second paragraph next following.

the king by the mothers side), when he served in the warres of King
Edward the third, beyond the seas, together with this prophesie: that
the kinges which should be annoynted therewith should bee the
champions of the Church. Duke Henry delivered this oyle in a golden
violl to Prince Edward, the eldest sonne of King Edward the third,
who locked up the same in a barred chest within the Tower, with
intent to be annoynted therewith when he should bee crowned king.
But the prince dying before his father, it remained there, eyther not
remembred or not regarded, untill this present yeere wherein the king,
being upon his voyage into Ireland, and making diligent search for
the jewels and monumentes of his progenitours, found this violl and
prophesie; and understanding the secret, was desirous to be anoynted
againe with that oyle. But the Archbishop of Canterbury perswaded
him that both the fact was unlawfull, and the precedent unseene that
a king should bee anoynted twice. Whereupon he brake of that
purpose, and tooke the violl with him into Ireland. And [p. 98]
when hee yeelded himselfe at Flint, the Archbishoppe of Canterburye
demaunded it of him agayne, and dyd receave and reserve the same
untill the coronation of King Henrie, who was the first king of this
realme that was anoynted therewith.

I am not purposed to discourse, eyther of the authoritye or of the
certaintye of these prophesies, but wee may easily observe that the
greatest part of them eyther altogether fayled, or were fulfilled in
another sence then as they were commonly construed and taken.
During the raigne of King Henrie the fourth, execution by fire was
first put in practise within this realme, for controversies in poyntes of
religion; in any other extraordinarye matter hee did as much make
the Church champion, as shew himselfe a champion of the Church.
But afterwardes his successours were entytuled Defenders of the Fayth;
and howe in action they veryfied the same, I referre to remembraunce
and reporte of later times.

[III]

Now it had beene considered that the tytle which was derived to
King Henrie from Edmund, whome they surnamed Crouchbacke,
would bee taken but for a blynde and idle jest: for that it was notorious
that the sayd Edmund was neyther eldest sonne to King Henry the
thyrd (as it was plainely declared by an acte of parlament) nor yet a
misshapen and deformed person, but a goodly gentleman, and valiant
commaunder in the field, and so favoured of the king his father that
hee gave him both the heritages and honours of Simone Mountfort,
Earle of Leicester, of Ferrare, Earle of Darby, and of John, Barron of
Monmuthe, who to theyr owne ruine and destruction had desplaied

seditious ensignes against the king.[98] And further to advaunce him to the marriage of Blanch, Queen of Naverne, he created him the first Earle of Lancaster, and gave unto him the coun[p. 99]ty, castle and towne of Lancaster, with the forrestes of Wiresdale, Lounsdale, Newcastle beneath Linne, the manner, castle and forrest of Pickering, the manner of Scaleby, the towne of Gomecester, of Huntendone, &c., with many large priviledges and high titles of honour[99]

Therefore King Henry, upon the day of his Coronation, caused to be proclaimed that he claymed the kingdome of England, first by right of conquest; secondly because King Richard had resigned his estate, and designed him for his successour; lastly, because he was of the bloud royall, and next heyre male unto King Richard.

'Haeres malus indeed,' quoth Edmund Mortimer, Earle of March, unto his secret friends, 'and so is the pirate to the marchant, when hee despoyleth him of all that hee hath.' This Edmund was sonne to Roger Mortimer,[100] who was not long before[101] slaine in Ireland, and had been openly declared heyre apparent to the crowne, in case King Richard should dye without issue, as descended by his mother Philip from Lionell, Duke of Clarence, who was elder brother to John, Duke of Lancaster, King Henries father. And therefore the sayd Edmund thought himselfe, and in deed was, neerer heyre male to the succession of the crowne then hee that by colour of right clayming it, carried it by dynt of force.

But such was the condition of the tyme, that hee supposed it was vaine for him to stirre, where King Richard could not stand. Whereupon he dissembled, eyther that he saw his wrong, or that hee regarded it, and chose rather to suppresse his title for a time, then by untimely opposing himselfe to have it oppressed and depressed for ever. To this ende hee withdrewe himselfe farre from London, to his lordshippe of Wigmore, in the west partes of the realme, and there setled himselfe to a private and close life. Idlenes and vacancy from publike affaires he accompted a vertue, and a deepe point of wisedome to meddle with [p. 100] nothing, whereof no man was chargeable to yeelde a reckoning. In revenues he was meane, in apparell moderate, in company and traine not excessive (yet in all these honourable and according to his degree), so that they which esteemed men by outward

---

[98] The battle of Evesham (1265), at which Monfort was killed, reversed the fortunes of the barons struggling against the crown, 1263–7.

[99] A: 'homour.'

[100] Hayward seems here (as he certainly does below) to confuse the young Edmund (1391–1425), who succeeded as fifth earl of March and third earl of Ulster upon his father Roger's death in battle in Ireland in 1398, with his uncle, Roger's youngest brother, Sir Edmund de Mortimer (1376–1409). Roger may have been declared heir presumptive in 1385. His son and heir was now about nine years old.

[101] July 1398.

appearance only could see in him no great shew, eyther of wit and courage in his minde to be feared, or of wealth and honour in his estate to be envyed. And thus, whilest a greater enemy was feared, he passed unregarded, making himselfe safe by contempt, where nothing was so daungerous as a good opinion, and raking up those coales in obscuritie for a time, which shortly after set all the realme on fire.

King Henrie presently, after his coronation, created his eldest sonne Lord Henrie, being then about xiii. yeares of age, Prince of Wales, Duke of Cornewall, and Earle of Chester, and soone after he created him also Duke of Aquitaine.[102] Afterwards it was enacted, by consent of all the states of the realme assembled together in parlament, that the inheritance of the crownes and realmes of England and of Fraunce, and of all the dominions to them apperteyning, should be united and remaine in the person of King Henrie, and in the heires of his body lawfully begotten; and that Prince Henrie, his eldest sonne, should be his heyre apparant, and successour in the premisses; and if he should dye without lawfull issue, then they were entayled to his other sonnes successively in order, and to the heyres of their bodyes lawfully begotten.

The inheritance of the kingdome being in this sorte settled in King Henrie and in his line, it was mooved in the parlament what should be doone with King Richard. The Bishop of Caerliel,[103] who was a man learned and wise, and one that alwayes used both libertie and constancie in a good cause, in his secret judgement did never give allowance to these proceedings, yet dissembled his dislike, untill he might to some purpose declare it. Therefore, now being [p. 101] in place to be heard of all, and (by order of the house) to be interrupted by none, he rose up and with a bould and present spirit uttered his minde, as followeth:

'This question, right honourable lordes, concerneth a matter of great consequence and weight; the determining whereof will assuredly procure eyther safe quiet, or daungerous disturbance, both to our particular consciences and also to the common state. Therefore, before you resolve uppon it, I pray you call to your considerations these two things: First, whether King Richard be sufficiently deposed or no; secondly, whether King Henrie be with good judgement, or justice, chosen in his place. For the first point we are first to examine whether a king, being lawfully and fully instituted by any just title, may uppon imputation eyther of negligence or of tyrannie be deposed by his subjects. Secondly, what King Richard hath omitted in the one,

---

[102] Poitou and Aquitaine, after the peace of Brétigny (1360), were known as the Duchy of Guyenne. Guyenne, the ancient Aquitaine, had been conferred upon Gaunt in 1389; he was reconfirmed as duke of Guyenne in 1390.

[103] Thomas Merks.

or committed in the other, for which he should deserve so heavie judgement. I will not speake what may be doone in a popular state, or in a consular, in which although one beareth the name and honour of a prince, yet he hath not supreme power of majestie; but in the one, the people have the highest empire, in the other, the nobilitie and chiefe men of estate, in neyther, the Prince. Of the first sorte was the common wealth of the Lacedaemonians who, after the forme of governement which Licurgus framed, oftentimes fined, oftentimes fettered their kings, and sometimes condemned them to death. Such were also in Caesars time the petit kings of every citie in Fraunce, who were many times arreigned uppon life and death and (as Ambiorix, Prince of the Leodienses, confessed) had no greater power over the people then the people had over them. Of the second condition were the Romaine emperours at the first, of whome some, namely Nero and Maximinus, were openly condemned,[104] others were sodainelie [p. 102] surprised by judgement and authoritye of the senate. And such are nowe the emperours of Germany, whom the other princes, by their aristocraticall power, do not onely restrayne but sometimes also remoove from theyr imperiall state. Such are also the kinges of Denmarke and Sweveland, who are many times by the nobilitye dejected, eyther into pryson or into exile. Such likewise are the dukes of Venice, and of some other free states in Italy. And the chiefest cause for which Lewes, Earle of Flanders, was lately expelled from his place, was for drawing to himselfe cognisance in matters of life and death, which high power never pertayned to his dignitie.

'In these and such like governmentes, the prince hath not regall rights, but is himselfe subject to that power which is greater then his, whether it be in the nobility or in the common people. But if the soveraigne majesty be in the prince, as it was in the three first empires, and in the kingdomes of Judea and Israell, and is now in the kingdomes of England, Fraunce, Spaine, Scotland, Muscovia, Turky, Tartaria, Persia, Aethiopia, and almost all the kingdomes of Asia and Afrike, although for his vices he bee unprofitable to the subjectes, yea hurtfull, yea intollerable: yet can they lawfully neyther harme his person nor hazard his power, whether by judgement, or els by force. For neyther one nor all magistrates have any authority over the prince, from whome all authority is derived, and whose onely presence doeth silence and suspend all inferiour jurisdiction and power. As for force, what subjecte can attempt, or assist, or counsaile, or conceale violence

---

[104] Marginal note here: 'Tranquil. in Caligula. Tacitus, in proaemio.' From this point onward throughout this speech, *A* (like all the QQ) bears scattered but copious marginal references to texts, both scriptural and from classical antiquity, cited by the bishop. It is clear that for Hayward, Carlisle's oration amounted to a legal brief crafted on the civil law pattern.

against hys prince, and not incurre the high and heynous crime of treason?

'It is a common saying, 'thought is free;' free indeede from punishment of secular lawes, except by worde or [p. 103] deed it breake foorth into action. Yet the secret thoughts against the sacred majesty of a prince, without attempt, without endevour, have beene adjudged worthy of death; and some who, in auriculer confession have discovered their treacherous devises against the person of their prince, have afterwardes beene executed for the same. All lawes doe exempt a madde man from punishment, because theyr actions are not governed by theyr will and purpose; and the will of man being set aside, all his doings are indifferent; neyther can the body offend without a corrupt or erronious minde. Yet, if a mad man draw hys sword upon his king, it hath bin adjudged to deserve death. And least any man should surmise that princes, for the maintenance of theyr owne safety and soveraignety, are the onely authors of these judgementes, let us a little consider the patternes and preceptes of Holy Scripture. Nabuchadnezzer, King of Assiria, wasted all Palestine with fire and swoord, oppugned Hierusalem a long time, and at the last expugned it, slue the king, burnt the temple, tooke away the holy vesselles and treasure; the rest hee permitted to the cruelty and spoyl of his unmercifull soldiers, who defiled all places with rape and slaughter, and ruinated to the ground that flourishing citty. After the glut of this bloudy butchery, the people which remayned he led captive into Chaldaea, and there erected his golden image, and commaunded that they which refused to worship it should bee cast into a fierye furnace.

'What crueltye, what injustice, what impiety is comparable to this? And yet God calleth Nabuchadnezzer his servant, and promiseth him hyre and wages for his service. And the prophetes Jeremiah and Baruch[105] did wryte unto the Jews to praye for the lyfe of him, and of Baltasar hys sonne, that theyr dayes myght bee uppon earth as the dayes of heaven. And Ezechiel [p. 104] with bitter termes abhorreth the disloyalty of Zedechia, because he revolted from Nabuchadnezzer, whose homager and tributary he was. What shall we say of Saul? Did he not put all the priestes to execution, because one of them did relieve holy and harmelesse David? Did he not violently persecute that his most faithfull servant and dutiful sonne in law, during which pursuite, he fell twice into the power of David, who did not onely spare, but also protect the king, and reprooved the pretorian souldiers for their negligent watch, and was touched in heart for cutting away the lappe of his garment, and afterwards caused the messenger to be slaine, who

[105] Marginal notes clustered here: 'Ierem. 25. 9.; Ezech. 29. 18.; Ierm. 29. 7.; Baruch, 1. 11.'

upon request and for pitty had lent his hand (as he said) to help forward the voluntary death of that sacred king?[106]

'As for the contrary examples, as that of Jehu, who slue Jehoram and Ahazia, Kings of Israell and Juda: they were done by expresse oracle & revelation from God, and are no more set downe for our imitation then the robbing of the AEgyptians, or any other perticuler and priviledged commaundement. But in the generall precept, which all men must oridinarily follow, not onely our actions, but our speeches also, & our very thoughtes are strictly charged with duety and obedience unto princes, whether they be good or evill. The law of God ordaineth[107] that he which doth presumptuously against the ruler of the people shall dye; and the prophet David forbiddeth to touch the Lords anointed. 'Thou shalt not,' saith the Lord, 'rayle upon the judges, neither speake evill against the ruler of the people.' And the apostles do demaund further that even our thoughtes and soules bee obedient to higher powers. And, least any should imagine that they meant of good princes onely, they speake generally of all; and fur[p. 105]ther, to take away all doubt, they make expresse mention of the evill. For the power and authoritie of wicked princes is the ordinance of God; and therefore Christ told Pilate[108] that the power which he had was given him from above, and the prophet Esay calleth Cyrus, being a prophane and heathen prince, 'the Lords anoynted.'[109] For God stirreth up the spirit even of wicked princes to doe his will, and (as Jehoshaphat sayd to his rulers) they execute not the judgement of man, but of the Lord.[110] In regard whereof David calleth them gods,[111] because they have their rule and authority immedyatly from God, which if they abuse, they are not to bee adjudged by theyr subjects, for no power within theyr dominion is superior to theirs. But God reserveth them to the sorest tryall: 'Horribly and sodainly,' saith the wise man, 'will the Lord appeare unto them, and a hard judgement shall they have.'[112]

[106] Here the QQ show a more extensive marginal insert, offering further precedents from classical antiquity, the text of which is: 'So did *Domitian* put to death *Epaphroditus*, *Neroes* libertine, because he helped *Neroe* (although in love) to kill himselfe. So did *Severus* kill all the killers of *Pertinax* his predecessour: and likwise *Vitellius* did put to death all the murtherers of *Galba*. *Theophilus* Emperour of Grecia caused all those to be slaine, who had made his father emperour, [by] killing *Leo Arminius*. And *Alexander* the great put to cruell execution those that had slaine *Darius*, his mighty and mortall enemy.'

[107] Marginal notes as follows: 'Deut. 17. 12.; Psal, 105; Exod. 22. 28.; Act. 23. 5.; Rom. 13. 1. 13.; Tit. 3. 1.; 1 Pet, 2. 13, 14, 17; 1 Tim. 2, 2.'

[108] Marginal notes: 'Rom. 13. 2.; John 19. 11.'

[109] Marginal note: 'Cap. 45. 1.'

[110] Marginal notes: '2. Chro. 36. 22.; 2. Chron. 19.6.'

[111] Marginal note: 'Psal. 28.'

[112] Marginal note: 'Sap. 6.'

'The law of God commaundeth that the childe should be put to death for any contumely done unto the parents. But what if the father be a robber? If a murtherer? If for all excesse of villanyes, odious and execrable both to God and man? Surely he deserveth the highest degree of punishment, and yet must not the sonne lift up his hand against him, for no offence is so great as to be punished by parricide. But our country is dearer unto us then our parentes, and the prince is *pater patriae*, the father of our country,[113] and therefore more sacred and deere unto us then our parentes by nature, and must not be violated, how imperious, how impious soever hee bee. Doth he commaund or demaund our persons or our purses, we must not shunne for the one, nor shrinke for the other, for (as Nehemiah saith)[114] 'Kinges have dominion over the bodyes and over the cattle of their subjectes, at their pleasure.' Doth he enjoine those actions which are contrary to the lawes of God? We must neyther wholy obey, nor violently resist, but with a constant courage submit our selves to all manner of punishment, and shewe our [p. 106] subjection by enduring, and not performing. Yea, the Church hath declared it to bee an heresie to holde that a prince may be slaine or deposed by his subiects, for any disorder or default, eyther in life or else in government.[115] There will be faultes so long as there are men, and as wee endure with patience a barren yeere, if it happen, and unseasonable weather, and such other defectes of nature, so must wee tollerate the imperfections of rulers, and quietlye expecte eyther reformation, or else a change.

'But alas, good King Richard, what such cruelty? What such impiety hath he ever committed? Examine rightly those imputations which are layde against him, without any false circumstance of aggravation, and you shall finde nothing objected, eyther of any truth or of great moment. It may bee that many errours and oversightes have escaped him, yet none so grievous to be termed tyranny, as proceeding rather from unexperienced ignorance, or corrupt counsaile, then from any naturall and wilful mallice. Oh, howe shall the world bee pestered with tirantes, if subjects may rebell uppon every pretence of tyranny? Howe many good princes shall daylye bee suppressed by those by whome they ought to bee supported? If they leavy a subsedy, or any other texation, it shall be claimed oppression; if they put any to death for trayterous attemptes against theyr persons, it shall be exclaymed cruelty; if they doe any thing against the lust and liking of the people, it shall bee proclaimed tyranny.

---

[113] Marginal note: 'Quintil in declam.; Cic. offic. lib. 1.'

[114] Marginal note: 'Nehem. 9. 37.'

[115] Marginal notes: 'Alphons. a cast in lib. de haeresi. in verb. Tyrannus. Dominie.; Soto lib. 5. de just. et jur. q. 1. artic. 3.'

'But let it be, that without authority in us, or desert in him, King Richard must be deposed: Yet what right had the Duke of Lancaster to the crowne? or what reason have we, without his right, to give it to him? If hee make title as heyre unto King Richard, then must he yet stay untill King Richards death, for no man can succeed as heyre to one that [p. 107] liveth. But it is well knowne to all men who are not eyther wilfully blinde or grossely ignorant, that there are some now alive, lineally descended from Lionell, Duke of Clarence, whose offspring was by judgement of the high court of parlament, holden the viii. yeere of the raigne of King Richard,[116] declared next successour to the crowne in case King Richard should die without issue. Concerning the tytle from Edmund Crouchbacke, I will passe it over, seeing the authors thereof are become ashamed of so absurde abuse, both of theyr owne knowledge and our credulity, and therefore all the clayme is now made, by right of conquest, by the cession and graunt of King Richard, and by the generall consent of all the people. It is a bad wooll that can take no colour: but what conquest can a subjecte pretend against his soveraigne, where the warre is insurrection, and the victory high and heynous treason? As for the resignation which King Richard made, being a pent prisoner for the same cause, it is an acte exacted by force, and therefore of no force and validity to binde him. And seeing that by the lawes of this land the king alone cannot alienate the auncient jewels and ornaments pertaining to the crowne, surely hee cannot give away the crowne it self, and there-withall the kingdome.

'Neyther have we any custome that the people at pleasure should electe theyr king. But they are alwayes bound unto him who by right of bloud is next successour; much lesse can they confirme and make good that title which is before, by violence, usurped. For nothing can then be freely doone, when liberty is once restrained by feare. So did Scilla, by terrour of his legions, obtayne the lawe of Velleia to bee made, whereby hee was created dictator for fourescore yeeres. And by like impression of feare, Caesar caused the law Servia to be pro-mulged, by which he was made perpetuall dictator. But both these lawes were afterwardes adjudged void. As for the deposing of King Edward the 2., it is no more [p. 108] to be urged[117] then the poysoning of King John, or the murdering of any other good and lawfull prince: we must live according to lawes, and not to examples. And yet the kingdome was not then taken from the lawfull successour. But if we looke backe to times lately past, we shall finde that these titles were more stronge in King Stephen, then they are in the Duke of Lancaster.

---

[116] 1385.

[117] A: '... Edward the 2. is no more to be urged ...,' a listed 'faulte.'

For King Henry the first, being at large liberty, neyther restrained in body nor constrained in minde, had appointed him to succeed (as it was uppon good credite certainly affirmed). The people assented to this designement, and thereupon, without feare and without force, he was anoynted king, and obtained full possession of the realme. Yet Henry (sonne of the Earle of Anjowe) having a neerer right by his mother to the crowne (notwithstanding his father was a stranger & himselfe borne beyond the seas), raysed such rough warres upon King Stephen that there was noe end of spoyling the goods and spilling the bloud of the unhappy people, besides the ruynes and deformities of many cities and holdes, untill his lawful inheritance was to him assured. It terrifieth me to remember how many florishing empires and kingdomes have bin by meanes of such contentions eyther torne in peeces with detestive division, or subdued to forren princes, under pretence of assistaunce and ayde. And I neede not repeate howe sore this realme hath heertofore beene shaken with these severall mischieves; and yet neyther the examples of other countries, nor the miseries of our own, are sufficient to make us beware.

'O English men, worse bewtiched than the foolish Galathians, our unstayed mindes and restlesse resolutions doe nothing els but hunt after our owne harmes. No people have more hatred abroad, and none lesse quiet at home. In other countries the swoord of invasion hath been shaken against us; in our owne land the fire of insurrection hath bin kindled among us. And what are these innovasions, but whet[p. 109]stones to sharpen the one, and bellowes to blowe up the other?

'Certainely, I feare that the same will happen unto us which Aesopp fableth to have been fallen unto the frogges: who, beeing desirous to have a king, a beame was given unto them, the first fall whereof did put them in some feare, but when they saw it lye still in the streame, they insulted thereon with great contempt, and desired a king of quicker courage. Then was sent unto them a storke which, stalking among them with stately steps, continually devoured them. The mildenesse of King Richard hath bred in us this scorne, interpreting it to be cowardise and dulness of nature. The next heyre is likewise rejected. I will not say that wyth greater courage we shall finde greater cruelty, but if eyther of these shall heerafter be able to set up theyr side, and bring the matter to tryall by armes, I do assuredly say that which part soever shall carry the fortune of the field, the people both wayes must goe to wracke.

'And thus have I declared my minde concerning this question, in more wordes then your wisedom, yet fewer than the weight of the cause doth require, and doe boldly conclude that wee have neyther power nor policy, eyther to depose King Richard, or to elect Duke

Henrie in his place; that King Richard remaineth still our soveraigne prince, and therefore it is not lawfull for us to give judgement upon him; that the duke whom you call king hath more offended against the king and the realme, then the king hath done, eyther against him or us. For being banished the realme for ten yeeres by the king and his counsaile (amongst whome his owne father was chiefe), and sworne not to returne againe without speciall lycense, he hath not onely violated his oath, but with impious armes disturbed the quiet of the land, and dispossessed the kyng from his royall estate, and now demaundeth judgement against his person, without offence proved, or defence heard. If this injury and this perjury doth nothing move us, yet let [p. 110] both our private and common dangers somwhat withdraw us from these violent proceedings.'

This speach was diverslie taken, as men were diversly affected betweene feare, hope and shame. Yet the most parte did make shew for King Henrie and thereupon the bishop was presently attached by the Earle Marshall, and committed to prison in the Abbey of S. Albones. Whose counsaile and conjecture then contemned, was afterwardes better thought upon, partly in the life time of King Henrie, during whose raigne almost no yeere passed without great slaughters and executions, but more especially in the times succeeding, when within the space of xxxvi. yeares, twelve set battailes upon this quarrell were fought within the realme by English men only and more then foure score princes of the royall bloud slaine by one another.

Then it was concluded that King Richard should be kept in a large prison, with all manner of princely maintenance, and if any persons should conspire to reare warre for his deliverance, that he should be the first man who should suffer death for that attempt. Then the actes of the parlament holden at Westminster in the xi. yeare of King Richard were revived, and the parlament houlden the xxi. yeare of King Richard was wholy repealed.[118] And they who were attainted by that parlament were restored againe to their fame and honour, and to their landes without suing lyuerie, and to such goods whereof the king was not answered, except the rents and issues which had beene received out of their lands in the meane time. Hereupon Richard, Earle of Warwicke, was delivered out of prison, and the Earle of Arundelles sonne recovered his inheritance. Many others also that were banished or imprisoned by King Richard were then fullye restored againe to their countrie, libertie and estate.

It was further provided that none of those which came in ayde of King Henrie against King Richard should for [p. 111] that cause be

---

[118] I.e., the acts of the 'Merciless' Parliament (1388) supplanted those of Sept. 1397, when Richard had moved against Warwick, Gloucester and Arundel.

impeached or troubled. Also, the king gave to the Earle of Westmerland the countie of Richmond, and to the Earle of Northumberland
he gave the Ile of Man, to be houlden of him by the service of bearing
the sworde wherewith he entred into England. Divers other of his
followers he advaunced to offices of highest place and charge, some
upon judgement and for desert, but most part to win favour, and
perhappes projecting a plot for friends, if times should change. For in
many actions men take more care to prevent revenge, then to leade
an innocent and harmlesse life.

It was further agreed that the procurers of the death and murther
of Thomas, late Duke of Gloucester, should be searched out and
severelie punished. And judgement was given against the appellants
of the Earle of Warwicke and the Earle of Arundell, that the Dukes
of Aumerle, Sussex, and Exeter, the Marquesse of Dorset, and Earle
of Gloucester, who were present, should loose their degree of honour
for them and their heyres; that they should likewise loose all the
castles, mannors, lordshippes, &c. then in their hands which sometimes apperteined to those whom they did appeale, and that all the
letters patents and charters which they had concerning the same
should be surrendered into the Chancerie, and there be cancelled;
that for all other their castles, mannors, lordships, possessions and
liberties, they should be at the grace and mercie of the king; that they
should give no liveries, nor keepe any retinue of men, but onely such
officers as were meerelie necessarie for their degree; that if any of them
should adhere to Richard, the deposed king, in giving him ayde or
encouragement against the judgement of his deposition, then he should
incurre the paines and forfeitures of high treason.

And because it was a clamorous complaint among the common
people that many officers had committed greevous extortions and
wrongs, eyther by the open maintenance or secret connivence of these
lords: [p. 112] first, those officers were remooved, and that corruption
taken away with integritie, which briberie had wrought in placing
(for money) men of bad qualitie in high degrees of office and service.
Then, proclamations were made that if any man had been oppressed
by these lords, or by any officers under them, he should proove his
complaint, and receive recompence. It was made a question whether
it was not meete that these noble men should be put to death. The
importunitie of the people and the perswasion of many great men
drew that way, but policie was against it, and especially the opinion
of clemencie, which seemed needfull to the setling of a new risen state.

In this parlament also, the Lorde Fitzwater appealed the sayd Duke
of Aumerle, sonne to the Duke of Yorke, upon points of high treason.
Likewise, the Lord Morley appealed John Montacute, Earle of Salisburie, and moe then twentie other appeilants waged battaile. But the

king, purposing to laye the foundation of his realme by favour, and not by force, gave pardon and restitution alike to all, uppon sureties and band for their alleageance. And in a sweet and moderate oration, he admonished and, as it were, entreated the one part, that ould griefes and grudges should not be renued, but buried together with the memorie of former times, wherein men were forced to doe many things against their mindes. The other part he desired to be more regardfull of their actions afterward, and for the time past, rather to forget that ever they were in fault, then to remember that they were pardoned. No punishment was laide uppon any, save onely the Earle of Salisburie and the Lord Morely, who had beene in especiall grace and favour with King Richard. These two were committed to prison, but at the sute of their friends they were soone released. The rest the king received freelye to favour, but most especially the Duke of Aumerle, and the Duke of Excester, Lord Governour of Calice. The Duke of Aumerle was cousen germane to both the kings. John Hol[p. 113]land, Duke of Exceter, was halfe brother to King Richard, and brother in lawe to King Henrie, whose sister, the Lady Elizabeth, he had taken to wife. The greatest matter that was enforced against them was their loyaltie unto King Richard (a grievous crime among rebels), because they did not onlie stomacke and storme at his dejection, but stirre also more than others, and assaye to raise forces on his behalfe. The dukes bouldly confessed the accusation, that they were indeed unfortunately faithfull to King Richard, but as those who are once false doe seldome afterwards proove soundly firme, so they that have shewed themselues true to one prince may the better be trusted by any other. The king did rather admit this as a defense, then remit it as a fault, affirming that such examples were not to be misliked of princes. So he entred with them into great termes of friendship, and put them in place neerest his person, endeavoring by courtesie and liberalitie to make them fast and faithful unto him. This fact was diverslie enterpreted, according to mens several dispositions, some admiring the kings moderation, others disliking and disallowing his confidence. And indeed, although these meanes have to this purpose prevailed with some, yet the common course may move us commonly to conjecture that there is little assurance in reconciled enemies, whose affections (for the most part) are like unto glasse which, beeing once cracked, can never bee made otherwise then crazed and unsound.

Furthermore, to qualifie all prejudice and hard opinion which other princes might chaunce to conceive, King Henrie dispatched embassadours to divers countries neere unto him, to make it knowne by what title, and by what fauour and desire of all the people, he atteyned the kingdome. To the court of Rome hee sent John Trevenant, Bishop of Hereford, Sir John Cheney, Knight, and John Cheney,

Esquire; into Fraunce hee sent Walter Shirlowe, Bishop of Durham, and Lord Thomas Pearcy, Earle of Worcester; into Spaine [p. 114) he sent John Trevor, Bishop of S. Assaphes, and Sir William Parre; and into Almaine he sent the Bishop of Bangor, and certaine other. Most of these princes (as in a matter which little concerned eyther their honour or their harme) seemed eyther not to regarde what was doone, or easely to bee perswaded that all was doone well. But Charles, King of Fraunce, was so distempered at this dishonourable dealing with his sonne in lawe King Richard, that by violence of his passion he fell into his oulde panges of phrensie. And at the last, by helpe of phisike returning to the sobrietie of his sences, he purposed to make sharpe warre upon that disloyall people (as he termed them) for this injurie against their lawfull and harmlesse prince. Many noble men of Fraunce shewed themselves verye forwarde to enter into the service, but especially the Earle of Saint Paule, who had maryed King Richards halfe sister. So letters of defiance were sent into England, and great preparation was made for the warre.

Likwise, the newes of these novelties much abashed the Aquitanes (who were at that time under the English subjection) and plunged their thoughts in great perplexities. Some were grieved at the infamous blemish of the English nation, who had disteyned their honour with the spot of such disloyall dealing. Others feared the spoyle of their goods and oppression of their liberties by the Frenchmen, against whose violence they suspected that the realme of England, beeing distracted into civill factions, eyther would not attend, or should not be able to beare them out. But the citizens of Burdeaux were chiefly anguished in respect of King Richard, partlie fretting at his injury, and partlie lamenting his infortunitie, because he was borne and brought uppe within theyr cittie. And thus in the violence, some of theyr anger, some of theyr grief, and some of their feare, in this sort they did generally complaine.

[P. 115]'O, good God,' said they, 'where is the world become? Saintes are turned to serpents, and doves into divels. The English nation, which hath been accompted fierce onely against theyr foes, and alwayes faithfull to their friends, are now become both fierce and faithlesse against their lawfull and loving prince, and have most barbarouslie betrayed him. Who would ever have thought that Christians, that civill people, that any men would thus have violated all religion, all lawes, and all honest and orderlie demeanure? And, although the heavens blush at the view, and the earth sweat at the burthen of so vile a villanie, and all men proclaime and exclaime open shame and confusion against them, yet they neither feele the horrour, nor shrinke at the shame, nor feare the revenge, but stand upon tearmes, some of defence for the lawfulnesse of their dealing, and some of excuse for the necessitie. Well, let them be able to blinde the worlde, and to resist mans revenge; yet shall they never be able to escape eyther the sight or vengeance of almightie God, which we daily expect, and earnestly desire to be powred upon them.

'Alas, good King Richard, thy nature was too gentle, and thy governement too milde for so stiffe and stubborne a people. What king wil ever repose any trust in such unnaturall subjectes, but fetter them with lawes, as theeves are with irons? What cariage heereafter can recover theyr credite? What time wyll bee sufficient to blotte out this blemish? What other action could they have doone, more joyfull to theyr enemyes, more woefull to theyr friendes, and more shamefull to themselves? Oh, corruption of times! Oh, conditions of men!'

The Frenchmen were nothing discontented at this discontentment of the of the Aquitanes, supposing that opportunitie was then offered to get into theyr possession the Duchie of Guian,[119] if eyther power or pollicie were thereto applyed. Hereupon Lewes, Duke of Burbon, came downe [p. 116] to Angiers, who from thence sent many messengers to the chiefe cities of Guian and, by faire speeches and large promises, solicited the people to change alleageance. On the contrarie side, Sir Robert Knowles, Lieutenant of Guian, endevored with all diligence to represse the mutinous, to staye the doubtfull, to confirme the good, and to reteyne all in order and obedience. But he profited very little: whether by the weakenesse of his owne arme, or stiffe necke of the people, it is not certainely assured. Neither did the Duke of Burbone much prevaile, when it was considered how ponderous the yoake of Fraunce was, above the English subjection. For all men were well acquainted with what tributes and taxations the Frenchmen were charged, having in everye countrie lieutenants and treasurours assigned, the one to drawe the bloud, the other the substance of the slavish subjects, whose crueltie and covetousnesse laide hold without exception uppon all, the one tormenting by force, and the other undooing by lawe. Thus stood the Aquitanes uppon tickle tearmes betweene obedience and revolt, as a shippe which the winde driveth one way, and the tide another. Desirous they were to displease the English, but loath to endanger and undoe themselves.

Uppon advertisment whereof, King Henrie sent into Guian the Lord Thomas Percie, Earle of Worcester, whom he knew to bee faithfull unto him, and expert in matters of charge, having in his companie a strong and serviceable band of souldiers. Who, not by unseasonable exprobating their fault, but by reason convincing it, partlye with his wisdome and credite so perswaded, and partlye with his authoritie and forces so terrified the wavering people, that he

[119] Guyenne.

wanne them to his opinion, and confirmed them in their alleageance: the graver sorte with respect of dutie and faith, the rest with regarde and feare of daunger. Then hee received oathes of obedience unto King Henrye, and planted certaine strong garrisons in places of [p. 117] chiefe import, without molestation if they remained quiet, and yet of force to represse them if they should rebell. This done, he returned againe into England, where he shewed an excellent example of moderation in seeming rather to have found then to have made the Aquitanes dutifull subjectes.

No sooner could this stir be stinted, but another more daungerous and desperate did foorthwith arise. For diverse noble men who eyther had dissembled, or did repent, the furtherance that they used to the advauncement of King Henrie, did conspire together to compasse his destruction. The hystories of that time doe vary concerning the causes of this conspiracy, whether it were for favour to King Richard, as the nature of man is inclinable to behold sodaine misfortune with a pittifull eye; or for envy to King Henrie, as commonly wee can endure excessive fortune no where so little as in those that have beene in equall degree with our selves; or whether upon dishonours received in the late parlament; or upon disdaine to see others goe before them in the princes favour; many sought to revenge theyr unjust anger with lewde disloyaltye. Likewise, it is not assuredly knowne by what meanes the workers thereof were drawne together, and the secret devises of some imparted to the rest: whether one of them did perswade another to enter into the action, or whether all were induced by the same unconstant disposition and light account of faith, which being once falsed to King Richard was afterwardes, uppon every light discontentment, lyttle respected to any. But concerning these matters, the most current report is this:

There was at that time an Abbot of Westminster, one that applyed his studies, not as the most part, to cloake idlenesse and slouth under the glorious tytle of religion, but to enable himselfe for counsaile and direction in publique affayres; who, for the generall opinion of his wisedome [p. 118] and integritie, was in good favour and credit with King Richard, and did accompany him in his last voyage into Ireland.

This Abbot called to his remembrance a speach which hee heard once fall from King Henrie, when hee was but Earle of Derbie, and not yet come to any great stayednesse eyther in yeares or judgement, that princes had too little, and religious men too much.

At that time the riches of the Church were growne so great, that many began to looke upon them with an envious eye; but, least covetousnesse should shew it selfe with open face, policie was pretended, and the excesse thought daungerous both to the king and also to the cleargie, as verie like to cause want to the one, and wantonnesse in the other.

Heereupon many billes had beene put uppe in the parlaments houlden in the reigne of King Richard, that provision might be made to represse the increase of religious possessions, namely, that inquisition and redresse might be had against such religious persons as, under the licence to purchase ten pounds yearlie, did purchase fourescore, or a hundred pounds; and also against such religious persons as caused their villaines to take to their wives free women inheritable, whereby the landes came to those religious mens hands. Yea, it was mooved in open parlament that the king should seaze into his hands all the temporall livings of religious houses, as beeing rather a burthen then a benefite unto religion.

Uppon these and the like petitions, the Archbishop of Canterburie and the Archbishop of Yorke, for themselves and the cleargie of their provinces, were oftentimes compelled to make their solemne protestations in open parlament, that if any thing were attempted in restraint of the libertie of the Church, they would in no wise assent, but utterlie withstand the same; the which their protesta[p. 119]tions they required to be enrouled.

So, partly upon love to King Richard, and partly upon feare least King Henry would bee as ready to invade, as hee was to enveigh against the richesse of religious houses, this Abbot was the first man that blew the coales, and put fewell to the fire of this confederacy. And first hee observed a farre off, then hee searched more neerely and narrowly (and yet warely, too) howe the myndes of certaine noble men were affected, or rather infected, agaynst King Henrie, tempering his speeches in such sorte that if matters sorted to his minde, hee myght take them upon him; if his courses were crossed, he might cleerely disclayme them. At last hee invited to his house, uppon a daye in Michaelmas terme, those whome he had sounded to bee moste sound for his purpose, the chiefe of whome were such as in the parliament before had in some sorte beene touched in reputation, although by pardon and reconcilement the harme did seeme to bee closed up. Theyr names were: John Holland, Duke of Exceter, of whome mention hath beene made before; Thomas Holland, his bro-thers sonne, Duke of Surrey; Edward, Duke of Aumerle; John Mon-tacute, Earle of Salisbury; Hugh Spencer, Earle of Glocester; John,[120] Bishoppe of Caerliele; Sir Thomas Blunt; and Magdalen, one of King Richards chappell, who in all poyntes, both of feature and favour, so neerely resembled King Richard that the lordes dissembled after-wardes that hee was King Richard indeed.

---

[120] Actually, Thomas (Merks), Bishop of Carlisle 1397-9.

These and some others were highly feasted by the Abbot, and after dinner they withdrewe themselves into a secret chamber to counsaile. Here the Duke of Exceter, who was moste hotly bent eyther to restore or to revenge the cause of his deposed brother, declared unto the rest the alleageance they had sworne unto King Richard, the honours and prefermentes whereunto they [p. 120] were by him advaunced; that therefore they were bounde both in conscience by the one, and in kindnesse by the other, to take his part against all men. That King Henry, contrary to both, had dispoyled him of his royall dignity, and unjustly possessed himselfe thereof, whilest they stood looking on, and shewed neyther the obedience of subjectes, nor love of friendes, as though they were men who knewe to doe anything better then to defend, and if neede were, to dye for theyr lawfull prince and loving patron. That King Henrie by violent invading, or fraudulent insinuating himselfe into, the kingdome of his naturall and leige prince, was but a tyrant, and usurper, and such a one as it was lawfull for any man, by any meanes, to throw downe, without respect whether he were a good man or evill; for it is lawfull for no man upon pretence and shewe of goodnesse, to draw soveraignty unto himselfe. That the lawes and examples of best governed common wealthes did not onely permit this action, but highly honoured it with statues and garlandes, and tytles of nobility, and also rewarded it with all the wealth of the suppressed tyrant. That this enterprize would be very profitable, and almost necessarie, to the common wealth, by extinguishing those warres which the Scots menaced, the Frenchmen prepared, and the Welshmen had already begun upon this occasion and quarrell. That he did not distrust but it might be accomplished by open armes, but he thought it more sure for them, and for the common wealth more safe, to put first in proofe some secret policie. And to that purpose he devised that a solemne justes should be challenged, to be kept at Oxforde in Christmasse holydayes, betweene him and twentie on his part, and the Earle of Salisburie and twentie on his part, to which King Henrie should be invited. And when he was most intentive in regarding their militarie disport, he should sodainely be surprized by men which without suspition might at that time be assembled, both for number and preparation sufficient for the [p. 121] exployt, and thereby King Richard presently bee restored, both to his liberty and to his state.

This devise was no sooner uttered, then allowed and applauded of the rest of the confederates. And so, resolving upon the enterprize, they tooke an oath upon the Evangelistes, the one to be true and secret to the other, even to the houre and point of death. The lords also made an indenture sextipartite, wherein they bound themselves to doe their best assay for the death of the one king and deliverance of the other. This they sealed and subscribed, and delivered to every lord a counter pane of the same; and further, they concluded what forces should be gathered, by whome, howe they should be ordred and placed, and to whose trust the execution should be committed.

When all thinges were thus contrived, and theyr hungry, ambitious mindes were well filled with the vaine winds of hope and desire, the Duke of Exceter came to the king at Windsore, and desired him, for the love that he bare to the noble feates of chevalry, that he would vouchsafe to honour with his presence the martiall exercise that was appointed betweene him and the Earle of Salisbury, and to be the judge of theyr performances if any controversie should arise. The king, supposing that to be intended indeed which was pretended in shew, easily yeelded to his request. The Duke, supposing his purpose now halfe performed, departed to his house, and so did the other confederates, where they busily bestirred themselves in raysing men, and preparing horse and armour for the accomplishment of thys acte.

When the Dutchesse of Exceter, King Henries sister, perceived the drift of the devise, and saw that the duke was uppon his journey, alas, good lady, how was shee distracted in minde, with a sharpe conflicte of her conceiptes? [p. 122] One waye she was mooved with nature towardes her brother, another waye shee was more strongly stirred, with love towardes her lord and husband; and both wayes shee was devided in dutie. 'And what,' sayd shee, 'is this love then against nature? Or above it? Shall I bee undutifull to my prince? Or is no dutie comparable to the dutie of a wife? Heigh, ho. In what perplexities (wretched woman) am I plunged, to see my two deerest friends in this case of extremitie, that (it is doubtfull which but) certainlie one must be ruined by the other.' Heerewith such a shower of teares streamed downe her cheekes that it drowned her speech, and stopped the passage of further complaint. Which when the duke espyed, he stepped unto her and, seazing softlie uppon her hand, used these wordes:

'What, Besse? Is it kindnesse to me, or kindred to your brother, that thus hath set your eyes on floate? Content your selfe, woman, for whatsoever the event shall be, it cannot bee evill to you, nor worse to me then now it is. For if my purpose prevaile, and my brother bee restored againe to his crowne, both of us shall be sure never to decline. If it bee prevented, and your brother continue still in his estate, no harme shall be doone unto you, and I shall be then sure of that distruction which I doe now continually dread, the feare whereof in expecting, is a greater torment then the paine in suffering.' When hee had thus saide, hee kissed her, and so leaving her to the torture of a thousand thornie thoughts, he tooke his jorney towards Oxforde, with a great company both of archers and horsemen. There he found all the rest of his complices, well armed and banded, except onely the Duke of Aumerle.

The king also, hearing that both the challengers and defendants were in a readinesse, determined the daye following to ride to Oxforde, according to his promise and appointment.

[p. 123] Now the confederates much marvailed at the stay of the Duke of Aumerle: some onely blamed his slacknesse, others began to suspect it; every man conjectured as he was diversly affected betweene confidence and feare. And in this confusion of opinions, they sent unto him in poste, to knowe the certaine truth. Before the messenger came to the duke, he was departed from Westminster towards Oxford, not the direct way, but went first to see his father the Duke of York, and carried with him his counterpane of the indenture of confederacy. As they sate at dinner, the father espied it in his bosome, and demaunded what it was. The sonne humbly craved pardon, and said that it nothing touched him. 'By S. George,' quoth the father, 'but I will see it.' And so, whether upon a precedent jealousie, or some present cause of suspition, he tooke it away from him by force. When he perceived the contents, he sodainely arose from the table, & with great fierce-nesse both of countenance and speech, uttered to his sonne these words:

'I see, traytor, that idlenesse hath made thee so wanton and mutin-ous that thou playest with thy faith, as children doe with stickes. Thou hast been once already faithlesse to King Richard, & now again art false to King Henrie, so that like the fish Sepia, thou troublest all the waters wherein thou livest. Thou knowest that in open parlament I became suertie and pledge for thy alleageance, both in bodye and goods. And can neither thy dutie, nor my desert, restreine thee from seeking my destruction? In faith, but I will rather helpe forward thine.' With that, hee commaunded his horses to bee made readie, and presentlye tooke his jorneye towardes Windsore, where the king then laye.

The Duke of Aumerle had no time eyther to consulte with his friends, or to consider with himselfe what was best to bee doone. But, taking advise uppon the sodaine, [p. 124] he mounted likewise on horsebacke, and posted towardes Windsore another way. It was no neede to force him forwarde; his youthfull bloud and his sodaine daunger were in steed of two winges, to keep his horse in Pegasus pace, so that he came to Windsore, & was alighted at the castell, before his stiffe, aged father could come neere. Then hee entred the gates, and caused them to be surely locked, and tooke the keyes into his owne hands, pretending some secret cause for which he would deliver them unto the king. When he came in presence, he kneeled downe and humblie craved of the king mercie and forgivenesse. The king demaunded, 'For what offence?' Then, with a confused voice and sad countenance, casting downe his eyes as altogether abashed, partly with feare of his daunger, and partly with shame of his discredit, he declared unto the king all the manner of the conspiracie. The king seemed neither rashlie to beleeve, nor negligentlie to distrust the dukes report; neyther stood it with pollicie to enterteine the discoverie with any hard and violent usage. Therefore, with gracious speeches he comforted the duke: 'And if this bee true,' sayd he, 'we pardon you; if it be feined, at your extreame perrill be it.'

By this time the Duke of Yorke was rapping at the castle gates; and, being admitted to the kings presence, he delivered to him the endenture of confederacie which hee had taken from his sonne. When the king had redde it, and was thereby perswaded of the trueth of the matter, he was not a little disquieted in minde, complaining of the unconstant disposition of those men, whom neyther crueltie (he said) could make firme to King Richard, nor clemencie to him, but uppon dislike of every present government, they were desirous of any change. So, being possessed of deeper thoughts then to gaze uppon games, he layde his jorney aside, and determined to attend at Windsor what course [p. 125] his enemies would take, and which waye they would set forward, knowing right well that in civill tumults, an advised patience and opportunitie well taken are the only weapons of advantage, and that it is a speciall point of wisdome to make benefit of the enemyes follie. In the meane time, he directed his letters to the Earle of Northumberland, his High Constable, and to the Earle of Cumberland, his High Marshall, and to others his most assured friends, concerning these sodaine and unexpected accidents.

The confederates all this time, hearing nothing of the Duke of Aumerle, and seeing no preparation for the kings comming, were out of doubt that theyr treason was betraied. And now, considering that once before they had beene pardoned, the guilt of this their rebellion excluded them from all hope of further mercie. Whereupon they became desperate, and so resolved to prosecute that by open armes, wherein their privie practises had failed. And first, they apparrelled Magdalen (a man very like to King Richard both in stature and countenance, and of yeares not disagreeable) in princely attire, and gave foorth that hee was King Richard, and that eyther by favour or negligence of his keepers, he was escaped out of prison, and desired the faith and ayde of his loving subjects. Then they determined to dispatche messengers to Charles, King of Fraunce, to desire his helpe and assistance on the behalfe of his sonne in lawe, if need should require.

The common people, which commonlie are soone changeable, and on the sodaine as prone to pittie as they were excessively cruell, most earnestlie wished the enlargement of King Richard and, earnestly wishing, did easely beleeve it. In which imaginarie conceit, being otherwise men of no deepe search, the presence of Magdalene most stronglie confirmed them. And so, eyther upon ignorance of truth, or delight in trouble, they joyned themselves in great troops [p. 126] to the lords, desiring nothing more then to be the meanes whereby King Richard should be restored, as in a manner resuming their first affections and humors towards him.

Then the lords of this association with great force, but with greater fame, as the manner is of matters unknowne, advanced forward in battaile arraye towards Windsore against King Henrie, as against an enemie of the common state, having in theyr company above fortie thousand armed men. The king, upon intelligence of theyr approache, secretlye with a few horse, the next Sunday night after newyeres day departed from Windsore to the Tower of London, and the same night, before it was daye, the confederates came to the castle of Windsore, where, missing their expected praye, they stood doubtfull and devided in opinions which waye to bend their course. Some advised them, with all speede to follow the king to London, and not to leave him any leave and libertie to unite an armie against them; that winter was no let but in idle and peaceable times; that in civill discentions nothing is more safe than speede, and greater advantage alwayes groweth by dispatching, then deferring; that whilest some were in feare, some in doubt, and some ignorant, the citie, yea the realme, might easilye be possessed; and that many armies whose furie at the first rush could not be resisted, by delayes did weare out and waste to nothing. Others, who would seeme to bee considerate and wise, but in verye deede were noe better then dastardes, perswaded rather to set King Richard first at libertie, for if their counterfeiting should be discovered before they possessed themselves of his person, the people undoubtedly would fall from them, to the certaine confusion of them all. Hereuppon they gave over the pursuite, and retired to Colebrooke, and there delayed out the time of dooing in deliberating, beeing neyther couragiouslye quicke, nor considerately stayed, but faintlie and fearefullye shrincking [p. 127] backe. And when they once beganne to relent, they decreased every daye more and more, both in power and in hope.

King Henrie, the next morning, after hee was come to the Tower, sent to the maior of the citie to put souldiours in armes for his assistance, who presentlye presented unto him three thousand archers and three thousand bill men, besides those that were appointed for defence of the citie. The king spent upon him many good speeches, and liberally loaded him with promises and thanks, and soone after he issued out of London with twentie thousand tall men, and came to Hounslowe Heath, abiding there and as it were daring his enemyes to joyne issue in the field, contemning theyr disorderlye multitude as a vayne terrour of names without forces. But the confederates, eyther for feare of the kings power, or for distrust of theyr owne, or else lingring, perhappes, after some succour out of Fraunce, refused the encounter, and doubtfull it is whether they shewed greater courage in setting up the danger, or cowardise in declining it when it was presented unto them.

So they departed from Colebrooke to Sunnings, a place neere Reading,[121] where Queene Isabell, King Richardes wife, did then abyde. To whom, upon the plaine trueth before declared, fame had falslye descanted that King Richard was escaped out of prison, and did lye at Pomfret with a hundred thousand armed men, and that King Henrie, for feare of him, was fledde with his children and friendes to the Tower of London. All which was as lightlye beleeved as it was vainlye toulde. Whereupon, shee defaced King Henries armes and plucked away his cognisance from those his servants that attended uppon her, and having in some sorte satisfied her womannish anger with this harmelesse spight, she and the [p. 128] lords departed together, first to Wallingforde, and from thence to Abington, stirring the people by the waye to take armour and to rise in ayde of King Richard, who was (saide they), and is, and should be their prince.

At the last[122] they came to Chichester, and there the lordes tooke theyr lodgings, the Duke of Surrey and the Earle of Salisburie in one inne, the Duke of Exceter and the Earle of Gloucester in another, and all the hoast encamped in the fields. But the bayliffe of the towne, suspecting all this countenance to be but the vaine flashe of a false fire, did in the night with about foure score archers beset and set upon the house where the Duke of Surrey and the Earle of Salisburie laye, who were men but of weake resistance by nature but, being put upon necessitie, shewed great manhood and persistance in defending themselves against the townsmen. The Duke of Exceter and the Earle of Gloucester, being in another inne, were not able by force to rescue their associates, whereupon a certaine priest of their companye set divers houses in the towne on fire, supposing thereby to divert the townsmen from theyr assault to the saving of their houses and of their goods. But this fire greatly inflamed their furie, and made them more obstinate in their attempt, crying out that they would never labour to rescue their losses, but to revenge them, and that with the bloud of the lordes those flames should be quenched. Then there arose confused clamours and noyses, all the towne being in an uproare and in armes, shooting fiercelie, and running upon the lords with a rashe

[121] A: 'Redding,' a listed 'faulte.'
[122] 7 January 1400.

and desperate rage, not caring to loose many, whereof they had many to spare.

When the Earle of Exceter and they that were with him perceived the force of the assaylants daungerouslie to encrease, and that it was impossible for a few to susteine the furie of so many so obstinately bent, they fledde out of the backe side, towards the campe, intending to bring the whole [p. 129] army to the rescue. But the soldiers, having heard a tumult, and seeing fire within the towne, supposed that the king was entred with all his puisance. Whereupon, being strooke with a sodaine and false feare, and wanting a commaunder of courage to confirme them, they ran away, and dispearsed themselves without measure. And so, whilest every man endevoured to save himselfe, all were brought to theyr confusion.

Thus, the Duke of Surrey and the Earle of Salisbury, & the lords & gentlemen which were in their company, were left to defend themselves against the townsemen as they could, who manfully maintained the fight, with great bloudshed of theyr enemies, from midnight untill three of the clocke the next day in the after noone. At the last, being inferiour both in number and fortune, the duke and the earle were wounded to death and taken, and the same evening theyr heades were stricken off and sent to London. There were also taken Sir Bennet Shelley, Sir Barnard Brokas, Sir Thomas Blunt, and 28. other lordes, knights and gentlemen, who were sent to Oxford, where the king then lay, and there put to execution.

The Duke of Exceter, when he found the army dispersed and fled, fled likewise with Sir John Shelley into Essex, lamenting the certaine destruction which his rashnesse had procured to himselfe, and to his friends, but moste especially to King Richard, if not as a party, yet as a cause of this unhappy tumult. Many times he did attempt to have escaped by sea into Fraunce, but he was alwayes driven backe by distresse of weather. And so, wandring and lurking in secret places, hee was at the last attached as hee sat at supper in a certaine friendes house, and led to Plashy, and there shortly after beheaded. So that a man might probably conjecture that the death of the Duke of Glocester was then brought in reckoning, who by his counsell and contry[p. 130]vance chiefly in the same place had been apprehended. An excellent example for all those which measure their actions eyther by their pleasure, or by their power, that revenge of injurious dealing, although it be prolonged, yet doth never faile, but commeth surely, although perhappes slowly.

This duke was a man of high parentage, of a franke minde, and wealth answerable thereunto, openly praiseworthy, but his secret actions were hardly spoken of. He was of consent to all his brothers vices, and of counsaile to many, yet somewhat the more close and vigilant man, and not so much partaker of his prosperity, as violently carried with the current of his misery.

The Earle of Gloucester fled towardes Wales, but was forelayed and taken, and beheaded at Bristow. Magdalene, the counterfeite of King Richard, flying into Scotland was apprehended and brought to the Tower, and afterward hanged and quartred with W. Ferby, another of King Richards chapleines. Diverse other lordes and knights and gentlemen, and a great number of meane and base persons, were in other places put to death, insomuch as the king, though otherwise of a very temperate and intreatible nature, seemed to shew too hard and haughty dealing in revenging his owne injury, or rather maintaining the injury that he had done.[123] The heads of the chiefe conspiratours were pitched upon poles, and set over London Bridge. In all other partes of the realme a spectacle both lamentable and ugly was presented to the view and terrour of others: bodies hewen in peeces, heads and quarters[124] of unfortunate, dismembred wretches putrifiing above ground, not al for desert, but many to satisfy either the mallice or want of King Henries friends; insomuch as many grave men openly gave forth that in short time, there would be cause to wish King Richard again, as being more tollerable to endure the cruelty of one, then of many, and to live where nothing, then where any [p. 131] thing, might be permitted.

The Abbot of Westminster, in whose house and in whose head this confederacy began, hearing of these adventures as he was going betweene his monastery and his mansion, fell sodainly into a palsie and shortly[125] after without speech ended his life. And, although in this enterprize fortune gave policy the check, and by a strange accedent which wisdome could not foresee overturned the devise, yet it is certainely affirmed that this abbot first stirred the stone which, rowling a long, was like to have turned King Henry out of his seate. The Bishop of Caerliel was condemned upon this treason, but the extreamity of his feare and griefe closed up his daies, and prevented the violence and shame of publicke execution.

And now King Richard, after he had abdicated his dignity, did but short time enjoy that sweet security which he did vainely expect. And first, all his goods which hee did give in satisfaction of the injuries that hee had done, were brought to devision and share amongst his enemies. Shortly after, he was remooved from the Tower to the Castle of Leedes, in Kent, and from thence to Pomfret, to the ende that by often changing hee might eyther more secretly bee dispatched, or

[123] *A*: 'injury he had done,' a listed 'faulte.'
[124] *A* misprints 'quarter.'
[125] *A*: 'hardly,' a listed 'faulte.'

more uncertainly found. Heere, being kept in streight prison, both innocent & ignorant of this offence, he was notwithstanding[126] made a party in the punishment. For King Henry, perceiveing that the lords so far prevailed with their late strategeme, that if their stomacke had bin answerable to their strength, & their bould[127] beginning had not ended in faintnes and sloath, they might have driven him to a hard hazard, caused King Richard to be put to death; intending to make sure that no man should cloake open rebellion under the colour of following sides, nor countenance his conspiracy either with the person or name of King Richard. Whether hee did expressely commaund his death or no, it is a question. Out of question, he shewed some liking and desire [p. 132] to the action, and gave allowance thereto when it was doone.

The most current report at that time went, that hee was princely served every day at the table, with aboundance of costlie meates, according to the order prescribed by parlament, but was not suffered to tast or touche any one of them, and so perished of famine, being tormented with the presence of that whereof hee dyed for want. But such horrible and unnaturall crueltie, both against a king and a kinseman, should not proceed from King Henrie (me thinke) a man of moderate and milde disposition, nor yet from any other minde which is not altogether both savage in humanitie, and in religion prophane. One wrighter, who would seeme to have the perfect intelligence of these affayres, maketh report that King Henrie, sitting at his table, sad and pensive, with a deepe sigh brake foorth into these wordes: 'Have I no faithfull friend that will deliver me of him whose life will breed destruction to me, and disturbance to the realme, and whose death will bee a safetie and quiet to both? For how can I be free from feare, so long as the cause of my daunger dooth continue? And what securitie, what hope shall we have of peace, unlesse the seede of sedition be utterly rooted out?'

Uppon this speech a certaine knight, called Sir Pierce of Extone, presently departed from the court, accompanyed with eyght tall men, and came to Pomfrete, and there commaunded that the esquire who was accustomed to sewe and take the assaye[128] before King Richard should no more use that manner of service. 'And let him,' quoth he, 'now eate wel, for he shall not eate long.' King Richard sate downe to dinner, and was served without courtesie or assaye, whereat he merveyled, and demaunded of the esquire why he did not his dutie. The esquire answered that he was otherwise commaunded by Sir

---

[126] *A*: '... offence was notwithstanding,' a listed 'faulte.'

[127] *A*: 'bloud' a listed 'fault.'

[128] 'To sewe' = to serve at table; 'to take the assaye' = to sample food and drink (as a precaution), before serving it to the king (OED).

Pierce of Extone, who was latelye come [p. 133] from King Henry. The king, beeing somewhat mooved at this acte and answere, tooke the carving knife in his hand, and strucke the esquire therewith lightly on the head, saying, 'The devill take Henry of Lancaster and thee together.' With that, Sir Pierce entred the chamber with eight men in harneys, every one having a byll in his hand. Whereupon King Richard, perceiving their drift and his owne daunger, put the table from him and, stepping stoutlye to the formost man, wrested the bill out of his hand, wherewith (although unarmed and alone) he manfully defended himelfe a good space, and slew fowre of his assailants. Sir Pierce lept to the chaire where King Richard was wonte to sit, whilest the rest chased him about the chamber. At the last, being forced towards the place where Sir Pierce was, he with a stroake of his pollax felled him to the ground, and foorthwith he was miserably rid out of his miserable life. It is saide that at the pointe of his death, hee gathered some spirit, and with a fainte and feeble voyce groaned foorth these wordes:

'My great grandfather, King Edward the second, was in this manner deposed, imprisoned, and murthered, by which meanes my grandfather, King Edward the third, obteyned possession of the crowne, and now is the punishment of that injury powred upon his next successour. Well, this is right for mee to suffer, but not for you to doe. Your king for a time may joye at my death, and enjoye his desire, but let him qualifie his pleasures with expectation of the like justice. For God, who measureth all our actions by the malice of our mindes, will not suffer this violence unrevenged.'

Whether these words proceeded from a distempered desire, or from the judgement of his foresight, they were not altogether idle and vaine. For Sir Pierce, expecting great favour and rewards for his ungracious service, was frustrated [p. 134] of both, and not onely missed that countenance for which he hoped, but lost that which before he had. So odious are vices, even where they are profitable.

Heereupon hee grew at the first discontented, and afterwardes mightely turmoyled and tormented in conscience, and, raging against himselfe, would often exclaime that to pleasure one unthankefull person, he had made both himselfe and his posteritie hatefull and infamous to all the world.

King Henrie, with great discontentment and disquiet, held the kingdome during his life, and so did his sonne, King Henrie the fifth, in whose time, by continuall warres against the Frenchmen, the malice of the humour was otherwise exercised and spent. But his second successour, King Henry the sixth, was dispossessed thereof and, together with his young sonne Henry, imprisoned and put to death, eyther by the commaundement or connivence of King Edward the fourth.

And hee also escaped not free, for hee dyed not without many and manifest suspicions of poison. And after his death, his two sonnes were disinherited, imprisoned, and butchered by their cruell unckle, the Duke of Gloucester who, beeing a tyrant and usurper, was lawfully slaine in the field; and so in his person (having no issue) the tragedie did end. Which are most rare and excellent examples, both of comfort to them that are oppressed, and of terrour to violent dealers, that God in his secret judgement dooth not alwayes so certainely provide for our safetie, as revenge our injuries and harmes; and that all our unjust actions have a daye of payment, and many times by waye of retaliation, even in the same manner and measure wherein they were committed.

And thus was King Richard brought to his death, by violence and force, as all wrighters agree, although all [p. 135] agree not uppon the manner of the violence. Hee was a man of personage rather well proportioned then tall, of great beautie and grace, and comlinesse in presence. Hee was of a good strength, and no abject spirit, but the one by ease, the other by flatterie, were much abased. He deserved many friends, but found fewe, because hee sought them more by liberalitye then vertuous dealing. He was merveilous infortunate in all his actions, which may verye well bee imputed to his negligence and sloath; for hee that is not provident can seldome prosper, but by his loosenesse will loose whatsoever fortune, or other mens laboures, doe cast uppon him. At the last, hee was driven to such distresse that hee accompted it as a benefite to bee disburdened of his royall dignitie, for which other men will not sticke to put theyr goods, and lives and soules in hazarde.

He lived three and thirtie yeares, and reigned two and twentie. His dead body was embaulmed, and seared, and covered with lead all save his face, and carryed to London, and in all the chiefe places by the waye his face was uncovered and shewen, that by viewe thereof no doubt should bee made concerning his death. At London, hee had a solemne obsequie kept in the cathedral church of St. Paule, the king beeing present, and all the chiefe men of the cittie.

Then hee was conveyed to Langley Abbey, in Buckingham shire, about twentie myles from London, and there obscurely enterred by the Bishop of Chester, the Abbot of S. Albones, and the Abbot of Waltham, without presence of noble men, without confluence of the common people, and without the charge of a dinner for celebrating the funerals. But afterward, at the commaundement of King Henry the fifth, his body was taken up and remooved to Westminster, and honorablye entombed amongst his auncestors, [p. 136] with Queene

Anne, his wife, in expiation (as it is like) of his fathers violent and unfaithfull dealing. So hee whose life was alwaies tumultuous and unquiet could not readily finde rest for his bones, even after death. It was not amisse in regard of the common wealth that he was dead; yet they who caused his death had small reason to reckon it among theyr good deedes.

And thus doe these and the like accidents dayly happen to such princes as will be absolute in power, resolute in will, and dissolute in life.

This yeere Humfrey, the sonne and heyre of the Duke of Gloucester, dyed of the plague, as he returned out of Ireland where King Richard had left him prisoner; and shortly after, the Duchesse, his mother, with violence of griefe ended her dayes. This yeere also dyed Thomas Mowbray, the exiled Duke of Norfolke, whose death would much have been lamented, if he had not furthered so many lamentable deaths; but he overlived his honour, & saw himselfe accounted a person infamed, and of no estimation. Likewise about this time, John, Duke of Brittaine deceased, who had taken to wife Mary, daughter to King Edward the third, and by her had no issue, but by Joan his second wife he left behinde him three sons: John, Richard & Arthur. This Joan was afterwards married to King Henrie, as hereafter shall appeare. Also this yeere, Edmund, Duke of Yorke, departed this life, his honour not stayned, his fame not touched. He was a man very circumspect, and wary in his cariage, not carelesse of a good fame, nor greedy after a great; of other mens wealth not desirous, liberall of his owne, and of the common, sparing. He did not by obstinate opposing himselfe against the current of the time, rashly hasten eyther his fame or his fall, but by moderation attayned safely that degree of praise and honour which others, aspiring unto by desperate courses, wanne with ambitious death, without any other profit at all. He left behinde him [p. 137] two noble sonnes, expresse resemblencers of his integritie, Edward, who succeeded in his dignitie, and before was called Duke of Aumerle, and Richard, Earle of Cambridge. Edward, in the change of the state, neither constantlye kept his fidelitie, nor stoutlie maintained his treason. Richard tooke to wife the daughter and heyre of Roger Mortimer, whose mother Phillip was sole daughter and heyre to Lionell, Duke of Clarence, the third sonne of King Edward the thyrd, by which title and discent his posteritie claimed the crowne and kingdome of this realme from the successours of King Henrie, as heereafter more at large shall be declared.

Charles, King of Fraunce, lost no time all this while in making preparation to invade England, and to that end he had now raysed an armie royall, which was brought downe into Picardie, and in a readinesse to have beene transported. But it is verye like that this hast for the deliverance of King Richard did the more hasten his death; uppon newes whereof the Frenchmen, perceiving their purpose for his restitution to be to no purpose, gave over the enterprise, some being grieved that the occasion was lost of making spoile of so plentifull a countrie, others being well content to be discharged of that hope together with the hazard whereupon it depended. Shortlie after, the French king sent a solemne embassage into England, to treate, or rather intreat, that Lady Isabell, his daughter, who had bin espoused to King Richard, might with her dowrie bee restored to him againe. King Henrie most honourablie received these embassadours, and gave in answere that he would speedelie send his commissioners to Calice, which should fullye commune and conclude with them both of this and other weightie affayres concerning both the realmes.

Not long after, he sent Edward, Duke of Yorke, and Henrie, Earle of Northumberland, to Calice. Also, the French [p. 138] king sent the Duke of Bourbone and certaine others to Bulleine. These commissioners did often meete, sometimes at one place, and sometimes at another. The Frenchmen especially required that Lady Isabell should be restored, shewing that King Charles, her father, had given in charge that this, before all matters, and without this nothing, should be concluded. On the other side, the Englishmen desired that she might be married to Henry, Prince of Wales, King Henries eldest sonne, a man answerable to her in equall degree, both of bloud and of yeeres. But the French king denyed that he would any more joine affinity with the English nation, whose aliance had once so unfortunately succeeded. Then they entred into speech of a perpetuall peace, but heereto the Frenchmen would not agree. In the end, it was concluded that Lady Isabell should be delivered to King Charles, her father, but without dower, because the marriage betweene King Richard and her was never consummate, by reason wherof she was not dowable by the very treaty of the marriage. Also, the surcease of armes, which foure yeeres before had beene made with King Richard for the terme of 30 yeeres, was continued and confirmed for the time then unexpyred. Some authors affirme that a newe truce was taken, but these also are at difference. For some report that it was during the life of both the kinges, others that it was but for a short time, which hath more apparaunce of truth, by reason of the open hostilitye which the yeere following did breake foorth betweene the two realmes.

Shortly after, King Henrie sent the Lady Isabell, under the conducte of Lorde Thomas Pearcy, Earle of Worcester, in royall estate to Calice. She was accompanied with a great troupe of honourable personages, both men and women, and carried with her all the jewelles and plate which shee brought into England, with a great surplesage of rich giftes [p. 139] bestowed upon her by the king. At Calice she was received by the Earle of S. Paule, Leiuetenant for the French king in Picardy, and by him was conducted to King Charles, her father, who afterwardes gave her in marriage to Charles, sonne to Lewes, Duke of Orleance. And so was eyther rest or respite of wars procured in Fraunce, whilest neerer stirres might be brought to some stay.

For within the realme, the fire and fury of the late sedition was scarcely quenched and quiet but (that the common wealth should not cease to be torne by multiplying of divisions, one streight succeeding another) the Welshmen, upon advantage of the doubtfull and unsetled estate of King Henrie, resolved to breake and make a defection, before eyther the king could ground his authority, or the people frame themselves to a new obedience. And, having learned that common causes must be maintained by concord, they sought by assemblyes to establish an association, and to set up theyr owne principality againe.

To this purpose, they created for theyr prince Owen Glendor, an esquire of Wales, a factious person, and apt to set up division and strife. And, although hee was of no great state in birth, yet was hee great and stately in stomacke; of an aspiring spirit, and in wit somewhat above the ordynarie of that untrayned people, boulde, craftie, active, and as he listed to bend his minde, mischievous or industrious in equall degree; in desires immoderate, and rashlye adventurous. In his young yeeres hee was brought up to the studye of the common lawe of the realme, at London, and when he came to mans estate, besides a naturall fiercenesse and hatred to the English name, hee was particularlye incensed by a private suite, for certayne landes in controversie betweene the Lord Gray of Ruthen and him, wherein his tytle was overthrowen. And being a man by nature not of the myldest, [p. 140] by this provocation he was made savadge and rough, determining eyther to repayre or to revenge his losse, by setting the whole state on fire. Also, his expence and liberalitie had been too excessive for a great man to endure, which brought him to barenesse too base for a meane man to beare. And therefore, he must of necessitie doe and dare somewhat, and more daunger there was in soft and quiet dealing, then in hazarding rashlie. Heerewith opportunitie was then likewise presented; for troublesome times are most fit for great attempts, and some likelyhood there was, whilest the king and the lordes were hard at variance, that harme might easelie be wrought to them both. Upon these causes his desire was founded, and uppon these troubles his hope. But that his aspiring and ambitious humour might beare some shew of honest meaning, he pretented to his countrymen the recoverie of theyr free estate, the desire whereof was so naturally sweete that even wilde birdes will rather live hardlye at large in the ayre, then bee daintily dyeted by others in a cage. And opportunitie was at that time fitlie offered, or else never to be expected, to rid them of theyr thraldome, falselie and colourablie intituled a peace, whilest the one kings power was waining, and the other not yet fullye wexen, and eyther of them grew weake by wasting the other. Neither was there any difference which of them should prevayle, sith the warre touched both a like, insomuch as the overthrow would ruine the one, and the victorie the other. So hee exhorted them to take courage and armes, and first to kill all the English within their territories, for libertie and lordes could not endure together; then to resume their auncient customes and lawes, whereby more then armes, commonwealths are established and enlarged. So should they bee a people uncorrupt, without admixtion of forreine manners or bloud; and so should they forget servitude, and eyther live at libertie, or else perhaps bee lordes [p. 141] over other.

Heereuppon many flocked unto him, the best for love of libertie, the basest for desire of bootie and spoile, insomuch as in short time hee became commaunder of competent forces to stand openly in the fielde. And, being desirous to make some proofe of his prowesse, hee sharply set uppon his ould adversarie Reignold, Lorde Grey of Ruthen, whose possessions he wasted and spoyled, slew many of his men, and tooke himselfe prisoner, yet gave him faire and friendlie enterteinment, and promised him releasment, if he would take his daughter to wife. This hee desired, not so much for neede of his abilitie or ayde, as supposing that the name and countenance of a lorde would give reputation to the house that was then but in rising. But the Lorde Greye, at the first, did not so much refuse as scorne the offer, affirming that he was no warde, to have his marriage obtruded uppon him. 'Well,' sayde Owen Glendore, 'although you bee not my warde, yet are you in my warde, and the suing of your liverie will cost double the marriage money that elsewhere you shall procure.' The Lord Grey, being not very riche to discharge his ransome, and seeing no other meanes of his deliverance, at the last acceptecd the condition, and tooke the damosell to wife: notwithstanding his deceitfull father in lawe trifled out the time of his enlargement, untyll hee dyed.

The Welshmen, being confident uppon this successe, began to breake into the borders of Hereford shire, and to make spoyle and pray of the countrey. Against whom Lord Edmund Mortimer, Earle of Marche, who for feare of King Henrie had withdrawne himselfe (as hath been declared) to Wiggmore Castle, assembled all the gentlemen of the countrye; and meeting with the Welshmen, they joined together a sharpe and cruell conflict; not in forme of a loose skirmish, but standing still and maintaining their place, they [p. 142] endeavored with maine might to breake and beare downe one another. The courage and resolution of both sides was a like, but the Welshmen were superiour both for number and direction. For they were conducted by one knowne leader, who with his presence every where assisted at neede, enflaming his soldiours, some with shame and re-proofe, others with praise and encouragement, all with hope and large promises. But the Englishmen had no certaine generall, but many confused commaunders; yea, every man was a commaunder to himselfe, pressing forward or drawing backe as his owne courage or feare did moove him, insomuch as no doubt they had taken a great blowe that day by theyr ill governed bouldnesse, had not Owen Glendor presently, uppon the breaking up of the field, ceased to pursue the execution, and shewed himselfe more able to get a victorie, then skilfull to use it. But even to his side the victorie had cost bloud, and many of those which remayned were eyther wounded or wearie. The night was neere, also, and they were in their enemyes countrie, by which meanes our men had libertie to retire rather then runne away, no man being hoat to follow the chase. They lost of their company about a thousand men, who sould their lives at such a price that when manhood had doone the hardest against them, certaine mannish, or rather devilish women, whose malice is immortall, exer-cised a vaine revenge uppon their dead bodyes, in cutting off theyr privie partes and theyr noses, whereof the one they stuffed into theyr mouthes, and pressed the other betweene their buttocks, and would not suffer their mangled carcasses to be committed to the earth untill they were redeemed with a great summe of money. By which cruell covetuousnesse the faction lost reputation and credite with the mod-erate sorte of their owne people, suspecting that it was not libertie but licentiousnesse which was desired, and that subjection to such unhumaine [p. 143] mindes would bee more insupportable than anye bondage.

In this conflict the Earle of Marche[129] was taken prisoner and fettered with chaines, and cast into a deepe and vile dungeon. The king was solicited by many noble men to use some meanes for his deliverance, but hee would not heare on that eare; hee could rather have wished him and his two sisters[130] in heaven, for then the onely blemish to his title had beene out of the way. And no man can tell whether this mischaunce did not preserve him from a greater mischiefe.

Owen Glendor, by the prosperous success of his actions, was growne now more harde to be dealt with, and hautelie minded, and stood even uppon termes of equalitie with the king. Whereupon he

[129] This was actually Sir Edmund de Mortimer, uncle of the young earl, who at this date (1402) was only eleven. Sir Edmund was at this time the most powerful representative of his nephew's interests, which included the fact that the boy was male heir of Roger de Mortimer, Richard's heir presumptive.

[130] Sir Edmund's sister Elizabeth married Sir Henry Percy (Hotspur).

proceeded further to invade the marches of Wales on the west side of the Severne, where he burnt many villages and townes, slew much people, and returned with great prey, and praises of his adherents. Thus he ceased not this yeere to infest the borderers on every side, amongst whom he found so weake resistance that he seemed to exercise rather a spoile, then a warre. For King Henrie was then detained, with his chiefest forces, in another more dangerous service which, besides these former vexations and hazards, this first yeere of his reigne happened unto him.

For the Scottes, knowing that changes were times most apte for attempt, and uppon advantage of the absence of all the chiefe English borderers, partly by occasion of the parlament, and partlie by reason of the plague, which was very grievous that yeere in the north partes of the realme, they made a roade into the countrey of Northumberland, and there committed great havocke and harme. Also, on a certaine night, they sodainly set uppon the castle of Werke, the captain wherof, Sir Thomas Gray, was then one of the knights of the parlament. And having slaine the watch, partly asleepe, [p. 144] partlye amased with feare, they brake in and surprised the place, which they held a while, and at the last spoyled and ruined, and then departed. Whilest further harmes were feared, this passed with light regard. But when great perils were past, as if noe worse misfortune could have befallen, then was it much sorrowed and lamented. And in revenge thereof, the Englishmen invaded and spoyled certaine ilandes of Orkney. And so the losse was in some sorte repayred, yet (as in reprisals of warre it commonlye falleth out) neyther against those particular persons which committed the harme, nor for those which suffred it; but one for another were both recompenced and revenged. Againe the Scottes set foorth a fleete, under the conduct of Sir Robert Logon, with direction to attempt as ocasion should be offered. His first purpose was against our fishermen, but before hee came to any action, he was encountred by certaine English ships, and the greatest part of his fleete taken. Thus, peace still continuing betweene both the realmes, a kinde of theevish hostilitie was dayly practised, which afterwardes brake out into open warre uppon this occasion.

George of Dunbarre, Earle of the Marches of Scotland, had betrothed Elisabeth, his daughter, to David, the sonne and heyre apparant of Robert, King of Scottes, and in regarde of that marriage to bee shortlie celebrated and finished, hee delivered into the kings hands a great summe of money for his daughters dowrie. But Archibalde, Earle Dowglasse, disdayning that the Earle of Marches bloud should be preferred before his, so wrought with King Robert that Prince David, his sonne, refused the Earle of Marches daughter, and tooke to wife Mariel, daughter to the Earle Dowglasse. Earle George, not used to offers of disgrace, could hardlye enforce his pacience to endure this scorne, and first hee demaunded restitution of his money, [p. 145] not so much for care to obteyne, as for desire to picke an occasion of breaking his alleageance. The king would make to him neyther payment nor promise, but trifled him off with many delusorie and vaine delayes. Whereuppon hee fled with all his familie into England, to Henrie, Earle of Northumberland, intending with open disloyaltie both to revenge his indignitie and recover his losse. The Englishmen with open armes enterteyned the opportunitie; with whose helpe and assistance the Earle made diverse incursions into Scotland, where he burnt many townes, and slue much people, and daylye purchased with his sworde great aboundance of bootie and spoile.

Heereuppon King Robert deprived the earle of his honour, seazed all his goods and possessions, and wrote unto King Henry, as hee would have the truce betweene them any longer to continue, eyther to deliver unto him the Earle of Marche and other traytours to his person and state, or else to banish them the realme of England. King Henrye, perceiving such jarres to jogger betweene the two realmes, that the peace was already as it were out of jointe, determined not to loose the benefit of the discontented subjects of his enemie. Whereuppon hee returned aunswer to the Heralde of Scotland, that hee was neyther wearie of peace, nor fearefull of warres, and ready as occasion should change eyther to holde the one, or hazard the other; but the worde of a prince was of great weight, and therefore, sithe hee had graunted a safe conduct to the Earle of Marche and his companie, it were an impeachment to his honour without just cause to violate the same. Upon this answere the King of Scottes did presently proclaime open warre against the King of England, with bloud, fire, and sworde.

King Henry thought it pollicie rather to begin the warre in his enemies countrie, then to expect it in his owne, because the land which is the seate of the warre dooth com[p. 146]monly furnish both sides with necessarie supply: the friend by contribution, and the enemie by spoyle. Therefore, sending certaine troopes of horsemen before him, both to espie and to induce an uncertaine terrour uppon the enemie, he entred into Scotland with a puissant armie, wherewith hee burnt many villages and townes, cast downe diverse castles, and ruined a great part of the townes of Edenborough and Lith, sparing nothing but churches and religious houses. So that in all places as he passed, the spectacle was ouglie and grislie which hee left behind him: bodyes torne in peeces, mangled and putrified limmes, the ayre infested with stincke, the ground imbrued with corruption and bloud, the countrie wasted, the grasse and corne troden downe and spoyled, insomuch as a man would have sayde that warre is an exercise not of manhood, but of inhumanitie. They that fledde before the armie filled all places with feare and terrour, extolling above truthe the English foreces, to diminish thereby their shame in running from them.

In the end of September, the king besieged the castle of Maydens, in Edenborough, wherein were David, Duke of Rothsaye, prince of the realme, and Archibalde, Earle Dowglasse. The inconstancie of the one, and ambition of the other, were principall causes of all this warre.

During this siege, Robert, Duke of Albonye, who was appointed governour of the realme, because the king was sicke and unable to rule, sent an herauld unto Henrie, assuring him uppon his honour, that if hee would abyde but sixe dayes at the most, hee would give him battaile, and eyther remoove the siege, or loose his life.

The king was well pleased with these tidings, and rewarded the herauld with a gowne of silke and a chaine of gould, and promised him in the worde of a prince to abide [p. 147] there and expect the governour during the tyme by him prefixed.

The sixe dayes passed, almoste sixe tymes over, and no more newes was heard of the governour, eyther by presence or by messenger. Winter came on, and victuaile fayled, the country was colde and fruitelesse, and it rayned every day in great aboundance, so that partly by hunger, partlye by distemperature of the weather, the soldiers began to dye of the flixe. It is verie like that these accidentes stayed the governour from performing his promise, for pollicy was against it, to hazard his men in the fielde, when winter and want, two forceable foes, had given the charge upon his enemyes. Certaine it is that they mooved the king to remoove his siege, and to depart out of Scotland without any battaile or skirmish offred.

Both the wardens of the marches were all this time in Scotland with the king, upon which advantage the Scots did breake into Northumberland, and burnt certaine townes in Bamborough shire. The Engish men were speedilie up in armes, but the Scottes more speedily made theyr returne, or else no doubt they had been met with and encountered.

Agayne, when King Henry had discharged his armie, the Scottes, beeing desirous not so much of lyfe as of revenge, made a sodayne roade into England, under the conduct of Sir Thomas Halibarton of Dirleton, and Sir Patricke Hebburne of Hales. But all the harme which they wrought dyd rather waken then weaken the Englishmen, and they themselves were somewhat encouraged, but nothing enryched, by that whych they got.

Not long after, Sir Patricke Hebburne, beeing lifted up in desire and hope, resolved to undertake a greater [p. 148] enterprise. The people, which are easilye ledde by prosperous successe, in great companies resorted to him, but hee was loath to have more fellowes in the spoyle, then hee thought should neede in the daunger. Therefore, with a competent armie of the men of Loughdeane, he invaded Northumberland, where hee made great spoile, and loaded his souldiours with prisoners and pray. There was no question made what perrill might bee in the returne. Therefore, they marched looselie and licentiouslie, as in a place of great securitie, not keeping themselves to their ensignes and order. But the Earle of Northumberlands vice-warden, and other gentlemen of the borders in good arraye, set uppon them at a towne in Northumberland called Nesbitt.[131] The Scottes rallied as well as the soddainnesse did serve, and valiantlie received the charge, so that the battaile was sharpe and cruell, and continued a good time, with great mortalitie. In the ende, the enemyesranckes grew thinne, as being rather confusedly shuffled together then orderly and firmlie compacted, and when the vice-warden felte them weake in the shock and yeelding under his hand, with a companie which he purposelie reteyned[132] about him for sodaine dispatches and chaunces of warre, he fiercely charged and disordered them. Sir Patricke Hebburne, being cleane destitute both of counsaile and courage, ranne up and downe from one place to another, commaunding many things, and presently forbidding them againe. And the lesse of force his directions were, the oftener did hee change them. Anone (as it happeneth in lost and desperate cases) everye man became a commaunder, and none a putter in execution, so the rankes loosed and brake, and could not bee reunited, the victor hoatly pursuing the advantage. Then might you have seene a grievous spectacle, pursuing, killing, wounding, and taking, and killing those that were taken, when better were offered. Every where weapons, and dead bodyes, and mangled lims [p. 149] laye scattered. And sometimes in those that were slaine appeared at their death both anger and valure. Sir Patricke Hebburne thought of nothing lesse then eyther fleeing or yeelding but, thrusting among the thickest of his enemyes, honourably ended his life. Many other of his linage and the flower of all Loughdeane were likewise slaine. There were also taken Sir John and William Cockburne, Sir William Busse, John and Thomas Hablincton, Esquires, and a great multitude of common soldiours. On the English side no great number was slaine, and those of no great service and degree. And with these troubles, the first yeere of King Henrie the fourth ended.

* *
*

FINIS.

---

[131] 22 June 1401.
[132] *A*: 'which purposelie reteyned,' a listed 'faulte.'

LONDON.
Printed by John VVolfe, and are
to be sold at his shop in Popes
Head Alley, neere the
Exchange.
1599.

The Second Yeare of King Henrie the Fourth.
Written by the Foresayde Author.

[IV]

Now the king had discharged himselfe of his troupes but not of his troubles, his mind being perpetuallie perplexed with an endlesse and restlesse chardge, ether of cares, or greifes, or of suspicions and feares.

First his cheifest glorie had a mixture of greife, & the attonement[1] of his kingdome did oftentimes lie heavy at his hearte, for being gotten with bloud, it was held with horror, wherein was never tast of joy without a touch of a guiltie conscience. Then hee had not fullie satisfied himselfe by his late voyage into Scottland, supposing that his performance was nothing answerable to his power, and that hee had rather stirred the Scottes then stayed them from attempting against him, having noe lesse weakened himselfe by chardge, then them by spoile. And coming farre shorte of his owne purposes and hopes, hee thought himselfe alsoe shorte of all mens expectations. Alsoe hee was disquieted with the doubtfull obedience of his new subjectes, against whome his suspicion had somewhat increased his severitie, and againe his severitie had increased his suspicion, for knowing that many were discontented, hee could not esteem his safetie ether by theire fidelity or by his owne forces assured.

Likewise the unsettled state of the Irish did not a little vexe him, who since the departure of King Richard from them, ledd a dissolute and loose life, nether at their owne libertie, nor under any certaine subjection. And they who had beene ether lefte or sent for that service contenting themselves with appeasing the warres, did noe further indeavor fullie to end them. Of these many revolted to the Irish rebelles, among which the Veeres, whome Robert Veere Duke of Ireland had there planted, [fo. iv] did quite cast of with theire alleagance theire name, and calling themselves Mackswins[2] were altogether habituated into Irish.

But most especiallie hee was anguished with the reporte of the

---

[1] Reconciliation, or 'staunching of strife' (OED); 'pacification.'

[2] Many of the galloglasses, or foreign mercenaries, employed from an early period by certain northern Irish chiefs, had come to be identified with the family name of Macswine (MacSweeney). Although by Hayward's time such foreign adventurers were generally identified as English, his assignment of the name to the Veres is probably anachronistic.

Welch under Owen Glendor and with the incursions which hee made upon the English borderers whoe, being men accustomed to peaceable businesse, nether practiced nor provided for militarie exploites, ether by rash resistance or by fearefull and unseasonable flight opened unto him the wide waye both to his glorie and to his gaine, by whom they receaved larger losses in lesse then one yeare, then all England received in many when King Richard did raigne. Hereupon the king, having sent supplies to his garrisons in Fraunce and appointed forces upon the confines of Scottland, bent all his thoughtes to the strong suppressinge of these oppressours. To this purpose hee made present preparation for a voyage into Wales, being never more greived at any disgrace then that a man for his person emptie of reputation, for his estate and forces weake, and having noe incouragement or supporte from forreign princes, then that hee whoe was first a thiefe and then a traitor, should beare the reputation of an enemie in the feild.

In the mean tyme the Emperor of Constantinople[3] arrived in England, to require aid against the Turkes, the common enemie not only to Christianity, but even to mankind, with the weight of whose power his weake resistance was overchardged, being not of force to bridle [fo. 2] the furie of such a mightie and obstinate enemye. That therefore he was compelled to complaine to other Christian princes whom the cause did concerne, thoughe not soe presentlie yet soe deeply as it did himselfe. For albeit hee was next to the danger and therefore to bee first swallowed up, yet the decaye of faith touched all the faythful alike, and the losse of any one Christian countrie doth shake and enfeeble all the rest. And as at that time his countrie did feele that which a few yeares before it did not feare, soe it was like that other countries should in shorte tyme both feare and feele what they soe litle regarded to foresee. That many whoe lately supposed themselves ether beyond his reach, or more then his match, hee had in shorte tyme brought both within his compasse and under his commaunde. That hee had already taken the suburbs of Christendom, and then bent his batterie against the walles, which might bee sufficient to waken those whoe slept soe soundlie upon the sweete pillowes of securitie and peace.

The king in verie great estate mett with the Emperor at Blackheath, and entertained him with all honors and offices of courte. Hee shewed himselfe alsoe greived at his distresse, but expressed noe inclination to releive him, covering himselfe with many excuses, that hee was nether free nor able for such an enterprize, by reason of his new unsettled

[3] Emperor Manuel II Palaeologus (1348?–1425) succeeded to the throne in 1391, and spent the period 1398–1402 touring western Europe in a generally futile attempt to beg assistance from the Christian states.

state, wherein hee had not assured ether the faith of his subjectes or the frendshippe of princes nere unto him, but held them all [fo.2v] ether as open enemies or els as doubtful and suspected frendes. Soe partlie by meanes of disorders amonge Christians, partly because noe man regarding the harme of others, everie one is lefte to shifte for himselfe. But cheiflie, by reason of a great division in the church, the common cause of Christianitie was generallie neglected.

For besides the division betweene the Greeke church and the Latine, a miserable schisme was then alsoe raised in the Latine church, sometimes two, sometimes three popes standing and striving one against the other, in a zeal differing nothing from mortall malice. The occasioner of this schism was Pope Urban the vjth, who in the first entrance into his papacie was soe insolent among the cardinalls and princes under him, and soe ambitious in advancing his bloude, that the greatest parte of his cardinalls fell from him, and sett up another Pope named Clement who satt a xj yeares, after whome succeeded Benedict the xiij who ruled xxvj years. On the other side after Urbane succeeded Boniface the ix, then Innocent the viijth,[4] then Gregorie the xij, then Alexander the vth, then John the xiijth.[5] Among these the schisme endured untill the yeare 1414 when the Counsaile of Constance was called for the pacifying thereof, and in the meane tyme brake forth disturbance [fo. 3] and destruction in everie Christian countrie and common wealth. Princes were murthered and cardinalles racked, beheaded, tortured to death. Preists and prelates tooke the feild. Manie battelles were executed, many townes spoiled and defaced, much bloud shed, and (above all) manie contentions in religion were raised, all pointes almost being drawne into controversie and everie controversie prosecuted with extreame sharpenes of humour, so as there was scarce lefte ether number for more contentions, or place for worse. This was a principall meanes both to hinder the conversion of infidelles, and to helpe forward the subversion of Christians. But againe to our purpose.

The emperor after some staye in England received advertisement that the King of Aleppo had slaine in battaile Bassack the sonne of Balthazardan, and destroied Jerusalem & all the country adjoyning to it, and that upon event of this adventure hee converted to the Christian religion with ten thousand of his followers. Hereupon the emperor, revived in courage, departed out of England, having requited his courteous entertainment with modest behaviour, and being highlie honored at his departure with all ceremonies and reverence agreable to his degree.[6]

---

[4] Actually, Innocent VII.
[5] Actually, John XXIII.
[6] The emperor was in London between December 1400 and February 1401, before

Now the king was not negligent to send his ambassadors abroad furnished with instructions and meanes to receave frendes, to discover suspectes, to sound the determinations of [fo. 3v] enemies, and to winne the inclination of such as were neutrall, of whome notwithstanding hee gott nothing but generall words of courtesie, and promises at lardge. Alsoe supposing frendship by alliance to bee not only firme, but as the cause thereof inseparable, he sent his eldest daughter, Blaunche, accompanied with manie personages of honor, into Almaine, where shee was joined in marriage to William, Duke of Bavier, sonne and heire to Lewes of Bavier the Emperor. Also in the beginning of Februarie[7] he contracted mariage by his procurator with Jane de Navarre, late wife to John de Mountfort Duke of Brittaine, and as shee crossed the seas for England, her passage was verie dangerous by reason of tempestuous wether, which accident was esteemed ominous in both King Richards wives. The king received her at Winchester, and there having spent some time in devises of pleasures, upon the viith of Februarie the marriage was solemnized betweene them, and upon the xxvith of the same moneth shee was with all ceremonies of state, crowned at Westminster. This the king did not soe much ether for hope or neede of aide from the Brittaines as by new alliance to make the French king more assured unto him. But betweene men of equall both ambition and power, albeit alliance may easilie bee made (as was between Caesar & Pompey) yet frendshipp [fo. 4] cannot. To the same end hee tooke order for returning the Lady Isabell, late wife to King Richard, to the king her father into Fraunce.

This ladie, after the death of King Richard, continued without meane in mourning, unable in any sorte to settle her mind, in bearing soe sadd a blow of fortune. Shee estranged her selfe from all occasions of pleasure or of comforte, and was accompanied with a heavy traine composed to sorrow both in behaviour and attire. The house where she kept was sometimes with a sadd silence desolate and still, sometimes unquiet with loud lamenting, under coulour whereof they tooke libertie to speake at large, crying out upon the king and casting many curses upon him, and that so bitterlie and bouldly that it seemed they had forgott what it was to governe a state. They complained alsoe sometimes of the crueltie of King Richards death, which was constantlie reported to have beene by famine, sometimes of the base

returning to Paris for another year. Beyazit (Bajazet) I Yilderim (1347–1403), son of Sultan Murad I, ruled from 1389–1402, when he was taken prisoner by Tamerlane at the battle of Ankara, thus postponing the threat to the Christian capital. He died a year later, in captivity.

[7] The proxy marriage took place 3 Apr. 1402, the marriage ceremony itself at Winchester, 7 Feb. 1403.

manner of his buriall, without any honor usuallie observed to other princes, affirming that his bodie was first exposed to bee a publicke spectacle of his calamity and contemptibly prostituted to the homelie handling of all sortes of people; then that hee was as closelie convayed away as hee had been made away, being rather hidd under the ground then buried. 'And where then,' said they, 'are aunciente obsequies? Wherefore was not the herse carried with solemne representation of mourning, and some memoriall made of his virtues? Wherefore is not a tombe erected, and his image laid [fo. 4v] thereon expressing his princelie personage and his lively and lovely countenance? Doth envie alsoe follow the dead? Or was hee not worthy of these last duties of humanitie? If the heavens had not beene covered with darke and dropping cloudes, if the stones and pavements had not yeelded some moisture, there had beene noe token of teares, no sign of sorrow.'

These complaintes were performed in soe naturall a time of sorrow, that even they whoe felte not the loss seemed to have some sense of the greife. Yett were they not sufficient to ease the boyling affections of the yong princesse, but her haughtie disposition was desirous to tell the king his faulte to his face, to see with what countenance and wordes he would ether maintaine his actions or els excuse them. And having procured opportunitie of presence, first pouring forth in a sett silence great plentie of teares, in the end shee brake into these speeches:

'In seeking to obtaine our purposes of others, it is an ordinarie endeavour to move ether by prayers pittie, or by promises hope, or by threats feare. But as with men cruell and ambitious and in theire owne opinion mightie, these meanes are of litle force, soe with them whose miserie is beneath all releife they cannot bee of any use. Being now therefore in that distresse that there remaineth to mee nether thing to desire [fo. 5] nor thought to obtaine, I am come only to putt you in remembrance, what benefittes with what ingratitude you have requited, that in my heaviest mishappe, I may conceive this vaine satisfaction to have reproved you openly to your face.'

At these wordes the standers by made offer to interrupt her, some putting her back, others interposing betweene the king and her, others ministring unto him some matter of discourse, all unwilling to adventure upon his displeasure if in his owne hearing they should silently indure to heare his reproach. But the king as being confident ether in his cause or in his power, gave her leave to proceede and commaunded the rest to lend her a patient eare, whereupon the ladie, not anithing abashed, in this sorte continued her speech:

'I neede not by particulars putt you in mind of the honors and advancementes which King Richard dailie heaped upon you, onlie out of his owne princelie disposition, soe farre underserved by you, as not desired. But noe greatnes could satisfie your greedines, enoughe was nothing to him that desired all. How many of your dangerous both actions and speeches were ether freely pardoned or favourablie interpreted and not regarded? When you were discovered for a suspect, noe extremities were practised against you, when you openly held the feild with armes, and your children were in King Richardes power (by [fo. 5v] whose danger parentes are more terrified then by theire owne) not only noe harme but some honor was done unto them.[8]

'All which proceedings may bee justly blamed for loose securitie, saye alsoe if you please foolish. Yet this loosenes, being grounded upon love, is soe farre from purging your breach of faith, that it doubleth your dishonor. And albeit ambition (an unquiet humour) hath hitherto blinded your judgement, yet shame will shortlie cause you to discerne that you possesse onlie an appearance of honor sett upon you by a few flatterers which will easily bee escared[9] by those infamies which our just complaintes shall blazen throughe the world. Your owne conscience alsoe shall torment you and compell you to condemne your selfe to the severest punishments which treason and parricide cann deserve. And albeit it may seeme by successe that god in his secrett judgement hath furthered your proceedings, yett assure your selfe hee hath not favored them. But your dominion begunne with crueltie shall in you, or in your progenie, end with contempte. As for my dishonor, I will not offend the law of modestie in being overcarried with remembrance thereof, being fullie purposed to make light accounte of any disgrace of fortune afterward, yet I make litle doubte but it shall alsoe appeare to be instantly recompenced with revenge.'

When shee had thus ended, all whoe were in presence stood attentive to see whether the king were of power to governe his passions, or whether hee would breake forthe & declare himselfe. But the king, albeit hee felt himselfe in many pointes [fo. 6] touched to the quicke, yett was hee soe farre from being carried into turbulent change that hee would not by long & sett answere make any shew that her wordes were receaved with much regard, returning breifly: That when hee gave her libertie of speech hee was well assured into what rage and furie shee would fall, but was able to digest the injurie of her reproachfull tongue, governed by the weakenes both of her sexe and age, and of her distempered mind, wherewith how unjustly hee had beene charged, his patience did declare, and to men of indifferencie and depth of judgement hee had made manifest; that hee had noe further offended King Richard then in providing that King Richard should not offend him.

---

[8] MS marginal note: 'K. Henries eldest sonne was knighted by K. Rich. in Ireland.'
[9] Scarred, defaced (OED).

The king nether used nor admitted wordes of further provocation, neither would hee openly seeme ether to displease or feare her. In shorte time after hee made appointment for her returne into Fraunce. And soe upon the xxvth of July shee departed from Dover to Callais, from whence Huguenel, who had beene sent for her, advertised the French kings commisioners then abiding at Boleigne of her arrivall, upon the last daye of July. She was honorably accompanied with the English from Calleis to Lalingham where, encountring with the Earle of St. Paule and other commisoners for the French king, shee forsooke her horse, and entred into a tent erected for that purpose. Many French ladies came unto her, and went with her to the chappell of Longlingantes, but none entred with her besides the to the chapel of Longlingante, but none entered with her besides the commissioners of both the realmes. Here the Lord Thomas Percie protested that the king his maister had sent her to bee delivered to her father [fo. 6v] with intent that hee againe should be acquitted of all bandes concerning her marriage. Hee protested further that shee was then soe cleare a virgine as when shee was delivered to King Richard, and if any man would advow the contrarie, hee offered to justifie it upon his bodie by execution of armes, according to the lawes of combate.

The Earle of St. Paule thought best to beleeve that which hee thought best to bee beleeved, and thereupon returned answere that hee was soe well perswaded for that pointe, that there should need nether triall nor talke. Then the Lord Peircie tooke her by the hand and delivered her unto the earle, and the earle againe delivered unto him letters of discharge, according as before it had beene agreed. Then they departed from the chappell to the Frenchmens tentes where dinner was prepared, which being finished, the English companie returned to Calleis and the ladie departed with the Frenchmen to Bolloigne.

The Lady Isabell, framing her behaviour to the lowest descent of courtesie bestowed great giftes upon the lordes and ladies at theire departure, upon the ladies for favour, but upon the lordes only for fashion, for shee was not ether soe yong as not to perceave, nor yet soe carelesse as not to regard the treacheries that they had used against King Richard. But wronges must bee wincked at many times, and they that openly will frett or frowne have a meaning to loose their means of revenge. And albeit shee was reported to bee of sharpe conceite (ether because she was soe indeed, or that pittie did raise everie thing to the highest), yet it is not to be doubted but shee receaved instructions, when as being of soe simple age she could [fo. 7] expresse the arte of experienced yeares. The French king her father receaved her, and deceived King Henrie who expected to have gained his amitie thereby. But these two kinges were soe full of jealouzies on both sides that their frendship could not long indure. And impossible it is that old displeasures by new desertes should sodainly bee appeased.

And now wee will leave this yong ladie to her meaner but surer honors in France, where shee lived to see the House of Lancaster first exceedingly flourish, then sodainly fall, and that cheifly by the working of a ladie of Fraunce who seemed to bee raised in reveng of her dishonor, for King Henry the 6th took the Earles daughter of St. Paule to wife,[10] whose raigne was the most apparant cause of his ruine.

After the feast of the Epiphanie a parliament was held at London,[11] wherein the statute of Lollardes was made, wherebie it was enacted that if any did preach doctrine which should bee judged hereticall, and should persist to maintaine theire opinions before the bishop of theire diocesse, they should bee degraded and delivered over to the secular power. This statute was presentlie putt in execution upon one William Sawtrie,[12] parish preist of the church of St. Scithe in London, who because hee could not frame his conscience ether to beleeve as others did, or to speake otherwise then hee did beleeve, was putt to death by fire in Smithfeild, being the first man that was burned for religion in this realme. Upon increase of these executions the religion which hee professed in ensuing ages did mightily increase, for death only for conscience of religion doth alwaies most stronglie stirre pittie to the one side, and envie to the other, which affections being unable[13] to helpe those that are past all remedie, or to hurte those that are above their power, they straightwaies turne from the [fo. 7v] persons to the cause, wherein the inclination of men being once settled, they become resolute for death, perswading them selves that thoughe a man looses of his yeares in this world, that is more then manifoldly recompenced by coming the sooner to heaven; that althoughe it be painfull to die in health yet few in sickenes die with ease, and a man might happily with lesse thankes to god, and more adventure to his soule, die as painfully and violentlie many other waies; that seeing many upon their death beddes did account it a great blessing to suffer death for religion, they would never be greived to goe to that death which they should afterwardes happilie have desired.

Alsoe in this parliament many stricte statutes were made against the Welshmen forbidding any of them to purchase landes or tenementes within England, or within English townes of Wales, or to injoy other office or libertie in any cittie, burroughe or franchised

---

[10] An apparent error: Henry VI married Margaret, daughter of René (1409–80), duke of Anjou and king of Sicily.

[11] Jan. 1401.

[12] Marginal note: 'The first man that suffered as a Lolarde.' Sawtre, a priest from Norfolk, was burned at Smithfield 2 Mar. 1401.

[13] MS: '... being being unable.'

towne; that noe Englishmen should bee convicte at the sute of a Welshman, but by judgement of English justices, and by verdicte of Englishmen of the next venue; that no Welshman should take distresses[14] within the counties adjoyning to the Marchesse of Wales, nor arrest the people of those countries coming into Wales; that noe Welshman should beare defensive armes in markett townes, churches, assemblies or highewaies; which statutes seemed to deprive the Welshmen of all the libertie and priviledge of subjectes.

These proceedings were much against the advise of many who perswaded the [fo. 8] king that the wild witte of that untrained people would more easilie bee reclaimed by clemencie and justice (vertues most amiable where they have not beene usuall) then by severitie litle shorte of crueltie; that noe people will indure unequall conditions any longer time then necessitie doth bind them; that it was noe pollicie to seeke his will by driving a feirce people to seeke theire remedie by a desperate resolution of revolte; that desperate subjectes are more dangerous then discontented, because both are displeased with the present state, but these only expecte a change, they will worke it with all possible power; that they whoe hope for noe good, they feare noe evill. And indeed, these hard lawes being hardly executed, did much harden the mindes of the Welshmen, whose stiffe nature incivilitie had made by these meanes intractible, & prone to breake all patience of subjection. Soe they who before ether held alleigaunce or brake out only upon licentiousnes then knitt into one strength, and to runne all fortunnes for theire common libertie, holding it necessary ether valiantlie to oppose against these greivances, or els by yeelding unto them to open a way for many more.

'What,' said they, 'shall wee soe litle esteeme the desire of libertie, which nature hath made of such vertue as nether force can winne nor flatterie weaken, nor tyme weare out? Have wee our ancient libertie in noe estimation? Is our courage abased more than our fortune? Doth vertue and libertie allwayes end together? That which heretofore wee yeelded unto them was subjection, not slaverie, not submission [fo. 8v] to bee more hardly intreated then outlawes. Nay, then, goe too, wee must & wee will, there remaines some life of dying libertie. Wee will not yeeld one inch to those who cann measure out such large elles, but since wee have in some sorte recovered our free estate wee will with all obstinacy endeavour to retaine it. Heretofore wee have beene able ether to vanquish or to wearie them when they were more mightie, and wee more weake, they being united and wee scattered. But now they are more divided then wee, having more traitors among themselves then enemies with us. And albeit wee had noe hopes to

---

[14] Legal seizures of property, intended to compel satisfaction of an obligation (OED).

incourage us, yett extreame hatred must make us desperate; all
enemies are to bee resisted because they seeke theire owne glorie and
our spoile. But speciallie wee are to stand against those who desire to
bring us to their absolute devotion. Wee have weapons and wee have
handes; lett us take courage alsoe to disburthen our selves of bondage
ether by victorie or by death!'

Soe they resolved with losse of their lives to recover or to end the
losse of theire libertie, being overcarried indifferently with hate and
disdaine, two mightie passions to drive on disordered desires. But
upon advertisement that great preparations were made against them
in England, feare (which maketh men subtle to search into all counsailes) enforced them to doe that which at the first they thought
unnecessarie, by seeking to bee supported by others. And knowing
the disposition of the French at that time against the English, they
commended theire cause under many argumentes of equitie to the
King of Fraunce, [fo. 9] before whome they laied sometimes theire
owne ether innocencie, or desertes, sometimes the injuries done by
theire enemies: what example it would bee ether of his confidence to
his other frendes if they were helped, or of discouragement if they
should bee abandoned; that the law of honor and clemencie did bind
him to theire releife which, the more freelie and readilie hee did afford,
the more agreable it should bee to true magnanimitie; that he gave a
greivous sentence against the common condition of this life, if hee
denied compassion to men in distresse; that soe many of them as
should perish throughe defaulte of his defence, of soe many hee should
lose the honor and service, being all readie in any danger to adventure
for him.

The French king entred into counsaile whether it were more expedient for him to adjoyne to the side, or to attend the issue with an idle
eye. Some, knowing what it was to undertake the prosecution[15] of a
tumultuous war, perswaded the king that it was a dangerous advise
to move & declare himselfe ether upon the reasons or requestes of
rebelles, whose hopes being measured by desire more then judgement
are for the most parte deceavable; that it was the custome of the
popular sorte to enter easilie into warre and afterwardes, perplexities
increasing, to seeke an end with undiscreet desires; that it was better
to permitt the English and the Welsh to weare out themselves by a
long warr, then by interposing his aid to drive them to conditions of
peace; that ether being neutrall, hee should bee honored of bothe, or
that being intire in Fraunce, he might more stronglie attempte the
possession of [fo. 9v] Guian, or that some other waies the travailes
and perplexities of the one and the other would in shorte time raise

[15] MS: 'protection,' probably a scribal error.

occasions favourable to his desires; that neutralitie is then onlie com-
mendable when there is noe feare of the victorie of ether parte, for
then it bringeth not only suertie, but sometimes (the warrs having
weakened both) advantage.

Others were of opinion that supportance should not bee denied,
but deferred onlie, untill the king might discerne what traine these
affairs would take; that in the meane time hee might entertaine theire
requestes with wordes and hopes in generall, nether denying nor
assuring his aide, not omitting alsoe to cast amongst them some seedes
of sedition and hate; that holding his helpe in some difficultie and
suspence, hee should the more kindle both theire desire & estimation
of the same; that in case they should bee more dangerouslie distressed,
that assistance which they could not obtaine as frendes, they might
easilie bee intreated to accepte as subjectes. For it often happeneth in
civill seditions that men will submitt themselves rather to strangers,
then to theire soveraigne, esteeming it more tollerable to stoope under
the power of any other then of him who houldeth himself injured by
them. 'And thereby,' said they, 'wilbee cast into our armes not onlie
glorie, spoile, enlargement of empire (things honorable and great) but
the meanes to bee revenged of all our former wrongs. Whereof wee
may hold the best assurance if wee nether lett goe occasions, nor runne
before them. For us the mulberie tree buddeth last but [fo. 10]
bringeth forth fruite with the first, soe they who attend the true season,
albeeitt they enter late into action yet shall they in good time execute
& atcheive.'

Against both these opinions the Earle of St. Paule used a fable, that
once there was a shower of raine which washed away the wittes of all
them upon whome it fell. Now certaine wise men, foreseeing this raine,
crept into caves because they would not bee wett therewith. When
the shower was over and had made the rest fooles, they came forth
againe, and begann to make some shewe of theire wisdome. But the
fooles were soe farre from honoring them, that they handled them soe
rudelie as they wished they had beene alsoe made fools. 'Soe,' said
hee, 'if wee will make our selves soe wise as to shrinke from this shower,
and shunne the common condition of our neighbours, assuredly they
will all hate us, and upon occasion declare against us. And if wee have
not altogether abandoned the hope of recovering Guian, and expelling
the English out of Fraunce, there is noe meanes soe proper as by
maintaining enemies, especiallie rebelles, against them, which may
hold them soe busied as to attend both greater and nearer matters,
they shall bee inforced to lett that goe. Further, this may bee an
occasion for us to fasten foote in England which, not many yeares
passed, with exceeding great both industrie and expence wee did
attempte. But if wee are not movable by hope, yet feare should enforce

us to provide that the King of England growe not greate. For if ether by denying or deferring our aide, hee shall obtaine his purpose in Wales, hee [fo. 10v] will not easilie bee bridled in Fraunce. The desire of riches and of rule is immoderate, hee will never stand content with the present but will aspire to inlarge his state. It perteineth to cowardes to spend much time in deliberation. Opportunitie cannot brooke delaies; wee must not stand upon long advise after the occasion bee once fairelie offered.'[16]

This advise prevailed with the king as being both conceited and bold, whereupon hee resolved to declare himself in aid of the Welsh, and according to the state of affaires to gather frute from theire necessitie, or at least to draw them soe farre into faulte as there should bee noe hope of reconcilement with theire king. To this end hee forthwith dispatched James, Earle of March and his two brothers, with xij hundred knightes and gentlemen, and an answerable band of ordinarie souldiers, for valour, pollicie and discipline bearing good reputation and hope. They tooke shipping at the mouth of the River Seine,[17] and beganne to crosse the seas with xxxty saile, but were soe crossed in theire way with contrarie & tempestuous windes that they could by noe meanes approach the coast of Wales. Soe they came before Plymouth a litle within evening, and leaving parte of theire shipps riding at anchor, with the residue they entered the haven. Here they surprized a few small vesselles loaden with fish and corne. Then they landed and beganne to forrage & [fo. 11] fire certaine of the next villages, running scattered here and there, whethersoever hope of spoile did lead them.

The greedinesse of the French was a great means of advantage to the English, for being more thirstie after pillage then bloud, and respecting less endes principall then inferiour and accidentall, they gave liberty to the English to collecte themselves and to cutt in peeces many of theire enemies whoe in hungrie hunting after prey (as greedie men are seldome cercumspecte) ranged loosely from the maine companie. Alsoe by firing of beacons the people from all partes assembled in armes, and with well governed speede charged stronge upon theire enemies. Hereupon the French souldiers, some for want of experience in militarie affaires, others for care of the pillage they had gott, not only omitted to doe things requisite, but beganne to seperate, and fall into disorder, rather running then returning backe againe to their shipps. But there they found a farre greater confusion and disorder,

[16] Note that Waleran of Luxembourg, Count of St. Pol, had married King Richard's half-sister Maud Courtenay (issue of his mother's first marriage) but was subsequently prevented by Bolingbroke's accession from securing the territories to which his marriage had entitled him.

[17] This is probably the expedition of August 1403.

for presentlie after theire landing foule wether beganne to rise, which in shorte tyme increased to a fearefull tempest, whereby xij of the French shipps that had beene laid in the mouth of the haven were dashed to peeces, ether upon the rockes or sandes or one of them against another, and all the men in them perished by drowning.

Hereupon the French that were on shore made a desperate reckoning of theire safetie, all labouring [fo. 11v] in one distresse, and one increasing the feare of another. Theire enemies did drive them upon the sea, and againe the sea did drive them upon theire enemies, betweene which they stood in a miserable choice, ether to bee swallowed by the one, or slaine by the other, serving for example to men of action to manage theire adventures with forecast and care, and not to proceed upon dangerous hope that theire enemies are ether farr of, or fearfull and weake. But theire destruction by sea was nether soe plaine nor soe terrible, nor soe honorable to theire enemies; whereupon making choise of the least parte of theire calamitie, they putt from the shoare in theire smaller vesselles. Here many of them were cast away, many alsoe not escaping the furie of the sworde. The residue with desperate adventure recovered those shipps that lay at sea, which having long wrought against the rage of the storme by having roome to drive, & heaving their heaviest carriage over board, with much adoe were kepte alive. Then, leaving the English coast, they returned broken and disordered to St. Malos in Fraunce, where they imposed one upon another (as the custome is in infortunate successe) the faulte of the disorder. The broken wreckes, and the floting bodies of men and horses not only ministred large matter of contentment to the English, both for recompence and revenge, but this weake beginning did much increase both their courage and contempt against theire enemies.

The French king, not much dismayed with this adverse adventure, appointed [fo. 12] one of his marshalles called Mountmorencie and the maister of his crossbowes, with xij thousand men for a second voyage into Wales, giving them commission to deale at large according as occasion should open unto them. They tooke shipping at Brest, and the wind was soe favourable & soe full that in shorte tyme they arrived at Milford Haven in Wales.[18] Here they landed, and finding themselves in good condition of strength, beganne presentlie to thinke upon some enterprize, supposing that ether to lie still, or to march quietlie and doe nothing, would greatlie diminish theire reputation. Soe, leaving the castle of Pembroke, they made their first attempt against the towne of Hevefordwest, wherein the yong Earle of Arundell commaunded, whoe succeeded his father in all pointes aswell of vertue

---

[18] This landing actually occurred in early August 1405.

as of honor and estate. But albeit the force of the Frenchmen was great, and theire resolution to carrie the towne greater, yet the valour of the defendantes applied to the strength of the place surmounted them both, soe as all their sharpe assaultes were beaten backe with disadvantage. And this happened the rather for that they seemed soe hastily desirous to prevaile that they neglected the best meanes to prevail, supposing only by suddaine force[19] to make themselves maisters of theire purposes and hopes.

The Frenchmen, desperate of successe, forsooke Hareford, and tooke theire journey [fo. 12v] towardes Denbigh, and seldome hath any man greived for loosing his owne as they did for not getting[20] that which pertained to another, holding it for assured that it could not bee without losse of reputation that theire first enterprize did not succeed. In the meane time the most advised Welshmen, upon reporte of King Henries preparations, could not talke or almost thinke of any other thing then of his might and theire miseries; theire trembling thoughtes allwayes ranne upon the spoyling of theire countrie and upon the butcherie and captivitie of themselves, fearing to lose all and alsoe to bee lost.

But Owen Glendor (whome the Welshmen, giving title with authoritie, commonly called Prince of Wales) lett fall noe pointe of diligence to raise the feare of some and repress the feare of others, to a true temper of courage in all. And knowing right well that strength without discipline is nerer beastlines then manhood, hee imployed all his endeavours both in arming & trayning his followers, in transporting women and children into places of safetie, in using all meanes to confirme those that were forward, to drawe on those that were doubtefull, and to provoke those to open dealing who were frendes to him, and durst not declare themselves enemies to King Henry.

Before these hee laid the memorie of their auncient libertie, comparing it with the condition of theire base bondage, how honorable the one was and [fo. 13] how ignominious the other. To this desire of libertie hee added alsoe respecte of glorie, affirming that theire auncestors had often prevailed against the English forces, and ether chased them backe by a couragious chardge or, by advisedly induring, wearied them awaye. He proceeded further that not only opportunitie did invite them to confederate, but necessitie did injoyne them to adjoyne to theire frendes, and to become partakers of theire desires and hopes in whose dangers they were made parties; for the King of England, esteeming all by a few, did free none where some were in faulte, but wrapped up all alike in those rigours & severities which

[19] MS: 'by force by suddaine force.'
[20] MS: '... as they did not for getting....'

cruell princes in the height & pride of theire fortune are inclinable to use; that by cold neutrality they should manifestly incurre danger from both parties, by bearing themselves as forsakers of the English and not followers of the Welsh side, whereby they should bee esteemed open enemies to the one and false frendes to the other. 'Take, therefore,' said hee, 'weapons in your handes, and courage in your hartes: this is the time ether to recover that which wee have lost or to loose that which shall never bee recovered, and the greater our enterprize is, the greater shalbee ether our glorie if wee beare throughe, or the danger if wee fayle. For my parte, I will bee as forward to execute as to advise, considering that in our victorie doth consist not only the particular safetie of everie man, but the glorie alsoe and the libertie of all.'

[fo. 13v] These speeches in substance delivered by Owen Glendor, but (according to his nature) with vehement gesture and voice, breathed soe fresh life and courage into the rude multitude (by whome bould counsaile is alwayes accepted for noble and wise) that it seemed more necessarie to retaine them, then to provoke them. The remembrance of theire greene indignities concurring with theire naturall inclination were suficient to arme theire mindes with desperate purposes & desires. Soe having made themselves x thousand strong, and joyning companie with the French forces, they marched together throughe Glamorgan shire into Worcestershire, being raised into highe hopes both for the greatnes of their strength, and for the meanes which they supposed they had to maintaine it. Here they[21] harried a good parte of the countrie, fired the suburbes of Worcester, and begann to enterprise against the cittie, intending to make it the seate of the warre. But on the suddaine, advertisement arrived of the kinges nere approach with an armie verie strong and well appointed, and resolved to present themselves to a present encounter. Besides the soddainesse of his cominge (which in case of rescue is of great importance) his readinesse to fight did somewhat daunt those who before stood in best assurance. Hereupon they dissolved the seige, and retired [fo. 14] into Wales with such spoiles as theire hungry hast could gather up. The king followed with all his power, and found them imbattailed upon an highe mountaine, as nether willing to putt themselves upon the arbitrement of fortune nor altogether disposed to abandon the feild.

Some advised the king to charge upon them, affirming that they had not that advantage in place which hee had in men; that the same feare which drew them to that retreat (being well sowed) would easilie dislodge them; that they were almost contrarie counsailes to forbeare to fight, and yett to drawe soe neare to the enemie; that they could

21 MS: 'the.'

not retire without dishonor, dangerous to the whole substance of the warre. This opinion was advaunced cheiflie by those who beare least swaye, supposing by adventurous advice to raise a reputation of valour to themselves. But the king, whose deliberations depended cheiflie of himselfe, perceaving that without disadvantage hee could not approach them, not only in regard of the nature of the place but for that the condition of assailantes is allwaies worse then that[22] of those that defende, determined not to fight rashly against resolute men who, by how much greater was the inequalitie of theire adventure, by soe much lesse would they esteeme the losse of theire lives. Hee held it more assured to cutt of theire releife, and vexe them with incommodities, the [fo. 14v] probabiltie being great that partly for want, partly for that the armie was composed of different nations, they would draw to some disorder, which being well taken & followed, would do them greater dammage then a present encounter. Soe hee possessed himself of another hill nere unto them, stopped all passages, and attended the best opportunitie to enterprize upon them.

Here both armies remained, the one in full view of the other, governing themselves according to the proceedings of theire enemies. Betweene them there was a fair large plaine wherein many actions of arms were dayly executed: here were slaine the Lord Patroles of Triers, brother of the Marshall of Fraunce, the Lord Mattleton, the Lord Vale, and the Bastard of Burbone, with 5 hundred gentlemen of Fraunce, persons of speciall both hope and regard in the armie. On the English side was no notable loss, ether for number or for name.

After viij dayes, victualles grew scant among the Welsh, and all other things drewe to extremities and streightes. And the French could hardly indure the harde fare of that uncivill and unfruitfull countrie, which if all passages had beene open could not afford sufficient supplie to such a multitude. Hereupon they begann to lay downe theire hopes and to [fo. 15] submitt all other respectes to the safeguard of theire lives. Soe after some debatement betweene Owen Glendoer and the Marshall of Fraunce, they determined presentlie to remove the whole armie, which then begann to bee equallie oppressed with famine and with feare. And to avoide those difficulties which the nearenes of an enemie might worke upon advantage of retreate, they departed about the dead of the night in the most secrett silence that they could. But this, being done both sodainlie and in the darke, cast such confusion and stroake soe unappeasable a terror upon the souldiers, that if the king upon the first discoverie of theire remove had putt upon them the chase, there is noe question but hee had driven them to a ruinous rout. Butt he, not assured of theire intentes, forbare to execute so

[22] MS: 'worse then them ...'

happie an occasion, hoping (as indeed it happened) that for want of maintenance and paye, theire companies of themselves would disorder and dissolve. And thus it often falleth, that because the confusions of enemies are not alwaies knowne, the time is past for manie advantages before it is espied. And seldome it hath beene seene, that twoe so great armies soe nere placed together have departed without ether battaile or chase.

After this the Frenchmen were slowe in service, but readie enoughe in doing injurie to the Welsh, the penurie of the souldiers driving them to open insolencie and disobedience; for having noe meanes to maintaine [fo. 15v] themselves but pillage & praye, they became a greater terror to theire frendes then to theire enemies, and did more endamage them by entertainment & robberies then a professed ememie could have done by spoile, soe hard it is to entertaine discipline where paye is not performed. And thus the pore people, bearing the ordinarie infelicitie of an hired armie, were oppressed alike on the one side with theire enemies, and the other with theire aides, who were unto them like Ajax sheild,[23] which rather weigheth downe then defendeth those that beare it.[24] Att the last the Frenchmen, being prepared nether with money nor constancie of minde to indure out the length of the warre, and the Welshmen finding it a lesse weakening to them to have few soldiers then more then they were able to maintaine, a dangerous thing alsoe to call in greater forces to theire aide then they had power to keepe in order, they both agreed to breake societie, and the French, with litle thanke and lesse ether purchase or reward, mounted upon shipboard, and returned into Fraunce. And it is manifest that the intent of the voyage was ether for the spoile of England or dominion of Wales, if the enterprize had drawne to good event; for few will undertake the travaile and expence of forraigne warres but to gaine by those for whome they fight.

Now the Welshmen were lefte unto themselves, unable ether to resist or divert the kings forces, and reposing [fo. 16] noe other hope by yeelding unto him then might bee expected from an enemie provoked and revengefull. Hereupon they withdrew themselves into the mountaines of Snowden, and there scattered the warre, giving ground when they were pursued, and hovering at hand when they were given over, and by shifting allwaies into places of advantage endeavored at one time both to avoid battaile and to hinder the king from doing any thing of importance. By which manner of fight they kepte the English playe to litle purpose, delighting themselves with

---

[23] A wry bit of irony, whether intended or not: in the dedicatory preface to *The First Part*, Hayward had employed the image of Ajax's shield when invoking Essex's name to defend his book.

[24] MS marginal note here: 'Maintaining souldiers.'

this hope, that in time theire enemies would ether grow wearie or laye themselves open to some advantage; at least they were assured to winne tyme, which is the mother of manie mutations. Yet the king ceased not in close and firme order sharpelie to pursue them, throughe all waies & in all weathers, being alwaies ether the first, or with the first, in everie adventure. And whereas in actions of armes lingring is tedious and haste dangerous, to avoide tediousnes hee made choice to enterprize with danger. And by observing the carriage of his souldiers, and bearing his parte deepely in theire hardest adventures, he imposed upon them the strongest commaund, whilest every man affected both the imitation and favour of the king. For there is noe meane soe availeable to winne the souldier ether to labour or love, as when theire commaunders doe make themselves equall unto them in diett, in apparell, but cheifely in paines, which to theire seeming takes away theire constrainte. Insomuch as they esteeme not soe much the rewardes of theire generales as theire company & helpe, and doe more honor those whoe take paines with them [fo. 16v] then those who doe allowe them much idle ease. And albeit labours are distastfull at the first, and cause the souldier to murmure and repine, yet being alike hardened therein they beginne to conceave a good opinion of themselves, when they see they are able to surmount those things which are soe terrible unto others.

Herevpon you might have seene the standardes striving who should make most hast, & the souldiers in a glorious emulation contending to passe under all perilles, to climbe over all difficulties with their valour. They seemed many times to frett and to feare, that by the meanes of theire long & often restes, theire enemies should have opportunitie to escape, and if they could but find the warre they would (they said) in shorte time finish it. But what availeth it to bee resolute where courage cannot assure successe? For the Welshmen, well acquainted with the straight passages, the steepe cliffes, the craggie rockes, the hilles, the woodes, the fenny places, did easilie delude the devices and the endeavours of the English armie, whose wantes alsoe they much increased by destroying forrage, and wasting all the countrie which they were not able to defend.

Att the last, the king finding that the Welshmen held continuallie to this advantage of place, that there was more hazard then hope in those roughe and barren mountaines where horsemen could doe but litle service, that his soldiers by travail and want fell everie daye into change of distresse, that supplie of victuall came slowelie forward, that his traine of carriage was not [fo. 17] easilie to bee continuallie removed and guarded, that all difficulties did not onlie continue but increase, that the glorie would bee far lesse to bee victorious then the infamie would bee to bee beaten awaye, his obstinacie was overcome and hee yeelded to frame his counsailes according to the condition of his affaires. So, having burned a great parte of the countrie and hewed many in peeces who fell within the swing of his sword, and gathered a large prey of cattle, hee withdrew his armie to Worcester. But the Welshmen, perfectlie knowing the passages of the countrie, intercepted certaine of his carriages laden with victuall, which was an adventure of greater regard then it would have beene in a more plentifull place. Then, because winter approached, in which tyme it is hard taking the feild, the king dispersed his power and returned to London, expressing an expectation to accomplishe his desire with the favour of another time.

And albeit it often happeneth that [a] leader not attaining his intended endes may meritt praise in his proceedinges, yet was the king much disquieted that in this great enterprize the end was not answerable to the endeavour, and this was the more greivous unto him. By how much in former tymes his felicities had sailed with a prosperous gale, by how much alsoe the action was followed with a vehement desire, lastly by how much he had beene frustrated by an uncivill people, incloased in a barren and streight territory, never seeking to make theire fortune greater then theire virtue.

After this Owen Glendore gathered together his dispersed compan-ies, to whome many others resorted dailie, carried noe [fo. 17v] lesse by hope of pillage then by authority of his name. With these hee made continuall incursions upon the English borderers, not ceasing to execute such insolent outrages as hungry and angry souldiers full of desperate both wantes & revenge are accustomed to exercise upon theire enemies. They regarded not the innocencie of anie person, but rather supposed that the more innocent they were, the more should they manifest thereby theire hate. They desired alsoe to increase rather the hate of the English then to winne theire love, for that hate would putt them in hope of victorie, but love would bee the instrument to drawe on subjection. The king had appointed forces sufficient to have resisted the Welshmen if they had orderly joyned and charged together. But coming by companies ether too weake or too late they were soe farre from diminishing the feares of others that they were drawne into societie of theire feares. Doubtlesse that prince maketh warre to his great disadvantage, who vexeth a people that hath nothing to loose.

Whilest the king was in this sorte held busied in Wales, Aquitane grew unquiet, whence followed dishonour and losse to the English. For John, Earle of Clermont, sonne to the Duke of Burbone, laid seige to the castles of St. Peter, St. Marie and the new castle with soe livelie resolution and constancie of courage, that albeit the English assayed manie times to make rescue, sometimes assailing the armie and sometimes· disturbing the countrie of theire enemies, yet could they not remove him from his enterprize. And soe by advantage partly of the wavering minds of the Gascoines, who beganne now to shake aswell in faith as in courage, the kinges absence & delayes much abating theire affections, [fo. 18] partlie of the weakenesse of the English garrisons, daily wearing out & slowely supplied, in shorte time hee made himself maister of those holdes. And because one good or ill happ cometh seldome unaccompanied with the like, the Lord of Delabrech, alsoe joyning himself to the favour of tyme, assailed the Castle of Carlassin, and heaping upon the defendantes one necessitie after another enforced them to yeeld to composition. The souldiers of these places returned into England so pore and naked of all things as they seemed to beare the resemblance of rogues. Here they filled everie mans eares with justification of themselves and complaintes against others, afferming that throughe weakenesse of government & other despaires the rest alsoe will give up themselves in like sorte to the enemie. And it was assuredly beleeved, if after the yeelding of these peeces the[25] French had proceeded in good appointement to the rest, that many of them would have done the like, examples being of great effecte in all varigations of fortune.

But the English were soe blinded with hate and jealouzies among themselves that they litle regarded any common dangers. But all the meanes of remedie were past, which then wrought verie different effectes, for the better sorte with care of the common wealth were greatlie greived; others who disliked the present and desired change conceived a kind of joye at these misadventures, as being meanes to draw others to the like dislike and desire with them. Yett all had a touch of indignation and shame, and (as in like cases it ever happeneth) were much incensed against those whoe governed. Of whome, not knowing who were most in faulte, they blamed cheiefly the king for all, traducing him that being possessed with nearer feares, he permitted the [fo. 18v] remote parts of his dominions to bee lost.

Alsoe the Earle of St. Paule, whoe had taken the half sister of King Richard to wife, because hee had sent defiance into England supposed it would bee a checke to his reputation if his word were not seconded by his weapon. Hereupon hee assembled about xvj or xviij hundred men of armes, the greatest parte of noble race, and made provision of all thinges expedient for his exploite, purposing to shew his face to fortune, and according to the chaunces thereof to proceede. Soe aboute the end of the yeare he losed from Harefleet, & with a shorte & speedie course arrived at the Ile of Wight. The people upon the first feare (which allwayes is the fiercest) forsooke their houses and left all things

[25] MS: 'they.'

to the discretion of the enemie which ether by staye or carriage might bee a hinderance to theire escape. By this meanes he landed without resistance and forthwith fired foure cottages and foure small villages, and to grace this successe made foure knightes upon the feild, bearing himselfe with such proud joye as if fortune had cast her selfe at his feete. His soldiers alsoe filled the aire with such shoutes and cries as might easilie have perswaded some whoe knewe not what they had done, that they had atcheived some gallant victorie. But they did crowe too soone before daye, and theire cold speed in going forward was the cause that afterwardes they spedd soe coldly. For the earl, blinded with his owne hopes and not considering that feare soone diminisheth if the cause of feare bee not maintained, by remisse and unperfecte government of his advantage gave soe good respitt to the ilanders that, ether upon better consideration or upon a common custome of men [fo. 19] to conceave hope when they knowe the hardest of theire danger, they assembled in armes and resolved to putt their fortune in adventure.

The Earle had sent forth certaine souldiers to make discoverie whoe, returning unto him in extreame haste, reported everie thing farre greater then it was: how many thousandes theire enemies were, how good theire appointment, how resolute they were, how nere at hand for hard blowes. Hereupon the earle, being as prone to feare as hee had beene light in joye, determined not to attempte any triall, and soe in great confusion & hast returned to his shipps, which would have beene hard for many of his companie had not the night come on and covered his disordered flight. The weakenesse of this action cast upon him such a contempte even amongst his followers that it was a vaine thing to goe about to cover his cowardise with any coulorable excuse. In his return upon the seas hee came within veiw of certaine English shipps of warre; the same feare which drew both sides to prepare to fight, withdrew ether from giving the attempte. And this was the end of a strange warre, begunne with feare, continued without danger, and ended without losse, wherein was deserved the name nether of of enemie nor of enterprize. The like event may all expecte who presume more & adventure lesse then is expedient.

Now the king, albeit hee had hitherto carried himselfe honorably enoughe, and with good courage, yett were his atcheivementes farre under expectation. And albeit hee was held to bee of noe evill disposition, and in most pointes behaved himselfe both moderatly and uprightlie, not doing evill of himselfe unlesse hee did mistake it, as being apparelled [fo. 19v] in the fashion of goodnes, yet as the court never wanteth those whoe will worke ether upon the weakenes or necessities of princes, soe the continuance of his course imbouldned him to followe some indirect directions. Alsoe, being both new in state,

and by a new enforced title, hee was tied to respecte manie who would
not bee bridled, with whome hee held his pace rather as a good frend
then a good prince, ether permitting or not punishing many greivances
for theire sakes, and being noe authour of much offence, yet did both
indure & protecte those that did offend. Againe, many who had beene
his agentes to advaunce his cause, not finding effectes answerable to
expectation, begann to call into affection theire aunicent government.
Generally for one cause or other scarce was any man esteemed of witt
who found not faulte with pointes of government. And verilie nothing
is more burdensome, nothing more dangerous, then to undertake a
charge with extraordinarie opinon of worthinesse and deserte, because
not being able to satisfie such expectation (men desiring more then
cann bee done) all actions are therefore interpreted at the worst. For
who knowes a people that knowes not that upon suddaine liking they
will expecte wonders, which if they bee not soddainly answered, they
fall forthwith into wonderfull hate? Againe, ancient true descentes are
constantlie obayed, because time hath worne out both hatred and
contempte, but new erected titles, as they are soone [fo. 20] followed,
soe are they sodainly abandoned and loste. Lastly, as a wound when
the bloud growes cold paineth the bodie more then when it was first
taken, soe the dishonor of that alteration which the people felte not
in the heate of theire humour afterwardes grew to bee most greivous
unto them.

Upon these causes emulation and envie beganne to kindle, which
like unto fire alwayes drawes to the highest. And in a fume ether of
mutabilitie or of malice, the people were heard not only to murmure
that with such facillitie the king had attained his estate both against
the will of manie and above the expectation of all, but they beganne
further to looke into his evidence, to examine his title, and to bring
into question ether what right hee had to the state, or what necessitie
the state had of him.

In this humour they coursed, and discoursed in theire ordinarie
conferences that it was not the care of the common good, not the love
of lawes ether dashed or depraved which drew him to sett up a civill
discord (which cann never bee done with any lawfull meaning or
meanes) but that the corruption of the time served for a cloake to his
ambition, in laying an unjust gripe upon the crown. That in King
Richards time the common wealth was soe well settled that it needed
not to bee behoulding to him for uphoulding the same. For the prince
wanted noe obedience, the subjecte noe justice, and if severitie had
beene used against some few, it was for maintaining quiet [fo. 20v]
among the rest. The French were frendes, the Scottes noe enemies,
the Irish were reduced, the Welsh retained in good obedience, no
enemie was expected, none suspected, none respected; noe warrs were

feared, none towardes, but such as noe man would have conjectured. That hee in undertaking the state had shewed himselfe such a propper underpropper thereof, that hee had brought upon the same an univ- ersall face of confusion & trouble. And as the meanes were wicked whereby hee attained it, soe was it never governed with worse order. For as then nether by warrs was glory gotten, nor by peace quiet, noe subject was safe, no frend sure; great men were full of licentiousnes, good men of feare; many were inriched by lewd practises and many undone for doing well. That hee had taken order to keepe them busied, but tooke noe care to keepe them safe. For France had broken league, Scotland had made defiance, Ireland was lost, Wales lost more, ether throughe negligence or ambition of those that governed, then the peoples impatiencie to bee under commaunde; which being both attained and held with the valour and bloude of their auncestors, could not without shame bee soe lett goe. That by intestine warres (wherein only hee had beene fortunate) these mischeifes which the enemies could not, himselfe hath ether occasioned or done. That more nobilitie had beene destroied, and the realme sorer shaken (what with spoils [fo. 21] by enemies, what with charge of much unprofitable service) in two (too many) yeares of his raigne, then in twentie yeares which passed before. 'And thus have wee leaped,' said they, 'with the foolish fish out of the warme water into the flaming fire, and if hee continue this course of government wee shall shorte time find huge effectes of his politicke providing a mischeife for a remedie, or eles a remedie with a mischeife.'

These and the like speeches were at the first whispered by the better sorte, some talking by passion, some by errour, and some upon a sordid inclination to speake evill of those who are in highest place. Afterwardes they were broadly blasoned by the common people, whose nature is to bee open & free mouthed, as having small wisdome and litle to lose, soe most adventurous and least subject to danger. All men were possessed ether with hate or with suspicion, or with disdaigne, fruites ordinarily growing from civill discord, and soe much the more perillous and working in that they happened in a second degree, as all evilles are more dangerous in a second degree then in the first. In all those losses or dishonors which happened, many truthes were enlarged, many untruths invented, which were as readilie beleeved as if they had beene true. And the cause thereof was never imputed to the forces of the enemie, but to the want of foresight in the king. Generally, there seemed to want rather an authour, then ether cause or disposition to rebell. [fo. 21v]

And thus it falleth out[26] as in griefes soe in governmentes, the present

[26] MS marginal note: 'The multitude alwaies enclined to inovation.'

is allwayes esteemed most painfull, and as the diseased are desirous to
change chambers, but doe therewith change nether disease nor desire,
so they whoe are greived under any government are humorous of
alterations, but doe thereby find altered nether theire humour nor
theire harme. Hereupon Augustus used to say, that whosoever desireth
not a present state to bee changed, hee is both a good citizen and
a good man, because by often turning a commonwealth is often
overturned. Then what maddnesse is it for any people to attempte
alteration which they cannot ether rule as they would, or leave when
they list, and wherein they are assuredly lost if they doe not prevaile.
And if they doe, yett are they worse then they were before, for being
blemished for want of faith they are abhorred, or at least suspected,
even of those whome they did advaunce, and must alsoe satisfie with
theire substaunce a new lord and his emptie officers, who will use all
meanes to make the best hand of theire time.[27] But it is common to
men when theire evill destinie approacheth: it blindeth theire eyes
that they cannot see, it bindeth theire handes that it cannot helpe
making them oftentimes both contrivers & executioners of theire owne
mishapps.

And thus it befell to the English at that time whoe, feeling theire
greivances rather altered then eased by one change which they had
wrought, [fo. 22] beganne to turne their purposes to another. And
first they did cautelouslie[28] discover their discontentment, then they
broadlie talked theire pleasure, lastly they brake forth into seditious
actions, wherein boldnesse alsoe grew desperate by degrees. First
infamous libelles were throwne about, then secrett practises were put
to proofe, lastly armes were taken and ensignes openly displaied in
the feild.

And now, to beginne this divilles daunce, certeine persons practising
theire wittes as theire conceites were carried, cast forth manie rayling
rimes, stuffed with injurious wordes and full of offence (yett more
tasting of malice then of witt), partlie depraving the king, and partly
threatning him that King Richard was not soe destitute of frendes
that hee should long injoye the rewarde of his parricide. Of these small
beginnings great effectes did ensue, because men are commonly more
readie to prosecute an enterprise then to sett into it, and having once
broken beyond the boundes of obedience, noe certaine compasse doth
then conteine them.

The king at the first was more then moved at these indignities (as
thinges not only base, but not respective, seeme hainous unto princes)
and yett hee was not resolved in what sorte to make shew of himselfe,

---

[27] 'To make the best hand' = 'to make one's profit' (OED).
[28] Craftily, warily (OED).

wavering in varietie betweene anger and feare, whether hee should take severe punishment of this presumption, or suffer the vaine veine to vanish with time. [fo. 22v] Sometimes hee esteemed it noe pollicie to make light of any thing, sometimes lesse to feare all things. Hee discoursed with himselfe that it was lesse dangerous to dissemble such matters as will dissolve of themselves, then by blowing at the brand to cause it to cast forth a fuller flame; that hee who is sensible of every mans hate is unskillfull what it is to raigne; that against loud tongues there is noe better rule then to doe soe as they may not justly speake evill, whereby a man knowing upon what wings hee flieth, hee may contemne the base barking of curres beneath him; that happilie it served for his turne that free mindes should sometimes breake into biting wordes, for that dischardging thereby some parte of theire anger, the heate of theire actions is much abated.

But the sharpenesse of the kinges humour was much edged by some about him who affirmed that there was noe countermine but severitie against contempte; that the common people not held in feare would bee a terrour; that the resisting of injuries at the first maintaineth majestie, and holdeth honour in reputation, but patient bearing of them breedeth a bouldnesse to rebell. Hereupon hee caused inquirie to bee made whereby some of the lightest libellers were found out, and strangled to death at Tiburne. But the like happened hereby to the king, as the fable reporteth to have happened to a bearc [fo. 23] which, being stung by a bee, in revenge thereof did teare the hive, by which unseasonable execution of anger aginst one hee brought many hundredes about his eares. For these Hydraes heades soe multiplied by cutting of, and in such sorte this uncivill humour swelled by restrainte, that everie small accident (as it often happeneth) was like to raise a great disturbance.

Among others Sir Roger Clarindon, knight, and his esquire, and one of his yeomen were putt to death, for wordes pretended to intend treason.[29] This knight had beene in such favour with King Richard, and soe priviledgd by him above the ordinarie course and compasse of lawes, that hee scarce knew what subjection ment. Hee was but yong and lustie in yeares, respected both for his courage & comelinesse of person, sharpe witted cheifely in speaking sharpe, courteous and affable if hee were not stirred, but then roughe, rash and full of feirce courage, and thereby easie to bee intrapped. Hee was bastard sonne to the brave Prince Edwarde, and naturall brother to King Richard. In whose behalfe hee had carried himselfe much opposite to King Henrye, whilest hee was in private estate, and had broken upon him many bitter jestes, which manner of mirth men of highe stomach and

[29] May 1402.

degree in bloud beare long in minde, in whome the least woundes of honour doe closely rankle and many tymes greivously breake forth. Some others alsoe hated [fo. 23v] him not for any great offence, but for the great swaye and authoritie hee had borne. When hee was brought into publicke audience many great matters were objected against him sufficient to move the prince to indignation, or at least to give him colour to disclose the indignation which hee did beare. Some light matters were likewise objected, but (as in suspicions it is usuall) wrested to the worst sence, and agravated with the countenance & wordes of great men. But the only cause of his ruine [was] that hee had noe patience to dissemble the love and honor that hee did bear to King Richard, but had lett fall some speeches of the unfaythfull crueltie that had beene used against him, which because they conteined matter of truth, were the more easilie beleived to have beene spoken. In his answers hee carried himselfe carelesse and stoute, as disdaigning to submitt the estimation & dignitie that hee had borne to a new raised felicitie, & esteeming it more tollerable to indure all extremities, then to seeme to bee a sutour for favour. When hee was brought to the place of execution, with a firme countenance & voice full of spirit & harte he spake to the people to this effecte:

'I am come hither to suffer death as you see, and because in actions I have not offended, I am condemned only for wordes, not for incensing the people to turbulent behaviour, not for dangerous depraving the king or the state, but for praising and for pittying the life & death of King Richard of famous memorie, of whome I [fo. 24] suppose noe man cann thinke wthout greife, nor speake but in tearmes tempered with honour. Many worser princes this realme hath had, both for warre & for peace, hee bearing himselfe for the moste part victorious in the one, and not insupportable in the other, and in both his good partes surmounting his ill. But whatsoever hee was, it hath alwayes beene free to speake freelie of those whome death had freed both from hatred and harme, and greatest men have nothing greived to heare theire greatest enemies commended after death. There is noe power, noe authoritie, cann ether tye the tongues of men, or barre the libertie of theire thoughtes, the one whereof is the wittnes of honor, the other the judge. There is noe man able with the force & felicitie of his present time ether to extinguish the memorie of tymes past, or to stoppe the mouth of times succeeding. But it is time vainlie spent to repeat matters which cannot bee repealed; it is too great weakenesse in cases of extremitie ether to wish or to complaine. I have digested in my judgement the sorrowes of death, and doe esteeme noe man miserable but him who soe esteemeth himselfe by feeblenesse of his owne harte. I litle value the reputation & reporte of the present time, which for the most parte is full of errour, because few men are free from one passion or another; posteritie will give to everye man his due, and happilie some will not hereafter faile, who will make unpartiall mention of us all.'[30]

Having thus said, & seeming to take comforte in the [fo. 24v] innocencie of his cause, hee putt himselfe into the executioners handes and by him was beheaded, being lesse tormented with paine by induring death than others were with pittie and greife by behoulding it. For hereupon the people were heard to murmure against the king, that in soe great dangers & disorders of the state, hee would spend his time in weighing wordes, and wresting them to malicious meanings, and that in punishing many light offences hee exceeded the auncient boundes both of clemencie and of lawes. 'What?' said they, 'Are citties shambles? Are societies of men heardes of beastes? But wherefore is not Owen Glendore, wherefore are not the Welsh and the Irish arraigned for treason? Or because great offenders canne defend themselves, the anger which they have stirred must ease it selfe upon any that are offered? Hostility is more safe then subjection, and bloud were well spent against such bloudie judgements.'

This affection of the people was partly raised by the highe & firme courage of Sir Roger Claringdon, which is soe notable a virtue that even in evill deservers it winneth favour. But especiallie it proceeded from the memorie of Prince Edward his father, whome the people ever held in deare accounte. And it was nether improbably nor obscurelie surmised that this was the principall cause of his death, and that the king could not thinke his estate assured soe long as any of the progenie of Prince Edward were alive. There is noe doubte but [fo. 25] this knight was worthie of blame for his rash and undiscreete liberalitie of speech, but whether hee deserved punishment in soe highe a degree, especiallie according to the lawes of that tyme, all men made a question.

After this some others nere aboute the king closed more neare to him in a dangerous devise, for an iron was conveyed under his bedd cloathes having 3 pikes, round, slender, sharpe & standing upright, to the end that when hee should lie downe, hee might have thrust his bodie upon them. The king discovered the mortall instrument, but could never discover his mortall enemie the authour thereof; yet were certaine suspected persons torne upon the torture, but they confessed nothing, doubtfull whether innocentlie or obstinately secrett. And thus, as if the life of man were not shorte enoughe by nature, strange meanes are dailie devised to bring the same by violence to an end.

Hereupon advise was offered to the king to remove old officers, who commonlie esteeme them most by whome they were raised to most

30 See introduction.

estimation, and to strengthen his new fortunes with new frendes. But the king proceeded slowelie in this deliberation. And it may bee that this advice was ordinarie, because in tymes of change officers are most suspected, and are manie tymes the cause thereof. It may bee alsoe that it trenched more deepe, & reached into a secrett of state, intending to raise more enemies to the king. [fo. 25v] For they whoe never enjoyed offices have noe great cause to complaine if they stand without them, and are never soe thankfull for attaining them as they are revengefull whoe are dispoiled of them. Because men are not soe sensible of a benefit, as of a losse; and soe the worker of such change doth winne thereby few frendes and many enemies, and these more disposed to displease than those to defend.

This yeare the Lord Thomas Beauchampe, Earle of Warwicke (of whome mention hath been made before) departed this life: a man warie in taking, and both faythfull & fortunate in giving advise, of invincible stomach and somewhat aspiringe, yet to noe higher matters then hee was well able to rule. In the whole passage of his life hee had noe great cause ether much to boast of his fortunes, or much to blame them, having tasted of sweete & sower almost alike. Alsoe this yeare died the Ladie Katharine Swinsford, the 3d wife of John, Duke of Lancaster, father to King Henrie. Beyond the seas alsoe died Philippe, Duke of Burgoigne, & Duke Alberte of Bavier, Earle of Henaulte. The famous stone bridge over the River of Medewaye at Rochester, builded by the Lord Cobham & Sir Roberte Knowles, was this yeare finished.

The Thirde Yeare of King Henrie the Fourth.

[V]

This yeare in the moneth of March a blazing starre appeared,[1] first spreading the flames round, then stretching them towardes the north, which astrologers (whose arte & errour are nere neighbours) conjecture ether to cause or to portend some tragicall event.

About Whitsonntide[2] certaine persons, whose hopes depended upon noe honest meanes, did newlie confederate against the king, with whose majesty theire malice continuallie contended in increase. And to drawe some authoritie to theire attemptes, they gave forth that King Richard was living and desired the aide of his loving people; that by extreame violence of the time hee was constrained to keepe unknowne, but upon some declaration of his frendes hee would appeare, & royallie rewarde those whoe should bee readie to adventure for him. This was whispered uncertainely at the first, as in dangerous newes it is usuall; afterwardes it was confidently committed to the credulous eares ether of the weake sorte or of the turbulent & busie minded, the one being easie, the other being earnest for innovations. Among these, the reporte running variously concerning King Richards death, it was the more easily beleeved that hee might bee alive. The first brunt of this bruite much shaked the common people, wavering by nature & slowe to settle in a new subjection, but the king composed [fo. 26v] himselfe to a carelesse securitie, changing nether countenance nor place, ether through haughtinesse of courage, or because hee knew the truth lighter then the reporte. And indeed, upon apprehension of a certaine preist in Ware who was the principall both authour & actor of this devise, all the terrour vanished to a toye.

That priest had by secrett conference confederated unto him a few of the most carelesse, & wittlesse audacious, whome feare ether of povertie or of punishment might easily plunge into any enterprize, first by casting forth true yet seditious complaintes, partlie against the avarice, partlie against the arrogancie & ambition of divers officers, then by an inference both seditious and untrue in fastening all theire

---

[1] Hayward's choice of this well-documented comet to introduce a segment marked by thematic imagery of violent tempests, diabolical apparitions and the like, is another illustration of his preoccupation with dramatic narrative.

[2] 14 May 1402.

faultes upon the kinge. Hee had beene much imboldened, albeit not with open incouragement and aide, yet with much privie & particuler good will, but the greatnes of the adventure caused feare, and feare bredd delaies & diversities of advise. Hee had enrouled the names of many[3] as complices to the conspiracie with whome hee had never treated, & some whome by countenaunce hee did not knowe at what tyme they were confronted with him; his only hope of theire assistance consisted in that they had beene advaunced by the favour of King Richard, and by his fall (as thinges take encrease by the same meanes whereof they take beginning) they ether declined or stood at a staye. But the vaine man did weakely waigh the weake working of passed benefittes [fo. 27] in regard of danger & destruction that are present. Soe manie were dischardged whome hee had enrolled and hee, with Walter Baldocke, Prior of Lawnd in Leicestersheire, and certaine other graye friers were drawne forth to execution;[4] giving example to all private men how vaine it is to imagine that the multitude, althoughe discontented, will easily bee raised and that all they who accompany a man in his complaintes, will alsoe accompanie him in his dangers.

About the same tyme, eight other minorite or graye friers, men having nether learning, wisdome nor good intent, conspired to compasse the kings destruction. But because dangerous enterprizes, the more they bee thought upon, the more unwillinglie they bee undertaken, most times it falling that conspiracies not soddainly executed are some wayes discovered. Among these one Richard Firsbie, Doctor of Divinitie, a man bould in mischeife & without heed headie, being openlie demaunded what hee would doe if King Richard were present, and in life, hee answered stoutly that hee would doe as hee knewe all should doe, even stand for him against all men, even unto the death. For which brainlesse braverie he was hanged (otherwise then the rest) in the habitt of his profession, and with great difficultie did the brethren of his order obtaine that his bodie might bee taken downe & buried.

Soe the desperate rashenesse, or rather rage and fury, of these flingbrained friers [fo. 27v] (whome nether theire owne weakenesse nor the waightinesse of the adventure could any deale restraine) maketh the report more credible that this yeare in Danburie Church in Essex the divell appeared in likenesse of a graye frier, and with great rage[5] & terror of tempest did beate downe the toppe of the steeple, rend awaye the roofe of the church, & teare halfe the chauncell in peeces.

---

[3] MS 'enrouled the names the names of many'
[4] May 1402.
[5] MS: 'with great great rage ...'

It is certaine that religious men have had[6] theire handes in many mischeivous actions, not as corrupted by religion, nor alwaies for defaulte ether in government or in choice, but because they seldome runne a middling course. Noe men better, in case they take well, if otherwise none worse; there is noe middle condition betweene being an angell or a divell.

About the middest of August the king raised forces for invasion of Wales, with desire & hope to revenge himselfe upon the rebelles and to reduce the countrie to his absolute subjection. This armie was guided with his owne person & fortune, supposing that the reputation of his presence would bee not the meanest meanes both to incourage his soldiers & to terrifie the enemies. But Owen Glendor was nothing discouraged at this great preparation against him, for as hee was not minded by brunt of battell to putt himselfe upon one jumpe of triall against meane forces, soe this mightie multitude, in those fruitlesse places, was like to settle noe [fo. 28] long continuance. Upon this hope he withdrew himselfe into the mountaines & woodes, his accustomed places of retreite, where being clogged nether with companie nor carriage, hee easilie frustrated the kings furie against him. And as hee continuallie rather fleeted then fledd before the English armie, he ether consumed or carried away whatsoever might serve them to any use.

The king sharpely pursued them through many difficulte passages, many waies dangerous, but was himselfe more sharply pursued with a strange confusion of all crueltie & rage of weather, which did much increase the calamitie of the souldiers, being otherwise miserablie molested both with labour & want. Obscure & stormy cloudes continually covered the heavens, & wrapped the earth both in darkenesse & terrour, & being turned into raine, haile & furious windes, did worke most memorable & fearefull effectes. Villages were cast downe, churches & religious houses were torne, fired & defaced, many stronge trees were rent up and violently carried a great distance from the place where they grewe; the lightenings flashed forth such terrible flames, the thunder scoured the skies with soe fearefull roaringes, as if the whole frame of the world would have dissolved. From these broken cloudes, from this turbulent mixture of all weathers, proceeded strange noises & sightes, which did soe greivouslie affright the English armie that noe future day many times was expected. Upon the vigill of the Nativitie of St. Mary[7] [fo. 28v] the king, weatherbeaten & weary, pitched his tentes upon a plaine, purposing to favour & refresh his men, & happely to possesse the enemies with opinion of a fainting

6 MS: 'men have have had'
7 7 Sept. 1402.

courage, to embolden [them] thereby to attempte upon him. The wind was calme, the weather cleare, the place pleasant but very open; the soldiers were partly ridd of the terrour which the weathers wrath had stroke into them, hoping that all those extremities (as violent things are seldome permanent) were then blowne over, & joying in remembraunce of the miseries which they had passed. When the evening was closed in & the souldiers had settled themselves to rest, the cloudes somewhat clustred againe together, & it beganne a litle to blowe & raine, which did sodainly rise to soe highe a rage as if the heavens were resolved into wind & water. In this tempest the kings tent was violently overturned & his launce shaken downe, the pointe whereof pitched with soe full force against his bodie that if hee had not lien in his armour that night, hee had never worne armour daye after. It was commonly supposed that these prodigious tempestes were stirred up by divelish arte, & that the graye friers were workers of the same. But it hath beene familiar to our nation to surmise every extraordinary effecte to proceed from a supernaturall cause. I am rather of opinion that God stirr'd up these stormes to revive in the dull mindes of men the remembrance of His power, & that Hee did thereby rather threaten then beate the English nation, [fo. 29] foreshewing the tumultes & confusions which afterwardes did ensue.

The king with invincible stomach did long struggle against these stormes, esteeming his honor above his ease. His soldiers alsoe hee held by good wordes in painfull obedience, perswading them that these were the galleries, the gardens, the pleasant walkes of men possessing armes; that in such adventures & not in idlenesse and ease true valour was tried; that doing as men, whether they prevailed or whether they perished, theire labour or losse was gloriously imployed. Soe, partly by exhortation, but principallie by example, hee did not only receive theire patience, but incense them to bee excessive (whether all from the harte or some fawning for favour) in highe praising & prizing theire king: some extolling his princely personage, others his generous disposition, many his curtesy, all his courage, professing therefore that they could not otherwise bee dischardged of theire dutie but by sacrificing the traytors to his glorie & revenge.

Butt all this proved a vaine fitt of furie without any force, for in continuance of time such languishing diseases seazed upon the armie that manie died, & the rest begann to murmure that wthout any profitt they were made a prey to the mercilesse weather. Everie mans desire ether to overtake or meete with the enemie, inflamed with the presence of theire king, caused [fo. 29v] them to beare even to all extremitie, yet theire strength & courage was soe broken in the end that the king was constrained to give over his pursuite. And now hee had made full experience that it is a manifest abuse obstinatly to strive against weather & want, and to putt the souldier to indure more then hee is able, and that a fugitive & fleeting enemie in places of advantage is not to bee pursued with a maine armie, but with standing campes to bee wasted at seasons & by degrees. Thus the king, having fired divers base buildinges, with the spoile of a country ether barren or not husbanded returned againe into England, not without some discredite that hee could bee soe long held playe to soe litle purpose by a few both unarmed & untrained traitors. Here the souldiers reported many admirable adventures, strange stormes, soddaine terrours, aswell in uncouth noises as in fearefull apparitions, which they had ether heard or seene or eles imagined throughe feare.

Upon this retreit of the English army an occasion fell out which was apprehended by the Welshmen & hottly pursued, & yet fayled of theire hoped successe. Soe soone as the English were retired within the confines of the realme, they did presently disperse into the next villages, some upon necessity, and some for theire pleasure, for that there remained not many with the king. Whether this were conjectured or whether [fo. 30] advertised to the Welshmen, they determined to sett full upon the bodie of the English armie by night, with all the power they could possibly make. They knewe right well that there was a river betweene the English and them, but the passages thereof they knewe alsoe as well. Soe they marched to one of the passages, which they found stronglie guarded with archers & pikes, vigilant upon theire chardge, & yett not doubting any such attempte. These they tasted[8] only, and finding them both readie & resolute, they removed to another passage, which they found in like manner guarded. Here they charged very lively and stayed long upon the skirmish, but could not force it. By this time the alarme was hottly taken in the campe, and the king called in his dispersed companies by sound of trumpett and drumme, & provided for reenforcing the passages. The Welshmen, perceiving this, gave over their enterprize, seeming to rejoyce that they had done soe much as to putt the English only in feare. But if the passages ether had beene neglected, or could have beene forced, it was beleeved that the English armie would have beene shaken, and that before they could have had 3000 men in good appointment, the enemie would have sett 5000 in theire faces. And albeit the hazardes of armes bee uncertaine, yet the advantage of a suddaine surprize is verie great, and commonly importeth danger to those who will suffer themselves to bee soe overtaken.

In this meane tyme, the Scottes could not quietly bear the blowes which of late they had receaved of the English nation. For supposing that not the valour of the souldier, but ether the vigilancie of the one

---

[8] to tast(e) = to test, to try (OED).

commaunder or negligence of the other in apprehending or slipping some occasion had carried the successe, they abated thereby noe pointe of courage, but were rather incensed to prosecute revenge or death. This enterprize was most earnestly desired, urged, advanced by all, surmising (according to theire naturall impatience of delay) that the more roundly it should bee begunne, the lesse difficulte it would prove. For whereas there are two tymes of advantage to assaile an enemie, when hee is diverted to forraigne warres or eles divided within himselfe, it seemed that both these opportunities did then invite them, whilest the French, Irish & Welsh stood in open hostilitie, & the English remained doubtfull in obedience.

Hereupon the Earle Douglasse, with consent & furtherance of the Duke of Albanie, governor of Scottland, assembled a great power, exceeding the number of xxty thousand armed men, the veiw being taken, besides a supply of voluntarie youths (a loose complement of the warre) which flocked very fast unto him, some [fo. 31] upon a bould braverie only, and some cheifly for desire of spoile. In his armie alsoe were Lord Mordake, Earle of Fife, sonne to the governour of Scottland, the Earle of Anguis, Earle of Murrisse, the Earle of Orkney and divers other of the principall nobility of that realme, well reputed for valour and for honorable descent. This companie exceeding full of harte and of hope, upon confidence both of discretion in the commaunders and of the number, choice and good appointment of the soldiers, entered Northumberland about the middst of September, not by soddaine incursions & roades, but with banner displayed, making a brave head, in sett and composed order of battaile.

They had not farre marched within the Marches of England, nor made much wast of such things as the countrie people, unable to defend, could not take with them in theire flight, but out of a valley nere to a towne called Hameldon,[9] came against them Lord Henrie Peircie, Earle of Northumberland, and Henrie Peircie his sonne, whome the Scottes for his feirce courage commonlie called Sir Henrie Hotspurr. They were accompanied with George of Dunbarre, some-times Earle of the Marchesse of Scottland, but then revolted to the English side, and followed by all the gentry of Northumberland, and about eight thousand ordinarie souldiers. The two [fo. 31v] Peircies were appointed by the king wardens of the Marches upon Scottland, with charge not to attempte upon the Scottes, nor any waies to provoke them, but to observe theire motions, and to bee in a readinesse to resist any enterprize which they should make. And being without question of equalitie (the one the father, the other the sonne), they were not touched with envious emulation whereby services comitted

[9] 14 Sept. 1402.

to equalles are many tymes overthrowne. George, Earle of Dunbarre, had soe farr ingaged himselfe in service against his country that despaire of pardon had made him a most obstinate enemie to the same. And yet hee had beene sollicited to returne againe under many liberall promises of restitution of his estate, of redresse of his wronges and of good increase both in honor & entertainment. But hee much suspected that the promises of his countrymen would not be found soe faythfull as faire, which held him in respite of his resolution, fearing that hee should never enjoye those hopes, whereof hee had noe better assurance then the bare word of those that hated him at the corte, whereunto noe wise man (but upon necessitie) will ever trust, for many great mindes who accounte nothing dishonorable but losse, will a litle straine in breaking theire [fo. 32] fayth for accomplishment of theire desires. The souldiers which were imployed in this service were such as had beene trained and formerlie tried in those frontier warres, men of advised courage and assured execution of theire charge, whose discipline, favoured by fortune, had made theire valour alwaies victorious. Thus guided, thus garded, they made a bold head against theire enemies.

The Scottes, when some of theire forragers came fearefullie running backe, and advertised them that theire enemies were at hand, did hardly beleeve the reporte to bee true, being better disposed to spoile then to fight. But when they perceaved it was soe indeed, a tumultuous rufflinge did soddainely rise among the common soldiers, who did as litle like as they did looke for such present entertainement. Some ranne to the topps of hilles and trees to discover what forces came against them; some fell to addressing & bridling theire horses; everie man betooke him to his armour in hast, which hast, & the hastie calling that one made to another, did much increase the confusion & feare. The Earle Douglasse, finding this disorder among his souldiers, retired them to the toppe of a hill called Hallidowne Hill, nere to a towne named Woller, there to digest this suddaine surprizment, to collecte theire courage, and to arme theire bodies at better leasure. [fo. 32v] When hee first espied the Engish ensignes, hee was putt by them in remembrance of the honor which the yeare before his nation had lost, and thereupon seemed to boile with desire of revenge, resolving forthwith to comitte his case to the arbitrement of the sword. Soe hee beganne to advaunce himselfe, & with a confident and loftie cheare in this sorte inflamed his soldiers.

'Wee are assembled together in armes, fellow soldiers, to recover against our English enemies the harmes that wee have sustained, & the honor that wee have lost. And noe sooner are wee entred the confines of theire countrie, but occasion is presented unto us to regaine againe our glorie, or to double our disgrace. For if wee had proceeded without opposition of armes to outrage the harmelesse and unarmed people, wee had made proofe of crueltie, rather then of courage, and not regarding the right offenders, should have dischardged our wrathe upon the next at hand. But to this purpose have wee entred this action, not by suddaine incursions to purchase a litle refuse spoile, or wast a few base buildinges, but by open armes to chastice those who openly and by armes have dishonored us. Upon these men must wee hew out revenge; by this meanes our present resolution may recover that which heretofore our rashnesse hath lost.

'And many inducementes doe move me to presume or rather to stand assured that [fo. 33] our forces shall carrie the favour of this daye, for in number wee are superior to our enemies, in strength of bodie equall, in experience & skill of service not inferiour; there remaineth nothing but bouldnesse of harte, wherein it seemeth that wee stand in many tearmes of advantage. For because nothing is more frequent with excellent soldiers then to grow riotous by prosperous eventes, it is not unlike that the late successe of the English have turned theire courage into carelessnes and contempte of theire enemies, a most dangerous opinion to those whome it doth possesse, and alwaies foreshewing some calamitie to ensue. As for us, althoughe wee were rather beguiled then beaten, yet the greife of our overthrowe, as it hath made us adventurous to attempte, soe doubtlesse will it make us vehement & obstinate to bee victorious. And a shame it were that wee have dared them to meet us in armes, if wee shall not dare to abide theire blowes.

'Besides this, wee shall all find against us (to theire shame bee it spoken) many of our owne nation, whose treacherie our enemies doe cunningly converte to the advancement of their purposes, prevailing more by our divisions then by any valour in themselves. But they must never expecte true hartes from those who have beene longer their enemies then theire frendes. And questionlesse, upon nere approach of theire allies and frendes, uppon veiwe of those ensignes [fo. 33v] under which they are bound to serve, they will have theire falshood in detestation, & ether openly turne to us or, secretlie shrinking backe, nether worke nor wish us any great harme. Yea, the English themselves are not like to prove enemies dangerous to bee encountred, being discontented & divided into factions, obeying against theire willes those who rule wthout any right, kepte under only by terrour & force, weake workers of faythfull affections.

'But nether any nor all these respectes should soe much kindle ether our courage or our hopes, as the care of our country, which upon our overthrowe wilbe laid open (the walles, as it were, being beaten downe) to the spoile of our greedie and cruell enemies. Which of us had not rather die this daye in the feild, then to indure againe that sorrow & that shame which not long since wee were enforced to beare: our country peirced by mortall enemies, the open partes burned, the strong places battered, our good taken to spoile, our wives, children & whosoever were most deare unto us, ether miserably slaine, or shamefully abused, & led away prisoners? Which, whether wee are againe to suffer or presently to revenge, it lieth in the issue of this feild. It lieth this daye upon our handes to maintaine not only the honor but the safetie of our common state. Or if any of us esteemeth his life more precious, that alsoe is preserved [fo. 34] by valour. For if wee hould together, and manly maintaine our place, wee shall preserve both our honors and our lives; if wee scatter and flee, a base butcherie will forthwith ensue. Soe as in combate and in armes the valiant man[10] contendeth for glorie, the dastard alsoe must labour for his life. For my parte, as I was the first in advise, soe will I bee the foremost in adventure, being clearely resolved that safetie and victorie, for the most parte, are joyned together, and if at any time they are severed, an honorable death is farre better then life with reproach.'

The Scottes entertained this speech with great demonstration of fervencie and hope, shouting, acclaiming and calling aloud for the signe of battle, the least valiant, and such as afterwardes were observed first to give ground, being most excessive and hardie of tongue. For many were inwardlie nipped with remembraunce of theire former mishapps, fore-judging the successe of theire present adventure (as in such cases it is usuall) by event of those which latelie they had runne. Againe victorie, spoile, revenge were brave tearmes indeede, but depending upon doubtfull hope; but weapons, woundes & death they sawe to bee both certaine and at hand. Yett the lesse harte any of them had, the more hee endeavored to expresse, being afraid to bewray any feare, least thereby they should discourage [fo. 34v] others. Soe, with different courage, they ranged themselves[11] in arraye, and attended the directions of theire generall.

By this time the Earle of Northumberland, whose confidence had taken away all care of encouraging his souldiers, had advaunced his armie somewhat nere. But then, perceaving the great number and resolution of the enemie, hee thought it not fitt to sett the fortune of the state upon a carelesse cast wthout due preparing his men. Wherefore, making a stand, in this sorte hee quickened their courage, somewhat daunted at the first sight of enemies and armes.

'Companions and frendes, if I had new soldiers to directe, or you new enemies to encounter, I would after the example of other leaders use many wordes to sett your courage on edge. But you & I, having

[10] MS: 'the the valiant man'
[11] MS: 'with different courage, ranged themselves.'

taken sufficient triall ether of the other, and both of the enemie, this cercumstance shall bee nether laboured nor long. For hitherto you have soe behaved yourselves that I never wished better soldiers, nor could perceave you desirous of other commaunder. Behold alsoe your enemies, and aske your owne eyes if these bee not the men for whome not long since you searched in the verie bowelles and harte of theire country. And what effectes of valour (may wee thinke) will they shew abroad, whoe shewed so litle harte at home? [fo. 35] For by how much hope is lesse powerfull then feare, soe much lesse courage will men expresse in offending others then in defending themselves. When lately wee marched throughe the midst of theire dwellings, how often have I heard the soldier, full of Francke courage, saye, 'When will the enemy present himselfe? Where shall wee find him? What shall wee doe that wee may fight?' Loe, now they are crepte out of theire cavernes, and there they are come to answere your charge. Your wish, loe, here, & meanes for you both to exercise your vertue, and increase your glorie.

'Once since that time in this fashion did they enterprize upon us, but with what successe you all remember. And albeit they now looke bouldlie and brave, yet they are griped at the harte with ominous feare of the like event; for a partie lately beaten, howsoever hee carrieth his countenaunce & speech, doth long retaine a quaking courage.

'As for theire multitude, there is noe cause wherefore wee should bee moved; wee shall find them an untrained company of litle counsaile and great confusion, whose bouldnesse hath not gone beyond braggs. And if wee reckon the number of souldiers and not the names of men, wee shall find on our side the greater strength, because wthout conducte and courage, the greater [fo. 35v] the companie is, the greater alsoe is the confusion, and if wee have in our bodies one dragme[12] of our auncestors bloud, wee shalbee nothing dismayed ether at the multitude or preparation of our enemie. Wee shall never shrinke at such shadowes, but rather die in maintaining our place then yeeld one foote of ground upon any terrour, and this for noe other reward, but only to keepe our faith & fame. But I feare to detaine your forwardenesse too longe. It is now tyme to turne our tale to our enemies, whoe have already begunne theire flight, and doe seeke to secure themselves by advantage of place, presenting occasion to us (if it bee well followed) of a most worthy and memorable victorie.'

When the earle had thus ended, the souldiers drew theire swordes and, shaking them aloft, desired to bee sett within reach of theire enemies. Other clamours they gave none, which the generall conceived

___

12 'Dragme' = 'dram.'

to proceed rather from a grounded resolution then ether from dullnesse or distrust, suppposing that loude clamours and cries are not alwayes signes ether of resolution or of hope, but rather of the contrarie, like a great smoke from a small fire, or like froath & fome which proceed not from any sound or solidd substance.

Then the Earle sent his archers to the foote of the hill whereupon the [fo. 36] Scottes were mounted, with intent to dislodge them, and to drive them downe into the plaine. The Earle Douglasse, upon theire approach, sent forth his archers alsoe against them, but this encounter endured not long, for the Scottes were presently beaten backe, being both the fewer & the worser bowemen, the English at that time bearing reputation to bee the best shott in the world. Then the Earle Douglasse tooke launce in hand, and ledd forth his maine battell, marshalled in due order against the English. Whereupon the Earle of Northumberland alsoe advaunced forward with the bodie of his armie, to second and supporte his archers. Thus were both sides sett upon a mercilesse match, hatred, at that time almost naturall, doubtlesse hereditarie betweene the two nations, enflaming them to valour. The English had the advantage of the souldiers, the Scottes of men, supplying that in number which they wanted in worth. The English were incensed with hope, the Scottes with hate, they contending for glorie, those for revenge. The English were confident upon the favour of fortune which had often made theire valour victorious; the Scottes were headlong & furious, supported cheifely by despaire.

The English archers, as the Scottes came towardes them, gave ground & drew backe not fearefullie, not disorderly, but with a well measured pace fitting theire advantage, [fo. 36v] letting fly in theire retreat so thicke as haile among theire enemies. It is almost incredible to reporte the effectes of the English archerie that daye upon the Scottes: theire swordes were broken, theire launces shattered in peeces, theire armour which had beene three yeares in preparing was not sufficient, ether compleat or of proofe, to defend theire bodies. Hereupon not only the captaines but the ordinarie souldiers were heard to incourage theire fellowes not to abide the shott which galled them afarre of, but to close couragiously to hand blowes. But all this proved stomach without strength, for soe fast as they inforced themselves to runne upon the enemie, soe fast were they ether beaten downe, or beaten backe, and the unfortunate forwardenesse of some caused others to advise how farre it were best they should adventure. At the last, amazed and distracted with distresse, they rann ruinouslie up and downe, uncertaine what resolution to putt in practise, everie man being busy to helpe himselfe and deafe to harken to what was commaunded.

Earle Douglasse, generall of the Scottes, was wounded in five places

of his bodie and lost one of his eyes; which, when the soldiers understood, and perceaving that among theire companies was nether order
nor harte, they utterly disbanded, and comitted the safetie of their
lives to theire good footmanshipp, but was the accomplishment of [fo.
37] theire miserie and losse. For the men at armes (whoe had not
stroke one blowe before) then closed together, and with great heate
pursued the execution of the feild, first killing wthout respecte, afterwardes taking prisoners, and killing them too when better were
offered. Here were slaine the Lord Adam Gourdon, the Lord John
Swinton, whoe had beene false to both the realmes; alsoe Sir John
Lueston, Sir Alexander Ramsey of Dalehowse, and xxiij other knightes
of honorable note, and of gentlemen and common soldiers to the
number of x thousand. The chace was followed to the river Tweede,
the feildes being scattered all the way with scattered bodies, armour,
weapons and bloud. And because many of the Scottes nether knew,
nor had leisure to search the foardes of that river, they lost alsoe there
v hundred of theire companie, some beaten downe by theire enemies,
others borne downe by the weight of theire fellowes, others swallowed
up by the swifte violence of the streame.

There were alsoe taken prisoners the floure of nobilitie and chivalrie
in Scottland, to witt, Earle Douglasse, generall of the armie, Mordake,
Earle of Fife, eldest sonne to the Duke of Albanie who was gouvernour
of Scottland; also Thomas, Earl of Murrisse; Roberte, Earl of Anguis;
the Earle of Orkney, Athol, Mantz; the Lordes of Montgomerie,
Ershin, Graine, Sir John Steward of Emeunath, [fo. 37v] Sir Nicolas
Seton, Sir John Trogan, Sir David Flemminge, Sir William Pearson,
Sir Roberte Sentclere, and about lxxx other knightes and of gentlemen
& ordinarie soldiers about v hundred. Nothing was soe available for
the escape of the rest as the small number of the English, unable to
pursue all the broken partes of the chase. These prisoners did afterwardes turne this great victorie to a farre greater overthrowe to the
English, for whilest many contended to make them theires, they raised
more malice and thereupon more mischeife in England, by being
captives, then they could possibly have done if they had fortuned to
escape.

The Earle of Northumberland sent his prisoners to divers fortresses,
and determined, whilest his soldiers were hott and fleshed with
successe, and whilest the feare was fresh among the enemies, to surprize
all the country of Loughdeane and March, whereof the cheifest
lord[es] (the life of courage in the common people) were ether captured or slaine. So hee entred into Tinedale, wasted and forraged all
the country, the enemie not adventuring to appeare, or if att any time
hee shewed himselfe it was upon the sodaine, and as sodainly againe
vanished awaye, being never soe farre driven out of harte, never (as

the captines did reporte) attached with the like feare. The people all forsooke theire houses and villages, giving forth that it was better to leave the nestes then to suffer the birdes to bee therein taken. Divers [fo.38] places of defence were likewise abandoned, for they knew not in what strength they should repose assurance, when theire armies were not able to stand in the field.

The Earle, when hee could find abroad neither enemie nor prey, and loath to loose tyme, which should bee precious to those whoe have theire forces on foote, pitched his seige about the castle of Corklaves, a place at that time of good importe and commaunding a large country round about it. Hee appointed Henry Peircie his sonne, with a companie lightly armed, to rove up & downe to fire, slaye & spoile, aswell to busie as to terrifie the enemie. In the meane time hee prepared all meanes to carrie the peice, ether speedily by maine force, or at lengthes by mines and sappe, or finally by building fortes against it. It may bee that the earle supposed by this devise to drawe the Scottes into the feild, but it fell soe out (whether by decree of his destinie, or by the envie which his vertue had raised) that this seige proved not only a staye but a full stoppe and period to his fairest fortunes. And it was thought that had hee not stayed thereupon, but peirced further, & followed the feare whilest the enemie was therewith astonished, hee might have indamaged, if not endangered, the principall stake. Assuredly they are not well advised, who when theire advantage lieth in pursuite, will assaile any place that may hinder theire hast. [fo. 38v]

The captaine of the place, whose name was Sir John Greenlowe, being unfurnished ether of resolution, or of provision and power to maintaine his charge, entred into capitulation with the earle, that if the castle were not releived within 3 moneths hee would then deliver it into his handes. This tearme seemed exceeding long to the naturall impatiencie of the English souldiers, but for this the earle did requite them with the greater libertie to range abroad & seek adventures. The captaine advertised this agreement to the governour of Scottland, who therupon assembled the counsaile of state and entred into advise what was fittest to bee done.

The greatest parte were of opinion that it was better to suffer one castle to bee lost, then to adventure the remainder of the nobilitie, and the residue of the strength of the realme, upon one jumpe of triall; that theire advantage by winning would bee nothing soe great as theire danger by loosing; that they were more like to lose then to gaine; that the losse of soe small a peece might easily by favour of tyme bee recovered, but the misadventure of the whole could very hardly bee repaired.

The governour much blamed theire falling or rather fayling spirit, soe soone daunted with a few unprosperous eventes. He assured them with great vehemencie of speech that soe long as hee was in place, ether to counsaile or [fo. 39] commaunde, what losse soe ever did happen to the realme, none should bee throughe defaulte ether of courage or of cost; that in enterprizes of armes, nothing was soe certaine as change, especiallie if wee acquitt ourselves like men; that if none of the nobility would adjoyne unto him in defending every handbreadth of theire country, hee alone (he sware) would not abandon soe honest a cause.

This countenance of the governour, whether from the harte or only in shewe, much erected the courage of the rest. Howbeit his oath was nether broken nor kepte, yett verie nere and almost broken, for during the first two monethes hee made noe preparation, and beganne to cease talking of this businesse. And there is litle doubte but hee was weake harted, and did busie his thoughtes how by anie other meanes hee might bee ether ridd of the enemie, or at least make some advantage of this respit of time. But as ordinarily it falleth out that they whoe are most readie to fall doe meet with some unexpected staye, soe in the 3d moneth it happened that the enemies of the beseiged did that for them which all theire frendes were unable to doe. For the king of England did sodainly resolve to prosecute the warrs of Scottland no further, not upon distrust of successe, but ether upon some straine of envie, in that his owne [fo. 39v] performance in Wales was soe farre exceeded by the Peircies against the Scottes, or eles fearing that the victorie would not prove soe beneficiall unto him as the greatnesse of the generall would thereby prove dangerous.

For the Earle of Northumberland and his sonne at that tyme did hould rather a shadowe then any substance of favour from the king, ether soe ordered by nature that affections are seldome permanent, or because it is usuall that where greatest benefittes have passed, both parties growe soone weary, the one in requiting what he cann, the other still in expecting more. Verely, to men of judgement in these affaires, theire overgreatnesse did then threaten theire overthrowe. For being men valiant and ambitious, and living in a turbulent and discontented time, they seemed not safe, I will not say to bee advanced, but whatsoever the cause was, there wanted not occasion to countenance the cause.

For presently, after the kings departure from Wales, Owen Glendor beganne to assaile the borderers, first by roving pillages nether resisted nor revenged, by reason of his sodaine cominge; afterwardes by wasting of villages and charging himselfe with greater spoiles; lastly, increasing by successe both in bouldnesse & in power, by attempting against defensive places. Hereupon the king purposed to increase his garrisonns upon the frontiers [fo. 40] of Wales, aswell to restraine this licentious ranging, as alsoe that having forces both furnished and at hand, manie advantages which could bee nether contrived nor fore-seene would from the enemie bee offered unto them. For this service hee determined to drawe some soldiers from the north partes of the realme, ether because hee held them most sufficient, or to withdrawe strength and favour from the Peircies. For hee esteemed not himselfe fullie secured, unlesse hee did as well suppresse those whome hee held suspected, as oppresse his professed enemies.

Soe hee dispatched lettres to the earle, commaunding him forthwith to send parte of the forces which hee had in readinesse, whose fayth and fortune had beene sufficiently proved, for present service to bee done in Wales; that hee and Lord Piercie his sonne should retire with the residue into the Marchesse of England, and there remaine for defence of the same; that hee should not release the prisoners upon any ransome, to the end that the enemie might not sodainly recover strength, but that hee should keepe them safely to the use of the king. For as by right of armes they perteined unto him, so intended hee to make his best benefitt of them.

The earle knew not what construction to make of this resolution of the king, as one that could not conjecture what might move him to cast away soe certaine a victorie. He could not conceive that for want of good [fo. 40v] will to thanke his frendes, hee would releive and release his enemics; that hee was soe negligent of glorie as to rejecte her when shee offered herselfe, or soe ambitious thereof alone as to envie it to those whose glorie tended to make him great. Wherefore hee was bould with the king (and thought by reason of his services that so hee might), & under protestation of his duty and obedience advised him not to change an assured and almost present expectation for a hope that was both doubtfull & remote, not to leave an action more then 3 partes finished, to undertake another both long and of uncertaine event; that the victorie which lately they obteined against the Scottes was like a wound taken in the flesh, some losse of bloude which in shorte tyme would naturally bee repaired; but that which then they did pursue would bee like unto the losse of a limme, a maine maime unto the bodie of that state; that the service for Wales might more conveniently bee furnished out of the middle partes of the realme, aswell for that they were more populous and rich as alsoe placed in lesse danger of enemies; but if his souldiers were required upon opinion of theire valour, hee earnestly intreated the respitt of one moneth to accomplish that enterprize which was almost at an end.

As for the prisoners hee affirmed that in right they did belong unto him as the giust[13] of his fortune or purchase of his sword; that hee was

[13] The OED identifies this as Spenser's quasi-Italian spelling of 'joust' ('just').

perswaded that the king would never have made any claime but by suggestion of some whoe intended not to attaine the like, whoe tooke paines [fo. 41] for nothing but only to stuffe theire bellies with surfett, theire bones with ease, theire bagges not only with raking but with racking wealth from others; that if such persons would not cease to cast theire envious eyes soe farre into the lawfull ether rightes or rewardes of other mens labours, his advise was that they should bee appointed to sustaine the next enterprize the enemie did offer.

All this moved the king verie litle, for being guided by the most powerfull of all passions, feare, his intent was estranged not only from determining well, but from induring to heare thereof, soe much greater was his hate to suspected frendes, then it was to knowne and ancient enemies. Many alsoe advanced his doinges, some from weakenesse of judgement, others out of hatred against the earle, & most upon flatt flatterie, in soothing the king whatsoever hee said. But driving at particuler endes doth seldome further the common good.

Hereupon the king did more earnestly assaile the unwillingnesse of the earle, signifying that since his purpose was to commaund & not to perswade, it was the earles parte not to objecte, but to obey; that hee esteemed it sufficient that the misadventure of the Scottes had quieted those who wavered betweene desire of peace or warre, and stay'd the hast of the hottest of them from the like attempte; that hee was not soe vaine as to conceave that upon event of one battaile the strength of that realme might easily bee broken; [fo. 41v] that by subduing any parte thereof, hee should drawe a necessitie upon himselfe to maintaine a continuall warre in that place; that having at that tyme many warrs in hand, & being soe overburdened with charge that hee could not maintaine armies in divers places, hee held those fitt to bee first pursued which were both next at hand & nerest to an end.

Concerning the prisoners, he said that to a prince of generous disposition the victorie is vile, if the spoiles and ransomes bee not brought to his treasurie, because his subjectes are noe lesse greived by such a victorie, then they should have beene by an overthrowe, for by an overthrowe they indure the injuries of enemies, which by many meanes may bee resisted or avoided, but by such victories they incurre the insolencie of theire frendes, sometimes more intollerable, alwaies unreasonable, and in both new provision must againe bee drawne out of theire purses alike; that the most auncient and best ordered comonwealthes by conquestes accustomed to inrich theire treasuries, to make distribution among the people, to release theire contributions,

Hayward uses the term here and elsewhere as a substantive, meaning a 'right' or 'just reward.'

to make publicke triumphes and feastes; but since the spoiles were shared among theire souldiers, the states victorious doe first exhaust theire owne treasures, then fleece the people, and never secure themselves of the enemie; that hereby the victors many [fo. 42] tymes have litle advantage above the vanquished, because both sides stand in like neede of money, the one to wage new soldiers, the other to entertaine the old, the victories bringing forth litle other benefitt but to make the prince more bold to impose upon the subjectes, & them more willing to indure the burden.

The earle hereupon raised his seige, not as allowing the reasons of the king, but as yeelding to his authoritie, whereby the last and best parte of his victorie was unatcheived; not withstanding in regard of himselfe hee accompted it accomplished, because hee had it in his hand, and was commaunded to lett it goe. Nether was hee slowe and heavie to suspecte that these were but secrett subtleties, invented throughe envie to represse his reputation, and to drawe him from the glorie which hee was like to winne. Soe, the drifte being conceived, the dissembling was the more artificiall. But the violent humour, by suppressing, did swell and could not alwaies bee closely kepte from breaking forth into manifest shew. For the king was heard often to complaine of the obstinate and haughtie disposition of the earle and his sonne, and they againe of the kings ingratitude, and of his infortunate or rather envious advice in cutting of the course of their prosperous proceedings.

And thus were the first seedes of dissention [fo. 42v] sowne, which afterwardes brought forth much fruite of mischeife. And it may seeme that nether the king nor the earle cann bee excused, in adding fewell to that fire, which was more like to scorch and consume, then it was to warme them. Verely, to men whoe judge counsailes by eventes, everie misadventure may easily bee attributed to some oversight. But when God intendeth to chastice any personne or state, Hee permitteth them to runne into errours, whereby those calamities which come by His appointment doe seeme to proceede from corruption of counsaile.

This is manifest by divers prodigies which are reported to have happened this yeare ether as warnings or threatnings of those mischeifes which upon these beginnings did ensue. Such hideous tempestes did rage in divers quarters of the realme that men supposed them to transcend the force of anie naturall cause. From the feast of the Epiphanie untill the middest of Aprill a blazing starre did appeare. Many monstrous apparitions were seene, of divers coulors and in fearefull formes. Nere the towne of Bedford and Breklesward[14] many troupes of armed men seemed oftentimes in mornings and evenings

---

[14] A neighbourhood of ancient Saxon and Briton battlegrounds from the 6th century.

to sallie forth out of the woodes and to combate together in cruell sorte. These appeared onlie to such as stood farr of, but by those who drew nere they could not bee seene. Assuredlie, how soever [fo. 43] in regard of inferior causes some things are imputed to wisdome, some to follie, and some to chaunce, yet in regard of the first and highest cause all things are most certainely, most orderly, most justly decreed.

Upon the next daye after the Feast of St. Michaell,[15] a parliament was assembled at London, which continued the space of seaven weekes following. In this parliament the nobilitie and commons besought the king to have the personne of George, Earle of Dunbarre and those of his retinue commended to him to increase theire intertainment, and to bind them with other benefittes, in regard of the services which they had done to him & to the realme. The king made an honorable declaration both of theire desertes and of his love, and thereupon allowed the request as reasonable and just.

Att this tyme much wastfull excesse (a certaine argument of a sicke state) was used in England, and those riottes were in theire rushe, which ether long peace or disordered government (the nurses of licentious life) doe comonly ingender. Yong gentlemen being idle became prodigall, and consumed theire substance in all varietie of vanities too dissolute, yea altogether shamelesse. Especiallie there was used a deformed pride in apparell both of men & women, which commonly is a signe of some common calamitie to ensue. All did weare gownes with deepe and broad sleeves full of cuttes and curious workes, whereof some did hang downe to the feete, & the shortest to the knees. [fo. 43v] The courtier first brought up this invention whoe manie times did sharpe pennance for such uneccessarie expence. Next was the gentleman, not altogether soe excessive, yet straining to come soe nere as he could. Lastly they were taken up of everie puffie[16] youth, insomuch as the basest did often exceede the best, & servauntes went beyond theire maisters. Hereupon Thomas Ockham, a man of excellent learning & witt, did write these verses following:

> Now hath this land litle need of bromes
>   to sweepe awaye the dust out of the street,
> Sith side sleaves of pennilesse groomes
>   will it up licke, bee it dry or wett.
>   O England, stand upright upon thy feete;
> Soe fowle a wast in soe simple a degree
>   banish, or it shall sore repent thee.

Some good mindes, having better will to desire the end then judg-

---

[15] I.e., 30 Sept. 1402.
[16] 'Having an empty or unsubstantial air of importance' (OED).

ment to discerne the meanes of reforming these abuses, moved in this
parliament that by some severitie of lawes the people might bee
reduced to theire auncient frugall sobrietie in life, and to bee content
with honest sufficiency, the next neighbour to abundance, avowing
that as particuler offenders are only charged with particular faultes,
soe common misdemeanors doe redound to the blame and blemish of
the state. But the king was doubtfull whether these abuses could bee
repressed by lawes or not: if they could not, then hee esteemed it
better not to undertake the reformation, then to declare himselfe
unable to effecte it; if they could, yett hee feared that the repressing
of these pleasures would bee taken for some restrainte of libertie, and
that whosoever should bee ether pleasured or pleased with [fo. 44]
the punishment, the hatred thereof would bee laid upon him, which
as hee was content to beare for the necessitie of the state, soe otherwise
hee was not desirous to incurre.

Hereto others added that there are many abuses in a common
wealth which, if they should all by penalties bee repressed, the lawes
in shorte time would soe increase that some would bee abolished by
oblivion, the rest (which is worst) transgressed by contempte; that
thereupon the same might happilie bee said of the English, which was
once said of the Athenians: that they were ever writing of lawes,
and never observing them; that for this cause lawes should concerne
matters of cheife importance; that in other things which are nether
dangerous to the whole, nor prejudiciall to any but those whoe use
them, common modestie and civilitie must bee a law unto all, which
by two meanes cheifely is maintained: first by reproofe of great men,
secondly by theire example; that these were of greater force then
lawes, in reformation of abuses.

For whilest the Romanes were exercised with enemies both mightie
and nere at hand, necessitie did restraine them (as having nether
plentie nor rest) to a sober & moderate course of life. But afterwardes
the spoiles of theire victories spoiled them of theire vertues, being
inured by armes to consume the goodes of other men, and by royott
theire owne. Then were lawes made against stately buildings, against
the number & traine of retinue, against [fo. 44v] sumptuousnes of
household stuffe, against costlines of apparell, and against superfluous
furnishing of the table. To this end the lawes Fannia, Orchia, Dydia,
Oppia, Khamina, Licinia, Cornelia, Auxia, Julia, and also divers
edictes of censers were made. But what ensued? Where noe man was
free from offence, noe man was in feare of punishment. This caused
all excesses (as having broken throughe restrainte) to bee more licentiouslie practised. All sumptuarie lawes by common consent were
driven into dissuse, and the people (whose nature is more desirous of
that which is forbidden, then content with that which is permitted)

were the more ravished into royott and vanitie. Afterward examples did that which lawes could not, for Galba, Vespasian, Titus & certaine other moderate emperors, composing theire carriage to a sober severitie, drew the people by degrees from theire lavishing loosenesse to a staied fashion in life. And what marvaile is there of the auncient austerity within this realme, when 3 shillings was esteemed a prodigall price to lay upon a paire of hose for a king? The aptenesse to imitate and please the prince worketh more then ether penalties or fear.

This question being quashed, the statutes[17] that were made the yeare next before against the Welshmen were in this parliament part renued and confirmed, parte declared, and parte inlarged. The severitie of which statutes were soe farre from furthering [fo. 45] the kings affaires in Wales that manie esteemed them the greatest impedimentes to the same. For soe well may anie thing bee expected, as that rude natures may bee reclaimed ether to subjection or to civilitie by sharpe enforcement of lawes. After that divers other matters of more particularitie had beene enacted, never since that time either repealed or almost regarded, the king, deepelie besett with warres, and at a deepe sett for money (the whetstone of courage and without which swordes have noe edge) tooke advise to move the people for a subsidie.

This was oppenly opposed by many, who boldly affirmed that the king had undertaken by his oath at Dancaster to cause such paymentes to bee laid downe. 'And what will the people,' said they, 'not only thinke but murmure? Was this a faulte in the government of King Richard, and may it bee allowed or excused now? Was theire desire to have theire burthens not eased, but only altered? Is it the lighter grievance in that it is not commaunded, but demaunded, which from a king importeth a commaunde? Assuredly, there is noe reason to putt that soe soon into practice, which was lately thought fitt to bee chastised by armes, unlesse wee esteeme it more to satisfie the necessitie of our king, then to assure his state.'

Others answered that in times ether of great danger [fo. 45v] or great atcheivement, taxations and subsidies were inevitable burthens in any government; that greatest states have used them in greatest degree or eles could never attaine to any highe pointe ether of glorie or securitie; that they whoe have beene more sparing of them were most assured in shorte time to bee cast downe, and in the meane seasone to hould them selves in great suspicion and by supportance of theire frendes; that under the government of King Richard paymentes only were not disliked, albeit they were both frequent & great, &

[17] MS: 'the the statutes'

taken by unusuall meanes, but the imp[l]oyment of them was cheifely taken to harte, as being ether hatefullie or unprofitably expended.

'For men,' said they, 'are alwaies willing not only to impaire but to consume theire wealth, ether for increase of theire glorie, or upon necessitie of theire safety, hoping alwaies to recover that in peace which the warre hath wasted. But then especiallie doe they greive and grudge when they find themselves in warre and peace oppressed alike, in the one to beare or beat of the power of the enemie, in the other to supply the insatiable pleasures of men ether in favour or commaunde. And this last doth more wring, yea wrong, the subjecte then the first: for in that, how soever the event falleth, the intention is honorable; in this the finall intention is many times more displeasing then the charge. In that, men of action and service are maintained; in this, very often base quallified persons. Of that, some end may be expected; but of this, none at all.

'And therefore noe impositions have ever beene ether hatefull to people or hurtefull to prince, excepte twoe quallities do concurre: one that they bee excessive, [fo. 46] the other that they bee not honorably expended. The first whereof maketh them greivous, the second odious. But if they bee both moderate and alsoe necessarie, or if they bee great, joyned wth greatnesse and importance of use, the subjectes nether in right canne, nor in reason will repine against them. For the prince is a persone both of authoritie and trust to imploye the private goodes of the people for preservation of theire common good,[18] ether in maintaining order amongst themselves, or in repelling the attemptes of theire enemies, or in advauncing theire reputation and glorie. To these endes hee may call for publicke contributions; to these endes nothing that a man hath is to bee esteemed private; to these endes not only the goodes of the subjectes, but theire bodies and lives must bee adventured. For as the stomach cannot imparte nourishment to all the partes of the bodie, unlesse the partes alsoe take paines to furnish the stomach with daily supplies, soe is it impossible for a prince to sustaine the safetie of his subjectes, if they withdrawe from him theire travaile and supplie. It is impossible for a prince to preserve, much lesse to enlarge, ether the safetie or dignitie of his people, except hee receave meanes from them both to furnish his enterprizes and to maintaine the honor of his estate. All theire labour and liberalitie tending to these endes is in show for the king, but indeed for themselves.'

Upon these and the like reasons the king tooke harte to prosecute

---

[18] Marginalia: 'Subsidy.' This invented speech restates Hayward's support of the monarch's right to levy taxes for the common good, set forth earlier in his 'Epistle Apologeticall' written for the suppressed second edition of *The First Part.*

the motion, and the people had the honestie not to deny it. Soe they graunted unto him a tenth, & halfe of the cleargie, a tenth of all the burroughe townes [fo. 46v] and a fifetenth of the commons throughe the realme. The king againe, to requite the people, revived 3 statutes which had beene made under the raigne of King Edward the 3d. The first was that the commons of everie sheire should not furnish or convoye soldiers into Scottland or Gascoigne or any other place out of the realme upon theire owne private charge; the second that souldiers appointed for service out of England should bee at the kings paye only from from the time of theire departure out of the countie where they were chosen, untill theire returne; the third statute was that noe man should bee constrained to furnish or find men of warre (other then those whoe held theire landes by such termes and services) if it were not by common assent & graunte made in parliament. And thus both the king and the people held themselves contented, the king being furnished for the time with money, and the people in hope of after ease, willingly submitting themselves to the present burthen.

The king alsoe, for further supplie of future wantes, suppressed all the priories of strangers that were within the realme (excepte such houses as were conventuall) and seized theire possessions into his handes. This is the first invasion which I find to have beene made by any king of this land upon religious possessions. In succeeding ages the example proceeded further by degrees. First, small monasteries and other like religious houses of the value of 200 poundes by yeare & under were graunted by parliament to the king.[19] [fo. 47] These were in number 376, and the yearely value of theire landes at that time exceeded 32,000 poundes, which hath beene since much more then doubled. Theire moveable goodes, being sould to such as did apprize them, amounted to more then 100,000 poundes. Besides the decaye of hospitalitie, which was much lamented among the people, it was thought that more then 10,000 personnes lost theire livinges by suppression of these places.

In shorte tyme after all other religious houses of like nature were by acte of parliament graunted to the king, of which the true value is almost inestimable. After these followed chaunteries, free chapelles and such like. After all this many good morselles have at divers times beene snatched awaye from bishopprickes, deanries and other ecclesiasticall preferrmentes, and more have beene gaped for with greedie desire. Whether this decreasing bee now at a staye I have alwayes doubted; out of all doubte, noe man can assure.

Edmund, Duke of Yorke, of whome much mention hath formerlie beene made, this yeare ended his life, and was buried at Langley nere

[19] MS marginal note: '27 Henry 8.'

to his wife, daughter to Peter, King of Spaine. This yeare the conduite upon Cornehill in London was made, which before was a prisone called The Tunne, whereunto persones suspected of felonie, night walkers and other offenders were commonly comitted.

The Fourth Yeare of King Henrie the Fourthe.

[VI]

All this time the king insisted, the Peircies resisted, and both persisted: hee in stiffe demaunding, they in stoute denying the Scottish prisoners which had beene taken at Hallidowne, and Nesbite. For of all the captive captaines in those twoe conflicts, only Mordake, Earle of Fife, the Duke of Albanies sonne, was delivered to the king, and hee (as it was protested) under tearmes rather of honor then of right. All the residue were retained by the Peircies as theire owne proper purchase and prey. These Peircies at the first were the greatest furtherers of King Henries designmentes: for Henry Peircie, Earle of Northumberland and Lord Henry Peircie his sonne were the first whoe incouraged him to returne out of banishment, first who adjoyned unto him at his arrivall, and the principall countenance and strength to all his proceedings. Thomas Peircie, Earle of Worcester, was the occasion that the forces which King Richard brought out of Ireland, yea his houshold officers & servauntes, did breake & scatter from him. But they, being mightie and proude, were able to give him the kingdome, but could not bee content that hee should rule. In which case it often falleth that such great desertes are but [fo. 48] ill requited, not alwaies throughe the princes disposition, ether forgettfull or unthankefull, but for the most parte throughe theire owne presumption, who bearing themselves upon theire service become respectlesse of the prince, and arrogant among theire peeres, incurring thereby the indignation of the one and envie of the other.

This presumption standeth in 3 degrees, accompanied with soe manie degres of dangers: first, when men doe thinke that by reason of theire abilities they cannot bee spared; secondly, when they suppose that by reason of the greatnesse of theire desert, the prince is bound to indure them in all things and deny them nothing; thirdly, when they perswade themselves that they are of power to bridle the prince, and to hold him straightly to theire directions. But there is noe prince soe meanley manned but as hee thinketh hee hath some to spare, soe is hee willing to bee ridd of those from whose mounting mindes hee ether feareth danger, or findeth disquiet. Besides, a prince is desirous that men should rather esteeme theire services a dutie then a deserte, and his giustes[1] a favour rather then a reward. Lastly, there was never

---

[1] See above.

any man whose greatnesse depended upon his princes feare, that could escape evill adventure in the end. Hereupon it often happeneth to bee happier for a man to have received great benefittes from [fo. 48v] his prince without deserte, then to have performed great service without reward, because princes for the most parte love those better whoe stand bound to them, then those to whome they seeme behoulden.

And thus it befell to these Peircies at this time, whoe were the cheifest men (noe doubte) by whose counsaile and creditt the king mounted into majestie, by meanes of which service and deserte they grew to a haughtie behaviour, without due rule of themselves or regard to any other, omitting noe occasion & seeking some to inculcate to the king how bouldly they advised, how bravely they adventured on his behalfe, contemning others as men of noe meritt. Few they held for helpers, but none for authours of his advauncement, but themselves. This done verie often, became verie odious, which rubbed out the remembrance of theire fortunate forwardnesse, & brought them into light estimation with the king. Notwithstanding, hee continued his countenance as before, & used them in appearance honorably enoughe, but somewhat shorte of theire expectation. The desertes of the men (out of question) distracted him one waye, and the doubte of them another.

Affections being thus prepared, [fo. 49] both parties upon everie accident were ready to breake of, the king in love, the lordes in loyaltie, hee bearing himselfe upon his authoritie, they upon theire power and deserte. And now upon this occasion the king did resolutely demaund deliverie of the Scottish prisoners, and that with open wordes of menace and dispight. Whereupon the Peircies grew more proude & intollerable, & endeavored by divers demaundes on theire partes to checke or choacke his desire; soe they required many things not soe much with care to obtaine as with purpose to picke occasion to revolte. And the king, in graunting any of theire demaundes, gained nothing eles but that more instantly they importuned those things which they knew hee could not but deny. Att the last the Lord Henrie Peircie, by direction of the Earle of Worcestre his uncle, came to the king at Windsore, and being in presence his behaviour was humble and his wordes respective, but his harte was bigge and full of furious courage, whereby his voice trembled, his cheekes changed, & much paine it was for him to continue in modest temper. In this turbulencie of humour hee made open demaunde that the king would redeeme Edmund Mortymer, Earle of March, his cosen germane (for Elianor, the Lord Henries [fo. 49v] mother, was aunt to the Earle of March), whoe had beene taken prisoner in his service against the Welsh, and was then evill intreated by them, and shakled with iron in a filthie prison.

This motion moved the king not a litle, because it touched his tenure verie nere: for this Earle of March, before King Richardes voyage into Ireland, had beene declared (by right of his bloud) heire apparant to the throwne, for which cause the king would hardly have ransomed him out of hell, and yet would not have held him from going to heaven. He litle regarded which way hee did goe, soe as hee might not stand in his waye. And indeed many actions of the king induced many to bee of opinion that the Earle of March was rather protected than imprisoned in Wales, and that hereby the king was in some hope of his end by the enemy, without ether blemish or guilte of foule dealing from himselfe. Therefore, after a sullen silence hee returned answere, that the Earle of March was not taken prisoner in his cause, but in defence of his owne private estate; that albeit hee were taken in service of the realme, yet to burthen the publicke treasurie ether with the rashnesse, or cowardice, or infortunity [fo. 50] of all those whoe adventured in the warres, it is nether reasonable nor possible to bee perfourmed.

The Lord Henrie, having wordes at will, replied that the earle was taken in that quarrel wherein hee fought, and fought in that against which the enemies came, and that was against the realme and the king, and not (but in a common consequence) against him. That it was noe lesse reason that the king should beare the ransome of those whoe were lost in his warres, then that hee should receave the ransome of those whoe were taken, and if that bee impossible then is this unreasonable, for noe societie will allowe that one parte should beare all the hazard, and the other have all the hope. That in the Earle of March there was a speciall respecte, by reason of his nereness to the king in bloud, whereby hee might challenge a priviledge, if not of course yett of curtesie, above many others.

'I perceave then,' said the king, 'that your looke is one way, and your levell another, but the cases which you compare are nothing like. For in warre under any prince, the soldiers are not in tearmes of societie, but of service, whereunto they are bound, some by tenure, some by degree of dignitie, some by office, others for paye; the residue are voluntary followers for favour and thankes, in regard whereof all the avail of the [fo. 50v] adventure pertaineth only to him who setteth up the warre, and they whoe follow it cann challenge nothing but that which bindeth them to serve. Otherwise saylors might call upon the merchant for theire misadventures, and claime theire partage in the burthen of the shippe. Indeed, my bloud I have reason to respecte, but noe further then it is healthfull to my bodie, and rather then it should breede any dangerous disease I would make passage for it out of myne owne veines. Wee have already passed throughe many difficulte adventures and remaine untill now soe perplexed with some, as wee have nether pleasure nor neede to multiplie mischeifes, and to open occasion of moving new mutinees.'

'Well,' answered the Lord Peircie, 'whether the people stand in proper tearmes ether of societie or service, or of subjection, which hath a mixture of both, I will not debate. Assuredly they beare a deepe share both in the adventure and (as it is reason) in the charge, and yet are not free from obedience & commaunde, which if under the familiar tearme of service you intend to draw to an absolute subjection, assure your selfe that men cann spie & will speake how-soever they speede. It is true that bloud often causeth dangerous effectes, but especiallie when it is thrust out of the naturall place, for then of necessitie it [fo. 51] congealeth, it putrifieth, it inflameth, it ulcerateth, it infecteth profitable humours and maketh them pernicious. I[f] bloud letting bee a remedie, yet must [it] bee used both sparinglie & with judgement, not soe much in finding the vent, as in foreseing the event, and that with as good respecte to our honor as our health. For manie tymes it falleth that there is greater deformitie in the scarre then was ether danger or paine in the soare.'

The king perceaved the secret sence, but seemed not to perceave it, becuase hee would not seeme to bee touched with it, and loath hee was to blowe this cole any longer, least the flame of furie should not easily bee ruled. For his adversitie had taught him this lesson, to applie himselfe to the humour of those whoe were able ether to pleasure or offend him. Therefore, albeit hee intended nothing lesse then to graunt this demaund, yet would hee not make open shewe of deniall, but because it was both new & of waight hee said that he would deliberate thereon. But the Lord Peircie, taking deferring for a flatt denying, departed from the king bearing sensible markes of furie in his face, & having a full purpose to shake and stirre up whatsoever was in any place discontented & unsounde.

The king being unwilling ether to heare of this suite againe, or to bee charged wth cruell or unkind dealing, did openly [fo. 51v] publish against the Earle of March that hee did voluntarily suffer himselfe to bee taken, and therewith did falsely betraye both the honor and safetie of that parte of the realme, and the lives of those whoe adventured with him. This was commonly taken for an absolute devise, whereupon many who stared not before upon starres, & nether knew nor were inquisitive after titles to crownes, did then advaunce theire strengthes above theire private affaires, and knitt themselves against the king in the end. But especiallie the Peircies tooke this matter most hotly to harte, and made it the occasion to disavowe theire alledgeance, openly giving forth that the heire to the realme was unjustly dispoiled not only of his inheritaunce, but of his honor and reputation, and could not bee releived with that which was his owne. And indeed it is an errour in great personages to seeke shadowes & shiftes, ether for their subtleties or oversightes, because as they cannot long dazell soe many eyes as are sett upon theire actions, soe the deceipt being once discovered, it openeth a way ether to hatred or contempte. Alsoe it occsioneth some suspicion of feare which giveth encouragement to bold attemptes. Further, many cannot swallow an injurie & digest it too, & yet will not endure to bee scorned or [fo. 52] otherwise abused therein. Lastly, that prince canne expecte litle sinceritie & fayth, of whome men conceave opinion that hee is a deceavable dealer.

Now the Peircies, in this fitt of furie, dealte with Owen Glendor for enlargement of the Earle of March, and then confederated with both against King Henry. To this they were induced, or rather seduced, upon perswation that King Henry was the Mouldwarpe, whereof Merline did prophecie,[2] accursed by Godes owne mouth, & that they three were the dragon, the lion & the woolfe which should divide his realme among them. Hereupon theire deputies, meeting at the house of the Archdeacon of Bangor, agreed that an indenture tripertite should bee made which in theire lordes name they sealed & delivered, whereby all the middle parte of England between Severne and Trent south and eastwarde was assigned to the Earle of March. All Wales and landes beyond Severne westward were appointed to Owen Glendor. All the residue from Trent northward was allotted to Lord Henrie Peircie. Assuredly manie of these prophesies have beene devised by great men to serve theire turne, because nothing doth more forceablie ether drawe or retaine the common people then superstition, whereof the best experienced commaunders have made good use. But if the generalles themselves bee therewith touched, then is it dangerous, ether [fo. 52v] by causing them to lett opportunity slippe, or by driving them to unadvised attemptes. And with such like divinations, or rather deviations, this realme did much abound, untill by statute they were exiled; whereby hath beene occasioned many errours in princes, often ruine of noble families, & much destruction of the common sorte.

King Henrie, nether seing nor suspecting these practises against him, bent all his thoughtes about gathering a power for his accustomed chase in Wales, wherein hee pursued without victorie those whoe fledd without anie foile.[3] The Earle of Northumberland and his sonne, being advertised hereof by Lord Thomas, Earle of Worcester, buckled themselves likewise to theire businesse, and with great alacritie sett

_____

[2] 'Mouldwarpe' = 'mole.' The prophecy of the Welsh bard Merlin is reported, after Hall, by Holinshed (521/1/74) as a basis for the proposed division of the kingdom, and repeated by Shakespeare in *1 Henry IV*, III, i, 149-53.
[3] 'Foile' = repulse, or defeat (OED).

theire enterprize on foote. And first they made to theire partie those Scottes which had beene taken prisoners at Hameldone, promising to the Earle Dowglas the towne of Berwicke and a parte of Northumberland, and other townes & territories to the rest in case they obtained the upper hand. The Scottes did easilie imbrace this offer, & supported the Peircies with all theire power, not soe much for hope of recompence, as the desire for revenge; for both sides they hated alike, but the king they feared, besides. These forraigne forces being gotten, the Peircies thought fitt to give some countenance to theire cause at home, knowing right well [fo. 53] that without home-helpe they might shew theire good hartes against the king, but should never produce any great effectes. To this purpose, by advise of Richarde Scroope, Archbishop of Yorke, brother to the Lord Scroope whome King Henry caused to bee beheaded at Bristow (soe deepe doth violence strike into bloud), certaine articles were devised and divulged against King Henry, as doe ensue:

'Wee, Henry Peircie, Earle of Northumberland, Highe Constable of England and Warden of the West Marches towardes Scottland, Henry Peircie our eldest sonne, Warden of the East Marches of England towardes Scottland, and Thomas Peircie, Earle of Worcester, procurators & protectours of the common wealth, before the Lord Jesus Christ our supreme judge doe alleadge, say & intend to prove personallie with our handes against thee, Henry, Duke of Lancaster, unjustly & without title of right named King of England, and against thy complices & favourers: that when after thine exile thou didst enter into England, thou madest an oath unto us upon the holy gospelles at Dancaster that thou wouldst never claime the crowne or state royall, but only thyne owne inheritance & the inheritaunce of thy wife, and that Richard our soveraigne and thine should raigne during his life, governed by the good advise of the lordes spirituall & temporall; that thou hast imprisoned thy said soveraigne lord & our king within the Tower of London, untill for feare of death hee had resigned [fo. 53v] his kingdomes of England & Fraunce, and renounced all his right in the said realmes & other his dominions & landes beyond the seas, under coulor whereof thou hast crowned thy selfe king of the said realmes, & seazed upon all the castles & lordships pertaining to the kings crowne, contrarie to thine oath, and that therefore thou art perjured & false.

'Alsoe, wee alleadge, say & intend to prove that whereas thou didst sweare to us upon the said gospelles in the same place & time that thou wouldst not suffer any dismes[4] to bee levied of the cleargie, or

---

[4]'Disme' = var. of 'dime,' a tenth part, or tithe, usually a church tax; the fifteenth was generally a tax on personal property.

any fifteenes of the people, or any other tallages or taxes to bee levied in the realme of England during thy life, but by consideration of the 3 estates of the realme (excepte in cases of importance & for resistance of our enemies), thou, contrarie to thyne oath, hath caused many dismes, fifteens & other impositions to bee levied aswell of the cleargie & as of the cominaltie & marchauntes of the realme of England for feare of thy majestie royall; wherefore thou arte perjured & false.

'Alsoe, that whereas thou didst sweare to us upon the same gospelles in the foresaid place & time that our soveraigne lord & thine, King Richard, should raigne during the terme of his life in his royall dignitie, thou hast traitorously caused him, without consent or judgement of the lordes of the realme, by the space of xv dayes & nightes (which is horrible among Christians to bee heard) to perish & bee murthered with [fo. 54] hunger, thirst & cold within the castle of Pomfrett, wherefore thou art perjured & false.

'Alsoe, that thou, when our soveraigne lord & thine King Richard was by that horrible murther dead as abovesaid, thou by extort power didst usurpe the title & honor of the kingdomes of England & Fraunce, unjustly & contrarie to thyne oath, from Edmund Mortimer, Earle of March and of Ulster, the next & directe heire of England & of Fraunce by due course of inheritance after the decease of the foresaid Richard, wherefore thou arte perjured & false.

'Alsoe, that where thou madest an oath in the same place & time, & afterwardes at the time of coronation, to supporte & maintaine the lawes & good customes of the realme of England, thou fraudulently & contrarie to the lawes of the said realme hast written almost throughe everie sheire in England to choose such knightes for parliament as should bee for thy pleasure & purpose, soe that in thy parliaments noe justice should bee ministred against thy mind in these complaintes now moved by us, albeit that wee, according to our consciences (as, we trust, ruled by God) have oftentimes complained of them, as well cann testifie the right reverend fathers in God Thomas Arundle, Archbishop of Canterbury, & Richard Scroope, Archbishop of Yorke. Wherefore now by force of hand, before Our Lord Jesus Christ, wee must demaund our remedie & helpe. [fo. 54v]

'Alsoe, that where Edmund Mortimer, Earle of March & Ulster, was taken prisoner by Owen Glendor in a pitched & foughten feild, & cast into prison & there loaden with fetters for thy quarrell & cause, thou hast falsely proclaimed that hee willingly yeelded himselfe prisoner, & nether wouldest desire him thy selfe, nor suffer us his kinsemen to ransome & redeeme him, yett when wee had not only concluded with the said Owen for his ransome at our proper charges but alsoe for a peace betweene thee and the said Owen, thou hast not only publish'd us for traytors & subverters of the realme, but deceitfully contrived the destruction of our persons. For which cause wee defie thee, thy fautors[5] and complices as common traytors to the realme, and oppressors and confounders of the right heires to the crowne of England, which wee intend with our handes to prove, almightie God assisting us.'

These articles the Peircies shewed to divers noble persons & prelates of the realme, in whome they did perceave or conceave at the least ether signes or cause of discontentment against the king.

All theire frendes seemed well pleased with the attempte: many promised their aid, some confirmed the same by writing under theire seales, but most were rather foreward to drive on others then to be drawne on themselves.

[fo. 55] In the meane tyme the king was busied in assembling an armie, & having all things in a readinesse, beganne to advaunce forth towardes Wales. But it is not for nothing that the poetes faine Fortune to bee blind, because many things seeme[6] blindly to happen without ether forecast of foresight of our owne, and by actions intended to another end. For these forces gathered against the Welsh served the king to a greater purpose, for which otherwise it might have beene to raise, when it should have beene to use. And therefore they who suppose that all things were devised as they were done, doe oftentimes make that wisdome which is but happiness, and they who presume that theire owne counsaile is sufficient to guide a businesse of such varietie doe much misbehave themselves towardes God.

Now the Lord Henrie Peircie, accompanied wth the Earle Dowglasse & divers of the nobility of Scotland, sett forth in good appointment from the north partes towardes Scottland, such dailie drawing to them as obeying not for dutie but feare, were gladd they found commaunders to follow. The Earle of Northumberland, by reason of sickenesse, stayed behind, but promised to followe them upon his amendment. The Lord Thomas Peircie, Earle of Worcester, had the government of the prince Henrie, the kings eldest sonne, who then kept house in London; & hearing that the game was on foote, in most secrett manner he departed from the prince, & adjoyned to his nephew at [fo. 55v] Stafford. Most of the other confederates sate still, giving rather ayne[7] then aide to ether partie. Humphry, Earle of Stafford, had given his seale unto the Peircies, but his persons & followers hee carried to the king, and soe did divers others, ether dissembling at the first, or afterwardes changing theire mindes.

When the Lord Henry Peircie first tooke the feild, hee gave it forth

---

[5] Adherents, partisans (OED).
[6] MS: 'seemes'
[7] 'Ayes,' i.e., assurances.

that his journey was to aide the king against the Welsh. But after that the Earle of Worcester was come unto him, they declared openly against the king. To the soldiers they pretended the common libertie and glorie and wealth of the realme (usuall ensingnes of rebellion), which was governed by a tyraunt, they said, & not by a true and lawfull king, exhorting them that they would nether spare labour nor life in soe honorable an action. Among the common people they dispersed letters wherein was conteined that theire taking of armes was principallie to putt better government in the common wealth, because the paymentes which had beene graunted to the king for defence of the realme were expended to unprofitable endes. Secondly, it was for the suertie of theire owne personns, because by reason of the malice of theire enemies, they durst not approach the kinges presence until by entreatie of the lordes of the realme they might bee permitted to purge [fo. 56] themselves by judgement of theire peeres.

Many credulous conceites did highly commend both theire fayth to the state & theire foresight for themselves. But the king hereupon sent abroad his letters likewise, that hee marvailed much, seing the Earle of Northumberland & the Lord Henrie his sonne had receaved for defence of the Marchesse of the north most parte of the moneis which had beene graunted to him by the cleargie and cominaltie of the realme, that they should complaine of the unprofitable expending of the same. And whereas they gave forth that they durst not approach the presence of the king with[out] mediation of the lordes of the realme, he protested that as hee was not privie to any cause, soe was hee free from any conceite of such displeasure against them, & therefore hee offered them publicke fayth, or pledges if they pleased, that they might come unto him & returne safely without impeachment. But this could not satisfie the pride of the Peircies: it was not safetie but soveraigntie which they did regard. Soe they resolved to advaunce theire adventure, & dislodging from Stafford they marched towardes Shrewsebury, with intent to draw nere to Owen Glendore, with whose forces if they could have knitt they had sett up a side very hard to have beene dealte withall. They alsoe published in the countries where they went, that King Richard was alive & in theire company, whome if any man desired to see, hee [fo. 56v] should forthwith come in armour to the castle of Chester. This they did because King Richard was in those partes especiallie favoured; but as it wrought something wth men of fleete & fleeting apprehensions, soe to men of deeper search & less mutable, this varietie of devise made theire intent more doubtfull & suspicious.

Now the king, being upon the frontiers of Wales, provided soe well that the Welsh could not starte forth in any great companies to joyne with the Peircies. Alsoe, the Earle of Northumberland, having recovered his health, sett forth with a good power towardes his brother & his sonne, as it was conceaved, but towardes the king as it was given forth. But the Earle of Chester and Sir Roberte Waterhowse, houlding it best in an action of doubtfull construction to projecte against that designe whereof the event is most dangerous, with a strong hand putt themselves against him upon his waye. Hereupon the Earle, having noe desire ether to trust them as frendes or to try them as enemies, retired backe to the castle of Wakeworth. A manifest note of destruction at hand, when confederates ether cannot or dare not joyne & continue together.

The king, leaving upon the frontiers of Wales sufficient forces to watch the Welsh enemies & to hould them playe,[8] [fo. 57] turned sodainly upon the Peircies, & used such diligence in his march that his approach prevented the fame of his setting forth. Hee found them embattled before Shrewsbury & readie to give assaulte unto the towne; but upon discoverie of the kings ensignes they brake of that enterprize, and withdrewe to a litle village not farre distant called Berewicke. Here they armed theire soldiers as well with courage as with steele, partly with hope of victorie, and partly with despaire ether of pardon or escape. 'Behould,' said they, 'the standard of the usurper, who proudly advaunceth upon us ether to receave present vengeance for the bloud which hee hath shedd, or to increase his reckoning against another daye. Wee must now resolve to playe the men, for if wee turne our backes, wee have noe holes to hide us, noe houldes to defend us; the sworde will followe us & the gibbett stand before us, soe as if wee escape a base butcherie, wee shall runne upon an infamous death. Our safetie, our glorie consistes only in valour, first if wee overcome, next if wee die rather then bee driven from the place of our chardge; the first whereof will mo[u]nt us to the height of our hopes, the second will free us from the tyrantes malice. For it is more honorable to die by the sword then by the sentence of the enemy.' There were then as cheife captaines of the armie the Earle Dowglasse, the Barron of Kinderton, Sir Hugh Browne, Sir Richard [fo. 57v] Vernon, knightes, & divers others both of courage & pedegree, all which, with xiiij thousand choice souldiers, made a solemne vowe to Lord Henry Peircie to spend theire last breath & bloud rather then abandon theire charge. In this heat of humour theire desire was forthwith to returne and shew theire faces to theire enemies, yea to tast them with theire horsemen, & happely to draw them thereby to fight before they had recovered the wearinesse of theire travaile. And sure theire courage was great, and theire resolution firme, which putt the Lord Henry in hope of a glorious daye.

[8] 'Hold them playe' = 'keep them occupied or engaged' (OED).

The king brought his armie nere to the walles of Shrewsbury, and himselfe with a few followers entered the towne, being joyfull that his diligence had fallne soe well that thereby hee had snatched this morsell out of his enemies mouth, which might both feede & furnish & alsoe defend them for a good tyme. But scarce had hee thanked the townesmen for theire faythfull service, when hee was sodainely advertised that his enemies were returned, & that theire flagges did wave in the feild, & that they were soe full of francke courage that theire light horsmen beganne to playe upon his armie. Hereupon, being shorte in cercumstances, hee issued forth againe, and ranged his souldiers without the east gate, having his backe covered with the towne, & purposing to deale according to occasion. The [fo. 58] Peircies alsoe embattailed theire men soe nere unto him, that hee must have beene a good man at armes that should have parted them without blowes. Howbeit noe actions of hostilitie were attempted that night, but every man stood fast & kepte his quarter, expecting which side would beginne his hazard, or rather his follie. Only the Peircies sent unto the king the articles before mentioned, under theire handes & seales, with theire defiance annexed to them. To which the king returned answere, that these quarrells were utterly untrue & forged against him partly upon malice, which when it aboundeth there is nothing whereto it will not applie, & partly upon ambition to advaunce some secrett aspiring endes; that the worse theire cause was, the more need it had of these artificiall mantles and maskes; that whatsoever imputation might bee fastened upon him, the Peircies were nether competent judges to condemne, being sworne to his subjection, nor sufficient parties to accuse, being disloyall & perjured traytors; that upon these pointes hee would joyne with them in issue, not by wordes fitt for women, but by weapons, wherein lay the tryall of manhood, & howsoever hee might seeme to bee overcome by the one, yett was he confident that God would assist him in the other.

The messengers departed but thought his answere very generall & shorte, for in dangerous & extraordinary motions, it is not sufficient that a princes cause bee [fo. 58v] good, unlesse a good opinion bee conceaved thereof; and they whoe upon confidence that the goodnesse of theire cause will appeare in tyme doe neglecte to publish the truth thereof, shall many times overshoote themselves. But leaving the king to his owne advise, some other man might thus (meethinkes) have returned answere: 'You Peircies have objected many haynous matters against your king, but such only which hee did by your direction & helpe. What then? Shall hee only beare the blame, who beareth away the benefitt? Noe, verily, but they who were the causes of the mischeife must alsoe bee companions in the revenge. You see that now it beginneth to worke; God hath cast betweene you the apple of strife.

You see that vengeance is gone forth; it is doubtfull with whome shee will beginne, but doubtlesse shee will end in time with all.' But againe to our purpose.

The same daye many others went from the one armie to the other, some to learne intelligence, others to draw away followers, all under coulor of honest pretenses, having secrett instructions for[9] underhand dealing. Hereupon you might have seene upon the body of the guard many gentlemen & ordinaries of both parties communing together, ether renewing old acquaintance or entertaining new, & all with faire & familiar carriages, [fo. 59] notwithstanding the contrarie badges that they bare. The kings side perswadeth the other to respecte themselves, to abandon the traitors & not obstinately to sett up a miserable warre, wherein ether they must perish, or destroye those who loved them well. Againe, the Peircies side perswaded the other to forsake the tyraunt, to have a care of the common wealth, whereof hee had almost effected & still laboured the overthrowe, houlding it assured that there was noe meanes of supporting the one but by suppressing of the other. Thus ether provoked other to his partie, but scarce any one perswaded to peace. Some who aparte did behould these curious courtesies, & considering that upon the least signe of battaile these kind greetings would forthwith turne to boisterous blowes, with water in theire eyes did curse the crueltie of publicke discord which, vayling the sight of men ether with ambition or with hate, keepeth them from detesting to ripp up the entrailes of those whome country, whome parentage, whome religion and lawes hath united unto them. Some of these with an honest entent laboured both parties to sheath up theire swordes, but they whoe in this course undertooke most found themselves most overtaken in the end. And it was weakenesse in them to apprehend any hope that soe great mindes, having soe great endes, could by any meane meanes bee appeased. [fo. 59v]

Now the king, being noe novice in militarie affaires, did give not only allowance but authoritie to this enterview of the souldiers. But in the Peircies it was an errour, & turned much to theire disadvantage, for they whoe are inferiour to theire enemies ether in goodnesse of cause, or greatnesse of estate, or eles in opinion of courage, fortune & skill, should carefully restraine such entercourses, assuring themselves that they shall not winne one to theire side for the losse of tenne. And this danger is then especially to bee feared, when wee have to deale with an enemie who is not infected with the hatefull humour of pride, but cann apply himselfe to winne men, for because all men naturally

[9] MS: 'from.'

are desirous to preserve themselves, they are easily drawne to side with the strongest.

When night was come, everie man withdrew to his quarter, reposing his body & disposing his conscience against the next daye, because the enterprize seemed dangerous. The day following being Saturday and the Vigill[10] of St. Mary Magdalene, both parties perceiving the game to waxe warme sett theire battailes in order very tymely in the morning, purposing to breake theire fast upon the flesh of those who should come against them. And verily it might have beene wished that both the frendes & enemies of the [fo. 60] realme had seene them as they stood ranged in the feild; the one would have learned to honor, the other to value it as it was of worth. For there might have beene seene almost 40,000 men in arraye (the most English) not farre asunder, theire courage feirce, their countenance brave, a levell ground called Old Feild, otherwise Bullfeild, without any advantage, betweene them. Both closed theire men in two bodies, a maine battaile & a vauntguarde, & before theire vauntguard they placed certaine troupes of horsemen, in a forlorne hope, the number on both sides being competent, which when it exceedes, the residue doe but breede confusion. The Peircies committed theire vauntgard to the Earle Dowglasse & his traine of Scottes, whoe instantly desired that charge. The kings vauntgard was ledd by Humphrye, Earle of Stafford, that day made Highe Constable of the realme, a man fresh in yeares & of singular courage, yet more fitt for execution then to directe.

Now albeit the king had hitherto carried a confident countenance & his forces were sufficient to encounter his enemies, yet as it commonly falleth when extremitie is at hand, hee had a checke of doubt, not without cause, that fortune might change upon him, having good experience of her mutabilitie by such things as shee had taken from others & cast upon him. Hee held it a manifest [fo. 60v] defecte in judgement to putt the whole body of his state upon adventure of battaile against men both furious &, such as most of them, beside theire horse & armour had nothing to loose, if by any milder meanes the contention might bee composed. Hee doubted alsoe the fidelitie of many whoe then did temporize & speake him faire, whome hee knew right well hee should find rebellious in case his affaires should have hard successe. Further, hee knew hee had many forraigne enemies who without the supporte of a domesticall faction would never enterprize to invade him. For these reasons hee thought it needfull to doe all things surely, & soe, howsoever the advise were taken, the event should bee honorable.

In this deliberation some advised the king to fortifie Shrewsburie

[10] 21 July 1403.

& to retire somewhat backe, yet not soe farre but that hee might beare a hand over his enemies in cutting of supplyes, & putting his power upon them upon everie advantage; for a litle delaye would soone make those ether wearie or wise, who then flocked fast to the enemies, & promised to themselves all the wealth of the land, & noe lesse fast would they shrinke from them when they should find nether provision nor paye.

This counsaile was so displeasing to others that they affirmed plainely that [fo. 61] was full of treason, & that the authours therof were worthy of the reward for giving the first onsett upon the king. They spurred him to present battaile, upon consideration that if they should give leave for the frendes of his enemies to adjoyne unto them, the warr would growe long, or eles they must fight a more uncertaine battaile.

To this the king answered that noe man should bee blamed for giving advise, especially when it is required. 'I daylie call you,' said hee, 'to the counsaile, and heare diversities of opinions, & yett doe not suspecte all those whome I doe not follow.' Therefore hee gave thankes to all for theire good meanings. But in retiring (he said) hee should seeme to give up both his country & his cause; for considering the force that fame is of, hee could not goe backe but it would bee reported that hee ranne away, which would cause those who hated him before to contemne him alsoe. And noe lesse did hee allow to committe the whole state of his affaires to one stroke of fortune, to sett a kingdome at stake against nothing, to jumpe upon a desperate bargaine, whereby hee should bee lost if hee were vanquished, & a looser if hee did overcome. Wherefore hee thought it best to delay the present encounter, by making some overtures of peace which would assuredly coole & happily quench the desire of battaile. For civill disturbance having noe further proceeded may bee appeased easily enoughe, but if bloud [fo. 61v] bee once drawne, the wound is hardly healed, and never without a skarre. And albeit hee had upon pointe of honour untill that tyme forborne to make offers of peace, expecting that this enemies should beginne the demaund, yet whosoever shall weighe dangerous dependances upon the losse of a feild will nothing blame him for avoyding to determine his debate by censure of the sword (especially against his subjectes), if without running from it hee may make a good end. For a small losse in battaile much changeth the mindes of subjectes, causing them to have the enemie in regard, & the prince in contempte, yea to murmure & practise to demaund, to deny more bouldly then before, & to storme if ether any thing bee done or doe happen against theire liking.

For these reasons the king (his souldiers resting under theire weapons) dispatched the Abbott of Shrewsbury & one of the clarkes of the privie seale to the Lord Percies, furnished wth instructions to perswade them to peace, & to offer them pardone if they would descend to any reasonable agreement. In the meane tyme he lost noe tyme, but first veiwed well the maine body of his armie, then encouraged the cheifest in chardge, whose valour might enflame the rest to fight well.

The Abbott of Shrewsbury declared [fo. 62] to the lordes that the king had not thrust himselfe among them against theire willes, but was sent for by them, & by them placed in his estate; that seeing him more noble then the rest, they should give him some time to make tryall of his vertue, and whether hee would shew himselfe worthy of King Edward for his grandfather. In a word, hee delivered the truth soe wisely that the Lord Henry Peircie was moved therby to waighe with himselfe all those things which ether feare or hope could put into his head, & to consider that the name of a king within his owne realme was of such majesty that it was like to drawe the maine power to his parte. Hereupon hee beganne not only to listen, but to leane unto peace. But in very truth the king had deferred this overture too long. For now necessitie having kindled the courage of the souldiers & banished all apprehension of feare, they were resolved (winking at any cercumspecte respecte) valiantly to runne some dangerous adventure. Notwithstanding, the Earle of Worcester did accompanie the Abbott in his returne, whoe declared largely to the king what theire greifes were, & what theire desires. Many demaunds were made for particuler persons, and some alsoe for the common wealth, but of these they stood least which manifested the end of theire endeavoures.

[fo. 62v] After some debatementes the king was not strange to acknowledge in many pointes both his owne errours and theire greifes, to promise alsoe reformation of the one & remedie of the other, & large favour to those who were willing to reduce all things into order by quiett, rather then by tumulte to sett them more out of frame. This was so seriously & soe sincerely delivered as noe man would suspecte the fayth of his meaning. But the earle distrusted him nothing the lesse, for hee was perswaded that noe man who putteth his prince in feare cann safely repose assurance in his worde. Againe, hee forgott not how the king before had fayled in his fayth, whereby a man procureth disadvantage that hee shall not bee beleeved in his truest intentes. Notwithstanding, hee dissembled his doubtes, & left in the king an impression of hope, that without bloud or blowes this stirre should bee reduced to a quiet staye.

When the earle returned to his company hee found them all changed in cheare, the Scottes for the hope which they should loose, the English for the danger wherein they should bee left if weapons were laid downe. Some were stroke into a sad silence, shaking the head, biting the lipp, & scratching where it litle itched. Others fell to flatt raging, that they should bee at the courtesie [fo. 63] of those whome they had soe much provoked; others with a learing laughter asked theire fellows into what country they would runne, in what place they had most pleasure to hang, & to what quarter of the realme they would bequeath their quarters. The earle alsoe did litle favour the pacification, & therefore related with a sparing reporte all the kings offers & agreementes. 'Only,' said he, 'hee passeth generall promises both of pardone & favour, if wee thinke it safe to stand to his pleasure for performance of them.' Hereupon a counsaile was called; the colonelles and captaines alsoe were sent to the soldiers, to imparte that unto all which did most nerely concerne all. These forthwith answered that they were readie to dispend the last droppe of theire bloud in that cause, desiring theire generall not to abandon them in that danger whereinto hee had drawne them. This disposition of the soldiers being reported to the counsaile, they were soone resolved in theire opinion.

One said, 'in play hee that giveth over the sett is accompted to lose it, which is not more true in any other game then in this. You have undertaken to deliver the state from the malice of an usurper, from whence proceede the greatest mischeifes which usually happen; if you now relinquishe you dishonor yourselfe, you discreditt the cause, you discourage all those who have [fo. 63v] beene all readie to adventure with you. For all men will attribute this yeelding ether to favour or to feare, of which your beginning hath cleared you of the one, & nothing but persistance cann free you from the other.'

Another said, 'the power of our enemies lieth upon our face, & behind wee have noe place of retreite. These parlies are but meanes partly to sound & partly to suaie us, for if they cann ether perceave in us any feare, or bring us to securitie, they will fortwith chase us even into the sea. The better way therefore is this: wee are now within sight of them; doe but sett us within reach, & happily within an houre or twoe wee shall fall to some agreement; for wee shall never bee good frendes untill wee have skuffled a litle together. Wee have hitherto only stirred theire galles, which must alsoe bee purged. For, having thus farre proceeded, there is no way to perfecte frendshippe but first to become theire perfecte enemies.'

'Nay,' said another, 'lett us rather abide untill they come to bind our handes & fetter our feete, & lead us to theire open scaffoldes & gibbettes, there to glutt theire crueltie as well with our shame as with our bloud. Or eles lett us packe out of the land & picke our teeth fasting in forraigne countryes, whilest they [fo. 64] keepe state in our houses, & fill theire purses with our revennues. Or if this choice doth not please us, lett us trye the maine chaunce, or rather because wee have noe choice, lett us imbrace necessitie. Doe wee not see both theire wealth & theire weapons bent against us, breathing out nothing but dire revenge? What moderate advise shall wee now pursue? Noe, noe, these meanes have already puffed theire pride; there is now noe mediator but the sword; the only reconciler now is death. What? How shall wee bee esteemed worthie of the two honorable titles of Englishmen & gentlemen, if wee cann putt on the patience to beare our selves soe base, and behold them soe insolent as heretofore wee have done? If throughe cowardice in saving our selves, wee cast away all this people who adheare unto us? Wherefore you that have taken upon you the common defence must forthwth not resolve, but dispatch, for the matter will beare noe longer delay.'

These speeches, being the verie bellowes of the warre, did move more by vehemency then by weight, and against those who thought best to entertaine the treatie of pacification for a time, aswell for advantage of drawing theire confederates unto them, as for avoyding the curses and clamours of the comon people, as lastly for that in weightye affaires which are accompanied with many mischeifes, [fo. 64v] men must rather bee drawne by necessitie then runne headlong upon will.

To these cold considerations the Earle of Worcester made answere that this advise was overcercumspecte, or to speake the truth too fearefull; that it wanted fortitude and magnanimitie, not only the sinewes but the very soule of militarie adventures; that this pointe was discussed at the entrance of this action, & for the present they were to resolve not whether they should beginne, but how they should proceede. 'But what,' said hee, 'will bee the event of this our treatie? Free pardon? Say alsoe, if you please, favour and advauncement! For all these are promised indeed, & the wordes sound well when they are fairely spoken. But where is our assurance? If wee request any other pledge then the promises & oathes of them whome wee have openly charged with perjurie, wee are heard noe further & are challenged for dishonoring the majesty royall. As for clamours & cries, wherewith wee feare to bee overwhelmed as authours of the calamities of publicke discord, there is noe man (I suppose) but will accompte them authours of the warre who are authours of the wronge. But wee shall winne tyme hereby, and herewith libertie for our associates to come in: I will not speake of our associates & I would that the voluntarie shrinking away of some of them had not made many [fo. 65] in our companie to waver, but lett us rest assured that if men ether discerne or feare any fearefullnes in us by reason of our readines to yeeld, nether will they stirre whoe are behind nor they staye who are already come; but the one will bee content never to have beene the kings enemies, the other will contend who shall first bee reconciled his frendes. As for the king, what with his countenance to allure, what

with his authoritie to commaunde, what with his abilitie to wage &
rewarde (wherof in wordes hee was never niggard), his power will
dayly receave increase. Now therefore, that wee bee not abused by
those who hate us at the harte to give way unto them, untill wee
bee cast into forraigne countries, chased into forrestes & cottages,
contemned by our basest & condemned by our proudest enemies, lett
us have recourse to armes in tyme; which as they were at the first
justly taken, soe are they now of necessitie to bee used. Trust not the
deceaveable promises of a perjured tyrant; doubte not your assured
forces; presume not upon uncertaine supplies, least wth Aesops dogg
you not only misse that for which you gape, but loose that which is
in your mouth. Wee have seene the boyling courage of our companions; wee have heard theire undaunted desires; lett us followe the
streame & make noe doubte of a good event. For fortitude is commonly
supported by fortune, but if wee deferre our dispatches [fo. 65v] this
swelling heate will soone asswage, partly upon the generall nature of
all vehemencies, which are of shorte continuance, partly upon the
naturall impatiencie of our English nation, which if it presently seeth
not the imagined effectes, doth from out of liking grudge & give
over.'[11]

The Lord Henry Peircie, finding himselfe disappointed of much of
his supplies, & it to bee impossible that his armie wanting paye would
long continue soe great as it was, with these wordes knitt up the
resolution:

'Hee that entereth the cariere purposeth to runne, & they who
skipp themselves in a warre as assailantes must adventure the onsett,
otherwise all theire preparations are nothing eles but vaine & vaunting
braveries. And in two cases especiallie delayes breed disadvantage,
one when the enemie is of power, the other when the cause is not
commonly favoured. It is dangerous to give a mighty enemie tyme,
& in such attemptes as are never applauded untill they bee atcheived,
rashenesse is a lesse fault then remissenesse, & quicke courage a better
vertue then cold & quaking consideration. Seing therefore in such a
cause against such an enemie wee are entred into enterprize, wee will
linger noe longer & suffer our selves to bee devoured by degrees in
doing nothing. Lett them cast doubtes that feare; the best tyme to
talke of peace will bee when wee shall have the advantage of warre.
Gentlemen, [fo. 66] followe me & stand by mee this daye, with
resolution to winne honour by victorie or by death. Plucke up your
hartes against those who would plucke them out. Come on, lett us
goe! If this first successe fall out favourable, it will cutt of the course

---

[11] MS marginal note: 'The nature of the English.'

of a long & ruinous warre. If otherwise, it shall end our care of whatsoever shall hereafter happen.'

This resolution was received with marvailous alacritie, first of the captaines, then of the souldiers, especiallie of the Scottes, whoe were in great feare of loosing both theire labour & theire hope. Herewith the signe was given, & the souldiers with a maine course tooke the feild. The king, perceaving the great game beganne to be plaied, with noe lesse courage made head against them. Then were strooke upon both sides the notes of furie, the soundes of slaughter, the harmonie of hell: trumpettes, fiffes, drumms, musicke sutable to the mirth in hand. The kinges side cryed 'St. George!' The other parte being confident in theire generall, to whome they bare great honour, cried 'Esperance Peircie!' The archers of the Lord Henrie Peircie beganne the battaile, dischardging against the kings archers as it had beene by way of salutation; whoe were againe soe roundly answered that both parties were shrewdly shaken & galled, without any apparant great oddes.

Then the Earle of Stafford, whoe never found anything too heavie, beganne [fo. 66v] with the kings foreward very openly & in loose troupes to chardge upon the head of the enemie. But the Earle Dowglasse, a more beaten soldier whome former overthrowes had instructed to make a true valuation of the valour both of himselfe & of his enemies, without ether pride in the one or contempte of the other (the two banes of unexperienced courage), cloased his troupes in firme squadrons, whereby hee did not only beare the first furious brunt of his enemies, but in shorte tyme broake them, & forced them to fly in such disorder that all his souldiers showted 'Victorie!' Many gentlemen of the kings side were there lost; among which the Earle of Stafford, being borne downe, could not bee releived, leaving example that rather warie then hott commaunders are to bee placed in the front.

Upon this defeate a thousand cries & noe fewer advises were presented to the king; notwithstanding, hee stood fast with his maine battaile, and nether moved nor seemed to bee moved. Divers of his owne partie, seing him stand still and looke on soe long when hee saw the bodie of his vauntguarde broken & the sword to surfett upon the bodies of his men, could not tell what they might thinke, & I beleeve that some forejudged him of feare. But the king perceaved that the great impatiencie & heate of his [fo. 67] enemies did drawe them to disorder; for hee saw the Scottes, who were in the foreward, on the kings side, soe violent in persecuting theire advantage that theire great troupes dissolved, some pursuing those that fledd, some chardging those that stoode, & some dispoyling those that were slaine. Many alsoe did breake from the maine battale ledd by the Peircies (which hitherto had not fought) & dispersed themselves aboute those loose actions. Hereupon the king beganne to advaunce the bodie of his maine armie, & that with soe resolute a countenaunce that all men might discerne that hee wanted nether patience to staye nor courage to take his tyme of advantage. And there is litle doubte but hee had soone shaken the armie of his enemies & chased them out of the feild, had they not beene releeved by certaine troupes of Welshmen, whoe after the kings departure from the borders of Wales brake forth &, hearing of this battaile towardes, resolved that they would daunce at the feast. These, when the first was most hott, assailed the kings armie on the flauncke, & then joyned with the lordes, whereby they had some respitte to call in theire companies & to rallie them in the best manner.

Then beganne a mercilesse matche. The soldiers on both sides were able men, well experienced, orderly ranged, & sufficient in number. The commaunders were equall in discretion, courage & felicitie. And this battaile [fo. 67v] being accounted the definitive sentence of the whole cause, both parties were obstinately bent to overcome. The Lord Henry Peircie shewed admirable effectes not only of skill, both in taking & framing occasions to prevaile, but alsoe of valour in perfomance with his hand. The Earle Dowglasse, as resolute a man[12] as breathed that daye, with directe courage brake into the midest of the kings armie, & making way with his sword pressed soe valiantly upon the person of the king that hee strake him downe, and slue many nere unto him. But the king was recovered & withdrawne from that danger by the Earle of Dunbarre, which was not amisse for the safetie of his life. For the Earle Dowglasse in this rude rage overthrewe the kings standard, & slue Sir Walter Blunt the bearer thereof, & three others apparelled in sute like unto the king, affirming that hee marvailed to see the king soe often to revive. Alsoe about the kings standard were slaine Sir Nicolas Langford, Sir John Cockaine, Sir John Calverlay, Sir John Massie, Baron of Padington, Sir Hugh Mortimer, Sir John Clifton, Sir Hugh Sherley, the two brothers Nicolas & Robert Gentelles, with many other knightes & gentlemen of worth. Whereupon the rest, seing theire enemies in the midest of them & theire cheifest men beaten downe, were upon the pointe to have taken the running retreite, & stood looking aboute [fo. 68] whether any had begunne the race.

When these fearefull tydings were brought unto the king, it was not needfull to bidd him stirre. For scarce taking time for fresh supplies, hee hasted to the place of danger, & both with presence & perswations incouraged his souldiers to stand fast & keepe theire ground unlesse‾

---

[12] MS: 'as a resolute a man'

they would bee esteemed ether fearfull or false. But when hee saw that wordes were too weake to oppose against weapons, and that nether by authoritie nor intreatie hee could prevaile, hee resolved to add effectes. And partly upon dispaire of a more honorable end, & partly upon hope to recover theire hartes, with a brave behaviour he opposed his brest & sides to the danger, sometimes crying to his companie that if any manly bloud remained in them they should not forsake him, sometymes bidding them goe & reporte to theire frendes that they lefte him fighting in Shrewsbury feildes. This veine of valour provoked them all to have in memory theire fayth & theire fame, whereby in shorte time they recovered both theire order & ground, & drave the enemie from his advantage. The king adventured soe farre that daye that hee slue xxxvj of his enemies with his owne handes, and it is most certaine that as well necessitie & as honour enforced him foreward. Alsoe, the yong Prince Henrie, who was then first fleshed in bloud, being litle above xvj yeares of age, did behave himselfe farr beyond opinion. For albeit [fo. 68v] hee was sore wounded in the face with an arrow, yett ceased hee not to presse into places where the medley was most thicke, engaging himselfe soe deepe in the danger that the bearing of him out was the cheifest meanes whereby the souldier maintained his place.

Thus was the battaile brought againe upon even hand, & the victorie did hang in equall ballance. The souldiers on both sides stood fast with obstinate courage, entending & contending to beate downe, breake and beare backe those who came against them; & they who there tainted theire swordes on ether parte had cause afterwardes to boast of theire courage, having stood the triall in soe dangerous a place. The furiousnes of this conflicte made the length thereof to bee more admirable, for it continued 3 long howers with great mortalitie and indifferencie of fortune. Indeed, light skirmishes may bee maintained a great space of tyme; alsoe, if one armie consistes of footemen & the other of horsemen the battaile betweene them may bee long, because nether the footemen are able to drive away the horsemen, nor the horsemen able to breake the great battailes of the foote. But for two battailes on foote to stand soe long in full fury (for in truth it is but fury & rage which is called courage) it is not usuall.

Att the last the Lord Henrie [fo. 69] Peircie, whose valour could not bee vanquished but by death, as hee laboured in the front of his armie by all meanes to breath fresh spirit into his soldiers, making cleare way before him & pursuing his enemies too farre, was environed by them, & sodainly slaine by an uncertain arme. This greatly abated the heat of his soldiers, to see themselues deprived of the glory & hope of all the armie, to see him slaine whom they esteemed invincible. The king, feeling them to fainte, cried aloud 'St. George! Victorie!' and therewith charged so livelie with fresh supplies that hee peirced their battaile & utterlie disbanded them. Then fortune turning her hand, they whoe were foremost in the battaile were last in the flight, & they whoe a litle before feared no mans countenance, throughe extremitie of feare rather flewe then fledd. On the other side, with the more difficultie and losse the victorie was obteined, with the more implacable furie it was followed, and the execution was the greater, because in civill warres there is noe advantage in taking prisoners. The feildes were strawed[13] with dead bodies, the wayes were embrued with bloud; everyone lay slaine where it was his chaunce to bee overtaken. Many climed upon trees to escape thereby the horsemens rage, but they were with bitter scorne cast downe by the archers.

The king was unable to moderate the [fo. 69v] victorie, insomuch as the riotous souldiers[14] followed the vanquished side into townes and villages, where if they saw any man bearing presence of a souldier, personable and yong, they forthwith slue him. And anonn, being gorged with bloud, the[y] converted the slaughter to spoile, breaking open houses, and under coulour of searching for traitors leaving noe roome unrifled, noe closett close. Much rascallie people who never approached the danger now joyned themselves to the souldiers, & were most forward in all kind of mischeife, insomuch as the miserable condition & shew[15] of a country overrunne by an enemie was then to bee seene. On the kings parte above 1600 were slaine, besides 3000 greivously wounded, of whome many died afterwardes. On the Peircies side aboue 5000 perished, & few of the Scottes escaped alive. O pore England, how unhappic wert thou to incurre the errour by dismounting thy naturall prince, & stouping under the soveraignitie of one who had noe right, whereby thy limmes were oftentimes in this sorte bathed in the bloud of thy children, & such as might have sufficed to encounter the proudest enemie in the world!

The Earle Dowglasse was taken, who once before had beene taken the same [fo. 70] yeare in fighting against the English. In the first battaile hee lost one of his eyes, in this he brake one of his genitalles, by falling from the cragge of a mountaine in his flight. Hee abated nothing of his courage, but declared by his countenance what stomach he bare, in regard whereof hee was freely released by the king. Alsoe Thomas Peircie, Earle of Worcester, was taken, who behaved himselfe abjectly, not daring to speake, but with silence & teares begged life. And albeit some putt the king in remembrance of his former services, yet would hee not bee entreated, such excuses being esteemed frivolous

---

[13] 'Strewn.'
[14] MS: 'souldier.'
[15] MS: '... condition condition & shew'.

to procure his pardone. Soe upon the second daye after the battaile hee, with Sir Richard Vernon, the Baron of Kinderton, & some others, were condemned & beheaded at Shrewsbury, & theire heades sent to London. When reporte was made unto him of the death of the Lord Henry Peircie noe newes was soe pleasing, noe mans head did hee veiw & reveiw with like contentment, his mind being then at ease & free to rejoice. The bodie was first delivered to the Earle of Furnivall to bee buried; then it was taken up & reposed betweene two milstones in Shrewsburie, & there kept with armed men, & afterwardes quartered. The head was sent to London & the quarters to other citties of the realme, but this was afterward [fo. 70v] objected against the king for being soe cruell to a slaughtered enemie, upon whome the victorie might have fell.

This Henrie was a man of a brave spirit, for his age wise & fortunate in his enterprizes, but his excessive desire of glory did always ravish him into highe and difficulte attemptes, seeming to bee delighted with dangers rather for themselves then for any benefitt they could afford, & preferring new incertainties before any certainties which hee had atcheived. Hee never complained of wearinesse, hee never shewed countenance of feare, his bodie being able to indure labour, & his bouldnesse to undertake action, soe farre as it was possible hee could bee followed. In speech hee was eloquent, soe much the more gracefull because it was naturall, & not by arte, [of] all men generally by divers allurementes much favoured, but most especiallie by courtesie & liberalitie, two strong enchauntmentes to gaine affection. Hee had done great services for the king, but was in the end ill repaid, yet rather throughe his owne ambition then the kings ingratitude, thoughe that bee not clearely to bee excused. One reporteth that a litle before the battaile hee called for his sword, & that it was tould him how it was lefte at Berwicke, a litle village next unto them; that hereupon hee replied with a sighe that then his plow was come to the last furrowe, for it [fo. 71] had beene foretold him by a wizard in his country that his overthrowe should bee at Berwicke, which untill then hee tooke for the strong towne upon the frontiers of Scottland. It is certaine that his death swayed the victorie, & that it is a faulte in a generall to adventure his person too farre, but it is not to bee tearmed adventuring when the maine battaile marcheth to the chardge, and the generall departeth not from his office & place.

This feild thus famously fought, thus fortunately wonne, the king departed from Shrewsburie towardes the north, from whence this tempest did arise. When hee came to Yorke hee was divided in advise how to deale against the Earle of Northumberland: whether hee should prosecute extremities or temper himselfe to a milder course. One waye hee was moved with the sharpe & bleeding greife of his disloyaltie, which had brought him to the jumpe of loosing all; on the other side hee was loath to drive him to a desperate resolution. And as hee did not hope that ever hee would bee faythfull, soe was hee not like to prove a more dangerous enemie then at that time hee might bee, for hee had in his power the towne of Berwicke, the castles of Alnewicke, Wakeworth, & other defensive places of Northumberland. Soe as it stood at his discretion to have carried all that countrie to the Scottes, & having entertained many Scottish souldiers into his strongest houldes, & [fo. 71v] Scotland being upon his backe, hee could not want ether forces to make head, or assurance of retreite if successe should faile.

Hereupon the king conquered his patience to applie his counsaile to his cause, & rather to dissemble old injuries, then draw on new. Soe hee sent to the earle commaunding him to dischardge his company & forthwith to come unto him. The earle, taking the commaundement of a king for a safe conducte, obeied & came to his presence. His behaviour was humble & submisse, as being in feare, his speech cleane altred from wonted tearmes. Not that hee behaved himselfe ether arrogantlie in former tymes, or basely then (althoughe in truth hee was not farre from both), but few doe soe moderate themselves in theire prosperitie that a change is not discerned if adversitie doth fall. Many things hee excused, & for some craved pardon. But the king admitted noe excuse, nether receaved him otherwise then as one who sued for pardon, notwithstanding hee shewed noe countenance of great displeasure, because hee meant to use him as hee might. Soe the king, with wordes of moderate favour, pardoned him his life, but comitted him to custodie for a time. The varietie of fortune which afterward he ranne, shallbee declared in the proper place.

[fo. 72] The king having settled his affaires in the north returned to London, & entred the cittie in verie solemne state. All seemed to rejoyce at his prosperous successe, but many wished from theire hartes that his affaires had remained a litle more doubtfull, as desirous that still hee had beene held in feare. For they suspected that being delivered from soe great enemies, hee would the lesse esteeme his frendes, & that being freed from feare, hee would become a terrour to others, that having noe warres to busie himselfe, hee would passe the tyme in making & undoing men, & in altering matters which could not bee amended. But in shorte tyme after, the Welsh, being desirous both to revenge theire harmes & to qualifie the kings glorie and joye, brake into the English borders, slaughtred all that stood in theire waye, forraged the feildes, burnt & beat downe many villages, & without any encounter returned loaden with spoile & with joye. And hereby it was conjectured what those forces might have done together, when being separate they were soe dangerous.

The king was desirous to make a voyage into Wales, for repressing these robberies rather then warres, but hee wanted money, which is of more strength then steele in execution of armes. Many perswaded [fo. 72v] the king that this defecte might both easily & lawfullie bee furnished out of the excesive abundance of the cleargie. These perswaded the king that in tyme of extremitie, especiallie of publicke extremitie, nothing is private to any man: all things must bee applied to the common necessitie; as the good dieting of a bodie doth not alwaies consist in full feeding, soe the right ordering of the church was not alwayes ether in increasing or maintaining the possessions thereof, but as humours in the bodie must sometymes bee abated, so happilie the cleargie may at tymes bee lighted of that heavie load wherwith immoderate devotion doth overcharge them, least it bring them to idlenesse & pride, the twoe most dangerous diseases of the church; that if this might bee ether requisite or tolerable at any tyme, then surely at that present, when the possessions of the church were soe excessive that it seemed to lye sicke of the surfett; that for this cause the diminishing would bee not the cutting downe, not the cropping thereof, but the pruning away of superfluous braunches. Some knightes & gentlemen were soe forward in this advise that they tooke horses & money from certaine bishops, who ether for private occasion or upon duty attended upon the king, [fo. 73] of which bold beginnings the progresse many tymes is furious, & the end mischeivous.

But Thomas Arundell, Archbishop of Canterbury, a man having much noble alliance, of strong courage & in good creditt & favour with the king (all which were litle enoughe), crossed this counsaile by affirming bouldly that nether any Christian prince hath priviledge to pull from his subjectes what hee please, nether is it pollicie for a prince to desire to bee soe esteemed; that they whoe, ether to flatter theire prince or to further theire owne ambitious hopes, endeavour to arme him with such authoritie, doe manifestly abase his honor, & will draw him in the end to bee hateful to his subjectes & contemptible to his neighbours, in making them wearie to continue, & these warie not to come under such subjection; that a prince is more highly honored when hee cann say that his subjectes are most assured unto him, of whome hee is soe lovingly feared, soe freely served, & soe willingly obeyed that they readily undertake any charge, & presently forgett it when it is past; that the cleargie of England hath alwayes beene soe forward in advauncing the service of theire prince by voluntarie contributions, & in doing all things requisite for the supportance of his estate, that it was noe lesse needles then odious [fo. 73v] to presse them with extraordinary power; that it was more honour & assurance to the prince, & better justice before God & the world, in that sorte to releive his wantes then by using any peremptorie power; that this course was never suggested by vertuous & grave counsellors, but by glorious parasites of meane judgement & lesse honestie, in some authoritie without any deserte who, to seeme to bee servauntes of regard, nether care nor know what they advise; that these cann spie and speake of the pride & idlenesse of a few, but nether of the labour nor wantes of many other; that theire leane devotion cann easily esteeme the hill of the lord to bee too fatt; that theire envious or ambitious eye did judge other mens estates farre greater then they were; that they never talked of altering the use of any thing which they esteemed either superfluous or not well imployed, but only of sweeping it cleane awaye, singing the Babylonian song, 'Downe with it, downe with it, even to the ground!' That it was not the lives but the livings which they respecte; that if any of these profane Dyonisians would upon theire private authoritie use violence against the cleargie of his province, hee protested by noe small oath that by stroke of steele they should understand the price of theire sacrilegious spoiles.

Now althoughe princes doe naturallie dislike that any of his subjectes should ether use or menace force, yet the king tooke pleasure at the archbishops angrie answere, or at least seemed soe to doe, partly to avoid occasions of stirres, & partly to hould the cleargie well contented, two pointes regardable by those who without just title are new in state. For as in a bodie unhealthfull a small distemper sufficeth to shake forth corrupte humours, & to acte secrett surfettes & greifes which may move to extremities, soe in a government both unsettled & unjust, wherein many are discontented & most indifferent (those being unsound, & these unsure), a small disturbance may suffice to draw affaires to the highest danger. And as the cleargie was at that time of great power in themselves, and great authoritie with the people, soe were they regarded not without great cause, even as Dyonisius, albeit hee nothing regarded any Sophist, yet because such men were in great estimation with the people hee alwayes held them nere unto him. Soe the king tooke order that his followers should behave themselves more modestlie afterwardes, & required the archbishop to raise some supplie from the cleargie. The archbishoppe pleasantly returned answere that hee would procure him the bishops blessing. Soe hee [fo. 74v] assembled the cleargie, & with good wordes on his parte & good willes on theire, obtained for the king a tenth. Assuredly the difficultie of houlding the livinges of the cleargie did plainly threaten that they should have a time to bee gone. This meanes for reteining them served only for the present, but nothing could have better secured theire perpetuitie as to have moderated themselves within the goulden meane. Even as Pittalus of Mitelene, when his citizens did offer him many thousand acres of land, accepted only one hundred, saying 'Give not that unto mee for which many will envie mee &, more, desire to take from mee.'

King Henrie with this money furnished up his forces, & sent them into Wales under the fortune & charge of Henry his eldest sonne, of whose brave beginnings all men begann to speake, & to heape many hopes of his honorable proceedings. This armie was greatly both increased & adorned with a serviceable & gallant traine of yong noble men & gentlemen, whoe upon theire owne pleasure & charge followed the prince. For besides the naturall inclination of men to fixe theire eyes upon the rising sunne, the yong prince was by nature apte to allure many followers. Hee was comely, pleasant, martiall, amiable not only in his vertues but even in his youthfull vices, carefull & industrious when hee was imployed, when hee had nothing to doe wanton & wilde, yett in [fo. 75] noe such degree as that it was ether blemishe or hinderance to his honor. Hee was of an enterprizing spirit, yet never moved warr but first offered faire conditions of peace. Hee had some ambitious humour, but in soe honorable a temper that hee never envied any mans worth, for the confidence hee had in his owne. Hee was reasonable learned, very inquisitive to understand affaires, of an excellent witt, which excelleth all learning beaten out by studie. Hee was in stature stately, majestically milde in countenance & speech, in all his behaviour nether popular nor proude, but seemely sweete. These giustes of nature, with other things which out of warre are accounted levities, as exercising among the souldiers, apparell not differing from the common sorte, courage & forwardnesse in the feild, did raise both love & reverence of all the armie. Many conceived an opinion of him that hee could enterprize nothing, but it was soe favoured by fortune that even his rashenesse sorted to his glory. His age, scarce ripe & yet sufficient for such a charge, did marvailouslie sett forth what hee did.

The prince, entring Wales, first planted standing campes in such places as might most conveniently commaund both the passages & covertes of the fleeting enemies, [fo. 75v] who sett all theire assurance in such advantages. Then with a strong & serviceable band hee chased them over all the countrie. By this meanes many of them were daylie cutt in peeces. Theire cattaile alsoe, upon which they lived, & which in barren mountaines & woodes could not long bee preserved alive, were in shorte tyme ether taken or consumed. Hereby the forelorne wretches were driven to such distresse that horses, doggs & all filthy flesh which nature doth abhorre, necessitie made most savourie & sweete. When this foode alsoe fayled, many perished with pure hunger; many alsoe, more then halfe starved, crepte out of theire caves, looking like shadowes rather then men, & desired theire enemies to dispatch them at once. In a worde, theire companies were disbanded, theire courages broken, & noe remnant of the rebellion did appeare.

Some write that Owen Glendor, destitute of helpe, desperate of hope, equallie fearing both his enemies & those who had beene his firmest frendes, upon feare that they would make his head ether the objecte of theire revenge, or the price of theire pardon, lingered this yeare in deserte & unfrequented places, in miserable want of all naturall necessities, & that being a long tyme pined, hee lastly perished for want of foode. Whether this [fo. 76] was true, or whether surmised as an end agreeable to him who alwayes more greedily gaped after majestiie then after meate, by whose cruell spoiles many were pined & pinched to death, I will not determine. For others reporte that the summer following, hee forraged the countries adjoyning unto Wales. But it is very like ether that the yeare was mistaken, or that some roades being made by scattered relictes, they passed under the name of theire accustomed leader. On the other side the bardes of Wales, the preservers of the Welsh antiquities, have delivered to posteritie that when Owen heard of the hard adventure of his confederates at Shrewsbury, whether upon despaire of future successe or whether upon meere melancholie that his absence was accounted the cause of the losse, hee forsooke his followers & was never after seene in Wales, some surmising that hee fledd out of the countrie, others insinuating I know not what fabulous disparition.

Howsoever hee died, hee was a man full of courage & practise, & of highe enterprizing thoughtes, very hardie in undertaking perilles, & noe lesse resolute in the middest of them. His body was never tired with toile, nor his spirittes abashed nor abated with infortunate successe. Hee patiently could endure all extremities of weather, hee was not slavish to his bellie, [fo. 76v] but held nature content with what was necessarie. For sleepe hee made noe difference betweene day & night, but what tyme was most free from his affaires hee bestowed in refreshing & resting his body, not upon a soft bedd, remote from noise, but upon the ground amidst his troupes, covered with a soldiers cassocke. Hee marched alwayes foremost, & was with the first who gave the charge, & againe with the hindermost in the retreate. When any enterprize required nimblenesse of witt in working some sleight or giving a gleike[16] to the enemy (as to choose some advantage of place, to passe a river or streight, to give a sodaine charge, to avoide an unexpected danger,[17] or such like), hee was both fine & fortunate in his contrivance. In all his adventures his share was

---

[16] To give a gleek = to play a trick upon (OED).
[17] MS: '... unexpected danger danger ...'.

deepest in the danger, but the spoile hee wholly lefte to his followers, contenting himself with glorie & hope.

When the prince had thus extinguished the rebellion, hee returned to his father, of whome hee was entertained according to the greatnesse of his deserte, yet not soe much with demonstration of outward honor, as of inward joye. For hee supposed that the proofe of his sonnes fortunate courage would bee a principall meanes of his assurance, by much increasing terrour amongst his enemies, [fo. 77] love amongst his frendes, & respecte among those who were indifferent. Assuredly the king might then have said unto him, as Philip once said to his yong sonne Alexander, 'Sonne, goe seeke some larger limittes, for England will not bee sufficient to conteine thee!'

Upon advantage of these internall (or rather infernall) troubles, the Brittans rigged forth a fleete to adventure upon the English coast. This fleete was committed to the conducte of the Lord of Casselles, a baronne of theire country, a man well esteemed both for courage & knowledge in matters of enterprize. Theire preparation was soe secrett, & theire passage with soe good speede, that theire suddaine coming prevented the fame of theire setting forth. Soe they made theire descent upon Plimmouth, the inhabitantes whereof, insufficient for resistance, & having leasure litle enoughe to carrie away theire lives, left their houses & goodes to the pleasure of the invaders. The French, more desirous of bootie then of bloud, left the English to the pursuite of theire feare, & first spoyled the towne, then fired it, returning without any tast of an enemie.

[fo. 77v] The Englishe, not soe much greived at the losse as ashamed at the disgrace, resolved ether to die, or to aquitt themselves of this debte. Hereupon they sett forth a navie, under the conducte & good fortune of William Willford, Esquire, a man both provident & prosperous in his atcheivementes. With this navie hee coasted Brittanne, & there tooke fourty shipps laden with iron, oyle, sope and Rochell wine,[18] to the burden of one thousand tunne. Then hee landed his men at Penarche, & fired the towne & milles of St. Mathew, all done with the greater rage because it was done in heate of revenge. And albeit this might have largely satisfied the losse at Plymouth, yet hee proceeded further, & wasted the country the space of sixe leagues, charging his souldiers abundantly both with contentment & spoile. And thus both parties had better fortune to offend theire enemies, then to defend themselves.

Now the Earle of St. Paule, a man of an enterprizing nature, having often attempted against the English with great provision & litle proofe,

---

[18] Wine exported from the French port of La Rochelle. The Breton raid on Plymouth occurred 10 Aug. 1403, the English naval retaliation later the same month.

determined once againe to putt himself into the handes of fortune.
[fo. 78] So he procured authoritie from the king of Fraunce, assembled
8 hundred men of armes, 5 hundred Genowaies with crosse bowes, &
one thousand Fleminges on foote, which proude power hee brought
before the castle of Marke, three leagues from Calleis within the
territorie of the King of England. The Captaine of the peice was Philip
Hale, Esquire; the garrison consisted of lxxx archers, & xxiiij other
soldiers, men readie & resolute to maintaine theire charge. The earl
applied divers engines, and used many encouragementes to his souldiers, assuring them that they should not find theire enemies the same
men in theire fortresses as they were in the feild. 'For even wild
beastes,' said hee, 'being shut up forgett theire naturall feircenesse,
& nothing more then confidence of place maketh men carelesse &
forgettfull of theire accustomed valour.' Notwithstanding, some being
fearefull to execute theire charge, the residue endeavored in vaine,
being continually beaten upon with shott & stones from the castle, &
sometymes borne backe with push of the pike.

The earle, having enterprized the most parte of the daye without
[fo. 78v] successe, retired his tired souldiers towardes night, & lodged
them within the towne, fortifying all the passages thereof, & appointing his scoutes and watches for feare of releife to his enemies from
Calleis. The daye following, hee gave a sharpe assaulte, wherein Sir
Robert Barington, knight & cousen to the earle, & divers of theire
company, lost theire lives. Notwithstanding, the French soe obstinately continued theire assaulte that with maine force they entred the
out[er] courte of the castle, and therein tooke many sheepe, horses &
kine, whereby the remainder of the enterprize seemed more feasable.
The same day an hundred archers came from Calleis on horsebacke,
to discover all the advauncementes of the earle. And having discovered
the course of his carriage, towardes night they sent unto him an
herauld, assuring him that the day next following, they would bee his
guestes at a dinner. The earle returned answere that hee was provided
to give them entertainment, and they should undoubtedly find theire
welcome warme.

[fo. 79] Soe they returned, and the next day issued from Calleis cc
men at armes, cc archers, ccc men on foote, with x or xij charriottes
laden with victuall, & artillerie. These marched forth in good order
of battaile under the courage & conducte of Sir Richard Aston, knight,
Lieutennte of the English Pale for the Earle of Somersett, Captaine
Generall of those Marchesse. As they passed in theire array, Sir
Richard did ride continuallie up & downe, before the front & along
the flanckes, moderating theire hast, for feare of spending theire breath
& strength before they should come in face of the enemie. Hee used
also divers encouragementes, as hee thought best agreable to theire

dispositions & desires. Hee putt them in remembrance of theire valiant atcheivementes in Fraunce, whereby they had purchased a great opinion of theire valour, that they were sett forth aswell by theire owne desires as by his direction.

[*Here the account breaks off. There then appears a notation in another hand:* 'I found this peece among Sir John Heiwoods papers which I bought written in his owne hand, 1628, out of which this was coppied.']

INDEX OF PERSONS

[This index lists the historical persons appearing in Hayward's narrative, as well as names drawn from scripture and antiquity mentioned in his text by reference only. Abbreviations used below: Archbp = Archbishop, Bp = Bishop, CJ = Chief Justice, D = Duke, E = Earl, K = King, L = Lord, LC = Lord Chancellor (Keeper), LT = Lord Treasurer, Q = Queen